LUND STUDIES IN SOCIAL WELFARE
III

Sven E Olsson
Social Policy
and Welfare State
in Sweden

Sven E Olsson

Social Policy
and Welfare State
in Sweden

Second, enlarged edition

Arkiv förlag

Redaktionskommitté:
Per Gunnar Edebalk
Gunnar Olofsson
Sune Sunesson

Publisher:
Arkiv
Box 1559
S-221 01 Lund

Contents

Acknowledgements

First and foremost: without the exceptional support, encouragement and patience of my family, this book would never have been completed. However, family life has also made possible participant observation in my field of research, both of child welfare policy and personal social services for the elderly.

Given the scope and nature of the essays included in this book, it is more than conventionally necessary to absolve other persons of any responsibility for the errors of fact, interpretation or language, that they contain. Such errors as remain are due to my mistakes and stubbornness. However, these essays have definitely benefitted from comments by a number of teachers, students and other friends. A complete listing would be impossible but I cannot refrain from singling out my present and former colleagues – economists as well as sociologists, labour market experts as well as welfare researchers – at the Swedish Institute for Social Research (SOFI), University of Stockholm, and the community of sociologists and social policy researchers in the Nordic countries.

In particular, Walter Korpi's critical yet optimistic perspective on the basic nature and development of western societies, his emphasis on power and inequality as fundamental concepts in social scientific research, has provided guidance of the utmost importance. Since 1975, I have had the good fortune to be a member of SOFI: for a brief period investigating the social stratification of bingo players in Sweden (with Paavo Bergman), later as a participant in the project "Industrial relations, strikes and trade unions", and from the early 1980s in the project "Social Policy in an International Perspective". Of course, I am particularly indebted to my colleagues in the latter project. Throughout these years the secreterial staff of SOFI has been a tremendous help. At SOFI, moreover, special thanks to Gösta Rehn, who has been a source of inspiration during the long hours of nocturnal research.

9

In the spring of 1980, Walter Korpi persuaded me to join Peter Flora's research project on "The Development of the West European Welfare State Since World War II" located at the European University Institute, Florence – a step that still gives me great pleasure. This international research environment strongly influenced by the sharp profile of its project director, became an eye-opener for a student more familiar with the industrialized countryside of Southern Scandinavia than with the classical metropoles of continental Europe.

Without the extraordinary support of Peter Flora and Patrick Hort, my father-in-law and a translator by profession, I would never have started to write in English. A year as a Fulbright Visiting Scholar at Mount Vernon College and the Brookings Institution in Washington DC during the academic year 1987/88 was another eye-opener – to the existence of poverty and destitution in the midst of excessive wealth – but also provided an opportunity to become less unfamiliar with English as a foreign language. Likewise, apart from being a scholarly environment, the International Study Group on Trends in the Welfare State, and the editors of the *International Review of Social History* have been instrumental in overcoming the language barrier. In this context, I would also like to mention the inquisitive students of the Social Welfare Seminar at the International Graduate School, University of Stockholm.

Here, it is pertinent to add that the Commission for Social Research, Ministry of Health and Social Affairs, Sweden, has provided generous financial support from the mid-1980s onwards (A87:91; A84:51).

Finally, I would like to thank the editors of *Arkiv* with whom I have had the privilege to work for two decades. Without Gunnar Olofsson's strong support and constructive criticism at crucial junctures this book might never have gone to press.

Once again, a big hug to Rebecca, Josia, Jacob and the rest of the family.

Introduction:
Facets of Welfare State Developments

In much current comparative welfare state research the Scandinavian experience is a controversial subject of interpretation. Of the Nordic countries, Sweden is often regarded as the world's foremost welfare state, and therefore a topical object in social scientific research.[1] The perception of Sweden as a model welfare state generates a number of intricate research questions. First, it necessitates a reasonable definition of the welfare state. What particular aspects of the contemporary state should be included into the delineation of this institution? Second, in a comparative perspective, is it really true that Sweden has been or is the leading welfare state?

The studies collected in this volume deal almost exclusively with the Swedish welfare state in terms of the dilemmas, ideas and systemic solutions that agents of change have articulated in this area of social action. Thus, in focus are the challenges that for more than a century have been faced by social actors and the institutionalized outcomes and non-outcomes of these processes. In Sweden these actors have run from the teetotallers, liberal intelligentsia and royal civil servants of the late 19th century, over the contemporary collective actors – unions, employers and farmers associations, political parties, etc – to post-modern green and neo-liberal political activists.

Who were the creators of the Swedish Welfare State Model? How did this model come into being? And what are the prospects for this model? These questions, as well as the discussion about actors, dilemmas, ideas and systems in the evolution of Swedish Welfare State Model form the underlying theme of the present studies.

The book contains four studies that focus on different aspects of Swedish social welfare policies during the past century. These studies have evolved in the context of comparative social research projects, something which hopefully has contributed to a wider perspective than domestic case studies generally provide.[2] Hence, this introduction, will (1) trace the research traditions and research communities, their theories and research designs, out of which my studies have grown; (2) present the specific research projects, to which these studies belong, their objectives, and the results of these endeavours; and finally, (3) discuss some topical problems that have arisen after these specific studies were completed. The studies included in this book are descriptive, explorative and interpretative rather than excersises in formal hypothesis testing. Without further elaboration, theoretical eclecticism is used as an alternative in a field where theories are abundant but empirical cases few, and where theories are overlapping as much as divergent (cf. European Journal of Political Research 1989).

1. From Bismarck to Thatcher: The Welfare State Research Cycle?

The set-up of the German social insurance programs a little more a century ago has generally been taken as the starting-point of the welfare state, although general public education, for instance, was an earlier (welfare) state activity in some countries in Europe and North America (Girvetz 1972; cf. Heidenheimer 1981). In 1881 in the Berlin Reichtag of Imperial Germany, the Emperor proclaimed the Allerhöchste Botschaft, which announced that more than repression was needed to ameliorate the social conditions of the working class, and that he, with God's help, desired to create something positive for the workers: social peace through social insurance against occupational injuries, illness and old age.[3] His Chancellor, Prince Otto von Bismarck, did not have to invent these social insurance schemes – there had been forerunners in Austria and Belgium, though not in Sweden – but Bismarck was the first to implement them on a large scale.

Somewhat later unemployment insurance was added to the initial trio – the first such national laws were passed in France and Norway in 1905 and 1906 respectively (Heidenheimer et al 1975:189; Kuhnle 1986), but public-sponsored unemployment insurance on a cantonal level had existed in Switzerland since 1893-4 (cf. Maurer

1981:764). Ever since then these four bulwarks have been regarded as the cornerstones of social security[4], giving the welfare state from the start a certain male-labourite feature with the absence of a "gender dimension".[5] These components of social security grew at varying rates throughout the first half of the present century in the advanced capitalist world, in Europe and North America but sometimes most notably in the Pacific, in Australia and New Zealand (cf. Castles 1985; Davidson 1989).

However, it is particularly in the second half of the 20th century that we have witnessed an overwhelming expansion of public endeavors in the realm of welfare, parallel to the staggering expansion of consumer capitalism throughout the West. The welfare state – a state which assumes responsibility for citizen welfare in the context of a market economy and a plural polity – was explicitly a part of the commitment put forward by the Western allies during or immediately after World War II, epitomized for example in the Atlantic Charter, and the Beveridge Plan. In the UK, it was in particular the 1948 inauguration of the National Health Service – "Mr. Bevan's Dream" (Townsend 1989) – that came to symbolize the welfare state and a new relationship between the "ukanian" Crown (Nairn 1988) and its subjects. Thus, the British case was a different welfare state emphasizing public services more than social insurance and full employment, although the latter two were also important aspects of the Beveridge Plan.

There was a time when social scientists and historians spoke about the development of the welfare state as a – Roman – road from Bismarck to Beveridge, a peaceful evolution from an industrial class-model to an all-embracing citizen-model of welfare, but also from a social security state to a social service state. Only for a short period after the Second World War, however, was this domain uncontested; setbacks followed in particular with regard to an institutionalized commitment to full employment (Therborn 1985). Nevertheless, social provision under state tutelage became a typical feature of postwar developments in most Western countries. State intervention in the distribution of welfare through social transfers for large-scale income maintenance programs, state-regulated prices in agriculture and housing, and state-provided schools, hospitals and other medical and personal social services, were seen as a means of countering the social injustices created by redistribu-

13

tion through the market. However, the boundaries of the welfare state have never been fixed and have always differed between the nations that regarded themselves as models of social development.

For a short while the welfare state seemed to be an integral element of Western Society, the outcome of a blissful marriage between capitalism and democracy. Hence, when the partners began to quarrel in the mid-1970s and divorce emerged as a serious alternative, social research approached this field. Once again, it was the development in the UK, and to some extent in the US, associated with the rise of Margareth Thatcher and Ronald Reagan to state/world leadership, that prompted the growth of what has been labelled a "sociology of welfare" (Taylor-Gooby 1989) or a "sociology of social security" (Sigg 1985).

Thus, it is no coincidence that so much food for thought in this research field has been inherited from British scholars – both recently and from the early postwar epoch. Out of the Beveridge plan and the hopes created by the Attlee Government came T H Marshall's evolutionary scheme of citizen rights, Richard Titmuss' various "divisions" and "models" of welfare, Asa Briggs' widespread definition of the welfare state, etc. One example of the impact of this tradition is empirical Scandinavian welfare research and the comprehensive component approach that is so typical in level-of-living investigations (cf. Erikson & Uusitalo 1987; Erikson & Åberg 1987). More relevant for the articles in the present volume is the influence of this tradition on a growing number of quantitative and qualitative historical and political sociologists working in the field of comparative welfare state research. The three scholars mentioned above are frequent reference-points in the latter type of research. Basically, these British researchers were all concerned with state welfare, and held that state power could bring about desired effects on the distribution of material resources without undermining the underlying stability of the socio-economic system. Towards the close of the 20th century this is a position that has become extremely controversial in politics as well as in the social sciences.

14

1.1 Grand Theory vs. Middle Range Theory in Welfare State Research

Conceptually, the welfare state is nebulous. Apart from a number of ad-hoc explanations of its existence, explanations not based on explicit theoretical arguments, there have been few successful attempts to pin this concept down. Besides the above-mentioned ambiguity between a social security and a social service state, the theoretical logic has been hampered by the duality of the welfare state concept. This has led to ambivalence on where to place the emphasis: on the first, (re)distributional component, on welfare goals and outcomes, or on the second, institutional aspect, on input, implementation and output, on the state. So far, the most fruitful mix of welfare and state are the proposals that emanate from the Titmussian triad of an industrial achievement-performance, an institutional redistributive, and a residual model of welfare (cf. Titmuss 1974). This proposal has been re-dichotomized by Mishra (1977:101) and Korpi (1980:303), who have tried to specify the most salient features of the models. Still, these endeavours have not produced any definite delineation of the borders of the welfare state (cf. Therborn 1989; Flora 1986; Persson 1986;Rose & Shiratorei 1986). Furthermore, the above-mentioned ambivalence has been coupled to a discussion about the relationships between equality, poverty, security, liberty, and solidarity. For example, Korpi and Esping-Andersen have contrasted the egalitarian and the solidaristic aspects of the institutionalized welfare state (1987; cf. Esping-Andersen 1985).

In mainstream social analysis, however, the theoretical approach for a long time followed the dominant structural-functionalist paradigm. In its grand version, the increasing scale and complexity of the modern social structure required a correspondingly large amount of universal co-ordination and regulation, i.e. structural differentiation. In this basically organic, harmonious, and evolutionary theory, the development of a modern welfare state was seen as an adaptation to changing conditions, i.e. integration. In its minor versions, where social actors more often were allowed to take part in the social processes, the welfare state – irrespective of how it was set up and what its outcomes have been – has nevertheless been regarded as a indispensable corollary of industrialisation and technological development, or as a development of enlighten-ment in the form of a sequential expansion from universal civil rights over all-embracing political rights to an all-encompassing social citizenship.

The main contribution of grand theory is to provoke new ques-tions and new points of departure. The radical renaissance of the late 1960s – conflict-oriented or non-equilibrarian grand theories like (German) critical theory, (later post-)structuralism, marxism, or feminism – questioned the general validity of the structural-functionalist school that had dominated sociological theory in the 1950s. Although the welfare state was seldom the central object of these theories – sometimes they even completely neglected these aspects of the "modern state" – they still provoked a number of responses, the more productive ones, on another "middle range" or empirical level. For example, it is noteworthy that an author from the marxist tradition like Gough (1975) started out from an angle – i.e. state but in particular social expenditure – that partly ran parallel to the dominant trend in comparative welfare state re-search.

Empirically it is fair, however, to say that Harold Wilensky pioneered the latter field of research with his 64 nations study (1975), although others had made similar attempts to capture welfare state developments in cross-national terms.[6] In *Industrial Society and Social Welfare*, co-written with Charles Lebeaux, Wilensky set out his main, structural-functionalist perspective: it is a study of the impact of industrialization on the organization of social welfare and the growth of the social work profession in the US (1958; 1965). Here too, we find the early textbook notions of "residual" vs. "institutional" forms of welfare (1965:138).

This dichotomization was not further developed by Wilensky in his cross-national investigation of social security spendings. There, his perspective changed slightly – the subtitle is "structural and ideological roots of public expenditure" (emph. added) – and in particular the testability of sociological theories in the "middle range" was underlined (1975:51; cf. Merton 1948). Thus, his basic affluence and demographic-growth perspective, which explains the similarity of advanced welfare states (including a few in Eastern Europe!), had to compete with ideology and political system theories in order to spell out the divergences in spending levels among nations that were socio-economically similar, i.e. rich nations.[7] Of course, the author's perspective came out as a winner – "politics does not matter" to borrow a simplifying slogan – but there are definitely important qualifications in this analysis, concerning for example the impact of middle and working class mobilization (cf. Wilensky 1975:65 and 68-9).

1.2 The Welfare State: "Core" and "Essence"

Wilensky devoted a whole chapter to the definition of the welfare state: "the essence of the welfare state is government protected minimum standards of income, nutrition, health, housing, and education, assured to every citizen as a political right, not as charity" (1975:1) echoing both the boundaries of the (old) US federal agency in charge of social affairs – the Department of Health, Education and Welfare – and a traditional American obsession with minimum protection for the poor alone. The definition is not particularly "beveridgean": there is no emphasis on full employment programs as part of the core of the welfare state. Furthermore, in Wilensky's emprical analysis, education – due to its supposedly regressive distributional impact – and housing, where data were "thin", were omitted. Basically, Wilensky's study – not least his smaller sample of 22 rich nations – concentrated on social security spending, an indicator that has been criticizised as much more multidimentional than Wilensky ever perceived (Korpi 1989).

Wilensky's *The Welfare State and Equality*, together with a few other books and articles definitely spurred a great deal of interest in this field of social research.[8] They were published at the right moment, at a time when most advanced industrialized countries were experiencing strains on the public budget after the "first oilshock" and a general downturn in economic growth in the mid-1970s. In a survey of welfare state research done in the early 1980s, roughly 80 out of 100 titles in the bibliography had been written after the publication of Wilensky's path-breaking work; and in many articles, it was social security programs, their costs and enlargements, that made up the empirical data to be analyzed (Shalev 1983). Hence, Wilensky's handy empirical definition of the

17

welfare state survived, as is apparent for example from a later standard work in this tradition, where the "core" of the welfare state is very close to Wilensky's delimitations (Flora & Heidenheimer 1981:8-9).

However, in his vast HIWED-project, focussed on the Western and Central European welfare states, Peter Flora tried to transcend Wilensky's social expenditure approach. Here, apart from public income and outlays, the importance of the growth of public employment as well as of social insurance coverage, the numbers of people included under such programs, is evident (Flora et al. 1983; Alber 1982). Flora continued these efforts in his welfare state project based at the European University Institute in Florence (see section 2.3 below). Similarly, Korpi, in his study of social policy development in 18 OECD countries – a sample fairly close to Wilensky's 22 rich countries[9] – programmatically called for the inclusion of preventive job creation programs and later explicitly rejected the social expenditure approach as too narrow (cf. Korpi 1980; 1989). The three research projects mentioned here were perhaps the most ambitious and comprehensive within the tradition of comparative quantitative historical sociology that started in the aftermath of Wilensky's trend-setting study.[10]

Another large-scale research project or program in this field, is of course the more qualitatively oriented historical-sociological investigations by Theda Skocpol and her associates (e.g. Skocpol et al. 1988). A further example from the late 1980s of a similar comparative and qualitative approach is *The Comparative History of Public Policy* (Castles 1989a). However, it is in particular the former, dubbed "Chicago School of historical social policy analysis" (Castles 1989b), with its emphasis on the autonomy of state officials in the process of policy making, that has provoked a number of responses. This research basically concentrates on US social policies, although there are examples of cross-national studies (Orloff & Skocpol 1984; Weir & Skocpol 1985). However, the definition of what constitutes the "core" or "essence" of the welfare state is not notably different from that of quantitative sociologists, and, together with the explicit rejection of competing macro-sociological theories, this probably explains the considerable interchange between these two research orientations (cf. Amenta & Skocpol 1987).

18

While there were no major disagreements concerning the definition, of what ought to be included as empirical observations, there
was of course fundamental opposition over the starting point and
interpretation of research. The proposition that "politics doesn't
matter" was rejected as utterly false by what in the late 1980s has
been called the "new orthodoxy" (cf. Schmidt 1989). However, to
depict the latter view, that "politics matter", as a uniform theoretical approach would also be misleading. The early rejection of
Wilensky's findings gave rise to the "Social Democratic model",
more adequately the power resources approach (Kopri 1983; 1985),
but it would be improper to equate this with the "new orthodoxy".
Neither the standard work on the welfare state from the early 1980s
(Flora/Heidenheimer 1981), nor the works of Theda Skocpol and
her associates can be included under the latter label, although they
definitely belong to the former. Common to this theoretical current
is a focus on agency in contrast to structure, but within this
research community there is as much divergency as in the earlier
paradigm: apart from Social Democracy, the roles of broad-based
catholic parties, of weak and scattered rightist parties, of the new
middle class, of state bureaucrats, as well as of a general political or
corporatist consensus, have been singled out as major factors in the
making of the postwar welfare state in Western Europe (cf. Alestalo, Flora & Uusitalo 1985; Therborn 1985). In the 1980s, not only in
Sweden but throughout the Nordic countries this theoretical current had far-reaching influence on welfare state research. The
theoretical debate outlined above has been the context in which the
studies presented in this volume have evolved.

2. The Structure and Content of this Book

Research knows no borders, according to academic orations. Still,
it is appropriate to stress the external and internal international
contexts in which the four case studies included in this volume –
focussing on the dilemmas, ideas and systems that engage actors in
this area of Swedish social life – have emerged. One of them – the
third article – is a direct offspring of one of the above-mentioned
projects (see section 2.3). Along with the close relationship between
social science and social development, the local coordinates of

individual researchers and the research environment in which they interact should not be played down (Wittrock 1989). As specified below all four studies in this book are related to the broader comparative research community on the welfare state.

2.1 In Search of an Early Welfare Intelligentsia

In Sweden and, more naturally, elsewhere, Swedish social policy is often equated with Swedish social democracy. This is particularly true of the period after World War II. The decision to include a study focussing on social policy prior to World War II stems from the inadequacy of a short-term perspective on the welfare state, and a dissatisfaction with the treatment of the earlier period of social policy in Sweden. In order to compare Sweden with other countries, the contribution of Social Democracy to social policy needs to be formulated in historical terms (cf. Alestalo & Kuhnle1987; Kuhnle 1978). Although still in the form of "preliminary notes", this essay on late 19th and early 20th century social policy developments complements the other three studies which are primarily concerned with postwar developments.[11]

The study is a search for a trajectory of an early social policy tradition, its foreign influences and domestic roots. The study rejects a widespread view about the non-existence of a pre-social democratic social policy thought. In contrast to some other studies from the 1980s that have taken up this issue (cf. Therborn 1986; Baldwin 1989), the study concentrates on the development of ideas and the environment – in particular the social popular mass movements – in which those ideas emerged, on the bearers of this mode of thought struggling with the dilemma of the "social question" from the 1880s into the first decades of the 20th century. This chapter does however not center on legislative or social expenditure developments. Thus, the focus in this chapter is on the coordinates of non-academic thought, and the welfare intellectuals in civil society.[12]

The outcome of this study is an emphasis on the early turnabout of Bismarckian "repressive" or paternalistic social policy into a domestic emancipatory and, in social terms, extremely broad-based liberal humanitarian vision. For many years, its figure-head was the MP and publicist Adolf Hedin, by the way the only native hero in the eyes of August Strindberg (Lagercrantz 1979:162). This radical liberalism continued into the first decade of the 20th century, organized around the National Association of Social Work (Centralförbundet för socialt arbete; CSA) but became increasingly involved in poor law reform and played down social insurance as a policy alternative. A turning point came with the 1913 Parliamentary decision, when this social policy discourse was overruled by a broad political consensus. This circle of liberal intellectuals (soon civil servants and politicians) then proposed "workfare" – at wages below the market rates – instead of welfare. This was implemented as state policy from the start of World War I, and soon generated a head-on collision with the labour movement especially during the 1920s. In response, a new social policy intelligentsia began to emerge in the labaour movement, and in an academic surrounding close to the latter.

The intellectual origins of the specific Swedish mix can be located to the 1930s in a critical realignment that managed to integrate and civilize what was to be a Swedish model of workfare. This approach (which ushered in the active labour market policy associated with the names of Gösta Rehn and Rudolf Meidner), together with social insurance, a wide sphere of "socialized consumption" (envisaged by Alva and Gunnar Myrdal in the mid-1930s but closer to realization with the "strong society" from the 1960s), important subsidies and regulations in such fields as housing and agriculture (significant already in the first red-green "cow-trade"), and internationally high tax levels, led to the formation of the "Swedish – Social Democratic – Model of the Welfare State". However, this transition is only intimated, and not the object of analysis in this study.

2.2 Early Post War Reforms

"Working Class Power and the 1946 Pension Reform" is the essay that most explicitly refers to the above-mentioned power resources model, as it discusses the role of Social Democracy in the making of the early postwar Swedish pension system.[13] In focus here is the thorough reformation of the basic pension scheme.

However, the power resources approach is in no sense a mono-factorial theory, and thus the contributions of other forces – both inside and outside the Social Democratic labour movement – in the intense process of postwar reform are quite extensively considered. Since one rebuttal of the power resources approach has concluded, that the role of Social Democracy in this pension reform process was rather marginal, while the centrality of the Swedish right wing has been completely neglected (Baldwin 1988), I have tried to elucidate the broad political spectrum of reform interests in this process. Of special interest here is not least the early emergence of self-aware lobbyists – a mobilization – among the retired when one of the foundations of the Swedish Welfare State Model was erected (cf. Elmér 1960).

In this essay I also stress that the welfare reform process at that time should not be analyzed primarily in terms of single programs but must be seen in its totality, as pensions were not the sole issue on the agenda. On the contrary, it was a "reform wave" that included sweeping changes in child welfare, sickness insurance, education, housing and labour market policies and in this process all political and many social forces – apart from political parties, public bureaucracies as well as "private" organizations – had to relate themselves to the investigative process in this field of action. Nonetheless, with Heckscher (1984) I underline the decisive weight of the Labour movement as well as the alliance between workers and farmers in this reform wave.

2.3 Postwar Sweden

The third and largest study in this book is one of twelve "country chapters" in the series of volumes from the above-mentioned Florence project on the "Development of the West European Welfare State Since the Second World War" directed by Peter Flora (1986-7).[14] Related to these national welfare state profiles was the ambition to produce macrosociological analyses which bore on theoretical discussions in political sociology. However, the project did not contain an explicit, common theoretical perspective – weberian, marxian, or the current vogue. Instead, the project was conceived as an empirical study, a data collection program, in order to describe the development of the welfare state between 1950 and 1980. Of course, data are heavily loaded with theoretical (in this field most often administrative) connotations, they are constrained by the prison-house of classification, and the project director suggested certain criteria in selecting data. Here, he was still close to his earlier proposed definition of the welfare state, and it is a definition of the welfare state close to common sense that still prevails (cf. Flora 1986:V).

However, the outline and strategy of the project were intensively discussed at a number of colloquia in the early 1980s. In particular, the centrality of social insurance programs can be ascribed to Flora's approach to the welfare state, while for example the inclusion of labour market policies is one outcome of collaboration within the project. Basic to Flora is Stein Rokkans "conceptual map of Europe", his insistence on taking a longterm perspective on the development of the welfare state (Flora 1981b). However, in his discussion of the postwar welfare state, Flora also employs Titmuss' models as a guide for inspection (1986:XXI). Another important question raised by Flora is whether the welfare state had changed from being a "solver" to a "generator" of crisis (Flora 1981a).[15]

However, here it is necessary to underline that these country chapters were never intended to produce a "Rokkanite" analysis of domestic postwar social policy. Instead, within the confines of the standardized guidelines, each author was free to select his own theoretical starting-points (without dwelling too much on the pros and cons of the perspective(s) chosen) and to develop his own mode of operationalizing the peculiarities of the national welfare state.[16]

The chapter on Sweden is, in a fairly broad sense, an overview of the welfare state 1945-1985. An attempt is made to a systematic treatment and presentation of a multitude of social programs, ranging from basic pensions to child allowances, from eduation to housing, in terms of expenditure developments, coverage, and financing of cash and in-kind social benefits during the period 1950-1980 (part II). Here, the 1960s stand out as the breakthrough period for the peculiar mix of Swedish welfare policies.

Other dimensions of the welfare state are, however, treated more arbitrarily although the evaluative part (III) attempts a fairly strict summary of the main results from the level-of-living investigations

(1968-1981). In the explanatory part (IV) the roles of economics and demography are less dominant than the role of socio-political forces: social class, political parties, labour market and similar organizations, as well as the emerging interest organizations and pressure groups based on the welfare state itself (pensioners, tenants, disabled, but also more powerful professional groups like the medical profession and the top welfare bureaucrats) are all briefly treated as causal correlates.

Discussions of the "Swedish model" generally point to the close ties between labour market organizations and the realm of politics. However, in an analysis of a welfare state that grew considerably between 1950 and 1980, it would be wrong to ignore the new modes of institutional interaction, and the emergence of collective actors related to the built-up of the welfare state: Thus, one aspect of the question whether the welfare state has changed from being a solver to a generator of crisis (from the perspective of the 1990s, an even more extensive treatment would have been desirable). Furthermore, the fourth section of this chapter includes three brief cases studies of welfare reform focussing on the political process. Unfortunately, all of them date back to the 1940s and '50s, which has to do with the availability of secondary sources at the time of writing.

The fifth part of this chapter deals with the "crisis and prospects for the welfare state" in the first half of the 1980s. Welfare state developments are discussed in terms of institutional changes and adjustments, policy options, social expenditure projections, and the legitimacy or credibility of the contemporary welfare state (i.e.opinion polls). The conclusion reached is very much an answer to the perception of a crisis of the welfare state. In Sweden, instead of a crisis it is suggested that the welfare state was consolidated or "matured" in the early 1980s as social expenditure stagnated in real terms and few new social programs were added to the existing stock. This conclusion is considered indirectly in the fourth essay, through the concepts of privatization and decentralization, as well as in the final pages of this introduction.

2.4 The Dialectics of Privatization and Decentralization

The discussion of the political process behind welfare reform, which was broached in the third chapter of this book, is approached again in its concluding essay. The main object of this study is the actual development of private initiatives – the growth of private pension insurance, private health centers and hospitals as well as health insurance, private child day care, etc. – and actual trends towards decentralization in the realm of welfare.[17] The definition of the two notions – of privatization and decentralization – is guided by the theoretical controversies in comparative welfare state research, not least Titmuss' "divisions of welfare". The close ties between these two notions are emphasized, but throughout the essay they are threated as distinct empirical entities: private and commercial initiatives in the realm of welfare are separated from trends towards decentralization within the public sphere, i.e. administrative and fiscal changes from higher to lower levels of the state. Furthermore, in focus are also some mixed forms of private and public welfare, in particular co-operative arrangements for child day care.

The conclusion reached in this chapter is that compared for example to the UK and the US, privatization in welfare practice up to the mid-1980s in Sweden was a rare phenomenon while as an ideological theme it was prevalent and associated with the neo-liberal right. Nevertheless, it points out the blind spots not least in the Swedish welfare model: apart from private welfare, the existence of, in the words of Titmuss, both occupational and fiscal welfare. Like privatization, decentralization was also a major bone of contention among the social and political forces in Sweden. After six years in opposition, Social Democracy regained the helm in 1982 – and was reelected in 1985 and 1988 – and succeeded in wrestling the decentralization theme out of the hands of the earlier, non-Social Democratic proponents, the Centre Party, and turning it into a weapon against the privatization theme. Within Social Democracy, however, there have been divergent interpretations of decentralization, and a flickering interest in privatization. Nevertheless, the possibility of a synthesis between marketization and decentralization within the public sector is pointed at.

2.5 A Short Summary

The studies in this volume focus on the agents of change in the field of social welfare, the dilemmas these agents have faced at various points of time during the last century (from the social question of the 1880s to the 1980s crisis of the affluent society), the ideas that have been put forward in the realm of welfare, and the solutions – in particular in terms of social security programs but also other types of public welfare programs – that have emerged as a result of these developments. Furthermore, an important shift of hegemony has taken place during this century, from a basically radical-liberal reform "movement" or "intelligentsia" – with deep roots in civil society but without the hegemony over the various bodies that made up the late 19th and early 20th century state – to a party or movement, Social Democracy, based on intense popular mobilizations but with an unsurpassed grip for almost fifty years (most of the time from a strong minority position or, for almost a third of this period, in formal cabinet coalitions) over the political executive, though without a similar hold over the state bureaucracy. A series of "historical compromises" – between peasants and workers, labour and capital, blue and white collar wage earners, as well as between proletarian politicians and urban upper middle class civil servants – were the social basis for the build-up of the institutional model of welfare that has come to characterize the Swedish system in the postwar period. This model is summarized here as a blend of (1) an active manpower policy keeping unemployment at an exceptionally low level internationally, and encouraging wage labour in the economically active population, (2) a comprehensive social security network closely related to active labour force participation, (3) a large public service production sector – more or less a monopoly – in the spheres of health, education, and personal social services, (4) significant public regulations and subsidies in such areas as agriculture and housing, and (5) a system of extensive resource extraction – i.e. taxation – to finance this public household (cf. Davidson 1989:15 & 29). Of course, the more traditional – residual – social welfare practices, addressed towards specific target groups such as juvenile delinquents, drug addicts, broken families, etc., could be added to this overview, but in this context they are of minor importance.

Before saying a few words about the prospects for this model, I will briefly discuss the theoretical implications of this study. In the final pages, I will again stress the expansionary nature of the Swedish Welfare State Model, which has not been appreciably affected by the crisis of the welfare state. This can of course be interpreted as a confirmation of the proposition that "politics doesn't matter". Despite the fact that the format of these studies does not allow any definite theoretical conclusions, I would argue that such an interpretation would be superficial, in particular as competing theories have less to offer in the Swedish case.

Sweden was fertile ground for Social Democratic welfare reform from the mid-1940s onwards. Already from the 1880s, the liberal welfare intelligentsia in civil society had been a strong proponent of state reform, and managed to secure support from the farmers – a significant political force. Also later on, the farmers were an important coalition partner in social policy, this time in the shift of hegemony in the early 1930s, when the Social Democrats took command in the realm of politics. Despite the clash in the 1920s between the Social Democrats and the liberal welfare intelligentsia (the latter now in control of the welfare bureaucracies), the political regrouping in the early 1930s and the compromises formed throughout that decade – not only in politics but also on the labour market – prepared the ground for the consensual agreements in the field of welfare reform that followed in the mid-1940s. However, the conflicts remained as regards the financing of welfare reform, and the narrow but decisive victory of the left in the 1948 election came after a battle launched by Social Democracy to maintain their fairly recent social policy hegemony. Other crucial electoral victories followed, again a narrow one in 1958-60 – the superannuation pension program – and a more comfortable one in 1968.[18] The confrontation over a superannuation pension program is generally regarded as the exception from an otherwise consensual evolution of the early postwar welfare state. However, these decisive electoral conflicts made possible a subsequent hegemony in the field of social policy that formed the basis for other reform agreements, the consensus of Swedish social policy. Equally important was the build-up of new welfare bureaucracies under Social Democratic hegemony (cf. Rothstein 1986). Furthermore, the first postwar decades were years of continuous economic growth, which enhanced the possibilities of welfare reform. When the non-social-ist parties, after victory in the election of 1976 and after thirty years in Parliamentary opposition, for six years occupied the cabinet seats, they did so almost without challenging traditional welfare policies. Although they had to face macro-economic difficulties, these did not affect social policy until the end of their reign in the early 1980s, when these scattered parties to the right of the political spectrum in Sweden failed to win a decisive welfare election.

Thus, in the paragraph above I have tried – simultaneously – to summarize the evolution of the Swedish welfare state and to indi-cate the contributions of other theories than those emphasising class politics and class coalitions in this field of social research: in particular the historical role of mobilization and interest articu-lation among the urban middle strata and the independent farmers in late 19th and early 20th century Sweden, while theories empha-sizing economic growth – as well as demographic growth – point to an important precondition for the consensus and compromises that dominated welfare reform in the postwar period. However, I have also pointed out the decisive conflicts that made possible a hegemony out of which a consensus on welfare policy could be reached. The independent role of state bureaucrats seems to be of minor importance in the postwar Swedish case, while the built-up of labourite welfare bureaucracies as an institutionalization of class compromises is of crucial importance in understanding the work-ings of the Swedish Welfare State Model. So much about the past; what about the future?

3. At the End of a Road?

Apart from trends towards decentralization and privatization, what happened to the welfare state in the 1980s? We can discern at least two perspectives. Firstly, theories of a "maturation" or "consolida-tion". These notions echo the idea of irreversibility as well as of stagnation or status quo. Secondly, the concept of crisis so often proposed from the second half of the 1970s. Does crisis better encapsulate what was going on? Or should we – instead of crisis, maturation, consolidation or stagnation – think in terms of a major transformation, as for instance Wolfe (1989) has suggested?

In these concluding pages, those recurrent questions are considered in a discussion of three indicators that are widely used in welfare state research: (1) social expenditures, (2) public employment, and (3) the enlargement or retardation of social programs/rights. Throughout, I will focus on the Swedish case.

In comparative terms, Sweden is still one of the leading spenders on social welfare (cf. Alestalo and Uusitalo 1990; OECD 1985). However, as shown in graph 1, in terms of spending, public social policy outlays as a percentage of GDP were virtually unchanged in the first half of the 1980s. Since then, particularly in 1987, there has been some increase, mainly due to a major reform of sickness insurance and the build-up of the child day-care service (see below). The most costly sub-program, the national health service, has not increased its running costs (at constant prices) in the 1980s. Likewise, public outlays on education has been fairly constant. In the late 1980s, the costs of the national superannuation program overshadow the basic pension program, these being the third and fourth largest social programs. The major conclusion is thus, that no major retrenchment has occurred, and in a field like child care there has even been expansion in the 1980s. In this sense, it is fair to talk of a consolidation of the Swedish welfare state.[19]

Another indicator of welfare state development is public employment which has continued to increase throughout the decade, as personal social services to the elderly and to children have expanded. In the course of the 1980s some 250 000 persons – mostly women – have joined the public sector as employees in the health and social sector. In terms of public employment, there is thus no indication of a stagnation of the welfare state. But I prefer to see this in terms of a transformation of the Swedish welfare state – as Wolfe has suggested – as more people are employed in this sector to take care and administer other people's lives, whole sectors that used to be family or personal obligations are being "socialized".

However, it is not the central state that has been "transformed"; here the number of employees has decreased. It is in the regional and local authorities that a growing number of persons have become employed from the 1960s onwards: para-medical personnel to care for the elderly and the disabled, teachers and nurses to look after the young generation because the vast majority of adults in active age groups are gainfully employed. However, it is highly debatable whether the implication of this transformation is, as Wolfe, following mainstream critical theory, suggests, that the state has "colonized the spheres of everyday life". Instead a counterhypothesis is offered: most of these new, local welfare state institutions – public child day care centres, public education, training centres for disabled and other hard-to-employ, and day centres for elderly people – are not signs of a breakdown of the voluntary community (the diminution of a sphere outside the immediate control of the state or the market) but a reinvention of – intermediary – institutions on the borders of state and civil society.

Figure 1. Social welfare expenditure as a percentage of the gross domestic product at market price in the years 1970 - 1987

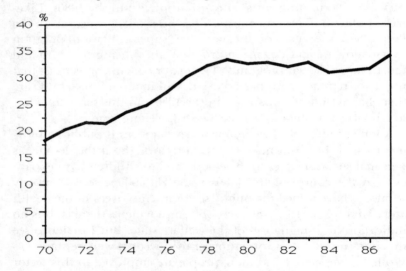

Source: SCB: The Cost and Financing of the Social Services in Sweden in 1987.

Furthermore, in the postwar period, the welfare state was inaugurated with broad social insurance programs, from the late 1940s to the early 1960s, while the growth of the social service state followed after the latter date. However, one aspect of the early postwar reforms was to rationalize the structure of local administration, and to make the local authorities more efficient in carrying out welfare reform. Basically, the social service state is run by the municipalities and county councils, which are independent tax-raising bodies in the Swedish administrative structure. These authorities represent a historical closeness between state and citizen, but it is a matter of dispute whether this closeness has disappeared with the fusion of municipalities – from some 2500 in the early 1950s to roughly a tenth of that figure in the 1970s onwards – as well as with the enlargement of the health sector.

3.1 Reforming Social Programs

In a few social programs, legislative changes have occurred or been proposed in the second half of the 1980s (see part V in the third study, as well as the fourth study for discussions about changes in the first half of the 1980s). Here, five programs will be singled out for a brief examination: sickness insurance, widow's pension, work injury insurance, parental insurance and child day care.[20]

In 1987, sickness insurance was reformed, and, for instance, the remaining initial no-benefit day was abolished. Furthermore, daily sickness cash benefits were converted to an hourly basis, a reform that the trade unions had demanded in order to rectify the arbitrariness of the system. The improvement concerned part-time and semiannual employment, and jobs with irregular hours. Thus, it is correct to interpret these changes as an extension of a social right (cf. Korpi 1989). However, the reform was fairly costly: together with an increase in the number of sickdays, it led to a 32 percent increase in the overall costs of sickness insurance, compared to a 21 percent increase in total social expenditure (current prices), between 1986 and 1987, and despite an increase in payroll charges, revenue has not been sufficient to meet outlays. Both before and after its implementation the change to "hourly benefits" was questioned by the parties to the right of Social Democracy, who have advocated other changes in this system in response above all to the increase in the number of sickdays.[21]

An abortive attempt was made in the early 1980s to reform the widow's pension scheme (cf. part V in the third study). A new Parliamentary Commission was set up in the mid-1980s, and quite soon after the 1985 election all political parties were prepared to support a proposal fairly similar to the one suggested a few years before. This time, no major social force took the opportunity to become the advocate of this elderly female minority. Thus, one of the oldest elements in the Swedish social security system will disappear over a transition period of thirty years. The Commission, set up with the object of reforming the entire pension system, has still to produce other reform proposals.

In contrast, despite widespread but divergent criticism, no reform has been proposed for the work injury insurance system. The trade unions are critical of the administrative procedures and bureaucratic practices whereby claimants have to wait for years for a final decision. on their status (Hetzler & Erikson 1983). But as the long-term benefits are more generous in this – comprehensive but selective – insurance system than in the universal sickness and disability pension program, a proposal by a state commission more than a decade ago to abolish this program has not reached the final stage of the political agenda. Despite the existence of complementary negotiated insurance schemes (collective agreements), the trade unions have never been willing to let this public scheme disappear. Compared to the widow's pension program, the occupational injury insurance program has much stronger defendants.

Parental insurance is another example of an enlargement of social rights. During the period 1989-91, the benefit period during which the insured are reimbursed at a 90 percent replacement level will be extended from 9 months to 18 months (in effect until a child is 1' year old). This proposal was part of a Social Democratic election promise in 1988 supported only by the Left Party Communists. Here, too, we find a welfare program that indicates that in some respect the welfare state is still expanding.

This is also the case concerning the even more controversial child day care program proposed by the Social Democrats in the mid-1980s. Here, the ambition is that every child above the age of 1' – thus after the general paternal insurance expires – shall have a place at a public day care center as of 1991. The notion of a "social right" to a day care place has been proposed, for instance, by the LO, but so far the government has not acted. Furthermore, in the second half of the 1980s, the number of places in public day care have increased considerably, but demand is still greater than supply. Despite decreased central state grants, the municipalities have put up the money needed to carry out this reform. However, the number of newborns has gone up, from roughly 90 000 a year in the early 1980s to some 120 000 in 1989, the labour turnover in this sector has been aggravated in regions with full employment, and it is a matter of much dispute whether the goal will be reached.

3.2 Still a Welfare Model?

This overview of these five sub-programs of social welfare indicates that it would be incorrect to talk about a stagnation of the Swedish system. Furthermore, total social costs have – with the exception of sickness insurance – more or less been controlled, but public employment has grown and there are a fair number of examples of growth and adaptation in the postwar system of social programs. Of course, some of these indicators do not tell us anything about the content of these programs, for instance whether the wage sum has risen while the money spent on program activities has fallen. Overall, whether these trends can be summarized as a maturation is a matter of dispute, but this has been done both on the Right and the Left of Swedish politics (cf. Zetterberg 1979; LO1986).[22]

Throughout these final pages, I have stressed the expansionary character – a "maturation", "consolidation" or "more of the same" (according to its critics) – of the Swedish Welfare State Model. Despite a slowdown in the growth of social programs and of social expenditure, both during the bourgeois years of the late 1970s and early 1980s but in particular during the economically more prosperous years of Social Democratic rule during the rest of the 1980s, the Swedish social policy has not been substantially affected by the crisis of the welfare state. This is a conclusion similar to the one proposed by a Pacific student of social welfare, who – based on the works of Korpi and Esping-Andersen, and after comparing New Zealand and Sweden over the last century – contrasts an "egalitarian" (generous income-tested cash benefits) welfare state model with a "solidaristic" (or universal earnings-related) social security state (Davidson 1989). Both egalitarian and solidaristic tendencies are inscribed in the Titmussian institutional redistributive model, but in contrast to the New Zealand Welfare State, in Sweden solidaristic aspects have generally dominated over egalitarian: the solidaristic model is strong on horizontal redistribution – over the life-span – and does not to the same extent emphasize egalitarian or vertical redistribution, from rich to poor. This is particularly true for the construction of the social insurance system, and it is the price paid by the working class for middle class collaboration.[23]

However, when the crisis of the welfare state from the mid-1970s constrained the potential for social politics, the "egalitarian" New Zealand welfare state rather abruptly regressed into a traditional residual welfare model (under a Labour cabinet!), while the "solidaristic" Swedish model (first under bourgeois, only later under Social Democratic political leadership) withstood attacks on its comprehensiveness. From the mid-1980s, Sweden, still with extremely low levels of unemployment, became an international answer to the "new pessimism" (Heclo 1981) concerning the future viability of the welfare state. In this period, the centrality of class power and coalition building have come to the fore again: more than ever has the Swedish Welfare State Model – petrified according to its critics – been identified with Social Democracy.

Nevertheless, there are naturally limits also to this type of welfare solidarity. In the 1980s, all the major social and political forces have had the ambition to change the welfare system. However, the direction of change has of course not been identical among the collective actors in this field, not least the political parties and major interest organizations. Furthermore, despite a fair number of reform initiatives during the 1980s, disputes within the labour movement have partly deadlocked the movement of change and adaptation to new circumstances. The official program of the Social Democrats is to decentralize and to increase efficiency in existing welfare services, but the interpretation of these goals have been the subject of bitter dispute between those who would allow some space for private initiatives, for example, in child day care and other personal social and medical services, and those who prefer to stick to the traditional centralist universal welfare paradigm.

Thus, the stability and the broad-based coalition of the Swedish Welfare State Model have their deficiencies. If the strategy of equality has its definite problems, there are also inherent limits to the internal strength of the welfare state coalition. The coalition that supported the build-up of this model in the 1950s and 1960s was very different from the one that in the early 1990s stands up in its defence. The latter is a notably wide coalitions but the question remains whether a centre exists that has the strength and vitality to give this coalition a sense of direction, or whether its various parts will block each other in the process of rejuvenating this model. For instance, in contrast to the 1930s and 1940s, in the 1980s no comprehensive investigatory process was initiated with the ambition to carry out reform in the welfare sector as a whole.[24]

So far, the Swedish welfare state model has survived, but the potency of structural change and adaptation is still an open question, although the optimist may point to the tax reform of the early 1990s as a recent sign of vigour. But despite a lot of talk about effective resource utilization in the fully developed welfare state, the decentralization strategy has become fragmented, while the theme of privatization has become a major bone of contention within the labour movement. Thus, the issue of whether the Swedish Welfare State Model will be renewed in a dignified or petrified manner − or even regress − is likely to come to the fore in the 1990s. Crucial to this outcome is whether the welfare state will be regarded as promoting social justice, efficiency, security, etc., or whether a cementation of existing inequalities and iniquities causes more powerful organizational alternatives to see the light of day.

I. Before Social Democracy: the Early Formation of a Social Policy Discourse in Sweden

> ...in Scandinavia the boundary between the state and civil society was increasingly crossed in practice without anyone thinking about it in theory.
> A. Wolfe: *Whose Keeper?* (1989) p. 157.

1. The Absence of a Theory of Social Policy in Sweden?

Few people, whether friends or foes, laymen or social policy experts, will deny that when it comes to social welfare and social policy, Sweden constitutes one of the most important test cases on the globe.* Sweden is a country where the practice of social policy has spread into most corners of society. Whether one likes it or not, Sweden is often taken as an example of the most advanced, fully developed or extreme welfare state. Viewed by friendly observers as an incarnation of the idea of the welfare state, Sweden stands as a pragmatic compromise between totalitarian socialism and unvarnished capitalism, a garden of social justice in a world of injustice. Adjacent to the presence of a working practicality is the absence of a concern with theoretical issues (Heckscher 1984). There has not been very much of a social policy discourse in Sweden.

A number of studies have focussed either on the actual policies carried out in social welfare and related fields, in particular labour market policies, or on the factors and forces behind the trajectory of the welfare state.[1] Several domestic social policy experts – as divergent as Per Holmberg and Hans L Zetterberg – have both complained about the absence of a social policy theory in Sweden, and have explained this in terms of the low level of academic institutionalization within this field of research (Holmberg 1970; Zetterberg 1980).[2] The ambition here is to make a modest contribution to uncovering some of the early, formative domestic ideas, and in particular their *environment* in Sweden, behind the advanced or extreme social practice. Thus, I am concerned with the soil in which the seeds of the Social Policy of Social Democracy grew, its early childhood, not its adult life. It is not even a study of the transition to a social democratic social policy although a paragraph at the end of this essay does touch upon that process (section 8.b). This essay is an interrogation into social policy "before" social democracy left a definite imprint on welfare policy in Sweden. Thus, the ambition is to refute a widespread conjecture concerning the – early – (non-existent) moral-spiritual topography of a Swedish social policy discourse.[3]

Ramesh Mishra's analysis of a specific domestic, Titmussian, social policy tradition in the postwar UK provided an example of the possiblity of such an analysis within the field of social policy (1977:3-24). However, here my ambition is to focus on social policy at the closing decades of the last century and the early years of the present one. Is it possible to detect such a domestic social policy theory tradition in Sweden, albeit earlier and thus closer in time to the original Fabian discourse? Is there a more or less hidden social policy discourse that has not been uncovered in its full scope despite – or maybe because of – the exceptional evolution of the Swedish welfare state practice? If so, which were its social and intellectual coordinates? What was the scope and peculiarity of this discourse? What was its special preoccupation?

The present analysis will thus focus on the way the early social policy discussion in Sweden framed (1) the relationship between markets, politics and civil society, (2) the role attached to social welfare in this relationship, and (3) the "boundaries" of social policy, the social division of welfare. This essay is accordingly not an attempt at a full coverage of the historical development of the Swedish social policy tradition. Instead, the subject is the formative moments of social policy, and the formation of a "welfare intelligentsia" in Sweden (sections 4-8). A searchlight will be provided through two notions – civil society and intellectuals – that hopefully will help to overcome the all too frequent binary/polar opposition of markets and politics in contemporary welfare state analysis.

2. Conceptual Interlude: Intellectuals in Civil Society

In the presumed absence of a coherent theory of social policy in the foremost welfare state, it is often taken for granted that state intervention has been the general medicine prescribed in particular by the Swedish labour movement. Of course, the political apparatus has been a preeminent instrument in the (re)distribution of resources – money as well as personel – among society's members. But it is far from the sole channel of means for subsistence. More or less (state or self-) regulated markets are central distributive mechanisms in contemporary capitalist societies. However, the economic and political spheres of society are in themselves hard to exactly define and delimit but nevertheless fairly easy to grasp not least in advanced Western societies. Their paradigmatic exactitude may differ considerably, nevertheless they are a common pair in a number of analytical social scientific languages.[4] To counterpose state and economy is, however, not enough, not even regarding a society sometimes characterized as a successful blend of extremely centralized state power (in the hands of the labour movement) and monopolized big business.

Here, the once fashionable concept of civil society will be introduced as a heuristic device. However, it will be coupled to a firmly established analytical framework in this field of sociology: Richard Titmuss rather unsystematic yet extremely influential ideas regarding the role of social policy in society. As is most clearly indicated in the Titmussian model of the social division of welfare (1958), but partly also in his three later models of social policy (1974; cf. Mishra 1977:101; Korpi 1980:303), there exists an intimate sphere of social relations separated from, but of course not completely independent of, economic and political human relationships in society: private welfare as opposed to fiscal, occupational and social welfare.[5] Here, by applying the triangular compass of markets, politics *and* civil society my intention is to locate social policy in relation to "voluntarism" and "charity" as well as to politics and business (cf. Rose 1986).

Following Wolfe (1989), civil society will here be used as an umbrella for intimate as well as distant social relationships between human beings in an "imagined community" (cf. Anderson 1983) within well defined frontiers: clusters of individuals in a territory and bonds – the often forgotten dimension of "loyalty" in Hirschman's terminology (1970) – between people in action that not necessarily are aimed at a market or directed towards the state.[6] Instead of a dichotomy – civil vs. political, private vs. public, politics vs. markets, or base vs. superstructure – human relationships in society are here viewed as taking place in a triangle composed of state, economy, and civil society. In contrast to analytical frameworks based on dichotomic antipodes, the inclusion of a third sphere is also a reminder of the existence of a multitude of social cleavages, some of these more dominant than others in different settings.

To introduce the concept of civil society in order to emphasise social relationships outside the market and not inside politics may invoke opposition from theorists in favour of supposedly likeminded notions: community, family, life-sphere, (again) private or intimate sphere, intermediary organizations, everyday life, life world, etc. This is not the place to delve further into abstract definitions. The conceptual ambiguities are overwhelming. Let me just propose that civil society has connotations that are broader than community and are less utopian and narrow than, say, life-sphere or everyday life.[7] Intense affective relationships such as love as well as loyalties promoting more or less organized and institutionalized cooperation and solidarity in wider circles than small groups are captured in this notion. An abstract analytical concept will not in a single blow solve or transcend the actual theoretical and empirical problems at work, but it may help to highlight aspects that otherwise tend to be forgotten or neglected.

After a short southern detour (section 3), I will in the following pages (sections 4-8) make an attempt to investigate the trajectory of the local theoretical social policy tradition in Sweden from its inception in the closing decades of the last century to the early "breakthrough" of social democratic welfare policies.[8] I will suggest the possibility of such a domestic social policy tradition through an examination of the environment in which ideas developed at the formative moments of some core areas of social policy, in particular in the intersection of social insurance and poor relief.[9]

This implies a focus on the role of intellectuals, and the kind of ideological independence and collective unity that takes hold in a given intelligentsia or segment of it; what has been labelled "ideological corporatism" (Mulhern 1981:viii). Intellectuals are those who create, distribute and apply culture, the symbolic world of man (Lipset 1960:311). In particular the first part of this definition will be highlighted: those who were on the creative edge of culture in contrast to the intellectual "mass" or "class" (cf. Gesser 1985). It is with the intellectual as social justifier or critic – in particular the "voices of dissent" – and the institutional setting of this elite, that I am concerned. Later on, the intricate problem of choosing intellectuals will be discussed (section 6). Needless to say in such an analysis of the domestic intellectual life of a country far from the centre stage, the imports of intellectual goods and cultural repercussions from the outside must be taken into account. Here and there notes about this importation will be inserted as well as the national roots and origins of the foreign social policy discourse will be indicated. Nonetheless, the general question to be posed will be: to what extent has there existed a domestic social policy discourse which may have left an imprint on the advanced welfare state.

3. Social Policy and Social Insurance: German Inventions

The idea of social policy originates from the crossroads of the commercio-industrial and socio-political revolutions. It is a late product of the Enlightenment tradition, one of many conscious efforts to come to terms with the unwanted effects of the great transformation of the twin revolutions: the contradictory movement of the destitution and mass insecurity of poor, uprooted and landless proletarians on their route from working the land to entering the urban fabric-market of contractual freedom. The threat of the combined free wage labourer and free "citoyen" was a durable underlying – and to a large extent also openly expressed – theme in most social thought of late 18th and 19th centuries.

The poor and destitute were kept under as strict control as possible by both the old and the new regimes.[10] Democracy in modern terms – universal suffrage and representative government –

was seldom the answer to the question of poverty neither from traditional intellectuals nor from ruling circles. Despite the existence of humanitarian and christian reform movements as well as a rich radical and socialist utopian tradition which tried to explicate the potentiality of (worldly) New Jerusalems, the dominant mode of thought – both the conservative defenders of the old social order and the proponents of the new liberal-capitalist society – viewed with suspicion and awe the capricious crowd or mob, which one way or another had to be disciplined and subordinated. It is in this context, social insurance – the private principle of mutuality put in a broader perspective – was invented from above. Hence, it is important to emphasize that social policy and social insurance was only one of many possible roads to the contemporary welfare state.[11]

Throughout Europe, but in particular in Germany, where a more organic and less individualistic culture prospered in an imperial greenhouse during the second half of the 19th century, important attempts were made to reconcile the rapidly emerging new economic order with a more positive but still authoritarian role for the new (nation-)state than what the liberal perception of the "night-watchman" entailed.[12] On the agenda was – parallelling the evolution of the theme of social policy – the build-up of a new, rational, civil administrative order to be distinguished from the old military-clientilistic state apparatus.[13] Although factory legislation was more advanced at the birthplace of the industrial revolution, the UK, than elsewhere in Europe, it was especially from Germany that the concept of *Sozialpolitik* spread. This concept is intimately linked to the set up of social insurance, albeit occupational safety and education become important state activities in many European countries from the mid-19th century onwards. Until the presentation of the Beveridge plan in the 1940s, no other single event had had a more profound influence on the discourse of social policy than Bismarck's initiative of 1881 (Girvetz 1972:514-5). Actually, this invention signals the formative moment of the discourse itself. The combination of rapid industrialization, imperial nation-building and the introduction of innovative social insurance laws gave the *Kathedersozialisten*, historical economists, or Socialists of the Lectern-Chair a considerable impact both inside and outside their native country.

41

In a crusade against free-market political economy as well as secular Marxian economic thought, this basically Christian ethical school of thought, suggested a new terrain of corporatist communality between the emerging social categories of the new social order.[14] In the German set up, social science and social action were intertwined not least in the theory and practice of the influencial *Verein für Sozialpolitik* (Social Policy Association), founded in 1872 (Ringer 1969:143-162). In effect this association became a non-parliamentary social reform party – the party of modernity – in Germany in the closing decades of the 19th century incorporating both social-conservatives as well as social-liberals. Unbridled capitalist industrial expansion should be curbed by an enlightened state bureaucracy favourable to public welfare.[15] The dominant figures of *Verein für Sozialpolitik* such as its moderate longstanding chairman Gustav Schmoller and the conservative Adolph Wagner, were outspokenly antagonistic towards socialist ideology, trade unions, and in particular the German Social Democrats. Both supported Bismarck's combined muffling of the electorally successful party of revolution and subsequent patriarchial social legislation. To them, enlightened despotism as well as social insurance were solutions to a certain historical weakness: the absence of a German nation. Thus, social policy was part of a national program for German-Prussian greatness.

Compared to the old means-tested poor relief system, the insurance principle meant that claimants/recipients were entitled to reimbursements from funds to which they had contributed during their working life as respectable workers and wage earners. Hence, the industrial working class was awarded a dignified or upgraded social status under Imperial state tutelage. Adding social to insurance implied a transcendence of the pure market insurance principle into a qualitatively new public relief system, in particular as the state created both a new bureaucracy, subsidized the new system and even acted as lender of last resort.

Thus, from its inception, state welfare and social insurance became a weapon in the struggle between organized social forces. But inside *Verein für Sozialpolitik* there were also leading figures that from the start advocated another strategy, a still integrative but less authoritarian and more tolerant attitude towards socialism. In particular Lujo von Brentano, who also supported the social insurance approach, came as well to defend equal participation of workers through freedom of association (trade unions) and the institutionalisation of class struggle (arbitration and collective agreements). This approach was more appetising for those interested in social reform in Scandinavia, at that time a cultural periphery of the most expansive continental European empire.[16]

4. Across the Baltic: Social Insurance Comes to Sweden

Throughout the 19th century Sweden was still one of the poorest and most backward nations in Europe. Nonetheless, it was a fairly egalitarian society, and, in terms of literacy, the population was advanced. Furthermore, the peasantry had never, not even during the 17th century Great Power Era, been subjugated by the feudal order; in the 19th century this made possible a limited degree of political freedom. Industrialization came late, beginning only in the 1870s at a time when a political-institutional representative reform had abolished the archaic Estate Parliament. At this time, young people in their best working age left the country *en masse* for North America, and the demographic structure became skewed towards the upper age brackets.

However, reactions to German social insurance legislation were swift in Sweden. Already in early 1884, the first comprehensive social insurance bill was introduced in the second chamber of the Swedish Parliament.[17] The bill was widely commented upon in the press and aroused considerable public attention (Kihlberg 1972:103-109). Although the bill was unanimously adopted by Parliament, the German social insurance principle was almost immediately openly attacked by a leading Swedish conservative senator and Manchester liberal: Hans Forssell (1843-1901). In a magazine for Nordic affairs, this brilliant historian and top ranking civil servant who admired Imperial Germany but vociferously opposed any state intervention in the relations between employers and employees, scrutinized German social policy experience during the 1870s and early '80s.[18] The latter was nothing to repeat in Sweden, but would end up in a devastating experiment in state socialism. Furthermore, he made fools of the *Kathedersozialisten*, and even criticized the military centralism and the dirigism so typical of

Bismarckian social insurance. In the view of Forssell, there was no space for state welfare in an industrial market system still underway. This would create largescale dependency and a huge bureaucracy, raise taxes, and overall be a threat to individual freedom and entreprenuership. In particular, a poor country like Sweden could not afford the luxury of work safety and workingmen's compensation, not to think of old age insurance (X 1884). The sponsor of the bill never replied in public.[19]

This bill was written by one of Forssell's antipodes in Parliament, Adolf Hedin (1834-1905), a charismatic and cosmopolitarian urban democrat, whose formative years followed in the aftermath of the European uprisings of 1848. His spiritual inspiration came from the radicalism of the French revolution. These sources were blended with native Geijerian democratic liberalism and a Scandinavian cultural nationalism similar to the "imagined communitarianism" of other peripheral European nations in-the-making (Berggren 1961).[20] Hedin was a frequent contributor to the emerging popular press, and for a short while editor-in-chief of *Aftonbladet*.[21] When the social insurance bill was introduced, for fiftheen years Hedin had been a very imaginative MP, in particular as an articulated protagonist of the rights of those without any rights, and actively intervened in, for example, the continuous revisions of the traditional Swedish poor laws (Nilsson 1965). Hedin was not much of a party man, but always considered himself a radical liberal. Already in the 1880s, he was called a "Tribune of the People" and his support among workers grew throughout his life to the point where he had hardly been buried before left socialists tried to wrest him out of the liberal net.[22]

In the 1884 bill, Hedin extensively surveyed European social legislation in the 1870s and early 1880s – from Denmark and Germany in the north to Italy and Spain in the south, from the western British Isles eastwards to czarist Russia and semi-independant Finland – and from the opposite of the political spectrum more or less accepted the unitarian Bismarckian social insurance approach (Hedin 1884a). Of course, he was critical of the latter's authoritarian tendencies, but emphasized its farreaching scope: compulsory state insurance in case of sickness, work accident, old age and invalidity. Compared to earlier attempts in other countries, the German legislation was superior.[23] Hedin also took pains to examine the ideological objections: both from the proponents of the Manchester orthodoxy – a doctrine that once made an important contribution to breaking up an old state despotism according to Hedin – and from those fearing socialism (Berggren 1965). As a liberal, Hedin indicated in the bill the necessity to rethink earlier anti-etatist positions, and without succumbing to their authoritarianism, he did not hesitate to quote Bismarck and a number of other European conservatives in favour of a new type of state involvement directed towards the labouring classes. Socialism as well as state interventionism should be viewed pragmatically.

However, the way he framed his concluding proposal and acted in Parliament is of particular interest for the future of the social policy discourse. In the bill, he pointed out the great variation in social legislation throughout Europe, but made no definite propositions regarding the boundaries between proper and improper state activity. However, in view of a future transition to full enfranchisement of the populace, he was prepared to accept new means of state involvement in – civil – society and new relationships between state and citizen.[24] Social insurance meant a radical break but Hedin did not choose total "statism". His pragmatic attitude towards state intervention is most evident in the case of sickness insurance. In the bill, this branch of social insurance had been deliberately omitted because, as he stated in Parliament, there existed successful voluntary associations actively enrolling new members (Hedin 1884b). But in a speech at the Stockholm Political Economy Club, he gave an overview of the German compulsory sickness insurance system without distancing himself from it (Hedin 1884c). Actually, as one of its few successful legislative proposals, insignificant but in effect already from 1891, the first Royal Worker's Insurance Commission came out in favour of state subsidies to voluntary sickness benefit societies.

Neither in the bill nor in the parliamentary debate did Hedin outline a definite organization of social insurance in Sweden. He simply proposed to the executive branch to investigate the issue and prepare relevant legislation. Tactics was not his strong side, but as a gifted and experienced politician, Hedin managed to make the bill acceptable to the great majority of farmers in the House who like himself were parsimonious with tax money, and who during the mid-19th century had ardently fought against central state interference in the parishes' poor relief practice (Nilsson 1965).

In an uncontested amendment the landowners made this acceptance utterly clear: they were prepared to trade municipal poor relief costs for state-financed benefits given to all types of workers, not just urban-industrial. Hence, this meant that from the start there was an implicit shift from worker's to people's insurance in Sweden. Thus, in theory, more or less the whole population was included as potential insurance contributors and beneficiaries, later endorsed by the analysis of the Swedish class structure made by the Workers Commission (Therborn 1986). In the Parliamentary debate in 1884, Hedin had no principal, only tactical, objections to this shift in coverage.[25] Quite the contrary: he was well aware of the difference between rapidly industrializing Germany and still basically rural Sweden. Furthermore, as an urban radical with a rural background in close contact with the emerging workingmen's organizations and other popular movements like the teetotallers – and to a lesser extent also the free-thinking Christians outside the ideological control of the Lutheran church – he managed to put forward demands that presaged what has later been distilled as a class or "worker's perspective" on social policy (cf. Therborn 1986).

Hedin ended his bill with a priority list which started with work accident regulations, followed by employer's liability in case of such accidents, occupational injury insurance and fourthly workers old age insurance.[26] Hence, the combination of Hedin's overarching opposition towards the still prevailing royal power and his detailed priorities regarding social insurance is important to emphasize: this way, he acted as a bridge-builder on social issues at a time when liberals and the still weak socialists were united in the day-to-day struggle for universal suffrage but definitely had divergent horizons regarding an ultimate desirable society. Hedin, thus, opened up a terrain soon to be explored by the Swedish intelligentsia, not least a future generation of Social Democrats. In the meantime, however, a group of slightly more traditional intellectuals took the lead.

5. The First Steps towards a Social Policy Discourse in Sweden

Social policy in Sweden, thus, emerged in the intersection between a German invention and a longstanding but controversial residual and patriarchial poor relief practice. In legislative terms, it took roughly three decades before the terms between the two were resolved.[27] Hedin's bill and active interventions in public events were, thus, the first steps taken towards the development of a social policy discourse in Sweden. As already mentioned, from the start the social insurance approach met with fierce theoretical opposition in Sweden. The contradictory viewpoints of Hedin and Forssell presented the arguments for and against social insurance, state intervention in the market, and the possibility of wealth creation and social progress in a modern capitalist society, but it never really developed into a full-fledged social policy discourse. Anyhow: 1884 was the moment of social policy in Sweden[28] – Hedin's bill passed Parliament almost without any opposition and later in that year, a Royal Commission on Worker's Insurance was set up by the Government in which Hedin became a very active member.[29] Although its immediate impact in terms of effective legislation was poor, the bill was not simply an episode, an origin to which certain phenomena can retrospectively be ascribed, but an *Ursprung*, an irruption so far without end, into a social order perpetually vulnerable to its impact.[30]

However, the formative years of a social policy discourse range from the mid-1880s up to the 1910s – in Sweden the breakthrough for social policy parallells the democratic breakthrough, the extra-parliamentary struggle for universal and equal suffrage as well as the growth of the social or popular mass movements – teetotallers, religious freethinkers, consumer co-operatives, and trade unions – under rapid industrial progress in towns as well as in the countryside – not to forget massive emigration across the Atlantic. Hence, modern politics was constituted along a clear frontline between a conservative, authoritarian, pre-industrial, and largely pre-bourgeois establishment and carriers of modernity, a new associational world of large groups of "deeply concerned people collectively grappling with basic questions of human life and of life beyond death" (Therborn 1989a:198).[31] In the words of Marshall Berman,

47

this formation basically occurred in a pastoral pre-modernity akin if of course not exactly similar to the underdevelopment of czarist Russia (1982:241). Although several attempts to take over social policy were made from various conservative elite circles, in particular one in 1888 by the King and his closest advisers, the party of order never succeeded (Englund 1976). It was the urban liberal forces that throughout this transitional period had the *intellectual* initiative on the social issue in Sweden (cf. Sellberg 1950).[32]

Thus, in contrast to Wilhelmine Germany, there was no important social conservative reform party despite the fact that, nine years after Hedin's bill, the first general treatise on social policy was published by a reform-minded academic conservative (see below – section 6.2). The "spiritual party of modernity" was liberal-minded, to some extent even "radical-democratic". Hedin is, of course, the obvious example, and he continued to be an active participant until his death at the time of the peaceful dissolution of the dynastical union with Norway in 1905. Although he was considered a "one-man show", during the course of the 1890s he was joined by several younger colleagues in Parliament, including Hjalmar Branting (1860-1924), the Labour leader, who all vied with each other in promoting social legislation. For example, in a bill from his final year Hedin and 21 cosponsors proposed the set up of a special Ministry of Labour and Social Affairs at Cabinet level.[33] However, it is once again important to stress that Hedin was something more than a mere legislator. Not only was he a frequent, regular contributor to the daily press, in the 1880s and '90s in particular to the *Dagens Nyheter*, but he was also a kind of Ombudsman of the common people.

So far parliamentary and legislative initiatives in the formation of a domestic social policy discourse have been almost exclusively focussed upon due to the centrality of Hedin. But cognitive developments are in no sense dependent upon legislative evolution. More important, outside Parliament interest in social issues grew continuously during the last decades of the 19th and first decades of the 20th century. It was the mass popular movements and its collectivist educational endeavours that proved to be fertile ground for social reform propagated by an urban radical elite. In Scandinavia, the social movements formed the audience to which avant-garde social thought appealled (cf Olofsson 1987; Alapuro 1988).

However, the popular mass movements were in no sense a unity, although memberships often were overlapping. In particular the "new" temperance movement – there was a first wave of mobilization on this issue in the 1830s and '40s – was the most rapidly growing popular movement from the 1880s onwards but also the religious dissenters rose impressively. None of the latter social movements had the ambition to be a Parliamentary party. This was, however, the goal of the least rapidly growing popular mass movement: Social Democracy.

There were both cooperation and competition between these organizations as well as conflicts over ends and means, both within the different temperance organizations, and between the religious revivalists on the one hand, and the workers' movements on the other.[34] However, here was an open, common ground and these movements were all fundamentally concerned with "basic questions of human life and of life beyond death" which often brought them together against the old regime. However, in particular the disciplined lifestyle of the world of sobriety became essential to labour organizing, in particular in the sectors of casual labour (cf. Olsson 1975:19). Nevertheless, total abstinence was a controversial tool and throughout his life the founding father of Swedish Social Democracy, August Palm (1849-1922), whole-heartedly fought this intrusion to the workman's most intimate sphere. However, several of the most competent trade union organizers – like the leader of the Iron and Metall Workers Federation Ernst Blomberg (1863-1911) – were convinced teetotallers, in contrast to their buoyant party leader, but these serious-minded men early on made their imprint on party policy positions. In this interzone, a crossover and interpenetration occurred between on the one hand a popular mass culture, and on the other hand avant-gardist or at least elitist social and ethical thought altogether in opposition to the dominant culture of mediocrity. This was, among other things, the early forum of social policy.

In particular a student organization in Uppsala, *Verdandi*, from its inception in 1881 was a stronghold of reform ideas and indispensable in the dispertion of these ideas.[35] In 1887, the conflicts between the academic establishment and the oppositional students reached a climax when several of their leaders were disciplined after an open lecture by a revolutionary marxist and sexual agi-

Graph 1. Yearly publication of social policy literature 1882-1907.

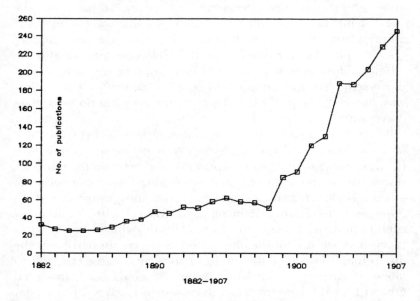

tator, Hinke Bergegren (1861-1936). *Verdandi* also held meetings with controversial Scandinavians like Georg Brandes and Bjørn-stjerne Bjørnson. Through a number of personal ties, *Verdandi* was associated with reform circles in the capital. In a series of booklets published by *Verdandi*, authors like Hedin and Wicksell went public. A number of foreign authors like John Stuart Mills were also translated. During its first half century, *Verdandi* published some 400 booklets which had a circulation of two and a half million copies, i.e. an average sales figure well above 6 000 copies per title.

Another indicator of the spread of these ideas is a bibliography covering social issues between 1882 and 1907: during these years, some 2 500 books and review articles about various aspects of social policy were published in Sweden, most of them of course in the first years of the new century (Thunberg & Herlitz 1907).[36] This is also an indicator of the relative importance of temperence and popular education within the early social discourse. This bibliography does claim full coverage, but for example no articles in the daily newspapers were included. Nevertheless, it is a fair indicator

50

Table 1. Rank order of social policy themes published in Sweden 1882-1907.

Themes	N:o of sub-sect.	N:o of reg item
Workers' question	17	389
Sobriety/temperence	11	346
Social hygiene	4	208
Popular education	7	184
Housing	4	180
Poor relief	8	166
General social question	4	131
Agrarian question	2	115
Womens' question	–	101
Socialism	–	89
Crime and criminality	3	73
Social history	4	65
Pol science & statistics	3	64
Taxation	–	58
Consumer Co-operative	–	50
Political economy	–	26
Emigration	–	22

Source: Thunberg & Herlitz (1907).

of the growth of this discourse. The number of items published on welfare issues steadily increased from roughly 30 books and articles per year in the 1880s (including translations), 60 per year in the 1890s to well over one hundred early this century (see graph 1).

Most of these publications dealt with specific issues such as child welfare, education, factory legislation, health, old age and invalidity insurance, but a few of them had a more general and principled approach (a few items from the latter will be the object of above all sections 6.2 & 6.4 and 8.1). The bibliography is divided into seventeen sections, their themes as well as numbers of sub-sections and numbers of registered items are shown in *table 1*. The most important theme is the workers' question, which among its seventeen sub-sections includes the history of the labour movement, working conditions in Sweden, vocational education, wages and work hours, industrial relations, arbitration, factory inspection as well as social insurance (almost 400 books and articles registered). Second in rank is sobriety (11 sub-sections; 346 items of which 30 included in the sub-section christianity and sobriety). Social hygiene – health – comes third, followed by popular education, and housing. Number six is poor relief including among its eight sub-sections a variety of charity, child welfare, foster care, work houses, and vagabonds (166 items). Thereafter follow in a sliding scale eleven themes ranging from general social questions including social policy (one sub-section on christianity and the social question), to emigration. As indicated, there was no separate section on welfare and christianity but the two sub-sections under sobriety and general social questions together with a few items included under charity (poor relief) make less than 100 items in toto. Thus, the outstanding feature of this survey of publications in this field is the voluminous dominance of the workers' question and sobriety.

As emphasized, the concept of intellectuals and the homogenity of social thought in a well defined segment of society – "intellectual corporatism" – is central to this study. In *table 2*, I will briefly present the most frequent social writers and their surroundings in the closing decades of the 19th century. Later in this article, two of them will be further scrutinized (section 6). The main environment for the great majority on the list in the early years of the present *siècle* will, however, be the object of section 7. According to the bibliography, the most frequent social writers – the "top ten" – consisted of the following (eleven) persons:

Table 2. The most frequent social welfare writers in Sweden 1882-1907.[37]

G H von Koch	(1872-1939)	editor and organizer, 50 items
G Sundberg	(1851-1914)	statistician/state com., 28 items
J Bergman	(1864-1951)	teetotaller, 21 items
S Wieselgren	(1843-1910)	teetotaller, 21 items
G Cassel	(1866-1944)	economist, 20 items
D Davidsson	(1854-1942)	economist, 20 items
J Leffler	(1845-1912)	economist, 18 items
A Raphael	(1850-1921)	reformer, 18 items
A Hirsch	(1879-1967)	poor law reform activist, 16 items
J Pettersson	(1866-1958)	teetotaller, 16 items
K Wicksell	(1851-1926)	economist, 16 items

Source: See table 1.

Outstanding on the list is G H von Koch who early this century became the principal organizer in this field, founder of *Social tidskrift* (Social Review) and a key figure within the National Association of Social Work (CSA – both the review and the association will be considered below, see section 7), and who like the majority on this list actively promoted sobriety. A few others on the list definitely belonged to this liberal-humanitarian center for the diffusion of a voluntarist social welfare ideology, in particular Hirsch and Pettersson (the latter a teetotaller) at the bottom of the "top ten" (the latter became a – liberal – Minister of Social Affairs in 1926). Apart from Wieselgren, Davidson, and Wicksell, all the others on the list contributed to *Social tidskrift* before 1908.[38] Apart from the important Emigration Commission reports, Sundberg, no. 2 on the list, also wrote a lot about Swedish demography primarily in statistical journals. The teetotallers had their own journals and publications to which both Bergman and Wieselgren frequently contributed, while the economist Davidsson, who was a tax expert, in 1899 had set up a scientific review for economists to which other professionals like Cassel and Wicksell also contributed (see below, sec. 6). Leffler and Raphael are typical of the early reformers as their writings appeared in a number of journals.[39]

Before the establishment of *Social tidskrift* in 1901, no review acted as a collective organizer of the evolving discourse. For example *Verdandi* had its series of booklets but no regular paper (and the booklets were in no way solely devoted to social issues). There were of course a number of other reviews set up at this time, but they became either general-popular or more academic like Davidson's *Ekonomisk tidskrift* (Economic Review) and Fahlbeck's *Statsvetenskaplig tidskrift* (Political Science Review). Charity, labour, temperence, and religious organizations were also all involved in disseminating social welfare issues as was the earlier mentioned and liberally minded *Nationalekonomiska föreningen (the* Economic Association). Social policy articles appeared in a number of journals, and roughly thirty journals have their abbreviations mentioned in the above-mentioned bibliography, but there was no organizational center of this early reform current.

Verdandi has already been mentioned as a stronghold of progressive thought. Otherwise, the old universities in Uppsala and Lund were no seedbeds for radical social reform[40]. However, it should be mentioned that already in 1893, Carl Livijn at the University of Lund presented the first dissertation in social insurance law: a rather dry survey of developments in European occupational injury insurance and work safety laws. Apart from the general introduction and a concluding section on voluntary accident insurance and self help, it is an extremely detailed examination of employer liability in case of work accident among his employees: the scope of liability, the evidence procedure, the content of liability, guarantees for the enforcement of liability, prescription, and the formal procedures of the court process. Livijn's dissertation is in no sense a general treatise but a systematic account of work safety legislation in Europe during the closing decade of the last century. For this reason, it is appropriate to mention its existence in the context of a presentation of the early breakthrough of a social policy literature in Sweden.

Finally, of utmost importance in supporting the establishment of a reform-minded social science intelligentsia through stipends, travel grants and publishing was the Lorén foundation.[41] Both Wicksell and Cassel as well as Steffen (see below – sections 6 & 8) benefited from this fund. This fund also sponsored the publication of social scientific investigations and the set up of a social science library at the emerging University of Stockholm. The Lorén money may be viewed as longterm investments, which gave some return from the turn of the century onwards.

6. Independent Spirits

In particular the 1880s marked a breakthrough of a new era in the intellectual life of Sweden: the cultural and religious orthodoxy under united state-church auspices was challenged by a heterogeneous European-influenced counter-culture which included natural scientists, artists and social philosophers. It was an age of independent spirits which through the educational program of the popular movements reached a fairly wide audience. The social policy discourse grew in this counter-culture of *literati* but it took two decades to emerge from this ghetto, and to create its own intellectual unity. Thus, in its early years this discourse was characterized by an absence of a 'collective organizer' – no key organiz-

54

ation, no main magazine, etc. Instead, in focus will be the independent spirits who were active in this field in the closing decades
of the 19th century. Adolf Hedin is already mentioned: he turned
50 when he introduced the social insurance bill in Parliament but
continued in this track for another twenty years. However, out of
the radicalism of the 1880s came several younger reform-minded
spirits, several from the *Verdandi* student club in Uppsala. One of
them will be considered in this section, while another will be under
particular scrunity in section 8.

There are no unequivocal criteria for selecting intellectuals.[42] A
fair number of "teachers, writers, and celebrities" (Debray 1981)
have already been mentioned as the most frequent contributors to
the appearance of a Swedish social policy discourse. In this section,
following Lilliestam, I will concentrate on a few profiles who were
central within the early social policy discourse, some of them still
remembered (not mainly because of their contributions to the
social policy discourse), others long forgotten.[43] These four men are
"representative" of the broad range of viewpoints within this
"(pre-)school of thought": the first a radical reformist, the second a
Kathedersozialist, the third a semi-populist liberal-conservative
reformer, the fourth an initially left-leaning mainstream economist.
In every sub-section, I will suggest an alternative to the one selected
in order to enhance the reader's ability to oppose my choices.[44]
Those who appear under later sub-headings hopefully indicate
changes over time, new themes, and the new frontlines of the early
20th century. Throughout, there is an absence of a proponent of
the model of "welfare capitalism" which if filled would probably
have improved the richness of the early social policy discourse.[45]

It may seem provocative to single out three future university
professors as "independent spirits" – Swedish academics are usually
considered as loyal civil servants (cf. Lönnroth 1984) – in the
formation of a Swedish social policy discourse. However, at that
time their discipline had not established academic chairs but
formed part of the controversial breakthrough of social science in
this country. The economists were not yet the high priests of
received wisdom. Furthermore, only the least influential and most
loyal to the Crown, reached his position through a traditional
straightforward academic education. Thus, there is a close link
between the institutionalization of social research and the early

formation of a social policy discourse in Sweden. In discussing the National Association for Social Work (section 7) and the Social Democratic Party (section 8), I will focus upon a few other social reformers – one of them social scientists as well – who were of theoretical importance in the early years of Swedish social policy.[46]

6.1 A Red Strindbergian Bull

Most important as a radical opponent to established culture among the independent social reformers was the budding economist Knut Wicksell (1851-1926).[47] He has been characterized as an early proponent of corporatist social reform primarily because of his publication in 1902 of a work on arbitration in industrial disputes (Lilliestam 1960:119). This is the closest he came to a formal treatise on the social question. Nonetheless, he frequently made controversial interventions on social questions.

Wicksell was the son of a Stockholm lower middle class entrepreneur, and like Hedin and Strindberg, the latter a friend from the student years in Uppsala, Wicksell early on became a red bull in the eyes of the defenders of law and order (cf. Gårdlund 1956:105). Another similarity was that like them he operated on a broad spectrum of public debate and provoked established common sense on moral and social issues as well as on defence and international relations. He studied mathematics but the main inspiration to his rebellious thought came from English neo-malthusianism through Drysdale's The Elements of social science (ibid 1956:46-59). As a student he also tried poetry but was too close to social policy to be accepted in the aesthetical avantgarde of the 1880s, "Young Sweden" (ibid 1956:113; cf Tjäder 1982:15). Already in early 1880, at the age of 29, Wicksell had shocked the narrow-minded academic community of Uppsala with an open lecture on alcoholism/drinking, poverty, celibacy, prostitution, and birth control. An academic controversy followed in its wake: Wicksell's secular views were repudiated as unedifying hedonism, the author was summoned before the Dean and sentenced. All of a sudden, this courageous red-hot agitator became a national fame. The speech was developed into a booklet and Wicksell travelled around Sweden. Through his lectures, publishing, and translations he reached a wide audience.[48]

The counterstrategy of the defenders of conventional wisdom consisted in either challenging this bogus thought in public, or closing the lecture halls. However, from this controversy stemmed Wicksell's life-long collaboration with the founding father of Swedish academic economics, David Davidson, who through his attack on neo-malthusianism forced Wicksell to take stock of the growing literature of theoretical economics.[49]

Poverty was at the heart of Wicksell's social thought. From a neo-malthusian viewpoint, he came to argue for birth control as the decisive solution to the misery of the common people. Nature set limits that human beings could not override. Overpopulation was the most urgent social problem: the ultimate cause of poverty. An enlighted population in command of Nature's scarce resources was the alternative to an overcrowded earth. In order to raise the living standard of the poorest section of the population above a mere subsistence level, diminution in the birth-rate was indispensable. This social program challenged sacred christian values, but it did not intervene in the commoner's daily struggle for bread and butter. Its explicitly utilitarian and rationalistic tone proved too individualistic and too middle class ethical to grow in the soil of the lower classes. Public education on birth control and a shrinking population were not the immediate answers to most labour activists. To them, the enemy "within" was less crucial to the ultimate solution of the social question than visible wordly targets (ibid 1956:93).

Wicksell, who was a friend of Branting from Uppsala, had a deep sympathy towards Social Democracy and in the mid-1880s, Wicksell started to give open lectures on socialism. He refuted marxism's scientific ambitions, its degrading of nature and over-emphasis of the social. In Wicksell's thought, a transformation to a socialist society was always secondary to the dimunition of the birth rate. The rhethoric of revolutionary class struggle did not impress Wicksell, who early on suggested a parliamentary road to power. State socialism was not his recipe and to him individual entrepreneurship was an essential wealth-creating force. He acknowledged the key role of the daily struggle for social reform by an independent labour party and urged the Social Democrats to become the strongest party of Parliament. This way, they would find out that the partial reforms they criticized from the outside would in the end prove beneficial to their adherents (ibid 1956:94; Lilliestam 1960:119-20). However, these reforms were always secondary to his perennial proposal.[50]

Apart from propagating a diminishing population as an answer to the poverty problem, Wicksell's most important works on issues related to social policy dealt with taxation and equity in state revenue extraction. On these issues, he was far ahead of time. He was critical of indirect levies and in favour of a complete tax reform: progressive taxes on earnings and property, income from work should be taxed more leniently than speculative profits and all taxpayers should have a say in the allocation of state resources. He was also a proponent of death duty (ibid 1956:175-8; cf. Kihl-berg 1972:83). His academic dissertation was a theoretical outgrowth of his popular booklets on taxation (ibid 1956:182)

6.2 A Manifesto of a Swedish Kathedersozialist

As mentioned, it took almost a decade before a general treatise by a domestic writer appeared in Sweden. Soon a few others were to follow. Cronologically, first out was a long forgotten loser, a persistant defender of the old regime, whose archaic theoretical foundations where profoundly destroyed by November 1918: the wealthy historian and social scientist, businessman, and politician Pontus Fahlbeck (1850-1923), who had published a path-breaking dissertation on the early constitutional formation of Europe.[51] In the late 1880s, Fahlbeck became involved in politics as an active protectionist, and was appointed secretary of the Royal Custom Commission, before he in 1889 joined the University of Lund as an assistant professor in history and political science. Already in 1892, Fahlbeck published a treatise on the Worker's Question in the tradition of Kathedersozialismus: Stånd och klass – en socialpo-litisk översikt (Estate and Class: a social policy overview). In contemporary limbo, it was "popular science" free from academic style, but written for the "higher" educated classes. However, the book is also a sign of its author's reorientation from a historical towards a social scientific approach: it is a treatise on the evolution from the old society to the new, from the absolutist royal-noble to the bourgeois order.[52] Modern society is founded on a three class model. A theme that soon came to recur in the famous Bernstein-Kautsky debate was at the fore of this book: polarization theory.

The book opens with two concepts: *liberté et egalité* – in French. Its focus is the threat posed by the working classes to the emerging social order: more than half of the book is devoted to a discussion of the merits of socialism and Social Democracy – to the social movement striving through class struggle for social equality and for a classless society. The book is written by a profoundly pessimistic mandarin, who openly admitted that the dusk of bourgeois society will arrive, although later than the proponents of the next, egalitarian-type of human social organization presumed.[53] In the meantime, there is an opportunity for the higher classes to create a new, even leading role and to prepare the ground for a peaceful transformation through social reform and increased egality.

In the concluding chapter, with the presentient title "What is to Be Done?", Fahlbeck outlines an ambitious program to (1) increase the national wealth, (2) raise the intellectual and moral level of the working class, and (3) solve the workers' question through social reform (1892:180-204). In a nutshell, this is Fahlbeck's priority list: first economic growth, then enlightenment and moral education, later mitigation of the worldly situation of the masses. Under the third category the author presented a number of measures starting with factory and safety legislation and ending with a plea for more and better social statistics (the latter due to the fact that regarding the social conditions of workers, "we live in darkness" – 1892:200). Yet, apart from low-cost legislative and administrative proposals as well as moral support and sometimes even small subsidies to voluntary associations such as cooperatives, (preferably non-socialist) trade unions, friendly societies and temperance associations, major economic reforms like social insurance were explicitly made dependant upon the development of Sweden's national wealth. However, regarding the legitimate role of state activities, apart from economic ones related to the actual affluence of society (i.e. private business), there are few explicit limitations in this program. The state is the association of the whole population (1892:187) and the municipalities are suitable instruments for common production (ibid 174). The liberty of the individual is not in danger in such a society, although all suitable persons are forced to work, as none can live off his fortune anymore: marriage, family and the private household economy still prevail (1892:177). Thus, to Fahl-beck, social policy was the conservative incarnation of the har-monious marriage between state and individual in a society all the more dependent upon market performance.

Almost twenty years later, Fahlbeck returned to the *Arbetarfrå-gan* (Workers' Question; 1910), and like so many other early bour-geois reformers he hesitated in particular towards state economic involvement. However, he was still critical of a one-sided market dependency. Instead, a closer, corporatist relationship between employers and employees within the firm would promote a desir-able communality.

6.3 A Humanitarian Free Raider

Of the four persons discussed in this section one was definitely an independent opinion maker but not at all an academic spirit: the retired officer and country squire, Baron Gustaf Adolf Raab (1844-1914).[54] When Raab left the army in 1895 – twenty years after the military officer's pension issue had been solved (Therborn 1989a) – he devoted himself fulltime to the general pension issue.[55] From the closing years of the 19th century, when the conservative majority in Parliament twice rejected a Bismarckian type old age and invalidity insurance, he managed for little more than a decade to keep alive a non-Parliamentary popular movement focussed on pensions. He appealed to the rich and powerful, who were fairly generous in financial support, but less impressive in contributing to organiz-ational work. The main exception was the liberal editor of the main daily in Gothenburg, Henrik Hedlund (1851-1932), who with perseverance supported Raab in writing as well as lobbying.[56] However, with a little help from the liberal labour associations in Stockholm and Gothenburg, Raab managed to set up a propagan-da committe – in reality consisting of himself but on paper also including Hedlund, and, at the start, also the insurance company executive and the master of the temperence order, Edward Wawrin-sky (see below – sec. 8b), as well as the chairman of the Stockholm branch of the labour association, a shoemaker namned Olsson whom Raab only reluctantly came to accept on the committee – which started to agitate for a compulsory pension reform. Typical for Raab was his avoidance of socialist and trade union support.

The basic ideology behind Raab's one-man-movement can be characterized as a blend of social conservatism – if not at all as elaborated as in the program of Fahlbeck – and an idealistic-optimistic liberalism close to the position of *Göteborgs Handels-och Sjöfartstidning*, which since the mid-19th century had sponsored social reform not least regarding temperence and poor relief parallelling the work of Hedin in the capital. Raab had no outspoken overall program but was concerned about retirement and public support at impecunious old age. To a former officer, the state as an administrative apparatus was a rational instrument to conduct general insurance practice. He insisted on the role of the insurance contributors, but was less concerned with the idea of "help-to-self help" which cost him the support of the CSA-people (see section 7). According to Raab's proposal, pensions should be paid by general contributions, but they would be paid out only to those in need i.e. below a certain income level (sliding scale). Raab relentlessly agitated for his idea, and he published as a fictiticous Royal Commission Report on the pension issue.[57]

Raab convinced the entire corpus of county governors to take up the formal investigatory process, got a considerable number of replies and could – accompanied by a Bishop – in 1906 present a full proposal to the King. In Parliament, Hedlund had succeeded in getting this proposal through his sub-committee, although it ultimately failed in full session. In particular, Branting was critical of the idea of contributions across the board which would hit the poorest most. However, Raab increased campaigning and in 1910 called a Conference on Retirement in Stockholm where a substantial number of activists gathered. The conference was the end to that movement.[58] However, as Elmér has pointed out, a remaining legacy of this proposal was the introduction of mechanical income-test in the Swedish social insurance system (1960:26).

6.4 The Mainstream Progressive View: Gustav Cassel

Gustav Cassel's *Socialpolitik* (Social Policy) is apart from Hedin's bill, probably the most influential early Swedish work on this subject matter (Boalt & Bergryd 1974; Wirén 1980). Cassel (1866-

1948), son of a Stockholm merchant, had received a degree in mathematics at the university of Uppsala in 1895 but soon changed his focus of interest from science to practical economics.[59] In order to get a proper education in economics, Cassel spent several years peregrinating supported by the Lorén foundation for social research. In 1898, he came under influence of German historical economists when he participated in Gustav Schmoller's and Adolph Wagner's seminars at the University of Berlin (Carlson 1988:147). Furthermore, during two summer visits to England in 1901-2, Cassel was inspired by Fabian thought, in particular the Webb's influencial work on industrial relations and trade unions (Cassel 1940:45-6).

After returning to Scandinavia, he lectured for a while at the University of Copenhagen, and finally in 1904, although considered too radical by the donors, Cassel was appointed to the chair in economics at the University of Stockholm.[60] From this position he came to operate on a world scale as probably the best knowned Swede – together with the ecumenian theologian Nathan Söderblom – in particular during the financial turbulence in the aftermath of the First World War and the "second Swedish Great Power Era".[61] Although active in public affairs for half a century, Cassel never joined any political party, and took pride in having four important activists from different party among his pupils.[62]

Cassel's *Socialpolitik* contains six separate lectures given at *Frisinnade klubben* (Free-thinkers Club) and at *Börssällskapet* (the Stock Exchange Association) in Gothenburg, partly repeated at that town's *Arbetarinstitut* (educational Worker's Institute), on invitation by liberal merchants in the main industrial port of Sweden (Cassel 1940:32). Published in 1902, it had a tremendous impact on the emerging liberal, humanitarian and Christian activists in the field of social work. This book is caught in the language of evolutionary progress: its focus is the individual emancipation through organic common participation in state and society. Cassel is critical of both dogmatic liberalism and socialism, of Marx and his obscurantist theory of value as well as of atomistic Manchester economics. Nevertheless, liberalism and socialism are, when the dogmas are put aside and their true practical sides of both come to the fore, regarded in this book as the ideologies of social policy. Cassel emphasizes individual responsibility in contrast to reliance on the state. However, "social policy does not hesitate to use coercion, either through public power or through voluntary-private (enskilda) associations, as this coercion will only create greater real freedom" (1902:19) writes Cassel in response to the proponents of the formal "freedom of labour".

In his social policy perception, voluntary organizations like cooperatives and trade unions have a central role; two out of his six lectures are devoted to these subjects. Both will make competition more social and efficient: the consumer cooperatives will organize the demand side, while the unions will make supply more uniform. However, when the associations cannot make further progress, it is time for state involvement, although Cassel in his critique of socialist ideology – rather tacitly – warned for an "over-belief" in the state. In a separate lecture devoted to the subject of public social policy, also included in the book, Cassel pointed-out at least ten different state activities that at that time were not on the agenda, from minimum wage to public work during business cycle downturns (1902:79-111).

In contrast to Wicksell, Cassel was no iconoclast.[63] For him, social policy was basically a means towards social progress and economic growth, as long as redistribution did not become an impediment to wealth creation. Although he never abandoned his views as put forward in his 1902 book (actually it was reprinted twice – in 1908 and 1923 – with the permission of the author) the debate leading up to the 1913 pension law may be viewed as a turning point in Cassel's writings on social policy (cf. Cassel 1940:134 and Carlsson 1987:176). From then onwards, the wealth creating powers were under urgent threat and, in particular, the state pension funds were viewed as an impediment to the workings of the capital market. In the case of trade unions, Cassel in his early work presages solidaristic wage policy – later in his life he became extremely critical of "trade union monopolism". For the rest of his life Cassel became a fervent opponent of state welfare, relief hand-outs and socialist ideology. In 1930, he published a book with the telling title *Understödspolitikens urartning* (The Degeneration of Relief Policy) in which public support to people on the dole was regarded as most harmful. Thus, in a decade Cassel turned from a social policy instigator to a critic of this mode of thought and practice, and this way came to portend the intellectual decline of the so far most important organizer of this discourse: *Centralförbundet för socialt arbete* (CSA).

7. CSA: a Collective Organizer

Cassel's *Socialpolitik* published in 1902, became the bible of CSA – to use the Swedish abbreviation of the National Association of Social Work – founded a year later. Here, the idea of voluntarism, preventive self-help, and individual responsibility as the heart of social welfare took root. In contrast to Baron Raab's retirement campaign with its stronghold in rural areas, and with its deep trust in the state as a collective insurance institution, CSA held its Tocquevillian ideological centre in urban civil society, the voluntary association of enlightened individual men and women. CSA's aim was to initiate and promote social progress and social work at a time when there were no central state coordinator and still more or less an absence of established policies in this field of action.[64] The association was launched by female philanthropists who missed a common forum for exchange of ideas and experiences. Hence, it early on managed to get substantial financial support from the court as well as from wealthy entrepreneurs in Stockholm despite the fact that the association used the word "social" at a time when even well-informed people had a hard time to separate it from the more dangerous notion of "socialism".

Officially non-partisan, CSA had a strong liberal and temperence profile.[65] Through its philanthropism CSA came to sponsor a judeo-christian humanitarianism renovated by an emerging bourgeois stratum in which an important role was played by enlightened and well-educated upper middle-class women involved in charity: Emilia Broomé (1866-1925), Karin Fjällbäck-Holmgren (1881-1963), Kerstin Hesselgren (1872-1962), Gerda Meyerson (1866-1929) Agda Montelius (1850-1920), and Anna Whitlock (1852-1930).[66] All of them belonged to the inner circle of the first CSA-generation, and held important official positions within the organization. In the surroundings of CSA, other early female social policy experts made important contributions, such as Anna Lindhagen (1870-1941), child welfare inspector in the capital and soon an important women's organizer within Social Democracy.[67] Ellen

Key was of course a – controversial – spiritual mother in these circles (Vennström 1984), and overall CSA must have been of some importantance as a role-model for early Swedish feminist public activity.

CSA's main activities can be summarized under five headings: (1) congresses and organizational endeavours; (2) publishing; (3) public education through exhibitions, a library, public lectures, etc (4) special education of social workers; and finally (5) social research (on home work, working hours, female industrial work, poor relief, etc).

Initially, CSA was an organization of philanthropic societies in Stockholm: thus, a collective organizer in civil society, however, with a clear direction towards public authorities. Later on it included a broader network of organizations, several of which had been set up by the CSA. These organizations were the offsprings of national thematical congresses on poor relief, housing, agriculture, female night work (cf. Carlsson 1986:233), criminal care, child welfare, unemployment, etc. CSA's first major convention focussed on poor relief and social insurance, and was held in Stockholm in late 1906. It was founded on an investigation of poverty and poor relief (see below), and in its wake followed *Svenska Fattigvårdsförbundet* (the National Association of Poor Relief) which became a subsidiary of CSA in poor law reform as well as municipal and voluntary poor relief.[68] Later followed similar associations of semi-public character like *Landskommunernas förbund* (the National Associations of Municipalities), Stadsförbundet (the National Association of Towns, where Palmstierna, another early close associate of von Koch – see section 8 below – played a leading role), *Lantingstingsförbundet* (the National Association of County Councils), and *Svenska Kriminalistföreningen* (the National Association of of Criminal Officials). Thus, CSA enlarged its role as a collective organizer in civil society by encroaching on public territory (Boalt et al 1975).

However, organizing traditional public tasks and authorities like towns, county councils, poor relief officials, etc, was not the only way CSA instigated public welfare. As indicated above, CSA's leadership was drawn from upper middle class circles in the capital: often civil servants with a social science education and with an interest in politics and temperence (Boalt & Bergryd 1974:31).

Likewise, of the "top ten" social writers at the turn of the century listed in section 5, two belonged to the first board of CSA (von Koch, and Pettersson) while a third was a close associate (Hirsch). They shared an upper- or upper-middle class background and were all liberal humanitarians affiliated with the temperence movement. Like several other leading CSA members they mixed journalism, writing, and lecturing, with organization-building. Furthermore, it is no exaggeration to say that the males of CSA came to staff the emerging welfare bureaucreacy. Thus, CSA's activists had the private economic resources, power-connections, the relevant skills and knowledge, and they also occupied key positions in the old administration, something which helped them to become the nucleus of the new welfare bureaucracy. This is in particular true of *Socialstyrelsen* (the National Board of Social Welfare), set up in 1913, and *Statens arbetslöshetskommission* (the Employment Commission orAK as was its hated abbreviation among Swedish workers) but to a certain extent also of *Socialdepartementet* (the Ministry of Social Affairs) in 1920.[69] Quite soon most leading male members also became MPs.[70] However, none of the above-mentioned female CSA key persons ever became civil servants in the welfare bureaucracy – or MPs – although some of them became members of various advisory committees in the state welfare sector.

Public education through exhibitions, a library for social literature, public lecture series as well as distribution of articles to the daily press were other important tasks of the early CSA. Soon, special education of social workers was supplied by CSA, as no national institution of higher learning in this field yet existed. However, in contrast to the German Social Policy Association, CSA was not particularly academic. But in the field of higher education, CSA came to remain after having managed to initiate voluntary and semi-public associations as well as public authorities in a number of specific welfare areas. In 1920, CSA set up an extra-academic *Institutet för social och kommunal utbildning och forskning* (School for Social *and Municipal* Welfare/Work Education and Research in Stockholm – e.i. footnote 4 in this essay). A year later a chair in economics and social policy at the University of Stockholm was endowed by CSA, and was to be coupled with this School and its dean. On the other hand, in Parliament a private member's bill by von Koch to establish chairs in social policy was blocked by leading Social Democrats (Andrén & Boalt 1987).

7.1 G H von Koch: Editor, Organizer and Social Reformer

Outstanding among the early CSA activists was G H von Koch, who was the spiritus motor of this association, and on its board for forty years.[71] He operated on a broad spectrum and was the brain behind most initiatives taken by CSA whether organizational or educational. von Koch came from a noble family which for at least two generations had belonged to the reform-minded circles in the capital (cf. Wirén 1980). During a study trip to Britain in the late 1890s von Koch became impressed by the Rochdale co-operatives and similar reform initiatives.[72] In the aftermath of this journey, he published a *Verdandi* booklet on consumer co-ops, and immediately became one of the founders of the national Swedish co-op association, which, however, soon came to be dominated by Social Democrats. When a private donor in 1905 offered CSA a large sum of money to investigate poverty and poor relief in Sweden, von Koch voluntarily left the co-op movement to head this investigation. However, he continued his involvements in other voluntary movements such as popular education.

Two years ahead of CSA, von Koch had established *Social tidskrift*, whose editor he was until its dissolution in 1917.[73] For three years the review became associated with "Students and Workers" as well as the co-op movement. This was not at all strange at the time, for co-ops were seen as part of the solution to the social question: a good example of voluntary organization and self help among the common people. As mentioned, Cassel devoted a special lecture to this subject as well as giving a lecture on trade unions. In radical liberal social theory cooperation on consumer markets was the counterpart to wage-earner unionization on labour markets.

However, as the journal of CSA, *Social tidskrift* came to have a lasting influence. As the founder of CSA and other voluntary associations in the social welfare sector – and through these organizations' repercussions on public welfare – von Koch influenced Swedish social policy, in particular poor relief and child welfare.

Social tidskrift came to follow developments in all sectors of social policy at home as well as abroad. Thus, the review had an inter-nationalistic approach and foreign social reports were a constant theme in the review. As the editor during its lifetime, no theme was too small for von Koch. However, the appearance of *Social tidskrift* marked an important shift of emphasis in the Swedish social policy discourse. All of a sudden, poor law reform came to the forefront, and the "German novelty" – social insurance – that Hedin had emphatically espoused but for almost twenty years had deadlocked in Parliament, in the first years of the new *siècle* definitely became second in rank.[74] Voluntarism, charity and private welfare reshaped on a higher order, and not state welfare *per se*, became fashionable some three decades after Strindberg's devastating critique of the charity ladies in *The Red Room* (1879).

Furthermore, it is noteworthy, that the social insurance approach never got a thematical collective organizer like poor law reform got in *Social tidskrift*. In Sweden, there was no journal that mixed the technicalities of social insurance with the overarching questions of social policy.[75] von Koch and *Social tidskrift* were primarily con-cerned with reforming municipal poor relief for the poor and destitute in general but in particular children and the aged. There was of course an intimate link between the two reform areas, but von Koch's eyes were kept on poor relief. To him, the distinction between the deserving and undeserving poor was central, and although he was in no sense a narrow-minded parsimonious tax-administrator and was always prepared to launch fairly costly public initiatives, he was keen on the principle that welfare was "help to self help". Individual responsibility was a key feature of his welfare approach, although he stressed (in controversy with the "passive" opponents of social reform) the necessity of preventive measures. von Koch was not an articulated social-christian, but he was close to this tradition and shared a world view with the proponents of a restrictive, responsible, even authoritarian and anti-hedonistic life style of the world of sobriety.

Thus, in its first years, von Koch never touched upon social insurance in the pages of *Social tidskrift*.[76] Others, like the head of the National Insurance Board, published a few articles about social insurance as well. But anticipatory "creative thinking" concerning social insurance – except concerning unemployment – was absent in the pages of *Social tidskrift*.[77] Social insurance never became the major alternative to the old municipal poor relief system, only a complementary instrument for those who could afford it and were prepared to save for their future. In contrast, as social insurance developed in Sweden, it came to symbolize irresponsible collectivist and anti-emancipatory social action for CSA (cf. Pauli 1913).

Apart from its humanitarian voluntarism and ecumenical evangelicism, von Koch's principal view on social policy got its inspiration from liberal economics. For instance, in the first edition of *Social Handbok* (1908) edited by von Koch, Cassel wrote its opening text on the economics of social policy, and they closely cooperated in the campaign against the 1913 pension reform (see section 7.3). However, when this manual was reissued fifteen years later, von Koch and Cassel recently had clashed on prohibition, and the latter was replaced by a run-of-the-mill professor in economics from the "Students and Workers" circles (1923).

Overall, *Social tidskrift* adhered to the principles of humanitarian philanthropy. The absence in the pages of *Social tidskrift* of party leaders like Staaff and Branting was a deliberate choice by its editor in his adherence to the principle of non-partisanship. In contrast to the dominant conservatism of the old regime, *Social tidskrift* was both reform-minded and oppositional but always simultaneously tried to challenge common sense and tried to be respectable within the confines of urban upper-middle class opinion. The role of radical social-christians on the fringe of the State Church within the *Social tidskrift* is symptomatic.

7.2 A Female Social Christian Welfare Theoretician

Ebba Pauli (1873-1941), who was a spinster throughout her life, belonged to the above-mentioned inner circle of female philanthropists active from the start of CSA.[78] After a year in Switzerland at the University of Geneva early in the century, Ebba Pauli returned to Stockholm and became a volunteer under the mentorship of Agda Montelius in *Föreningen för välgörenhetens ordnande*, as mentioned a founding member-organization of CSA (of which Montelius was vice-president 1903-09). For several decades, Pauli held no formal position within the latter association, but became executive secretary of CSA's far-reaching poor relief investigation chaired by von Koch.[79] For some years, they worked intimately and at the first Poor Relief Congress, Pauli held the main opening speech. Here, she developed an outspoken social-christian poor relief approach, which stressed social and human solidarity as well as a firm belief that the individual is responsible for his own destiny and worldly fate (cf. Lundkvist 1967). She had already developed this theme in a short booklet on social welfare in Switzerland (1904/5/6).

Thus, she was familiar with continental social thinking as well as with practical charity work, and she tried to combine the collectivist precepts of socialism with the moral codes of the Gospel.[80] According to Pauli, municipal poor relief could not be carried out without a deeply felt concern for human beings blended with a strong sense of authority and direction in social work. This was the spiritual message she delivered to the founders of *Svenska fattig-vårdsförbundet* in a country that still officially heralded the Christian doctrine and where the local practitioners of the Lutheran State Church most often were also involved in daily routines of municipal poor relief.

In 1907, Pauli became one of the first female members of a Swedish royal commission, and for nine years she served on the poor law reform commission of which von Koch (to his great disappointment) was not appointed by the Conservative government. Pauli once again became executive secretary, and came to outline their joint reform program, which fairly successfully made its way into actual legislation in 1918. During these years, she also came to participate in the poor reform lobby's critique of the pension reform. This reform was prepared by another state commission that worked parallell but not in coordination with the poor law reform commission. It is pertinent to mention that apart from the professional economists and "poor relief people", it was in particular womens' organizations like the Fredrika-Bremer Association and the Charity Association that vehemently criticized the apparent non-egalitarian sex differences in the pension proposal, and Pauli, although in no way the main proponent of the feminist position, openly shared these objections.[81]

When the poor law commission had finalized its work in the latter part of the 1910s, Pauli left her public plattform and continued with voluntary social work despite the hopes of von Koch that she would shoulder the task of being a "social" civil servant and join its pioneer generation.[82] Instead, she turned to publishing, and wrote a series of social-christian psycho-spiritual novel-pamphlets: *Eremiten* (The Hermit; 1919), *Våra barns moraliska uppfostran* (The Moral Education of Our Children; 1921), *Den vandrande människan* (The Pilgrim; 1930), etc. In these works, she outlined the wordly resposibilities of the modern followers of Jesus Christ. In practice more than in theory, she became a part of the European dialogue between christians and socialists. God, not men, would inaugurate his eternal realm, but this did not mean that christians could not espouse a social program and respond adequately to demand for social justice. But she never touched upon the crucial socialist goals such as the abolition of private property and the collectivization of the means of production.

Though her health was poor, throughout her life Pauli continued as a voluntary organizer. Together with Gerda Meyerson, secretary of the board of CSA 1903-06 and a key figure in its early years, Pauli was involved in the setup of the Swedish settlement movement, which, in spite of the hostility of Marxism towards religion, was an attempt to bring urban industrial workers in contact with Jesus the revolutionary and a theology of liberation. Here, they worked closely with Natanael Beskow (1865-1953), the rector spiritus of voluntary social-christian action and thinking in Sweden during the first half of this century.[83]

This movement was a bridge to the socialist working class movement, within which a national christian association (*broderskapsrörelsen*) was formed several decades later. Already in 1918, Beskow and Pauli founded an ecumenical and non-partisan *Förbundet för kristet samhällsliv* (the National Association for Christian Social Life) in which Pauli once again came to penetrate questions of social welfare, especially vagabondism and youth unemployment. Pauli did not contribute to the first edition of *Social Handbok*, but when it was reissued in 1923 she wrote an article on youth and juvenile care. She had for a long time been outside the Lutheran State Church establishment, but in the late 1920s she became involved in its social work in the capital. At the end of her life, although an invalid Ebba Pauli took the initiative to establish a private center for spiritual and psychological thought, education and meditation (Erica-stiftelsen; cf. 1953).

7.3 The CSA Economists

Up to the mid-1920s, CSA had a considerable impact upon social policy developments in Sweden not only through its critique of the treatment of the poor and destitute. Not least the theoretical weapons provided by the leading economists in the surroundings of or close to CSA made its imprint on the social policy discourse: apart from Cassel, in particular Eli Heckscher (1879-1953) and Gösta Bagge (1882-1951) became important opinion makers in particular after the general strike of 1909. Both of them had an upper-middle class background and both belonged to the early CSA-circles.[84] Bagge also contributed to *Social tidskrift* in its first years, worked closely with a number of CSA board members in a state agency, *Kommerskollegiums statistikbyrå* (which was the embryo to the National Board of Social Welfare), and was later instrumental in the set up of the School of Social and Municipal Welfare/Work Training and Research, where he created a chair for himself in economics and social policy (see above).[85]

Together, Heckscher and Bagge founded *Svensk Tidskrift* (Swedish Review) in 1911, a theoretical journal that indicates that the impact of the early social humanitarianism had reached its zenith already in the early 1910s. Furthermore, *Svensk tidskrift* also become a rallying point for the liberal economic critique of social insurance, not least the pension proposal. In its first years, Heckscher and Bagge devoted a fair number of pages to social issues. During these years Bagge was still working on his dissertation – under Cassel – but was an active participant in local politics in the capital. However, in contrast to the great majority of the CSA-people, he joined the Conservatives, another early sign of the break-up of the liberal-humanitarian welfare consensus.[86] During this time, Bagge himself characterized his position as "social-ethical", and he actively participated in the social-christian settlement movement (Olsson 1982)

Heckscher who was to become one of the world's leading economic-historians in the first half of the 20th century, was early on concerned with social issues.[87] However, he was critical of the empiricism of the German historical school of thought and an ardent supporter of neo-classical economic thinking (cf. Nyström 1982). In 1912, Heckscher wrote a programmatical article in *Svensk tidskrift* in which he discussed the necessity of economic growth as a precondition for the abolition of poverty. Like Cassel, he was concerned about the efficient use of the labour force, and in this perspective the trade unions could have an important role in equalizing wages and competition. However, he was also deeply concerned about the negative impact of redistributive measures on the wealth creating process. Both Bagge and Heckscher belonged to the transition period between the early breakthrough of a social policy discourse in Sweden and the establishment of a social democratic welfare paradigm from the 1930s onwards.[88] This transition is not the object of the present text, thus their full contribution to the Swedish social policy discourse will not be considered here. Instead, in focus is the contribution of the CSA-economists to the breakdown of the liberal-humanitarian welfare consensus. Paradoxically, initially this took the form of a unanimous position by both the "poor relief people", the womens' organizations and the traditional economists – including Wicksell – vis-à-vis the 1913 pension insurance proposal. In 1913, a new attempt had reached widespread support in all three political parties having been prepared by a Conservative cabinet, finalized by a Liberal and strongly influenced by the Social Democratic party leader.[89] However, it was a proposal that had emerged in the bar rooms of Parliament, and far from the lobbyists of the CSA.

It was a proposal that came to be strongly contested by the "poor relief people". They saw it as a complete disavowal of the preventive self-help principle, a breakdown of individual resposibility as no private savings for the future became necessary, and the creation of a new huge central bureaucracy with pension boards parallell to the municipal poor relief committees all over the country. The pages of *Social tidskrift* were opened up for critical voices. Likewise, after a meeting at *Nationalekonomiska föreningen* dominated by the chief actuarian on the royal pension commission, Lindstedt, von Koch managed to call an extraordinary session with Cassel as the main speaker. Cassel was emphatically critical of state financing of pensions, and argued that salaries should be high

73

enough to make workers' contributions possible. His views were endorsed by other academic economists like Wicksell, while von Koch – in a invocation of Adolf Hedin – spoke for the poor relief reform proponents. This welfare intelligentsia was also engaged in a press campaign against the royal proposal which culminated in an article by Cassel on the very day of the Parliamentary decision, which was immediately echoed in Branting's major speech in the House. Although this circle had a few articulated MPs, their views had no impact on the great majority of legislators. In particular their minority within the Liberal party is striking. However, the opponents of the pension reform did not give up their cause, and in the years to come their view points become more widespread.

Orthodox liberal economics was influential in the continuing controversy between the early 20th century welfare intelligentsia and the coming regents of Sweden in particular on, apart from pensions, what was to become the major feature of Swedish welfare policy: /un/empoloyment.[90] Soon after the beginning of World War I, some key persons from the CSA circle – in particular Järte and von Koch – for almost twenty years came to administer a "Swedish system" which instead of cash benefits to unemployed emphasized job creation – workfare instead of welfare – at wages below the market. In particular during the unemployment crisis in the early 1920s, this system became extremely controversial. However, it was forcefully defended not only by its administrators, no longer mainly intellectuals of civil society, but also by the high priests of liberal economics: especially Cassel and Heckscher (Carlsson 1988). Furthermore, in Parliament, it had a strong backing among the non-socialist majority. But Social Democratic minority cabinets twice resigned on the principle behind this administrative praxis, and in the trade unions and in the left-led municipalities an alternative mode of thought began to see the light of day, which soon came to attract a new generation of welfare intellectuals.

8. A Happy Marriage between Liberalism and Socialism?

Swedish Social Democracy is a product of the 1880s: the party was founded in 1889 after a few years of socialist agitation and organ-

74

izing among industrial workers. The second half of the 1890s was the "take off" period for unionization, and in 1898 a national Trade Union Confederation (the LO) was set up. The general strike of 1909 was a severe blow to the expansion of the labour movement, but the franchise reform in 1911 made the party equal to the conservative Right in Parliament. The party was still second to the Liberals which with Socialist support formed a government. Despite severe internal contradictions, from the end of World War I, both the party and the unions were on the move forwards.

In this section, the focus will be on response by Swedish Labour to the early domestic social policy discourse. In contrast to the dominant middle class perspective, within the international labour movement there was a workers' perspective on social policy, in which labour demands like the right to employment, work safety etc came to the fore. With local peculiarities this class perspective also appeared in Sweden (cf. Therborn 1986 discussed in section 4). But it is probably fair to say, as Gustav Möller did in a late chronicle, that the early Swedish Social Democrats had a very vague program if any concerning specific social policy issues (1959:113).[91] The few programmatical statements made in official documents from the early Party Congresses are cursory and tentative. Of course, in their agitation the early socialist condemned all types of cruelties of capitalist exploitation, but even on such close questions as work safety, the first trade unionists who entered Parliament were surprisingly inactive in the beginning (Sellberg 1950:156). Likewise, although the first Swedish Minister of Social Affairs, Bernhard Eriksson (1872-1951), a teetotaller and friendly society activist, entered Parliament on a Social Democratic slate as early as 1906, he cannot from the start be considered a "shadow cabinet spokesman" on social affairs.[92]

Eriksson is, on another level of generality, no exception from a larger pattern. In a survey of the early social policy discourse, it is important to emphasize, that the disciplined world view of temperance was an important constituent part of labourite ideology in Sweden. As mentioned above, the temperence movement was the fastest growing popular movement from the 1880s onwards. It culminated in the 1910s when roughly a fifth of the adult population (350 000) was enrolled, compared to a membership in the trade union movement of roughly 200 000 before the 1909 general strike (Lundkvist 1977). Until the 1922 prohibition plebiscite, which the teetotallers lost with the most narrow margin (49 to 51 percent), the labour movement grew in the shadow of the former. More important, many labour activists got their ideological and organizational skills in the temperance lodges. From the start, Swedish Social Democracy had a restrictive if not prohibitionist view on drinking and similar moral issues close to social policy.[93]

Branting was the exception to the general absence of a social policy expertise in early Social Democracy. He was an intellectual of the first Verdandi generation as well as a student of a leading insurance expert in the first Workers' Commission. To him, the abolition of poverty would disarm drinking as a social problem, and he succeeded in undermining the influence of the extreme prohibitionists within Social Democracy.[94] As a frequent participant in overall Swedish public opinion, an editor of the party's main daily from the late 1880s, as well as an MP from 1896, Branting almost daily intervened on a broad spectrum of socio-political issues. He never wrote anything like a general treatise on social policy, but came to formulate party positions not least on social insurance. Of course, several of his major articles took issue with the burning strategical question of social reform and social revolution, but Branting was neither a Kautsky nor a Bernstein. Hence, he was a very active participant in the royal commission – chaired by Lindstedt (see footnote 44) – and in the Parliamentary sub-committee that prepared the 1913 Old Age Pension Act. Thus, it is not a coincidence that Branting's main social policy booklet – published by the party Publishing House Tiden – simultaneously was his speech to Parliament the day the pension reform was enacted (1913).

At a time when Social Democracy and the trade unions were growing but still of secondary importance in the Swedish society, it was otherwise people in or close to the CSA-circles that came to participate in the early Social Democratic social policy formation. The most apparent case is the young Otto Järte (1881-1961), who in the second half of the first decade of the 20th century also became involved in the Labour movement as the Berlin correspondent of the party's main daily 1908-09. At that time, he was already a junior civil servant in the earlier mentioned embryo to the National Board of Social Welfare, in which he became a senior official for twenty years. While in Berlin, Järte became acquainted with the proponents of reformist-socialist state interventionism, and in those years, he belonged to Branting's inner circle of close advisers. In 1911, the same year Bagge, his student friend and colleague from the state bureacracy entered on a Conservative slate, Järte became a Social Democratic member of the Stockholm town council. This year, he was also appointed official investigator of unemployment, a choice by the new liberal Minister of Civil Affairs (the predecessor to the Ministry of Social Affiars) loudly applauded in the labour press (Edebalk 1975:77-8). Before he was expelled from the party as a "German activist" in 1915, Järte for example wrote about the advantages of social insurance in *Tiden*, the theoretical monthly of the Social Democratic Party (1909).[95]

A few years after Järte three leading urban liberal social politicans and MPs joined the ranks of Social Democracy. One of them was an established elderly statesman among the teetotallers and an early contributor to *Social Tidskrift*, Edvard Wawrinsky (1848-1924), the second the heir of Adolf Hedin but an outsider among the philanthropists, Carl Lindhagen, (1860-1946),[96] and the third a nobleman and for a few years the deputy of von Koch as organizer of social voluntarism (as well as the head of another CSA-subsidiary, the National Association of Towns) Erik Palmstierna (1877-1959). At the turn of the decade when the male franchise reform put the Social Democrats in a decisive Parliamentary position, they all joined the Social Democratic party. All of them made important contributions to various single social policy issues. For instance, Wawrinsky has been pointed out as an early proponent of a labourite workfare system (Steiger 1972). Furthermore, as mentioned Lindhagen was one of the most critical voices when the 1913 pension law was enacted – but none of them was social engineer combining social technicalities with an overarching social policy program.[97] However, Lindhagen was the most articulated utopian socialist to be in Sweden, but he briefly moved further left which nonetheless emphasized his outsider-position in regards to the emerging social policy discourse (cf. Sörlin 1986). Hence, this alert intellect was a sharp contrast to the only *Kathedersozialist* that joined the early Social Democracy.

8.1 A Social Democratic Kathedersozialist

From 1910 the parliamentary group of the Social Democratic party accomodated a lukewarm academic from Gothenburg: Gustaf Steffen (1864-1929).[98] Until then, Steffen for many years had been an independent spirit similar to the ones considered earlier (see section 6). He, too, belonged to the Verdandi generation, and had made a career similar to, but not as remarkable as, Wicksell and Cassel. Actually, if Cassel successfully managed to separate economics from the faculty of law at the university and make it an independent discipline, Steffen was a rather unfortunate empire-builder in academic sociology. Like Wicksell and Cassel, he had studied science in his early youth, but in Germany, however without taking an advanced degree.[99] In 1902, after lengthy trips abroad, he got a PhD from the University of Rostock, once part of Great Power Sweden, on a dissertation concerning consumption power and wages in the early phase of the English Industrial revolution, and immediately started to intrigue to get the open chair in economics at Stockholm University. There, like Cassel he was also considered too radical. Rather ironically, in an informal competition with Cassel, Steffen in 1903 got a chair in sociology and economics at the University of Gothenburg. After much reluctance, and after another unsuccessful attempt to get a chair in the capital of Sweden, Steffen in 1910 joined the Social Democrats and also became a member of the Swedish Senate.

Long before joining the Labour movement, and only a few years after Cassel's *Socialpolitik*, Steffen in the same series released seven booklets called *Sociala studier – försök till belysning av nutidens samhällsutveckling* (Social Studies – Attempts to Perspectivize Modern Social Development), in which several articles dealt with social policy.[100] Its focus was of course the "Worker's Question", but to Steffen social policy was something larger and more specific than this. Social policy cannot be limited to the solution of the Worker's question. In this work, Steffen presented a postwar view of what constitutes social policy: because of major societal change, the state had to be awarded a new task in society in general.

In silent polemic against Cassel, Steffen stressed that social policy is state activity in contrast to the wage policy of unions and the consumer policy of cooperatives (1906:28-9). Voluntary associations are of greatest importance for social policy, but above all are only examples. The only case when these associations can be regarded as instances of social policy is when they act as "movements for interventionist state social reform" (1906:29). Here, Steffen immediately added that not only central state but also municipal organized intervention were to be regarded as social policy. Like Cassel, Steffen criticizised the socialism of the Second International but not so much the Marxian theory of value as the theory of pauperization and breakdown, which in combination with the belief in the revolutionary solution made socialism outdated. To Steffen, the dissolution of private property was not a goal in itself but rather a question of the best possible societal organization, and here the state quite often proved to be the best available solution.

In contrast to the ideas of Wicksell and Cassel, Steffen's never became ingredients of public controversy, and his role within the CSA-circles was marginal. As a Senator (1911-16), Steffen made his voice heard on social policy issues. For instance, he became a forerunner on housing, an area in which next to nothing had been done by public authorities before World War I. Within the party and its parliamentary group, he was throughout his mandate a controversial figure. This *Kathedersozialist* immediately clashed with the emerging radical left wing. In 1913, when the crucial Pension proposal was on the Parliamentary agenda, Steffen clashed with the party chieftain, when he expressed doubts about state financed scheme, and openly advocated his preference for a Workers' Insurance based on contributions from employers and employees.[101] His early etatism was further diluted during the 1920s when he sat on the Nationalization Commission, and he became more sceptical in his overall belief in human progress. Although he never joined Cassel who passionately denounced most possibilities of politics, their youthful optimism was in both cases replaced by a pessimism of old age.

8.2 Towards a New Swedish Social Policy Discourse

The 1920s has been characterized as a period of stagnation in the social policy literature (Höjer 1952:132). However, it was in the decade foregoing 1932 that a new social policy intelligentsia began to emerge inside Social Democracy and at Bagge's and Cassel's Institute for Social Science Research. In the mid-1920s, Gustav Möller (1884-1971), within a few years second only to Per Albin Hansson in the Social Democratic party hierarchy, for two years held the position as Minister of Health and Social Affairs. It was a short experience, but his two decades of work in the same job were soon to begin. In the years before 1932 he wrote several election pamphlets on social policy, social insurance and unemployment.[102] According to one of his close collaboraters in the 1940s, he had as early as 1920 – during a visit to a Scandinavian labour conference in Copenhagen – been convinced by a leading Danish socialist reformist about the possibility of a social policy. Basically a universal social insurance program that was neither authoritarian nor just humanitarian but had a specific labourite edge (cf. Nyström 1983; Elmér 1958). Furthermore, Möller, who viewed with suspicion the traditional state bureaucracy, in particular in a speech in Parliament in 1926 thus tried to combine this social insurance program with an administrative approach close to the one prevailing in the popular social movements (cf. Rothstein 1985).

However, it was a long forgotten local politician in Gothenburg, the second biggest Swedish town, Ernst Jungen (1890-1981), who in 1931 presaged the turnabout in social policy that characterized the 1930s.[103] Jungen commented upon a few articles in the monthly business magazine *Industria* on the debate within the German Social Policy Association on the theory of social policy, in particular a series of articles by Alfred Weber, Max's brother. In his commentary it is the transcending character of social policy and the labour movement's experience of three decades of welfare policy in Sweden that comes to the fore. Explicitly, Jungen was a proponent of the perspective put forward by Eduard Heimann in *Soziale Theorie des Kapitalismus* according to whom social policy has a double edge: it is both conservative and revolutionary, it contributes to maintaining capitalism as an institution, even after social policy has started social renewal, which is its second great main task" (1931:471). This was not only a left perspective within the German Association, it was shared by many conservative etatists.

Contextually, Jungen's article must also be seen as part of the programmatic debate within Swedish social democracy in the aftermath of the turmoils of the 1920s. This is especially regarding to the writings of local revisionists located within the Social Democratic youth movement, which reached a climax at the party congress in 1932. Jungen argues against the overemphasis of nationalization as the royal road to socialism – even against those who interpret social policy as "immediate socialization".[104]

Like most members in the second generation of Swedish social democratic leaders, Jungen did not formally abandon the nationalization perspective (cf. Nyström 1989a). However, he attributed an equal place in the strategy of the labour movement to social policy and tried to raise the status of social policy. From the dual character of social policy follows a more elaborated version of the close relationship of labour party and unions in the transformation of state and society. Jungen stressed the necessity for trade unions to transcend immediate interest articulation regarding wages and work conditions in order to participate in the general struggle for equality and democracy.[105] Given such a unitarian strategy of social policy measures, which anyhow was unavoidable, Labour could step by step undermine the rule of private enterprise, and make an important contribution to the process of economic egalitarianism and democratization (1931:480).

A year later, and twelve years ahead of his path-breaking study of race in America (cf. Southern 1987; cf. Swedberg 1990), Gunnar Myrdal in two sequential articles in the Swedish avant-gardist cultural review *Spectrum* had outlined the "Dilemma of Social Policy".[106] Here, the development of the ideology of social policy is discussed in light of reform optimism, the belief in progress and the substratum of political philosophies. These factors were the background to the extensive social policy compromise that from the 1880s up to World War I is visible all over Europe, although varying between nations depending on power constellations. This compromise "created a whole bureaucracy and has in all senses become respectable" and achieved, taking its starting point as a point of departure for measurement, good results (Myrdal 1932:3-2).

Social policy was born, according to Myrdal, in the collapse, leveling-off and compromise of the liberal and socialist ideologies: a socialistically-weakened liberalism and a liberalistically-weakened socialism – a study of social policy is therefore a study of liberalism and socialism in simultaneous compromise and change (1932:3-6).

81

Liberalism was all the more generous to accept various kinds of state interventionism and regulations. Socialism – "even more changed by the social policy compromise" – departed from revolution for evolution, for small adjustments of the present system (3-10;4-19). However, from the end of World War I until the 1930s, social policy was also drawn into the general crisis which after 1929 characterized the Western world. Social policy came to be questioned both on the left and on the right: "however, what is even worse is that the enlargement of social policy has a tendency to provoke that conflict of interest between the social classes which social policy claimed to be able to remove (4:15).

Now, as a result of the Great Depression, this compromise has broken down. There is no contentedness with small adjustments of the present order inside Social Democracy: the more it gets, the more it demands, the level of expectation is rising, no satisfaction is visible. On the other hand, there is no forbearance on the other side of society's great divide.[107]

A way out for Social Democracy, or radicalism in the language of Myrdal, apart from the impossible nationalization road (phraseology, the religious symbols in the party programs, according to Myrdal) was to take serious a social policy critique that was radical and that is not limited to merely the curing of symptoms, but wants to reach the causes: a prophylactic or productive social policy which "dislocates the whole problematic and therefore is deprived of all interest for the just exhaustively-cited liberal anxiety to form social policy after old guidelines...and instead this type of social policy will come much closer to a socialist outlook (4-24-5).[108]

These articles were in a few years followed by a book that on the intellectual level signifies the breakthrough of the new discourse. In the "dilemma of social policy", Myrdal holds out the prospect of a new compromise, and it is nowadays an established truth that *Kris i befolkningsfrågan* (Crisis in the Population question; 1934) paved the way for a common ground for conservative natalists as well as radical reformers: here, Alva and Gunnar Myrdal proposed a productivist social policy – investments in the population, in particular, in families with young children – in order to overcome the gloom and doom of Swedish population statistics which showed a steadily declined national population. In their optimistic scenario, the state was the instrument to put things on a new course through socialized consumption.[109]

If their predecessors represented liberal optimists of the breakthrough of Swedish capitalism, the Myrdals represented a mode of thought which was founded on the inability of capitalist society to create jobs and security.[110] The Myrdals were formed by a market system that had been in constant crisis since the end of World War I, and they did not view the state as an intruder neither in the everyday life of civil society, nor in the economic sphere of society. To them, experts like themselves were just supporting people who had not yet been enlightened and saw only their own interests.

Finally, in these extremely brief and preliminary notes on the transition to a social democratic social policy discourse it should be mentioned that Gösta Rehn (1913-) – one of the founders of the Swedish labour market and solidaristic wage policy model – as early as 1939 in an article in the left student journal *Clarté*, emphasized the close relationship between social policy and wage policy in a "responsible" trade union strategy (1939/1988).

9. Summary:
The Rise and Fall of an Early Social Policy Discourse

Internationally, social policy has a long and rich pre-history in the poverty tradition. With the transformation of the "dangerous classes" into the organized working class new attempts were made in the economically leading countries to come to terms with the destitution of particularly the industrial workers. In the most authoritarian capitalist nation, Imperial Germany, a specific social policy discourse was born in the 1870s and '80s. Here, a compulsory social insurance approach was deliberately coupled to repressive measures to impede the growth of the organized Socialist Labour movement. It was an explicit etatist approach supported by the majority of the intellectual community although dissenting voices existed.

The Swedish discourse that rapidly followed in the wake of the German invention was simultaneously less despotic, less etatist, and less elitist. Although it was paved with a number of good but shifting intentions, it does not present a straightforward path to a sociological wonder of the mid-20th century world. Although the moment of social policy appeared in the form of a private member's bill in Parliament, its presence in public throughout the late 19th century and early 20th century has been firmly situated in this essay within the rapidly growing popular social movements as well as in the emerging social sciences, a counterculture of independent spirits, and a likewise emerging urban upper middle class. Thus, the discourse has a varied heritage spatially dispersed on several levels of the socio-economic structure, and culturally ranging from old as well as refurbished christian philanthropy to modern secular humanitarian world views.

The starting-point of this essay was the relationship between the practice of social welfare in Sweden, the model welfare state, and the assumed absence of a domestic theoretical practice of social policy, i.e. the relationship between social change and social theory. Departing from Mishra's discussion of the existence of a British anti-theoretical theoretical practice, throughout this article I have tried to elucidate the possibility of such a tradition in Sweden where theoretical ambitions were intertwined with practical concerns. Knowledge obtained from empirical social research should be spread to ignorant powerholders and, not least through the institutionalization of social science, also to both the lay people and professional social workers.

However, this discourse was formed in a geo-political periphery where the break-up of the old regime differed considerably from patterns prevalent in the leading European nations. Late 19th century social contradictions were a blend of pre-modern-rural and modern-industrial cleavages in which mass popular movements, in particular the world of temperance, played a crucial role in the formation of a domestic social policy discourse. The phase of the early social policy "breakthrough" was rooted in Sweden's domestic radicalism of the 1880s, not least the Uppsala student radicalism of *Verdandi*. Here, parochial radicalism was mixed with a cosmopolitarianism consisting of the imports of German imperial *Kathedersozialismus* but also the radicalism of the French revolution, Marxian socialism, Fabianism and Anglo-Saxon liberalism closer to mainstream economic thought.

This discourse's notably disciplined nature had, however, its foundation in rapidly growing social (counter-)movements that stressed individual responsibility, diligence and moral self-education: the teetotallers, the free-thinking Christians, liberal and later in particular socialist trade unionists, friendly societies and (consumer) co-operatives. Here was a space where an ideology and a social force could thrive that challenged both the established order – the throne, the altar and the sword if not the ultimate power of the moneybag – and at the same time preached the gospel of orderly behaviour.

It was in this environment that the intellectuals of the Swedish mix of liberalism and socialism saw the light of day, far from milieus which became greenhouses for either excessive market liberalism or the Lafarguian 'right to laziness'. Markets were accepted but were to be curbed by the state (the latter to be throughly embedded in society) and not allowed to intrude in civil society, where counter-movements early on mobilized against the threat of a drunken, copulating population. In civil society, respectable commons took pride in self-education, self-organization, and a conscious sense of responsibility among their people, in contrast to the pompous Victorian-Oscarian hypocritical and hedonistic lifestyle of the Crown and the upper echelons of society, and their religious subsidiary, the pharisaic Lutheran Church.

Social policy was one late 19th century incarnation of modernity, development and progress. This disciplined radical oppositionism was at first particularly articulated in the independent writer and MP Adolf Hedin. He was the outstanding domestic liberal intellectual of the second half of the 19th century, who in the later part of his life saw the fruits of his early endeavours, when a number of "independent spirits" like the bohemian neo-malthusian economist Wicksell made their dissenting voices heard. The 1880s and '90s were bonanza years for free-floating intellectuals who provocatively challenged the established order.

From the start, Hedin had an all-encompassing democratic social program that was far ahead of its time. One piece in this package was the radically transformed German social insurance approach, which in the hands of Hedin, with more than a little help from his fellow farmer-MPs, was turned into a people's insurance accepted by the Social Democrats long before the Second International subscribed to the German model. Instrumental in this process was of course the social-technological intelligentsia, not least the insurance experts that dominated the royal social insurance commissions for three decades. This universal insurance approach also attracted another one-man show, the military captain, Baron Raab, who for a decade travelled the country propagating for a compulsory retirement system.

Hedin was a father-figure for a whole generation of radical intellectuals in Sweden, whether liberal or socialist. He was a modern urban intellectual giant with a deep rural and pre-modern background, until the end of his life a radical liberal but with intimate bonds to the emerging socialist intelligentsia, in particular Branting and Carl Lindhagen. However, apart from social insurance, his social policy initiatives were continued in particular by a young generation of urban liberals. Thus, it was in these circles that social policy became a catchword in the battle against poverty and destitution. Early this century, another budding economist, Cassel, wrote the first textbook on social policy, soon followed by his contribution to the first social policy manual. Here, the voluntary but still collectivist approach – trade unions and cooperatives – got as much space as the compulsory but etatist; in the capital of Sweden his book became influential in urban philanthropist upper-middle class circles which early this century coordinated their charity operations in order to spur the interest for social reform. The centrality of this ideological unity follows from *table 3*.

The figurehead of this movement was G H von Koch, while an important part of the activists were "charity ladies" and suffragettes whose collective voice in this essay has been represented by Pauli. Although initially circumscribed to volunteers and humanitarian philanthropists, CSA – the National Association of Social Work – became a meeting point for all those municipal officeholders, civil servants, social teachers and writers as well as female, mainly social-christian, philanthropists that were actively involved in the business of social reform. In this institutional setting, the optimism of secular liberalism was blended with a similarly optimistic social-christian humanitarianism.

Initially, this broad reform movement definitely belonged to the left universe in Sweden. It existed in the borderzone between liberalism and socialism, though definitely closer to the former than the latter. It was a radicalism, and "intellectual corporatism",

Table 3. The development of an early social policy intelligentsia in Sweden.

EARLY RADICAL INTELLIGENTSIA	KATHEDER-SOZIALISTEN	LIBERAL HUMANITARIAN WELFARE INTELLIGENTSIA	1st SOCIAL DEMOCRATIC SOCIAL POLICY INTELLIGENTSIA	2nd Generation of SOCIAL DEMOCRATIC SOCIAL POLICY INTELLIGENTSIA
Adolf Hedin	Pontus Fahlbeck	G H von Koch	Hjalmar Branting	Gustav Möller
(Branting)	(Cassel)	Gustav Cassel	Bernhard Eriksson	(P A Hansson)
Knut Wicksell		Ebba Pauli		(Wigforss)
(Steffen)	Gustaf Steffen	Agda Montelius	Gustaf Steffen	
(Hamilton)		Eli Heckscher		Ernst Jungen
(Danielsson)		Gösta Bagge	Axel Danielsson	
(Bergegren)	(G A Raab)	Emilia Broomé	Hinke Bergegren	Gunnar Myrdal
(Palm)		Gerda Meyerson	August Palm	Alva Myrdal
		Jacob Pettersson		
Johan Leffler	(Leffler)	Otto Järte	Otto Järte	
Axel Raphael	(Raphael)	Axel Hirsch		
Karl Staaff		Erik Palmstierna	Erik Palmstierna	
(Gyldén)		(Wawrinsky)	Edward Wawrinsky	
		Kerstin Hesselgren		
Ernst Beckman	(Lindstedt)	Ernst Beckman	Carl Lindhagen	Gösta Rehn

circumscribed by its urban upper class nature, and the limitations of this approach were visible early on: its focus was not the immediate demands of Social Democracy or a broad-based national social insurance system – favoured by rural independents and under consideration in Parliament for more than two decades by now – but municipal poor law reform. These urban reformers, who in most cases also had a close affinity with the world of temperance, stressed individual responsibility and in particular help-to-self-help. For a decade, this movement in civil society was extremely successful in initiating reform and spurring public programs and institutions. Their journal – *Social tidskrift* – became the collective organizer of this discourse and successful to an extent that it became superfluous and ceased to publish when its editor joined the ranks of the central state bureaucracy.

However, the existence of former liberals within Social Democracy was not a sign of an early happy marriage between liberalism and socialism. Actually, in the 1910s, conflicts between the social policy avant-garde and the labour movement became more pronounced. This is evident in particular concerning the 1913 pension law, when the proponents of social insurance clashed with the proponents of "help to self-help". From the early 1920s the unemployment issue became another major bone of contention. These two cases signify a clear break between the traditions. The CSA people within the Unemployment Commission – liberal civil servants like von Koch and and the now ex-socialist Järte – came into sharp conflicts with the second (minority) Social Democratic cabinet led by Branting, which in the end chose to resign. Within a decade after this defeat, a new generation of – mainly Social Democratic – social policy intellectuals had started to formulate the new doctrines that were to dominate the build-up of the welfare state.

Thus, the social policy thinkers before Social Democracy ranged from the old, or rather middle-aged, Hedin to the young, and middle-aged, von Koch; a road from rural-common enlightenment to urban-noble education.[111] It was a discourse that spanned from secular, optimistic, far-reaching, almost unlimited state interventionism of the 1880s (when the state was more or less absent in this field) to an activist – partly christian – humanitarian voluntarism blended with still etatist and interventionist economic liberalism.

Conservative, liberal and radical authors – except Forssell – were all critical of social Darwinism and Manchester Liberalism, but had a positive view of the relationships between economic development, state intervention and the workings of civil society.

However, external as well as domestic events made several of them rethink their earlier positions. One after the other, they all hesitated as critical thresholds in the relationship between markets, politics and civil society were reached. In particular, the pension decision in 1913 and the unemployment crisis (after World War I and the Great Depression) are important examples of this tendency. Furthermore, the radical democratism and christian humanitarianism were replaced by the ethical value of temperance, which had become an overriding concern in these reform circles, and thus a more authoritarian attitude towards the common people came to flourish, in which individual rather than collective responsibility was stressed. But as long as the early 20th century reform movement was a pressure group in civil society advocating public as well as voluntary welfare, this liberal authoritarianism did not impede its impact outside its own circles.

This brand of early social policy thought faded away as a result of the upheavals of the world war, revolutions and counterrevolutions in Sweden's neighbouring countries, and not least the growing attraction of the domestic labour movement, and the latter's impact on the formation of a new state in Sweden. This discourse lived its life from the start of Swedish industrialization to the advent of political democracy in this country, thus during four decades of thorough transformation of Swedish society and culture. When *Social tidskrift* ceased to publish in 1917, and von Koch started his long career as National Poor Law Inspector, Sweden was still way behind the leading European countries in terms of social policy. Neighbouring Denmark, for instance, was a role model for those who looked for new examples abroad, and it was from this country that the coming generation of Swedish social politicians found lasting inspiration. Thus, the early social policy discourse constituted a not negligible transitional phenomenon in the interregnum between the old and the new regime in Sweden.

II. Working Class Power and the 1946 Pension Reform in Sweden: A Respectful *Festschrift* Contribution*

> The Great Social Democratic Celebration view of the development of the Swedish welfare state has to be repudiated and relegated to where it belongs, the lush vegetations outside the open *veld* of scholarship.[1]

Obviously, the small states of the Far North are important cases in social scientific discourse over the character and development of the welfare state. In particular the long reign of Swedish Social Democracy, and maybe even more the exceptional strength of trade unions in Sweden, belong to the sociological wonders of comtemporary capitalism. Industrial relations as well as social and labour market policies in Sweden have become a fashion in current social and historical analysis around the globe.

Rather surprisingly, there exist few studies on the origins and historical development of welfare policies in Sweden. For example concerning pension policy, an area in which Sweden in several respects was ahead of most industrial nations from early this century, the seminal work is still Åke Elmér's *Folkpensioneringen i Sverige* (The People's Pension in Sweden) published some thirty years ago.[2] The major weakness of this theses is its national focus, and the absence of a cross-national perspective. However, otherwise it is an outstanding analysis of the origins and social forces behind the Swedish pension system from late 19th up to mid-20th century. In Elmér's view, the background to the unanimous choice in 1913 of an all-encompassing, universalist pension scheme, instead of a worker's insurance, the decisive political weight was held by farmers and rural smallholders. In contrast, the unanimosity behind the pension reform in 1946 had more intricate reasons.

90

Conventional wisdom holds that this was basically a Social Democratic affair. The Labour movement had since the 1930s become the main political factor, and had already from the 1920s tried to reform the pension system against stubborn Conservative resistance. The general election of 1936 with the pension issue in focus, proved victorious for the Social Democratic party, and a State Commission led by a leading Social Democratic social policy expert was appointed to carry out reforms in all areas of social welfare.

However, it is evident that Social Democracy was in no sense the obvious force behind the pension reform that followed in 1946. The labour movement was split when the State Commission made its proposals, and was reunited only after most other socio-political forces had made their choices. In Elmér's analysis, the pension decision was done in the interplay between on one hand the Swedish Conservative party, now in favour of social reform, and the left-leaning emerging lobby organizations of pensioners on the other.

Recently, the Harvard historian Peter Baldwin has started to publish the results from his comparative study of European pension policy. Among other things, he questions the validity of conventional wisdom regarding the Social Democratic impact on welfare state developments in Sweden.[3] Despite the obvious merits and seriousness of his article "How socialist is solidaristic social policy?", his analysis of pension reform in Sweden in the mid-1940s must be seen in a broader intellectual context. I have had the good fortune to read the mimeograph version of Baldwin's dissertation. It is broad in scope, rich in detail, and sharp in focus. His conclusions are well argued and the whole is a fine example of sensitive historical analysis.[4] I highly appreciate and respect his ambition to write a non-Whiggish narrative, and both the discussion of the 1913 Pension law and the 1959 Superannuation law are nuanced interpretations of Swedish history. However, I cannot avoid the impression that, in presenting the 1946 Swedish pension reform as a specifically Conservative effort for social solidarity, he overdoes his point.[5]

Generally speaking, Baldwin questions a classical axiom attributed to one of the founding fathers of the social sciences, namely Marx's thesis that the working class has only its chains to loose and is accordingly the only class whose interest is not "particular" but "universal"; in the end, workers' emancipation means the emancipation of all mankind. *The Communist Manifesto* holds that the only class with a "total" societal interest is the proletariat, the wage-earners. Baldwin's dissertation opens with an illuminating general discussion of redistribution, solidarity and the Welfare State. In the article, the starting point is narrower, focussing on the issue that has caused some authors to note with astonishment that the Swedish Social Democrats were not united behind what posterity has come to regard as the most progressive pension proposal of the Scandinavian welfare state.[6] The most consistent backers were, instead, the bourgeois parties, in particular the conservative party (the Right Party). This paradox is resolved by reassessing the forces behind the pension reform, including a thorough investigation of the change of mind *inside* the Swedish Conservative Party in the mid-1940s. If the arguments are taken to their logical conclusion, then it is the bourgeoisie – paradoxically by pursuing its most immediate and narrow concerns[7] – and not at all the working class, that represents the "totality" of social interests, i.e. as the ideology of nationalism as well as mainstream economic theory have always proclaimed. The solution to this paradox and a real test of the Marxian thesis may be impossible, except perhaps upon the death of the proletariat. However, focussing on Baldwin's orientation and contrasting it with Elmér's traditional analysis, I will discuss this dilemma of the pattern of interest representation and welfare reform in 20th century Sweden: had social development in the mid-1940s reached a point where the working class had only its "vested interests" to defend and no chains to loose? Thus, rather than defending the general validity of a certain theoretical position, I question the particularity of especially Baldwin's theoretical criticism and empirical analysis. From the outset, four initial remarks have to be made. I do *not* agree that universal, tax-financed, uniform flat-rate pension benefits *alone* are the most typical features of the Scandinavian welfare model. Secondly, in the mid-1940s in particular it is wrong to confine the investigation to the pension issue. Several social reforms were on the agenda at that time; apart from pensions, they included sickness insurance, child allowances, and other forms of child support, education, housing, and labour market policies. Also, as will be argued later, the reforms in the mid-1940s are *not* the major source of Sweden's reputation as a model welfare state. Fourthly, and perhaps most important to note is that Baldwin throughout the article underestimates the role of the Agrarian party, and more generally, agrarian interests, in the process under review.

1. The Ghost of Beveridge

The target of Baldwin's critique is the 'Social' (democratic) interpretation of the welfare state: "The solidaristic welfare state is here explained by the triumph of the interests of the poor and the working class, spoken for by the labor movement and the Left. While social policy had earlier and elsewhere been motivated by the interests of the elites and therefore restricted in its intents, in Scandinavia and Beveridge's Britain, a new vision of universalist, solidaristic, egalitarian social policy was successfully advocated by the disadvantaged groups that stood to gain most".[8]

In repudiating the 'social' interpretation of the welfare state, with the Swedish pension reform in 1946 as a 'case in point', two mistakes are made: one methodological, the other analytical. The methodological flaw consists of the use of a particular, *national*, social policy *model* – the British Beveridge Plan – as the implicit yardstick for all types of European welfare state development. Baldwin incorporates three basic constituents directly from the Beveridge Plan as the essence of his own "solidaristic social policy" model: first and foremost, universal coverage; tax-financing as a secondary aspect; and lastly, uniform flat-rate benefits.[9] These formed the nucleus of the Beveridge social insurance model, which Baldwin adopts and applies as a scheme without considering its historical context and deep British roots.

Thus, he looks at the Scandinavian welfare state, with its universalism, and in particular the social policy of the Social Democrats, through Beveridgean spectacles. However, Scandinavia is not and has never been Britain. There has been some exchange of social policy ideas but, as Baldwin mentions but fails to understand, the Beveridge Plan was not very important in early postwar Sweden.[10] Thus, the welfare models of Britain and Scandinavia are worlds apart, and cannot be blurred into a common vision of solidarity and equality. Their roots are strikingly different and must be treated as such.[11] Otherwise one misses the remarkably different *potential* of the two "models".[12]

To the upper class liberal civil servant William Beveridge the aim was to create an all-embracing social security network in peacetime. Postwar Britain should not return to the inequalities and status differences of an archaic past. An already rich and powerful aristocracy should share at least a part of its wealth and authority with the common people.[13] The aim was to cultivate cross-class solidarity – the wartime solidarity of officers and soldiers – in peacetime between employers and employees (compared to Scandinavia, British social policy at that time was extremely sexist) – in marked contrast to the "backward" Scandinavian solidarity between peasants and workers, between the rural and urban poor. However, there is no reason to work backwards and from the cooperation in mid-20th century Sweden between workers and farmers – the political alliance between the Social Democrats and the Agrarian party – exaggerate the "solidarity" between the free peasantry and the emerging proletariat at the beginning of the century. Nevertheless, the "backwardness" of Swedish society set the structural parameters that made the 1913 pension law feasible.

From the late 19th century Sweden was not only rapidly industrialized but also democratized.[14] With increasing prosperity, the Swedish reformist labour politician Gustav Möller – party secretary from 1916 and Minister of Social Affairs in 1924-26 and almost without interruption 1932-51 – primarily wanted to achieve, not universal benefits so much as a rising standard of living, a modicum of security (*trygghet,* to use the key notion in Swedish social policy discourse).[15] There was of course no Roman road for social policy from 1913 to 1946; pension policy deadlocked in the 1920s but Möller did score successes with pensions in the 1930s, both in consensus and in conflict with the non-socialist parties. Changes were enacted in 1935 and 1937. To omit this sustained Social Democratic – and Liberal – interest in raising pension levels as well as in changing the system – and the corresponding Conservative resistance – is to distort the picture.[16] Möller's fundamental solution to these problems in the mid-1940s – in the pension system as well as concerning child and sickness benefits – was to introduce uniform, flat-rate benefits, the third element in Baldwin's solidaristic social policy model and the main link to the famous world forerunner of social security at that time. Universality and tax-financing were never major pension issues in Sweden at that time, although the general tax *level* was extremely controversial immediately after the war. This is a missing link to social policy reform that has not been fully investigated.[17] The battles over universality and tax-financing had been fought long before in Sweden, in the latter case in particular by the peasantry – as Baldwin clearly and carefully points out in his dissertation – and later also supported by the workers' movement.[18] Universality meant a people's insurance instead of a Bismarckian workers' insurance. Thus the *inclusion* of the peasantry and the rural poor in an otherwise industrial system was the novelty of the 1913 pension law. Tax-financing meant that the central government took over some of the costs for poor relief earlier paid via local taxes (primarily by wealthier farmers).

However, Möller's practical preference for uniform flat-rate benefits was new to Sweden. It implied a complete reconsideration of means-testing, which became more like an administrative income-test, an important change in principle as well as in practice.[19] During the first half of the 20th century this type of screening of relief applicants *slowly* changed from the identification of the poorest individuals to the *exclusion* of the very rich from benefits available to the great majority – "vertical universalism" in Baldwin's terminology (for an empirical illustration of this concept, see the respective pension "take-up ratios" for Britain and Sweden in *graph 1*).[20] This became particularly evident in 1937 with the new motherhood support system, in which all but one mother in ten were entitled to public provision. The well-to-do (upper class women) were excluded on grounds of "national psychology" (*folkpsykologi*).[21] Thus, a test was *also* used to screen out people at the upper end of the income scale.

In the pension system, from 1913, the well-off could claim their share by virtue of the premiums they had paid; everybody above the age of 67 was entitled to a pension benefit. In the early 1930s, about three out of four exercised their right to draw a benefit. The income-tested pension supplement was provided for a majority of over 67, particularly after the 1935 pension reform, that was approved by all the parties; still, those at the top of the wealth and

95

income pyramid were excluded from this extra allowance.[22] This order was reversed in each of the three alternatives proposed by the Social Welfare Committee in 1945: the current system should be abolished in favour of a uniform, flat-rate benefit for everybody. In addition, there would be an income-tested supplement (alternatives I and II) and/or an income-tested housing allowance (alternatives II and III).[23] Alternative III raised the pension level considerably, but still retained the testing practice. In 1951, when this new system had been in operation for three years, a majority of the old-age pensioners still did not qualify for the housing supplement.[24] If this is the criterion of universalism, Sweden has still some way to go. To conclude: the issue at stake in 1945-6 was the appropriate use of income-tests, *not* the principle of universalism[25].

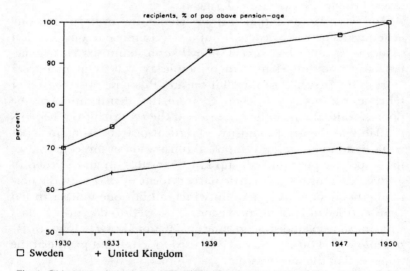

Fig. 1. Old-age pension take-up 1930-1950 in Sweden (represented by squares) and the United Kingdom (represented by plusses). *Source*: SSIB Data Files, Swedish Institute for Social Research (SOFI), University of Stockholm, Sweden.

The coincidental combination of these "Beveridgean elements" in British and Swedish early postwar pension *plans* tends to hide this basic underlying temporal dissimilarity. The outcome of welfare reform in Sweden and Britain in the mid-1940s – uniform, flat-rate social benefits – had very different lineages, which left their mark on the divergent futures of the two systems. Using the Beveridge Plan as a yardstick only confuses this fundamental incongruency. The reason why the 'social' (democratic) interpretation of the welfare state has been so powerful in recent social scientific discourse is not primarily its "Beveridgean" aspects. In contrast to Baldwin, I would argue that the "Scandinavian model" – as an example for the world, or at least for European Social Democracy – made its major imprint abroad *not* from the mid-1940s, but more than a decade later, in the 1960s.[26] A number of authors have blurred different aspects of Swedish modernization, some of which, such as technological progress and the regulation of industrial relations, were already apparent in the mid-1930s, others, like the welfare state, much later. When the international appeal of the Beveridge approach faded, the effects of another Swedish wave of social reform, in particular the introduction of more or less universal earnings-related pension and sickness (later also paternal) benefits, were recognised instead.[27] The combination of uniform, flat-rate social benefits with earnings-related benefits created an even finer and more comprehensive social security net and the welfare state managed to match the affluence of civil society.[28] The more recent prosperity of the Scandinavian countries, in contrast to the marked decline of the UK, as well as the remarkable differences in the strength of the Left, cannot be overlooked when appraising the use and abuse of presentday theories of the welfare state.

2. The Swedish Right and the Pension Reform in 1946

The second flaw in Baldwin's article is analytical. His major and undisputable contribution is his discovery of the relationship – the rational link – between the (future) class base of the Conservative Party (upper white-collar employees) and the internal ideological shift that occurred in that party in the mid-1940s. However, the *weight* he attributes to this relationship in the development of the

1946 pension law is debatable. First, it is important to distinguish between what a party wants, the ideology or party program, and what it can achieve in a given power constellation. Secondly, one should differentiate between events inside the Swedish Conservative Party and inside the Royal or Public Social Welfare Committee, which prepared the pension bill. Thirdly, it is important to assess the public process after the publication of the pension proposals, and the public debate they initiated before the final act was drafted in the Ministry of Social Affairs (and approved by various power centers inside the Social Democratic Party).

Baldwin's major mistake is to divorce the Conservative Party from its relationship to other political forces, thus ignoring the power context. He concentrates on the relationship between one social force (the new middle class) and the ideological shift that occurred within the party in the mid-1940s, together with the impact of this on policy making in Sweden at that time. In order to understand this shift, one has to grasp the decline of political conservatism in the Swedish culture.[29] The Right party of the 1940s was a shadow of its earlier strength and was challenged from all quarters. In 1928 it had still won almost as many parliamentary seats as the Social Democrats. After that election, Admiral Arvid Lindman formed the last Conservative Cabinet to date in Sweden with the support of 73 MPs in the directly elected Lower Chamber. In the Upper Chamber, another 49 Conservatives gave him almost unconditional loyalty. This was admittedly a minority government but the Conservatives far outnumbered the other non-socialist parties. After the 1932 election the situation was reversed (in the lower chamber) and throughout the 1930s and 1940s the party steadily declined, although it managed to remain the largest non-socialist party until 1946. (In the Upper Chamber the party remained the largest until 1952. For the distribution of seats in Parliament, see *table 1*.)

It is clear that a major programmatical shift occurred, particularly regarding social and economic principles, in the Conservative party in the mid-1940s, following major programmatic revisions by the Liberal, Social Democratic and Communist parties.[30] A new generation of Conservative activists, accompanied by electoral defeats, forced the party to rethink its position on a number of issues, including social policy. State intervention in the economy

Table 1
Distribution of seats in Parliament 1928-1948

	1928		1932		1936		1940		1944		1948	
	LC	UC	LC	UC	LC	UC	LC	UC	LC	UC	LC	UC
Conservatives	73	49	58	50	44	45	42	35	39	30	23	24
Liberals	32	31	24	23	27	16	23	15	26	14	57	18
Agrarians	27	17	36	18	36	22	28	24	35	21	30	21
Social Democrats	90	52	104	58	112	66	134	75	115	83	112	84
Communists	8	1	8	1	11	1	3	1	15	2	8	3

Source: SOS, "Riksdagsmannavalen".

and increased public responsibility became more acceptable to its adherents. The traditional critique of the "relief hand-outs" (*understödstagarandan*) was toned down and the idea of universal social rights gained respectability. The Conservatives backed all the major Swedish welfare reforms in the mid-1940s. However, they endorsed some of these proposals at a rather late stage and often added a proviso – such as that the economy must permit such an increase in public spending.[31]

The question remains, however, if it really was just a farsighted, strategic concern for the well-being of a potential Conservative electorate – the urban white-collar employees or the new middle class – that changed the party's social policy view?

The Conservative stance on the pension issue is obviously one piece in the Swedish welfare state puzzle, but far from the main one and definitely not the whole picture. Concerning urban white-collar employees, the party was clearly competing in particular with the Liberals. But also the Social Democrats were actively trying to attract the new middle classes. In the 1944 election campaign the Social Democrats, in a series of advertisements in the weekly press, for the first time specifically addressed white-collar employees. The ads focussed on demands such as full employment, higher wages, increased social benefits and improved education, while emphasizing that the Social Democratic party was the ally of all wage-earners – not just proletarian blue-collar workers – and best served the common interest of labourers and white-collar employees.[32] Thus, all the "urban" parties were preparing the ground in the early 1940s, and politicians from several parties were very active in the unionization of these groups. Perhaps the Conservatives were less hesitant than the Liberals to openly advocate the interest of upper-salary employees.[33] The new Liberal leadership, under the "Keynesian" economist Bertil Ohlin, took pains to stress reform, "social liberalism", and the situation of the poor and destitute. Regarding social reform, the Liberals tried to avoid confrontations with the Social Democrats. Besides attacking the Social Democrats on "socialisation" and "socialism", the Liberal party made a clear demarcation between its own progressiveness and the outmoded nature of Conservative policies. In its own view, the Liberal party was the sole bourgeois reform party.[34] In the Social Welfare Committee that prepared the pension bill, the Liberal representative sided with the majority of the Social Democrats in proposing a combination of income-tested *but* universal pension benefits (alternative II), while two Conservatives, one *Agrarian*, and one *Social Democrat*, together with one of the two *civil servants* on the Committee, backed the abolition of income-test except for housing supplement (alternative III).[35]

The Conservative party was not only under pressure from the Liberals. Another social group, the rural population, was a traditional supporter of universal social benefits. As mentioned, before the modern party system finally took shape, farmers in Parliament had opted for universal social insurance coverage and managed to convince the Conservatives to back the pension bill proposed by a Liberal cabinet in 1913, a reform that was also supported by most Social Democrats in Parliament.[36] In the 1940s, the Conservative party still had a strong backing in rural areas, in particular among the upper echelons of the landowning population. Since the 1930s, however, the Conservative party had lost its predominance among the non-socialist parties and was challenged in the rural electorate especially by the Farmer's Alliance, before 1932 a junior partner in the non-socialist camp. The Agrarians had gained confidence after "horse-trading" with the Social Democrats in 1933. Their independence was further underlined when they formed a government in the summer of 1936, followed in the autumn by the first formal red-green coalition cabinet with the Social Democrats. During the

100

wartime national coalition, the Agrarians also participated on an equal footing with their earlier superiors. In two decades, the party underwent a major transformation from the "poor country cousin" to a fairly respected gentleman at the King's table.[37]

Like the Liberals, the Agrarians also emphasized their reform-mindedness and even tried to outflank the Social Democrats "from the left" on welfare issues. The advocacy of social insurance in 1944 marked a turning point inasmuch as it was the first platform statement to advocate a broad social welfare policy rather than merely proposing improvements to existing social services in the countryside or benefits limited to rural groups. This coincided, however, with a more aggressive emphasis on the rural dimension – the name being extended to include "The Rural Party". The Agrarians were presented as the party of the "centre", between the bourgeois (i.e. the Conservative and Liberal parties) and the social-ist (i.e. the Social Democratic and Communist parties) – the golden middle way – but also as the sole reform party of the countryside. In 1944, the Agrarians lumped together all other parties as "urban".[38]

With the end of the surrounding war in sight in the 1944 election, the Conservative party was squeezed as regards social reform between the Liberals on one hand and the Agrarians on the other. The Conservatives approached the welfare proposals with reluctance and were basically vague and non-committal, except on a few natalist proposals. This stance contrasted markedly with all the other parties. In the mid-1940s the Conservatives then had to take this competition seriously. The electoral defeat in 1944 gave the party a new leader from the rank of big landowners who, as a group, were tentative about supporting expensive social reforms but were sensitive to rural opinion. Thus, there were many ten-sions in the party over the modernization of ideology; in the end the "elders" managed to keep the program of principles from 1919 intact, while the "urban youngsters" wrote and obtained approval for an "action program", pleading strongly for welfare reform.[39] Most noteworthy, perhaps, was the emphasis on the Conservative's role in the already enacted 1946 pension law, summed up in the slogan "The Conservative's line was the People's". The party was unanimous on this particular issue but that did not suffice to convince the electorate a few months later – the 1946 (local) election was yet another defeat (and for the first time since the advent of universal suffrage the party was not the largest on the non-socialist side).

In summary, how much credit can be given to the Conservatives for the final outcome of the Swedish pension reform? Their fair share: no less, no more. Together with the Agrarians they were the first of all parties unanimously to endorse alternative III, that much is evident. It is however, their role within the Social Welfare Committee that is at stake. How much did the two Conservatives push for what was to be known as "alternative III", later the pension law? Already in 1944 the junior Conservative representative on the Committee made it plain in a speech in Parliament that he would support a fundamental revision of the pension system.[40] In 1945, when the Committee was completing its work on the pension bill, the senior Conservative – a representative of the landowners and a vice chairman of the party – actively pushed for the elimination of income-tested pension.[41] The above mentioned programmatical development within the party opened the road to an unanimous party position. The party representatives on the Committee were thoroughly coordinated with the party leadership.

However, it is still not clear whether it was the Conservative representatives, the Agrarian representative, or one of the experts of the Committee that in the nick of time took the initiative to work out a new alternative (III).[42] In the Parliamentary debate preceding the almost unanimous decision the junior Conservative hinted at the role of "Committee members" in initiating the new alternative. However, it took him five years to stake a direct claim – after the Agrarian representative retroactively had tried to reap the glory.[43] Certainly all politicians were aware from the start of the prestige linked to this generous reform. In particular all the non-socialist parties were eager to minimize the role of the Minister of Social Affairs, who had a well-known record as the advocate of social reform within the Social Democratic leadership and when the law was enacted, was praised by several party back-benchers.[44]

3. The Social Democrats and the Pension Reform

Finally, there is one question that Baldwin fails to address: why was it so easy for the Social Democrats – and the Liberals – to switch and unite behind "alternative III"?

In the 1944 election, the Social Democrats were vague on the precise content of the pension reform: their discussions focussed on adequate benefits for all versus improvements for the neediest (the latter had been the tendency in the war period). This cleavage had been hard to bridge earlier[45] It was resolved in the aftermath of the proposals from the Social Welfare Committee and the public debate that followed. The regrouping behind "alternative III" was amazingly quick.

The main resistance came from the core of the Social Democratic leadership: the Prime Minister, the Minister of Finance, the future Prime Minister, etc. They naturally wanted the Party to take full advantage of the pension reform.[46] Concerning its content, apart from financial considerations there were redistributional objections but their minor weight must be seen in the light of the associated administrative drawback: income-test. Furthermore, the Minister of Finance in particular was aware of the need to foot the bills from the Ministry of Social Affairs, where the pension reform was by no means the only expensive idea. Finally, personal strains among the leadership grew in these years. In particular, the clashes between nos. 2 and 3 in the party hierarchy – the Ministers of Social Affairs and Finance – reached a dramatic culmination when the no. 1 – the Prime Minister and Party Chairman – died unexpectedly just before the opening of Parliament in the fall of 1946 – after the pension issue had been resolved but before decisions had been taken on sickness insurance and child allowances.[47]

The core of the party leadership was supported by economically responsible public opinion, i.e. in particular the Liberal press, which initially – like the Liberal party – stuck to the less costly alternative (II). Even some Conservative newspapers, in particular the leading *Svenska Dagbladet*, after the publication of the Committee's report, published editorials with this type of emphasis familiar to their readers. Quite soon, however, the editorials were coordinated with the Conservative party line.[48] The Agrarians and their press did not hesitate to back the proposal (III) put forward by their representative on the Committee. In time, however, the Liberal press, particularly its leading organs, not to speak of the Liberal party leader, had a hard time making up their minds (actually, the Liberal party switched its position after the Government). The longer the public debate went on, the more support non income-tested pensions received in the non-socialist camp.[49] Obviously, this unanimity contributed a great deal to the final outcome of the pension issue. But it was not only pressure from outside that made possible the swift change in the Social Democratic position.

As mentioned, *one* of the four Social Democratic Commissioners had backed the non income-tested proposal (III). He received firm support from the emerging pensioners' organizations affiliated to the labour movement (actually, his seat in Parliament belonged to the same town – Malmö – where these organizational endeavours had their centre). In 1944, these tiny associations had successfully lobbied Parliament and against the recommendation of a united sub-committee managed to get a more or less unanimous vote for an acceleration of the pension reform.[50] The organizations continued to lobby the party, the trade unions and SD parliamentarians.[51] After some uncertainty, most SD newspapers came out in support of the more generous alternative.[52] Finally, when the party executive made its decision, it also came out overwhelmingly for non income-tested, uniform flat-rate benefits.[53] The same strong support was found in the SD Parliamentary group.

Why? Why did the core of the Social Democratic leadership not receive any support from the party's MPs? Why did the former not make the question a vote of confidence? Were the latter more concerned about the well-being of a future electorate? Or did they fear immediate Conservative gains in the coming election? Or Communist gains, which at the time was an even more urgent threat?

Nowhere in Swedish society was any enthusiasm exhibited for a continuation of means-tested pensions. There was a strong commitment to self-education and responsibility in the organized labour movement but screening poor people was not a popular duty.[54] As mentioned, the means-test instrument had shifted from distinguishing between the poor and the rest of society to demarcating those at the top from the great majority of welfare recipients. Concerning pensions, the cost awareness argument did not take root, particularly as the difference between the two alternatives did not seem insurmountable in a milieu where even the most parsimonious came out in support of the more generous benefit. Also the powerful Trade Union Confederation (LO) supported non income-tested pensions. Pressure from pensioners in the trade union movement, as well as an ambition to work closely on social issues with the newly formed white collar confederation (TCO) – the LO and the TCO had meetings before sending their responses to the pension proposals to the Government – made it an easy choice for the LO. The non income-tested pension proposal was beneficial to its members as well as to other wage-earners. Furthermore, keeping the income-test might have led to a future rift in the LO. Finally, the LO was in more or less complete agreement on the pension issue with the Employers' Confederation (SAF).[55]

4. Conclusions

There is no need to repeat the arguments against analyzing the 1946 pension reform in Sweden as an either-or case of universality. However, the fact that the Conservative party was strongly united on the pension issue in the fall of 1945, just a few months ahead of the other parties – with the important exception of the Agrarians – cannot justify a scientific conclusion that is simply a repetition of the Conservative's election slogan of 1946: "The Conservative's line was the People's". This would be as ahistorical as the Great Social Democratic Celebration, putting the pension decision in the latter year out of context. Had it been the case that the Conservative party laid the foundation for the guiding principles of the presentday Swedish welfare state, then I am firmly convinced that the leading Conservative expert on postwar social policy, former party chairman Gunnar Heckscher (in the 1940s chairman of the party's youth organization, an active participant in the programmatical revisions at that time and later a professor of political science) would have made a point of this in his scholarly *The Welfare State and Beyond*.[56] He does not even hint at this. Is it likely that he forgot such an important, even decisive Conservative contribution? Hardly, just as it is unlikely that modesty (or rivalry with his predecessor Jarl Hjalmarsson) prevented him from mentioning this supposedly major role of his party in the making of welfare Sweden. Instead, he stresses the longstanding positions taken by Social Democrats (while mentioning the other participants in this process) as the key political factor in the development of the principles behind the modern Swedish welfare state.[57]

An analysis of these principles cannot be limited to the pension issue alone, in particular not in the 1940s when a whole series of social policy issues were on the agenda: apart from pensions, sickness benefits, child allowances, school meals, education, housing and maybe above all labour market policies. In all cases concerning income support, Gustav Möller opted for uniform flat-rate benefits. He did so with exceptional strength; for example, regarding sickness benefits he completely revoked the proposal put forward by the Social Welfare Committee and accepted by most pressure groups, and pursuaded the party to follow his line, even though he ultimately failed (after he had left as Minister of Social Affairs).[58]

Flat-rate benefits, so prevalent in the 1940s, must be seen in the context of the basically rural nature of Swedish society at that time. Although a growing group, urban white-collar employees were still a minority. It is definitely not unimportant that – as Baldwin has made plain – the 1946 pension agreement heralds the coming issue of the parameters of common interests between various categories of wage-earner.[59] But in the mid-1940s it was still the old communality between industrial labourers, agrarian smallholders and other segments of the rural population that managed to place its imprint on the principles of the Swedish welfare state. A decade later there was a different situation. But in both cases the Swedish labour movement had more than its vested interests to defend and pursue, and the Swedish working class still some chains to lose. As the recent study by Kangas and Palme indicate, there is definitely reason to analyze Nordic pension policy in a broad theoretical perspective, and not exclusively in terms of working class power.[60] However, to refute the "Social" (democratic) interpretation of the welfare state with the 1946 Swedish pension reform as a case in point, seems to be an exaggeration. There is no doubt, that the new social movement born in the closing decades of the last century, has had a say in the transformation of Swedish society in the current century. In the terminology of modern French historiography, in particular since the 1930s, a certain Social Democratic "mentality" has slowly been penetrating Swedish society, politics, and culture: easy to feel, harder to define and clarify.

III. The Development of the Postwar Welfare State

1. The Historical Legacy of the Welfare State in Sweden

1.1 From Poor Relief to Social Democracy: The Prehistory of a Welfare State-Model

The years immediately following World War II witnessed the beginnings of Welfare Sweden – the impact of the Keynesian solutions from the Great Depression blended with the development of late 19th and early 20th century social policy measures.* However, the tradition of public involvement in the provision of welfare had already been in existence prior to Swedish industrialization at the end of the nineteenth century as part of the maintenance of workdiscipline and work ability.[1] Poor relief has existed since the reformation, but always at a low level on account of the country's poverty and the strength of the free peasantry in both parliament and local government. Even so, until well into the twentieth century and the coming of the famous Swedish welfare state model, poor relief accounted for a large part of social expenditure.

In the course of the 19th century Sweden underwent an agrarian, commercial and industrial reorganization which greatly affected the relation between state and citizen. Following a parliamentary decision in 1842, compulsory schooling (*folkskolan*) was introduced, mainly financed and administered by the parishes, with some transfers from central government.[2] Central and local government provision of public health dates from the end of the seventeenth century, when provincial doctors pioneered community medicine. The first wave of expansion of public health, however, coincided with the foundation of the country councils (*landsting*) in 1862.

These were 25 representative regional bodies with tax-raising powers and responsibility for in-patient hospital services.[3] With the spread of industrialization and the development of the working class movement, parliament and the state bureaucracy became incresingly involved in the regulation of working conditions for adults (primarily women) and children, occupational safety and sickness, the care and maintenance of old people and babies, and the problems created by massive emigration. As in many other European countries the period from the turn of the century up to World War I saw the first breakthrough for social policy.[4] It was during this period of the 'social question' or *Arbeiterfrage* that the following laws were implemented, influenced as they were by the profound ties and conflicts between the new semi-urban proletariat, the rural poor and the free peasantry as well as the industrialists and older fractions of the ruling classes:

1889: Factory inspection act.

1891: Introduction of state subsidies to voluntary sickness benefit societies (further extended in 1910).

1901: Employers made liable for reimbursement in cases of industrial injury, changed to compulsory occupational injury insurance in 1916.

1913: Universal and compulsory old age and invalidity pension.

State responsibility for employment and housing increased at the end ot the war, and social expenditure rose considerably. Government was made responsible to parliament in 1917 and took the decision leading to universal suffrage in 1921. These political changes created conditions favourable for the development of state provision of public welfare. In 1920 the eight-hour day was implemented and a Poor Law reform restored the legal right to poor relief (abolished in 1871).

The 1920s were a period of political instability and minority governments. The main political cleavage was over the question of unemployment, and conflicts in this area ruled out any major welfare reform for over a decade.[5] From 1932 onwards the Social Democrats and the Agrarian Party collaborated, but it was not until 1936 that they first formed a coalition government. Outside parliament a major agreement on industrial relations was concluded between the trade unions and the employers federation in

1938.[6] The main concern of the new majority was to overcome depression by the implementation of Keynesian policies and the introduction of the following welfare measures between 1933 and 1938:[7]

- new state employment creation programmes;
- state subsidies to voluntary (trade union) unemployment benefit societies;
- a housing programme for families with many children including subsidies and interest-subsidized construction loans;
- the indexation of pensions to regional differences in the cost of living;
- maternity benefits to around 90 percent of all mothers;
- free maternity and childbirth services;
- state loans to newly married couples;
- the introduction of two weeks' holiday for all private and public employees.

Seen in terms of expenditure, social policy saw a sharp rise in state involvement from World War I onwards. Excluding the exceptional years of World War II, total public expenditure rose from 10 percent of GDP in 1913 to 23 percent in 1950. During the same period, social expenditure increased from below 4 percent to over 10 percent (see *Graph 1*). Social expenditure as a percentage of total public expenditure rose from 30 percent to 40 percent in the immediate postwar period, followed by a small rise to around 45 percent from the beginning of the Social Democratic era.[8]

At the outbreak of World War II the Social Democratic/Agrarian government was replaced by a broader coalition. The Social Democratic leader, already prime minister from 1932, Per Albin Hansson, headed a new cabinet drawn from four of the five parties represented in parliament, with the support of over 95 percent of the electorate. Only the Communists, who had obtained less than four percent of the vote in 1940, were excluded. Although Sweden was neither occupied nor directly involved, the war promoted decisive changes in the national administration. Emergency commissions made up of the labour market organizations and other relevant interest groups (chiefly agriculture), were established for every major social activity.[9] These commissions had the status of government agencies and their decisions were correspondingly binding. Organizations which had previously been more indepen-

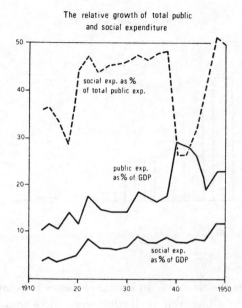

Graph 1

The relative growth of total public
and social expenditure

social exp. as %
of total public exp.

public exp.
as % of GDP

social exp.
as % of GDP

dent found themselves more or less incorporated into the administrative apparatus of government. The commissions were abolished after the war but nevertheless their existence influenced the development of core welfare institutions in the immediate postwar period.[10]

To summarize the development of social policy, a universal pension scheme, compulsory work injury insurance, employment programmes and state subsidies to voluntary sickness and unemployment benefit societies had already been adopted before, and in some cases several decades before World War II. However, the inadequacies of these programmes are illustrated by the fact that poor relief continued to play a major role in the social security system up to the postwar era, as can be seen from *Graph 2*.

So far we have primarily considered the legislative, administrative and financial changes in the development of the Swedish welfare state. In an examination of its historical roots we are confronted with a variety of conceptual approaches, many of them with specific Swedish ties.

111

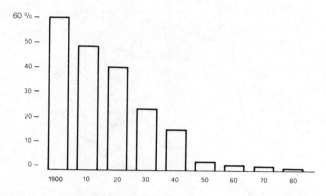

Graph 2

The relative decline of poor relief (a)

(a) Expenditure on poor relief as percentage of social expenditure excluding education

Firstly, there is the tendency to interpret events in relative terms, i.e. to equate the welfare state with conditions prior to industrialization, the result being that we invest the present political and social system with some form of continuity.[11] In the case of Sweden, a link may be forged with, for instance, the strong national administration built up in the sixteenth and seventeenth centuries during the period of absolutist monarchy. It is argued that the system's principles and institutions have not changed appreciably since the height of its strength as a European power. According to this exaggerated interpretation the foundations of the Swedish welfare state may be more accurately traced to the ideas of Gustav Vasa, the creator of the nation state, or to those of Gustavus Adolphus II and Axel Oxenstierna, his seventeenth century chancellor, than to twentieth century Social Democratic politicians.

The second approach is to emphasize the popular element in the Swedish state, i.e. the recognition of the free peasantry as an independent estate and the weight carried by independent farmers in the bicameral parliament (established in 1866 and replaced by a single chamber parliament in 1970). The widespread literacy in nineteenth century Sweden is likewise cited in support of this

112

thesis, as is the relatively uniform distribution of poverty, i.e. Sweden was poor but egalitarian.[12]

The third approach interprets the development of Welfare Sweden in terms of the Bismarckian model of social policy.[13] Here the expansion of state involvement in areas such as income maintenance, education and health (including workers' protection), is understood as a reaction to the social problems created by industrialization. The impact of the German model on the development of the Swedish welfare state, however, was more to stimulate parliamentary initiatives than to influence the actual content of decision-making.[14] The universal national pension scheme and the early pre-Social Democratic employment programmes can be regarded as specifically Swedish liberal welfare arrangements.

The fourth approach is to emphasize the Social Democratic tradition of 'the people's home'.[15] It was with this catchword that Per Albin Hansson launched the 44 years' och Social Democratic rule. This approach developed the idea of the 'three stages' in party policy: the struggle for 'political democracy' (completed with universal suffrage in 1921), the struggle for 'social democracy' (sometimes regarded as having been completed in the 1960s) and the current struggle for 'economic democracy'.[16] In this perspective the welfare state is linked above all to the second stage, that of struggle for 'social democracy'. It was the social reforms and the ambitious employment policy of the 1930s which created Sweden's reputation as a model for social welfare, enshrined in Marquis Child's book of 1936, 'Sweden – The Middle Way'. The main architects of social and economic planning during this era were Ernst Wigforss, the Minister of Finance, Gustav Möller, party secretary and for almost twenty years Minister of Social Affairs, and the two Myrdals.[17]

Fifthly, there is the interpretation of welfare growth in terms of the Beveridge model. The term 'welfare state' was coined during World War II, the German prerogative of power being contrasted with the democratic state, whose vast potential was mobilized for the first time.[18] According to this view the dramatic change during the war is considered as the real beginning of the Swedish welfare state.[19] But there are also links to the pre-war development as various state commissions for postwar social and economic planning – headed by such men as Gunnar Myrdal and Tage Erlander

113

Table 1   Major institutional changes in the Swedish welfare state, 1945-1982

Pensions

1948   Universal flat-rate pension
1959   Earnings-related compulsory supplementary pension
1976   Part-time pension and lower age of retirement

Health

1955   Compulsory earnings-related insurance
1963   County councils take over responsibility for state-provincial physicians
1967   County councils responsible for the whole health system including psychiatric care
1974   Cash benefits raised to 90% of gross earnings and made taxable; dental insurance

Industrial safety and injury insurance

1949   New safety law and central agency established
1955   Old compulsory industrial accident insurance coordinated with sickness insurance

Labour market and unemployment insurance

1948   Nationalization of local employment offices under a new National Labour Market Board,
        also supervising voluntary unemployment relief funds
1974   Cash benefits to non-insured

Family policy

1948   General child allowance
1974   Parental insurance replaced maternity benefits

Municipal poor relief

1957   Social Assistance Law replaced Poor Relief Law
1982   Social Service Law replaced Social Assistance Law

Education

1950   Ten-year experimental period with a nine-year compulsory school started
1962   Final decision implementing the nine-year compulsory school during another ten-year period
1964   New and extended study allowance system
1969   Open admission to universities
1971   Integration of upper secondary education

Housing policy

1948   Public loans and interest subsidies for housing construction, under supervision of a National
        Housing Board; housing allowances to families with children
1954   Municipal housing allowances to pensioners
1968   Interest subsidies replaced by 'parity loans'
1974   'Parity loans' abandoned and interest subsidies reintroduced

114

(who succeeded Hansson as prime minister in 1946 and remained in office for 23 years) – continued the work started in the 1930s. These were the proponents of the new institutional settings and the flat-rate social benefits inaugurated in the late 1940s,[20] to be discussed in the next section.

1.2 The Development of Welfare Sweden (1945-1980)

Although Sweden managed to remain neutral, World War II obviously set limits to the development of the welfare state, but in 1945 several changes occurred. Swedish industry, highly concentrated in the hands of a few wealthy families and groups, was not damaged by the war, and was in a good position to participate in the postwar industrial reconstruction in Europe.[21] On the political front, the broad coalition was dissolved in the summer of the same year and the Social Democrats formed a new government, which stayed in office (at times in coalition or with the support of the Agrarians/Centre or later the Communist Party) for more than 30 years. Formally the emergency administration was abolished, but in practice it was transformed and consolidated in the new, permanent institutions that were built up as the public sector expanded.

Conditions for social policy in the postwar epoch differed in two important respects from the earlier periods of welfare development. Firstly, until the late 1970s it was chaped under relatively favourable economic conditions: a rapid technological progress in both agriculture and industry; few industrial conflicts and a highly institutionalized wage bargaining system combined with a tremendous growth in the number and strength of unionized labour (both white- and blue-collar), both in the private and public sectors.[22]

Secondly, the mobilization of public resources (primarily new forms of taxation, but also the newly constructed administrative bodies) during World War II afforded the possibility of redirecting public expenditure towards non-military peacetime purposes.[23] As regards the growth of public resources the parties immediately after the war competed on tax policy issues, i.e. the extent of possible tax cuts and the structure of the postwar taxation system.[24] However, the increasing support for the political left and left-centre since

115

1932, together with the additional resources gave rise to a general consensus in support of social policy reforms.

Summarized briefly, the development of postwar welfare Sweden can be divided into five periods:

- The immediate postwar period: the institutionalization of housing and employment programmes and the introduction of flat-rate benefits;
- The second half of the 1950s: the introduction of earnings-related benefits;
- The 1960s and early 1970s: the expansion of public services;
- The mid-1970s: the extension of entitlement and improvement of benefit levels;
- The late 1970s and early 1980s: a period of adjustments.

A first wave of welfare reforms followed in the second half of the 1940s. Major decisions were taken and implemented in such areas as housing, employment policy and income maintenance. In the case of housing, residential construction had almost entirely ceased at the outset of World War II, and emergency measures (rent control in 1942 and low-interest loans to stimulate housing construction) were transformed soon after the war into a coherent housing policy. Housing construction and the housing market were brought within the competence of the state by prolonging rent control and by subsidiary loans coupled with a new law in 1947 which required all construction projects to conform with local government planning standards. The National Housing Board (*Bostadsstyrelsen*) was established in the following year as the central authority for the supply of dwellings and the handling of housing loans.[25]

Together with the insurance system, unemployment policy had been the corner-stone of Swedish social policy from World War I onwards. In the 1930s, however, the attempts to solve the economic crisis and the influence of Keynesian ideas meant that the whole issue of unemployment was reformulated as an 'economic' policy problem. Internationally, manpower policy is still regarded as part of this type of governmental policy. In Sweden, however, labour market issues have been closely bound up with welfare policies since the late 1940s, when the wartime institutions were transformed and the National Labour Market Board was set up as the central authority, coordinating the now nationalized local employment offices and supervizing the state-subsidized and unioncon-

116

trolled unemployment relief funds. Nevertheless, it was not until the late 1950s that the Board began to have an increasingly important role as new programmes were introduced and old ones expanded.[26]

In the field of income maintenance, the old means-tested benefits were replaced by flat-rate benefits.[27] Following this principle, three major reforms, basic pensions, general child allowances, and sickness cash benefits, were approved by Parliament in 1946-47 and were implemented, with the important exception of compulsory sickness insurance, in January 1948.

The introduction of universal flat-rate pensions, both for old people and the disabled (widows' and orphans' pensions remained means-tested for another ten years), and a child allowance was accompanied in the period 1948-1954 by income-tested housing allowances for pensioners and families. Sickness insurance was the exception: the original decision in favour of a compulsory health insurance system had envisaged flat-rate compensation to all employees, supplemented by a voluntary and heavily subsidized graduated insurance benefit. Due to inflation following the Korea boom, and conflicting opinions among political parties, the trade unions, inside the benefit societies, and particularly the Swedish Medical Association, the whole Beveridge-style system of flat-rate cash benefits and reimbursements to practitioners was postponed twice, in the late 1940s and early 1950s.

The 1953 Health Insurance Act marked the end of nearly a century of voluntary benefit societies; at the close of World War II these had covered approximately half the population. Sickness cash benefits were earnings-related and not flat-rate. However, this system was not entirely new: the voluntary but state-subsidized unemployment insurance benefits functioned in the same way, as did occupational injury insurance. The latter was administratively integrated with health insurance, although remaining legislatively separate. The 1955 system (still in force today) also introduced refunds for prescription costs, and covers all kind of out-patient care, medical and hospital treatment, etc. Maternity benefits (available since the mid-1930s), were also integrated into the insurance system.[28]

Some years later a compulsory earnings-related national supplementary pension scheme was establised. This proved to be the most

Table 2   T h e   m o s t   i m p o r t a n t   w e l f a r e   b o a r d s

Board	Established in	Year of co-ordination	Responsibility	Important legislative changes
National Board of Health and Welfare		1968	Central authority for social welfare incl. children and adolescents, treatment of alcoholics, public health and health care	Child Welfare Acts 1902 and 1924, Poor Relief Act 1918, Social Welfare and Assistance Act 1957
- Medical Board	1878			
- Social Welfare Board	1913			
National Social Insurance Board		1961	Central authority for social insurance; supervises the social insurance offices which pay out basic and supplementary pensions, child allowances, invalidity allowances and pensions, occupational injury life-annuities etc.	National Insurance Act 1963
- State Insurance Institution	1901			Occupational Injuries' Act 1901
- Pension Board	1914			Pension Act 1913
National Board of Industrial Safety	1949		Central authority for industrial safety and work hours	Industrial Safety Act 1949
National Labour Market Board	(1914)	1948	Central authority for labour market and regional development; supervises county labour market boards and local employment offices	Nationalization of local employment offices 1948
National Housing Board	1948		Central authority for the supply of housing, for housing loans and allowances	Family housing allowances 1948 in connection with child allowances
National Board of Education	1914	1964	Central authority for the school system: compulsory school, upper secondary school, adult education; responsible for training and re-training in cooperation with National Labour Market Board (a)	Nine-year comprehensive school from 1962 and changes in the upper secondary school from 1964-71
National Board of Vocational Training	1914			
The Chancellor's Office for Swedish Universities	(1893)	1964	Central authority for universities and other institutions of higher education	Open admission from the late 60s and early 70s
National Immigration Board	1969		Central authority for labour market and education problems of immigrant workers, and for refugee affairs	Voting rights in local elections given to immigrants in 1976
Statistics Sweden	(1764)	1879	Central authority for collecting information through surveys etc. on welfare and labour market issues	Labour force surveys, 1963 onwards; Level of living surveys, 1974 onwards

(a) According to a 1984 parliamentary decision, a new independent board will be in charge of this policy area from January 1986 (see Appendix volume).

controversial of the postwar social policy reforms. Parliament passed the Social Democratic proposal in 1959, after a governmental crisis (the end of the Social-Democrat/Agrarian coalition), an advisory referendum, a dissolution of parliament, an extra election in 1958, and a final dramatic vote in the second chamber, where the measure was passed by a majority of one vote.[29]

Together with the decisions on health insurance and earnings-related pensions, the flat-rate income maintenance programmes of the late 1940s were supplemented by earnings-related schemes to form the two guiding principles of present-day social insurance in Sweden.

From the early 1960s there was a forceful expansion in two important areas of public services: health care and education. Hospital treatment has always fallen within the competence of regional government in Sweden, but in the mid-1960s the county councils became the sole health authority, in that out-patient services and psychiatric care were transferred from the central government.[30] The municipalities also contributed to this development in providing care for the aged, children, etc.

The Swedish school system in the mid-1940s was rather old-fashioned, with a six-year compulsory elementary school followed by various forms of higher education from secondary schools to universities and professional colleges. Like most European countries, Sweden has extended the period of compulsory education up to the age of 16 (today, this is 17 or 18 in practice). A decision in this direction was taken in 1950, with the start of a ten-year "trial period". The final law on the implementation of a nine-year compulsory school was passed after several controversies in 1962, and was followed by various changes in the rest of the educational system.[31]

During the fourth phase of welfare development in the mid-1970s the above mentioned programmes were extended, often related to the expansion of manpower policy: a combined earnings-related and flat-rate parental insurance for both sexes, covering childbirth and early child minding coinciding with a major increase in public day nurseries; dental insurance for all adults covering 50 percent of indivudual costs; extended entitlements to old age and invalidity pensions combined with a general lowering of pensionable age; an expansion of education allowances under various employment creation schemes; and an extension of entitlements to housing allowances for all low-income groups and tax-credits to house owners. The fifth period of welfare state development will be dealt with in Section V.

As indicated, special welfare boards play an important role in the implementation of social reforms in Sweden. Peculiar features of the Swedish political and administrative system are the independent tax-raising power of the three levels of representative government (state, county, councils, and municipalities), and the sharp distinction between Ministries and Boards (*ämbetsverk*).[32] The boards are often headed by powerful Director Generals and are responsible for a well-defined field of operation. They are often set up after major institutional changes when parliament has approved important laws. *Table 2* summarizes the development of welfare boards with a brief picture of their administrative competences. These boards are funded by the state budget with the exception of the National Social Insurance Board and the National Board of Industrial Safety, which are mainly financed from social security payroll contributions.

Besides the central authorities, the health sector is run by regional country councils, which have their own tax-raising powers, and social provisions (old-age care, child minding, home services, etc.) are undertaken by the 284 municipalities, each of which has tax raising powers. The decentralized character of the Swedish tax system may have facilitated the rise of social outlays which will be considered in the next section.

2. Resources and Clienteles: Descriptions

2.1 Postwar Expenditure Growth: a Summary

In respect of expenditure growth the figures reveal tremendous changes during the development of the welfare state. In relative terms, public expenditure as a percentage of GDP increased from 24 percent in 1950 to 62 percent in the late 1970s (*Graph 3*). The rapid growth follows a linear trend with no unexpected variations. The same pattern is found in absolute figures at constant prices

(*Graph 4*). Throughout the postwar era there has been a continuous rise in public, particularly social welfare expenditure and
major changes in resource allocation.[33]

A disaggeration of public expenditure by economic category into
what is actually "used and produced" in the public sector and what
is just "passing through" gives us an overall picture of two more or
less constant and two changing categories (see *Graph 5*). The
shares of public consumption and interest on the public debt are
relatively stable, though the former has declined slightly. Consumption constitutes around half of public expenditure, while interest
on the public debt oscilliates at around 5 percent. In contrast,
transfers and subsidies, and public investments rose and fell respectively. For two thirds of the postwar period the unbroken OECD
series indicates an almost linear rise for transfers and subsidies,
while public investment is characterized by a marked decline from
the mid-1960s.[34]

Disaggerating public expenditure by level of government reveals
a pattern of stability in the first postwar decade (see *Graph 6*). The
municipalities were the main spenders, with 40 percent of total
public expenditure; followed by central government (almost one
third); social insurance (almost one fourth); and regional government (less than one tenth). From the 1960s, the overall trend shows

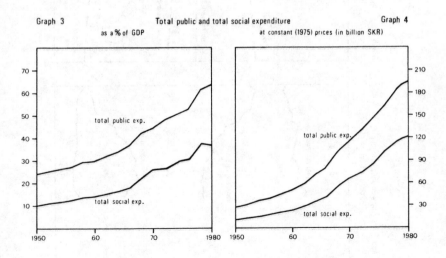

Graph 3   Total public and total social expenditure   Graph 4

as a % of GDP   at constant (1975) prices (in billion SKR)

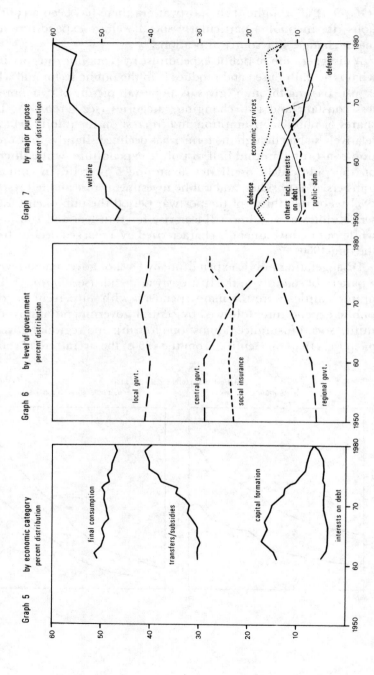

Total public expenditure

Graph 5   by economic category
percent distribution

final consumption

transfers/subsidies

capital formation

interests on debt

Graph 6   by level of government
percent distribution

local govt.

central govt.

social insurance

regional govt.

Graph 7   by major purpose
percent distribution

welfare

economic services

defense

defense

others incl. interests
on debt

public adm.

a marked increase in regional government outlays, closely related to the expansion of the health sector. By 1980, both regional and central government account for a sixth of public expenditure. In the 1970s, social security grew at the expense of central state activities. Only the municipal share remained almost unchanged throughout the period, contrary to the widespread dualistic conception of the trend as a change from central to non-central government spending. Nevertheless, the pattern of relative decentralization remains, if central government and social insurance expenditure is contrasted with that of regional and local government: a shift from a 52/48 in 1950 to 44/56 in the late 1970s.[35]

In addition to an analysis of expenditure data by economic categories and level of government, trends in public finance can also be examined in terms of functional breakdowns. This is a difficult task but on the basis of a careful investigation of Swedish expenditure figures up to 1958 and smaller follow-up studies covering from 1958 to 1980 we can obtain at least an approximate picture.[36] The changes shown in *Graph 7* are not dramatic, but the growing importance of the welfare state in relation to other public tasks is reflected there. Welfare constitutes the largest expenditure item during the entire period. Defence has dropped from just below 20 percent at the beginning of the postwar period to just below 5 percent in 1980. Economic services including transportation and the promotion of various infrastructural activities have been stable throughout the entire period, oscillating between 15 and 20 percent of total public expenditure. While non-allocated items (including interests paid on the national debt) have remained reasonably stable, general administration involving justice and internal order has moved from just below 10 percent to nearly 15 percent.

Public Employment

The expansion of the public sector, in addition to representing an explosive increase in costs and an enlargement and multiplication of social programmes, is also reflected in the changes in employment structure. Public sector employment (excluding state-owned firms in the competitive sector) rose from around 10 percent in 1950 to a third of the labour force 30 years later. The absolute number trebled from under half a million to almost one and a half million many of whom are part-timers.[37] This has also greatly increased the proportion of women in the labour force. The expansion in employment has mainly occurred in the welfare sector, particularly in public health and social services (see *Table 3*). This growth of employment in the public services has been accompanied by a sharp contraction in agriculture, leading to a social redeployment of the entire working population during the postwar era.

Table 3	Size and structure of public employment (a)										
	1950		1960		1965	1970		1975		1980	
	1,000	%	1,000	%	1,000	1,000	%	1,000	%	1,000	%
By level of government:											
General civil service, defence, and public enterprises (b)	274	(45.1)	316	(52.9)	356	296	33.4	406	33.9	441	30.3
Other central govt. financed (c)	31	(6.5)	62	(10.4)	82	117	13.2	137	11.5	173	11.9
County councils						171	19.3	257	21.5	353	24.3
Municipal councils						302	34.1	396	33.1	488	33.5
By function (d):											
Education	73	(15.4)	124	(20.8)	155	209	23.6	265	22.2	297	20.4
Health			137	(22.9)	176	243	27.4	329	27.5	425	29.2
Social services			51	(8.5)	81	162	18.3	233	19.5	298	20.5
Total public employment (e)	(475)	100.0	(597)	100.0		886	100.0	1 196	100.0	1 455	100.0
Labour force (f)	3 093		3 244		3 697	3 913		4 098		4 318	
Public empl. as % of labour force	15.4		18.4			22.6		29.2		33.7	

(a) The table is based on different series of official statistics which explains the incompleteness and inconsistencies. For the problems of public employment statistics, see A. Kruse, Den offentliga sektorns sysselsättningsutveckling i Norden under 1970-talet. NAUT-rapport 1983, 8, Nordiska Ministerrådet, Oslo 1983. Figures in brackets not comparable with percentage-figures without brackets.

(b) Public enterprises include a total of seven central government agencies (Post Office Administration, National Telecommunications Administration, Forestry). They exclude public enterprises in the competitive sector from 1970 to 1980, but not from 1950 to 1965.

(c) Mainly employees in the school system (143,000 in 1980), which is administered by local councils, but financed by central government, and employees in social insurance offices (ca. 15,000 in 1980).

(d) For the definitions of these categories, see SCB, Trender och prognoser 1980, IPF 1980, 4; figures for 1980 refer to 1979.

(e) The figures for 1950 and 1960 include employees in government-owned business enterprises in the competitive sector.

(f) The figures for 1950 and 1960 are not completely comparable with those for 1965 onwards.

2.2 Social Expenditure

The amount of money spent on welfare has grown in relation to GDP and in absolute figures (see *Graphs 3 and 4*). Its share of GDP more than trebled rising from 11 percent to 34 percent between 1950 and 1980. The exact amount of social outlays is not easy to summarize as they are taken from different public and semi-public sources.[38] On aggegated level, social expenditure includes most of the spending for education, health, income maintenance and social services. Taken together these give a rough picture of the welfare share of total public expenditure. Due to Swedish statistical classi- fication expenditure on housing is not included totally, which means that in general social expenditure is somewhat underestimated.

In order to investigate the development of welfare, a disaggrega- tion of social expenditures is given in *Graphs 8 and 9*. Income maintenance, although declining for the major part of the period forms the main part of public welfare outlays throughout the postwar era, i.e. between half and more than a third of all welfare expenditure consists of cash benefits. Education comes second up to the mid-1970s, growing during the two first decades with a peak in the early 1960s reaching almost a third of total social expendi- ture, but declining in the 1970s. Health expenditure (including hospital and out-patient services but not sickness insurance) in- creased its share from around 15 percent at the beginning of the postwar period to around 25 percent at the end. Social services are the fourth and smallest item of expenditure. They comprise such different things as benefits in kind to families and children, old age and invalidity services, employment exchanges and retraining programmes and industrial safety provisions.[39] Social services ex- penditure remained fairly steady at below 10 percent until the mid-1960s. After this time expenditure increased slowly, reaching a relative share of 15 percent at the end of the period. Social service costs partly follow the overall upward trend at constant prices (*Graph 9*), but the 'take-off' was retarded and can be dated to the mid-1970s. The overall pattern of social expenditure (see *Graph 8*), is consistent with Sweden's high level of public consumption expenditure (the highest among the OECD countries), but with lower levels of expenditure on transfer payments (these latter are, however, still high relative to other OECD countries).

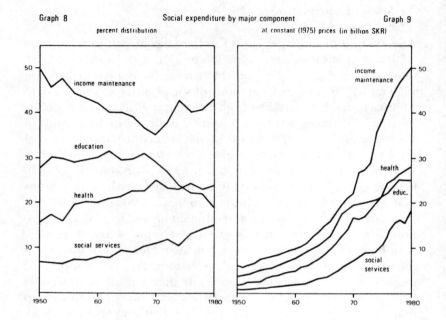

Graph 8   Social expenditure by major component   Graph 9

percent distribution   at constant (1975) prices (in billion SKR)

By breaking down income maintenance further into pension programmes, sickness insurance, occupational injury insurance, housing allowances and various family and children supplements unemployment insurance, public assistance (poor relief) – reveals the changing structure (*Graph 10*). *Graph 11*, which shows the distribution of income maintenance expenditure by type of benefit, reflects the relative shift from universal flat-rate benefits to earnings-related benefits. Up to the mid-1960s flat-rate benefits accounted for two-thirds of all income maintenance expenditure. During the first postwar years income- and means-tested benefits ranked second, with a peak in 1954 when they made up almost one-fifth of the total public redistribution system. From 1955 onwards, when universal sickness insurance was introduced, earnings-related benefits started to increase their relative share. This development was pushed forward by the second important earnings-related programme, supplementary pensions, which were introduced in 1959, the first pensions being paid in 1963. Sickness cash benefits were revised in the same year (and also in 1967). Throughout the period

126

earnings-related schemes strengthened their relative position, with flat-rate programmes deteriorating to a level just over a third at the end of the 1970s. Due to inconsistencies in the statistics, however, we should not exaggerate the differences between the two major types of income maintenance programme, even if earnings-related benefits obviously represent the chief item today.[40]

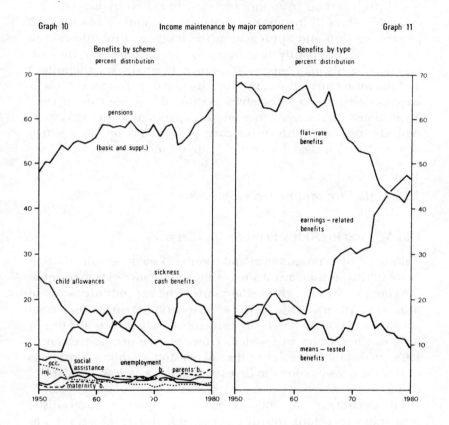

Graph 10   Income maintenance by major component   Graph 11

Benefits by scheme
percent distribution

Benefits by type
percent distribution

In relative terms, basic pensions have been the main expenditure item for the entire postwar period (see *Graph 10*). This is true despite a decline from over 50 percent in the 1950s and 1960s to around 40 percent in the 1970s. During the latter part of the period, supplementary pensions became more important and displaced sickness cash benefits as the second main expenditure item. Taken together, expenditure on basic and supplementary pensions never fell below half of total public expenditure on income maintenance.

Child allowances have dropped from second (during the first half of the 1950s) to fourth position (1980) as a social expenditure item. In percentage figures the drop is even sharper: from 25.2 percent in 1950 to 6.0 percent in 1980. During the second half of the 1970s, parental insurance (previously maternity benefits) increased its share of income maintenance expenditure, reaching 4.3 percent in 1980 and approaching the level of child allowances. Expenditure on family housing allowances, other family cash benefits (mainly maintenance allowances to single-parent families) and unemployment insurance (not included in *Graph 10*), oscillated between 1 and 4 percentage points throughout the period. Meanstested public assistance and occupational injury insurance ranked fourth and fifth in the early postwar period, after which time both diminished drastically in importance.

2.3 Single Programme Development

Old Age and Invalidity Pensions and Services

Taking pension programmes and connected services as the starting point of this section, again stresses the importance of retirement as the core provision of the welfare state. The expenditure development is given in *Graphs 12 to 14*. As mentioned earlier, universal pension rights are a governing principle dating back to the beginning of the century in Sweden. However, the decision taken in 1948, trebled the real value of the old pension, enabling pensioners to live on pensions for the first time, albeit at a low standard of living.

The decision meant that the early anticipatory universalistic principle – pensions for all citizens, not just employees – was maintained, that the meanstested elements were abolished and a flat-rate pension introduced, though it differed for single persons and couples. In the following years several improvements were made. Indexation was introduced in 1951, and income-tested municipal housing allowances became available on a nationwide basis in the mid-50s.

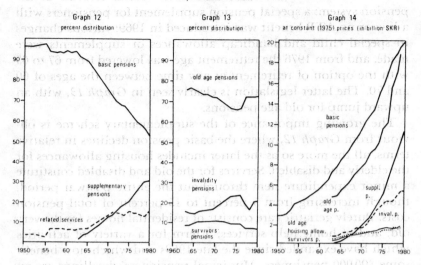

Expenditure on Pensions

Graph 12
percent distribution

Graph 13
percent distribution

Graph 14
at constant (1975) prices (in billion SKR)

An invalidity pension along the lines of the old age pension was provided from 1948 onwards, and the similarity between the two was preserved when the supplementary pension scheme was established. The similarity also holds true for survivors' pensions (widows and orphans), although they remained income-tested until the end of the 1950s. The relation between the three types of programmes are given in *Graph 13*, showing a growing role of invalidity pensions in the early 1970s, when the right was extended to the elderly (between the age of 60 – sometimes even 55 – to 65), with physically strenuous work or those unable to find a job on the open labour market.

In 1963 the national supplementary pension (*ATP*) came into effect, pensions paying (initially at a low level) to all three kinds of pensioners. Being an earnings-related benefit, the pension level is calculated on the basis of the previous earnings and years of employment (see Appendix volume). Employees are expected to receive an old-age pension which is equivalent to roughly 60 percent of their average income in previous years after 30 years of employment. The new pensioners of 1979 were the first to receive a full supplementary pension from the ATP system.

129

Since the late 1960s, there have been several reforms of the pension system: a special pension supplement for pensioners with a low or no ATP benefit was introduced in 1969; various changes in special child and handicap allowances or supplements were made, and from 1976 the retirement age was lowered from 67 to 65 with the option of retirement at any time between the ages of 60 and 70. The latter legislation is clearly seen in *Graph 13*, with an upward jump for old age pensions.

The growing importance of the supplementary scheme is obvious from *Graph 12*, where the basic pension declines in relative terms, all the more so as the latter includes housing allowances for the elderly and disabled. Services for the old and disabled constitute a minor expenditure item throughout the entire postwar period, though increasing from 5 percent to 15 percent of total pension costs. Purely geriatric care consists of residential homes for the very old, and of home help services; a term for a variety of activities which have expanded since the late 1960s and which now benefit some 300 000 pensioners. Municipal pensioners' dwellings are an intermediate form of housing care, which presupposes a high degree of selfhelp. About 60 000 of the country's 1.4 million retired persons live in residential homes and about 80 000 live in pensioners' housing. The great majority of persons over 65 live in ordinary housing. Since the end of the 1960s the numbers of beds in residential people's homes has hardly changed and instead local authorities are now constructing service buildings or ordinary apartments with access to social services. Besides this, improvement in handicap services also contribute to the rising service costs.

Health and Sickness Insurance

The administration of voluntary sickness insurance by local friendly societies was finally brought to an end in 1955, when a compulsory insurance scheme with earnings-related cash benefits was introduced, providing earnings-related sickness cash benefits, replacing low contribution related benefits (thus making it possible to separate benefits in cash and kind, see *Graphs 15 and 16*). Maternity benefits (see *Graph 19*) were integrated into the new system which in addition covers all kinds of medical benefits not covered by public health or fees. Important changes have since been made by parliament: the administrative integration of pensions and sickness insurance when sickness cash benefits were related to net earnings and simultaneously raised to 70 percent in 1963; the abolition of initial no-benefit days together with an improvement in replacement ratio to 80 percent of net earnings in 1967; the calculation of earnings-related benefits on the basis of gross income, thereby raising the level to 90 percent of taxable income in 1974, when, moreover, general health insurance was extended to cover dental treatment.

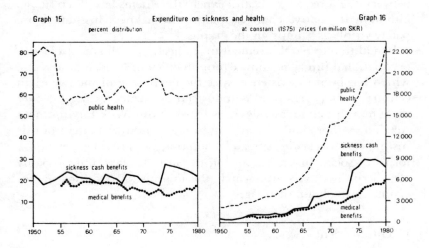

Graph 15
percent distribution

Expenditure on sickness and health
at constant (1S75) prices (in million SKR)

Graph 16

Health services, the major item, grew much more continuously during the postwar period, accellerating in the 1960s. Hospitals have been the responsibility of the county councils since the nineteenth century, and in the mid-1960s almost the entire health system became a regional public competence. The 1960s saw the start of a forceful expansion in the health sector, with new hospitals being built throughout Sweden. Seven regional hospitals, affiliated to medical schools for research and training and serving about one million people each, were created in order to offer a high degree of specialization throughout the country. Later on, public out-patient service was expanded in order to create a system of preventive health care, thus relieving cost pressure on the more expensive hospitals.

131

The fact that almost all health care is public entails heavily subsidized fees. Traditionally, fees for public medical treatment and hospital care have been very low. The introduction of compulsory health insurance in 1955 allowed universal access to medical services. The 'seven Krona-reform' in 1969, had similar goals whereby a low, uniform fee was introduced for the entire outpatient medical care system, including the majority of the private practitioners (reimbursed by sickness insurance included under 'medical benefits', see *Graps 15 and 16*). Since 1955 the relationship between the three major health expenditure items have been stable, although legislative changes, mainly in sickness insurance, are partly visible as 'jumps' in the graphs.

In addition to reimbursement in connection with fatal accidents, occupational injury insurance (not included in *Graphs 15 and 16*), which has been in existence since the beginning of the twentieth century, now covers serious industrial accidents lasting for over three months, and many deseases listed in the Work Environment Act. The minor changes in the overall expenditure pattern of this insurance reflects the spread of alternatives provided by newer forms of social insurance during the last 30 years, but probably also, according to recent research, the administrative difficulties for claimants to obtain their rights.[41]

Unemployment

The stress on employment programmes in contrast to reliance on unemployment insurance goes back at least as far as to World War I. This was confirmed when then National Labour Market Board (*Arbetsmarknadsstyrelsen, AMS*) was established in 1948, taking charge of the then nationalized local employment offices, and acting as superintendent of the heavily state-subsidised trade-union controlled unemployment insurance benefit societies. At the same time, the doctrine of active manpower policy was formulated as a measure to restructure Swedish industry with trade union support.[42] With the exception of the peculiar case of the first postwar decade, unemployment insurance has never been an important expenditure item on its own, while the sums spent on manpower policy have been considerable. In the early 1950s, unemployment was almost non-existent, apart from seasonal variations, but even so, the largest part of social expenditure was made up of cash benefits, which never accounted for less than 40 percent in the first postwar decade (*Graph 17*). The importance of the centralization of employment offices is shown by the expenditure on employment exchanges and careers' services which constitutes the second largest expenditure item up to the end of the 1950s starting at a level of 30 percent.

The situation altered around 1960, after the first postwar recession in Sweden (shown in *Graph 18*). From the 1960s onwards, the AMS acquired a powerful position in Swedish politics as the implementor of the active manpower policy. AMS' activities have grown immensely during the last two decades as new programmes have been added to old ones: training services, mobility allowances, educational allowances for retraining, employment creation schemes, regional development grants, occupational rehabilitation schemes, etc. (most programmes belonging to 'retraining' in *Graph 17 and 18*). Deliberate attempts have been made to integrate groups formerly outside the labour market. The proportion of women in employment has increased markedly. Despite many shortcomings, the position of the disabled has become stronger on the labour market, and persons with severe occupational handicaps have been given sheltered jobs. Since 1980, these jobs are offered by a special state enterprise (*Samhällsföretag*) with some 22 000 employees throughout Sweden.

In the 1960s the rise of employment programmes was in particular related to the regional unemployment problems in Northern Sweden, while the tremendous growth in the late 1970s was linked to the effects of the world economic crisis on Swedish economy particularly steel and shipbuilding (see *Graph 18*). In this period the relative importance of unemployment cash benefits grew somewhat, while public outlays on employment office and vocational guidance have been fairly stable since the 1960s. Otherwise the yearly fluctuations between expenditure items visible in *Graph 17* are mainly due to selective manpower measures to counteract unwanted consequenes of economic development.

Even if postwar manpower policy has been regarded primarily as part of a general economic policy, it is important to underline its social policy dimensions. Employment has been maintained and even increased over a long period unemployment rising to only 3 percent in the worst years.

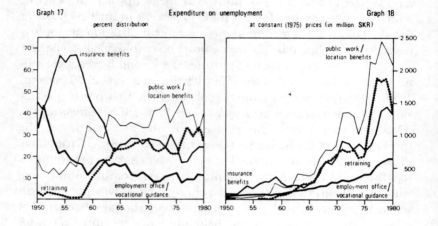

In comparative terms, unemployment insurance is underdeveloped both in relation to other forms of social insurance and by international standards. This is primarily due to the combined effects of trade union strength and the success of the active manpower policy. Despite years of parliamentary and governmental investigations and the many reports made by State Commissions, unemployment insurance has not been fully integrated into the national social security system.[43] It is still formally a voluntary insurance organized by unions and their benefit societies, although most unions have made it compulsory. From 1974 the insurance scheme was supplemented with a state administered unemployment assistance benefit for unemployed persons not enrolled in a benefit society, or society members not entitled to benefits.

Families and Children

While the importance of pensions, health and unemployment schemes has grown during the postwar period, the same is not true of family policy. Family policy was formulated in intense debate in the 1930s and culminated with the introduction of general child allowances in the immediate postwar years. Since then social expenditure on families and children shows a declining trend.

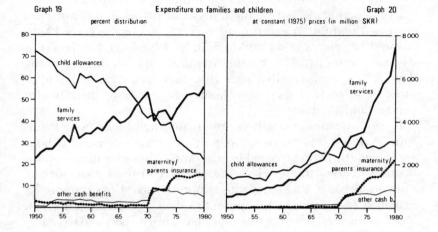

Graph 19 — Expenditure on families and children — Graph 20
percent distribution — at constant (1975) prices (in million SKR)

Looking at the internal composition (*Graph 19*) child allowances initially made up the dominant part, but steadily diminishing in importance, and constituting only a quarter of total outlays in the late 1970s. The reverse pattern is shown by expenditure on family services with just below 25 percent in the early 1950s and ranking first at the end of the period at around half of total family expenditure. Thirdly, the importance of parent's insurance, introduced in 1974, has grown over the last years.

In 1948 the old system of tax-deductions for children, which favoured the wealthy and had a negligible effect on the poor was replaced by a general child allowance. Unlike the basic pension, the child allowance has never been indexed; instead, parliament has augmented it occasionally, a mode of decision-making motivated by the minor role which the allowance plays in expenditure on childrearing. However, this meant that the real value (*Graph 20*) of aggregate expenditure on child allowances stagnated during the first ten years, while increasing also in real terms subsequently.

The main part of family services up to the mid-1960s was constituted by traditional public child welfare measures, a stable number of day nurseries, and subsidized school meals. After that, paralleling the sudden increase in female employment, the growth of family services is characterized by the expansion of municipal

135

day-care centres, built up with state support (see *Graph 19*).

In the period 1965-1980, the number of places in day nurseries increased tenfold, amounting to over 120 000 in the early 1980s. Around 17 percent of all children under school age had places at daycare centres in 1981. Another form of child minding is family daycare; the municipality hires child minders, who take one or more children into their own homes. In addition, there is also private family daycare.

In 1974, various motherhood and maternity benefits were transformed into a more uniform parent's insurance (equal for both sexes) and the period covered by insurance (giving earnings-related benefits at the same level as the sickness insurance or, for the nonemployed, a small flat-rate support) was also substantially extended (a minimum of up to 180 days – see Appendix). In absolute figures, parent's insurance has grown spectacularly, during the first seven years that it has been in operation (1974-1980) (see *Graph 20*).

Maintenance advances constitute the major part of "other cash benefits" (see *Graps 19* and *20*). They were mostly paid privately or after a court ruling, by the non-custodial parent. Today, however, they are often paid in advance by public welfare authorities in order to safeguard children from parental omission or inability to fulfill the obligation (this scheme has been in operation on a smaller scale since the late 1930s). Repayment is made to the government which recovers almost a third of the annual expenditure. The growth in expenditure on this item in the 1970s reflects the awareness of, and adaption to changing family composition. Unlike the general child allowance, advance maintenance is indexed, thus keeping pace with the overall growth of living costs.

Education

Generally speaking, education has always been a public competence in Sweden. In the old parallel school system pupils were divided at an early age between a closed academically oriented training system, and poor primary education. The system was much criticized even prior to World War II, and in the immediate postwar period measures were taken to modernize the system. Nevertheless, the final decision to introduce a nine-year comprehensive school for all children aged 7 to 16 was only taken in 1962, with its implementation planned over a ten-year period. Subsequent to the reform, girls' schools disappeared and education was formally equalized between the sexes. In the mid-1960s the upper secondary and vocational schools were combined to form an 'integrated upper secondary school' for those aged 16-20. These schools recruited almost 90 percent of pupils aged 17, mainly for courses lasting from two to three years. This meant that the length of schooling increased from an average of seven years in the late 1950s to eleven years in the early 1970s, i.e. that normal school leaving age rose from 14 to 18.

During the late 1960s and early 1970s municipal adult education was developed and entrance to university was broadened. Earlier forms of adult education, such as residential folk high schools, which were state subsidized but usually connected with the popular movements (temperance, free church and working class), have adapted to changing conditions and still offer courses which both complement, and provide alternatives to, the formal school system.

Changes in higher education occurred when the wartime baby boom reached university age. A university reform was proposed in 1968 and became effective a year later. It introduced strictly organized undergraduate courses (three to four years) in the arts and sciences, together with shorter occupational courses. University entrance was opened up to those with no formal qualifications but with five (later four) years of gainful employment and some language training. During this period the number of universities increased from four to six, one of the newcomers being Umeå in the far North.

In the late 1960s several satellite colleges were established, offering a wide range of undergraduate courses. This latter type of decentralization was taken still further in the 1970s, when all higher educational institutions were given equal status within an integrated tertiary educational system under the jursidiction of six regional higher educational authorities (högskoleregioner).

The rapid growth of education expenditure in the middle of the postwar period, when the compulsory school system was built up, is clearly shown in *Graph 21*. In real terms schooling absorbed five times more resources in the late 1970s than it had done 30 years earlier.

137

Graph 21

Expenditure on education
at constant (1975) prices (in million SKR)

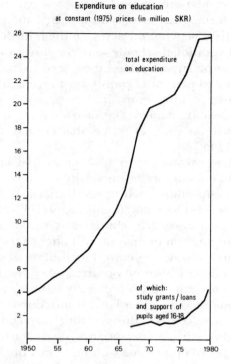

In the mid-1960s an extended child allowance was introduced for pupils in upper secodary schools aged 17-18, together with several income- and means-tested educatinal allowances for pupils up to the age of 20. At the same time a combination of general educational allowances and long-term, interest free study loans, irrespective of parental income, were introduced for university students. As a public 'expenditure' item, they have more than doubled in real value (see *Graph 21* and the Institutional Synopsis in the Appendix volume).

Already mentioned under 'families and children' were the more 'purely' social policy reforms in the field of education, such as free school meals, school health and dental services, and, most recently, municipal extra curricula recreational activities.

Housing

Housing policy developed out of the public control of both construction and the housing market, i.e. rent controls introduced at the beginning of the war and subsequently institutionalized by the National Housing Board set up in 1948. Rent control was gradually phased out from the late 1950s until 1975. In addition to the various forms of building control and urban planning at all government levels, housing policy entails the following economic support measures: housing construction loans, interest subventions, tax deductions for interest paid on housing loans, and housing allowances to subsidize rents for low income-earners.

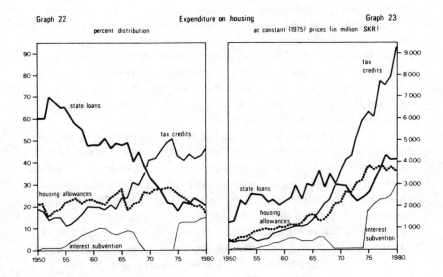

Graph 22 — percent distribution

Expenditure on housing

Graph 23 — at constant (1975) prices (in million SKR)

The promotion of housing construction by granting long-term and low-interest loans was introduced after World War II in reaction to the war and postwar housing shortages, migration and urbanization. Since the 1950s, over 90 percent of all newly constructed housing has been subsidized by the state in this way.

In relative terms (see *Graph 22*), the importance of loans as an 'expenditure' item has continuously diminished. At constant prices, however, (see *Graph 23*) they increased in the mid-1960s when

139

parliament decided that one million apartments should be built in a decade (mainly in the form of municipal multi-dwelling houses; the plan was pursued). A second increase occurred the late 1970s when a great many single-family houses were constructed in response to new market demands.

Interest subventions were initially designed to protect rents from effects of temporarily high interest rates but were soon regarded as a necessary complement to other housing policy measures in an economy with lasting inflationary tendencies. The role of these subsidies grew in the late 1950s and early 1960s. However, as they were technically difficult to operate, an attempt was made in the late 1960s to replace them by an altogether different system intended to adjust both interest rates and repayments on the loans to inflation. After a few years, the new system proved politically difficult to handle and in 1974 interest subventions were reintroduced. Immediately, they almost trebled in real value as compared to the year when they were temporarily abolished. In the 1970s their relative importance became almost equal to expenditure on both traditional housing allowances and the annual figure of public housing loans (see *Graph 22*).

In addition to providing loans and interest subventions, the state also supports owner-occupiers by granting tax credits (i.e. all taxpayers have a statutory entitlement to claim deductions for interest expenses). As a consequence of the reformulations of housing policy in the mid-1970s and the increase in the number of single-family houses, these tax deductions for house owners have become much more important in recent years. In the 1970s they became the outstanding item of housing 'expenditure' and in absolute figures trebled between the beginning and the end of the decade (see *Graphs 22* and *23*).

Housing allowances for low-income earners were introduced for large families and pensioners in the late 1940s and early 1950s (some small programmes existed as early as in the 1930s), and were subsequently extended to other groups in the 1970s. Expenditure on housing allowances for pensioners has increased steadily in real terms, while allowances for families first stagnated and then increased rapidly in the late 1960s and early 1970s. Subsequently the latter diminished and then stagnated again in the mid- and late 1970s.

140

2.4 Public Revenues

From the preceeding chapters we can see that there has been an increase in the public provision of welfare, either through the extension of existing schemes or through the introduction of new benefits and services. The public expenditure pattern for this period is one of rapid growth, in absolute and relative terms.[44]

A descriptive picture of the welfare state taken from the expenditure side only, would – at least in the long run – be misleading without the necessary information from the Treasury concerning public revenues. The relationship between income and outlays, however, is extremely complex and one should be cautious in comparing figures of the two sides of the public household. No single coordinating cashier exists, although the Minister of Finance plays this role in public opinion. Social security funds are tightly controlled by central government, but local government (municipalities and county councils) has a great degree of independence as regards taxation and borrowing although the latter is formally controlled by the Central Bank.[45]

This section gives a brief outline of the sources of public finance. As shown in *Graph 24*, total public revenues as a percentage of GDP have increased steadily from the early 1950s to the early 1970s, doubling their share from 25 to 50 percent. After a brief relative decline in 1972 as a consequence of economic recession, growth was resumed until the late 1970s when decline restarted (in relative terms). On average, total public revenues have grown annually by 6.4 percent, but growth rates have varied considerably. In the 1950s, revenues grew from 25 to 30 percent of GDP. In the 1960s, growth rates accelerated rapidly and were, with the exception of 1966, all above the average of the entire postwar period. In the 1970s, average growth rates were the lowest of the three decades and simultaneously had the greatest variations.

Comparing revenues with expenditure for the first 22 years after 1950, revenues exceeded expenditure and this surplus became more apparent in the 1960s. This helps to explain the continual demands for a reduction in income tax. These demands were not based on the traditional principle of a balanced budget, but on the Keynesian notion of deficit spending, first introduced by the Social Democrats in the early 1930s and defended intellectually by Gun-

141

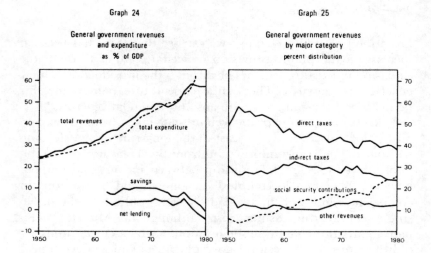

nar Myrdal in a 1933 amendment to the state budget. Countercyclical policies were formally introduced as a principle of budgetary policy in 1937.[46] These principles were never seriously questioned in the postwar years of full employment and inflationary pressure.

A look at the composition of revenues (*Graph 25*) shows that at the beginning of the period direct taxes were the dominant item (about one half), followed by indirect taxes (almost a third), and social security contributions (about a tenth). Towards the end of the period the shares became more equal, as a result of a broader and more differentiated tax base.[47] The relative shift from direct to indirect taxes applies to the whole of the twentieth century. It reflects a development from 'visible' to what were previously regarded as more 'invisible' forms of taxation, a pattern not unique to Sweden which may serve to avoid tax resistance.

The overall changes in the composition of public revenues conceal some important internal changes in the development of direct taxes. Corporate taxes have been of negligible size since the late 1950s, the share of the progressive national income tax gradually diminished over the entire period, whereas the share of the proportional local (municipalities and county councils) income tax

142

increased. Central government transfers to regional and local authorities have grown even more, increasing their share in local government finance from a fifth to a third.

On the central level, fiscal policy has been an area of contention between government and opposition throughout the postwar era, with the possible exception of the 1960s.[48] Demands by the opposition for lower income tax were raised nearly every year. At the same time, whenever a new major tax reform was introduced, the Social Democrats defended it on the grounds that welfare reforms force the state to find new sources of revenue. The first important clashes on fiscal policy occured as early as 1947, when the "war taxes" were incorporated into the peacetime taxation system (some of them were eventually abolished) and later in 1959, when a parliamentary decision on general sales tax was taken with only a very small majority (with extremely reluctant Communist support). Furthermore, the general payroll tax has been a matter of dispute since its introduction in the late 1960s. On the other hand, the replacement of the general sales tax by a value-added tax in 1968, and the continuous increase in social security contributions was, at least until the mid-1970s, supported by all major parties.

The enlargement of the public sector has meant increasing taxation, but in contrast with the other Scandinavian countries, particularly Denmark, there have been relatively few signs of a welfare backlash in the form of a tax revolt.[49] This is true even where the parties on both the right- and the left-wing have tried – sometimes successfully – to make tax issues politically controversial.

2.5 Single Programme Financing

As we have seen, the overall structure of Swedish public revenue has moved towards a more diversified pattern. This is reflected particularly in the fiscal balance of the welfare state. As the costs of welfare measures and social security are still to a considerable degree covered by the central government budget (only parts of it are funded locally) it is difficult to specify exactly how different programmes are financed.

Education is mostly financed out of general taxation on a fifty-

fifty basis by central and municipal budgets. This applies particularly to compulsory education and upper secondary education. Universities and research institutes are almost entirely financed by central government, while educational options which fall outside the traditional school system such as folk high schools, study circles, adult education etc. receive various types of government support.

Housing is financed both directly by transfer payments and indirectly by tax credits. In the last ten years, the main part of public support for housing has become 'indirect', i.e. interest on housing loans is tax deductable (as a consequence of the general tax deductions related to interest paid on loans). Directly, central government subsidizes from general revenues interest on housing construction loans, and contributes to municipal expenditure on housing allowances to pensioners, families with children and low income earners in general.

The provision, and to an increasing extent, the financing of public health services come within the competence of the county councils. Until the late 1960s, the financing of public health was shared on a seventy-thirty basis between the counties and central government. Since then the county councils' share has grown. Of this share a smaller amount comes from fees paid for services in hospitals or outpatient medical centers and from sickness insurance transfers to county councils. From the mid-1970s, employers also contribute to the health system.

The pattern of sickness insurance financing has changed (*Graph 26*) during the period. In the early 1950s, when the system was voluntary, central government financed a third of total costs. With the exception of occupational injury insurance employers did not make contributions to social security until sickness insurance became compulsory in 1955. From 1955 the employers' share of total revenue almost equalled central government support, while contributions from the insured continued to be the major component until the mid-1960s. Since then, employers' contributions have been the main source of financing, particularly since the mid-1970s, when contributions from the insured were abolished (except those from the self-employed). At the time of the most recent change in rules in 1974, the insured, employers and central government paid one third each.

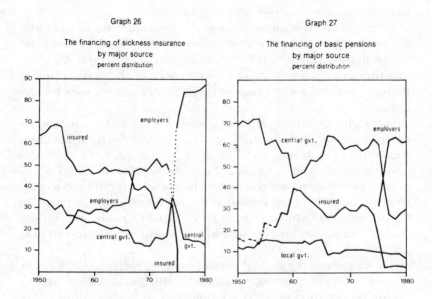

Graph 26

The financing of sickness insurance
by major source
percent distribution

Graph 27

The financing of basic pensions
by major source
percent distribution

Graph 27 shows the financing of basic pensions, i.e. old age and invalidity pensions, survivor's pensions and housing allowances. Until 1963 local government expenditure for basic pensions was totally absorbed by housing allowances. After 1963 these allowances were only partially financed by the municipalities. Following the 1948 reform, all basic pensions with the exception of housing allowances, were paid out of central government revenues, including an 'earmarked' amount (*folkpensionsavgift*) added to personal income tax. Until 1975, taxation was the main source of revenue, but in the late 1950s and early 1960s the earmarked contribution from the insured increased. In the mid-1970s, employers' social security contributions were introduced and soon became the major source of finance.

In the latter part of the period under review a new scheme, the national supplementary pension, was built up, financed by contributions from employers and the self-employed. This scheme is administered by four extra-budgetary funds. As a system which accumulates capital, not only contributions but also revenue from

145

interest important for its future fiscal balance.

Unemployment insurance is operated through voluntary organizations closely connected with the trade unions. Until the mid-1960s it was mainly financed by membership fees (see *Graph 28*). After this time central government revenues became the main source of finance until 1974 when employers' payroll contributions became payable.

Similarly, welfare programmes such as parental insurance, industrial safety, and orphans' pensions have been increasingly financed by employers' social security contributions. On the other hand, general child allowances have always been financed out of central government tax revenues. The costs for family services are usually shared between central and local government. Services for the old are mainly financed out of municipal taxation, and employment programmes are financed from the central government budget.

To summarize the overall development of social security revenues (including income maintenance, health, and social services but excluding eduation and most of housing), at the beginning of the postwar period benefits and services were largely financed by central and local government revenues and to a much smaller extent by individual contributions from the insured (see *Graph 29*). Employers' contributions did not exist, with the exception of the occupational injuries insurance, where they made up almost 100 percent. In the 1960s and 1970s welfare financing shifted away from the combination of government and individual contributions – the latter being abolished, excluding schemes for the self-employed, in the mid-1970s – and greater emphasis was put on employers' social security contributions. This is particularly true for income maintenence programmes, with the exception of child and housing allowances.

2.6 *The Growth of Welfare Clienteles*

The making of the Swedish Welfare State has its particular history which is quite different from its continental counterparts, this being especially true for the development of income maintenance. Although Bismarckian legislation on workers' insurance in Ger-

146

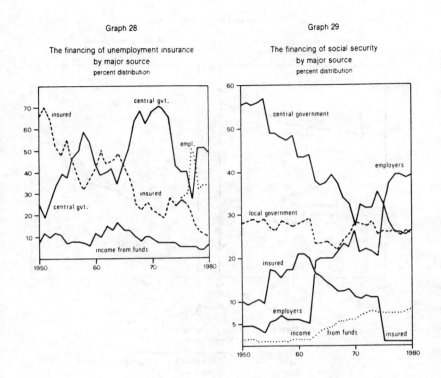

Graph 28

The financing of unemployment insurance
by major source
percent distribution

Graph 29

The financing of social security
by major source
percent distribution

many stimulated parliamentary debate and inquiry before the turn of the century, its impact on the eventual introduction of social insurance programs was diluted.[50] As regards the Beveridge model, Swedish social policy showed signs of universality well in advance of the appearance of the new social policy model in wartime Britain, due to the combination of rural backwardness and industrial modernization. Structurally, the existence of a large agricultural population alongside a growing working class was an important precondition for the steps taken, both groups being mobilized in the process of transforming poor relief into welfare policy.[51]

In 1913, Parliament decided almost unanimously to introduce pensions with just a tiny minority of voluntary welfare humanists and orthodox economists who feared the effects on work incentives and the long-term fiscal balance.

147

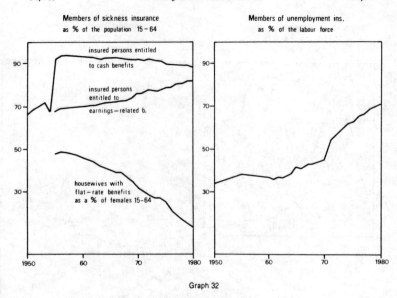

Members of sickness insurance
as % of the population 15 – 64

insured persons entitled
to cash benefits

insured persons
entitled to
earnings – related b.

housewives with
flat – rate benefits
as a % of females 15-64

Members of unemployment ins.
as % of the labour force

Graph 32

The clienteles of major income maintenance schemes
as % of total population

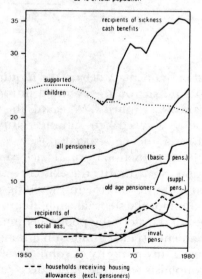

recipients of sickness
cash benefits

supported
children

all pensioners

(basic pens.)

(suppl. pens.)

old age pensioners

recipients of
social ass.

inval.
pens.

- - - households receiving housing
allowances (excl. pensioners)

Nevertheless, the early breakthrough of the notion of universality was not decisive, and it is important to stress the mixture of universal eligibility and widespread income-tested assistance inherent in Swedish social policy. Although social class and selectivity were rejected as alternative criteria for social welfare provision, they were not altogether absent from the pre-World War II system of social security. They still constituted a working part of the pension system and of family support, although with some modifications. In addition to the universal insurance schemes (pension and occupational injury insurance), another type of insurance characteristic of the prewar Swedish welfare system was state supported voluntary protection, such as sickness and unemployment insurance. Both of these had long-established links with popular movements i.e. the free church, the temperance movement and the trade unions. These represented a different kind of selectivity, excluding the very poor and weak. With all their apparent shortcomings, prior to the postwar era, the above mentioned provisions together with traditional poor relief formed a rudimentary system of welfare protection against social evils.

After World War II, the social security network was extended (see *Table 4*). By the late 1940s and early 1950s, all the major social categories had been covered in a minimum of social protection by means of basic pension, child allowance, sickness and maternity insurance. From this date we can speak of a victory for universalism, as all citizens and even all residents were involved in the system of social transfer. The idea of universal eligibility is also apparent in the earnings-related schemes, including the above-mentioned compulsory sickness insurance, where all economically active persons, regardless of employment status or occupation, are entitled to sickness cash benefits in relation to previous earnings, while the main part of the non-active are included on a flatrate basis, with the option of augmenting daily allowances on a voluntary basis. The self-employed are also included, though for a long time they were entitled to contract out from the earnings-related part of compulsory schemes. Universality also characterizes the other major earnings-related scheme, that of supplementary pensions, which was established in the early 1960s at the same time as youngsters in the upper part of the educational system were incorporated in the social security network.

In the late 1960s and early 1970s the (voluntary but very common) unemployment insurance and the basic and supplementary disablement pension were improved in order to cope with the worsening economic conditions. These improvements were particularly designed to protect elderly workers, although the amendments also affected other groups, e.g. unemployed young people, who also benefitted by the introduction of a general unemployment assistance in the mid-seventies. Apart from this, the organization of the unemployment benefit system has not been altered, though several state commissions have suggested that it be integrated with general social insurance, making unemployment insurance compulsory.[52]

Other changes in the latter part of the postwar era, shown in *Table 4*, are: the abolition of sexual discrimination in maternity insurance, i.e. its replacement by a parental insurance, with an equal entitlement for both parents to cash benefits after the birth of the child; and, the introduction of a general dental insurance covering all adults (young people are covered by the school dental service).

Due to the character of the Swedish social insurance system, consideration of the coverage percentages in relation to total or economically active population is not especially useful. Either all citizens/residents or all working people are entitled to benefits and the coverage is accordingly one hundred percent. A thin minority of the economically nonactive are not entitled to sickness cash benefits (*Graph 30*). This group has tended to grow slightly, thus reflecting the changing pattern of education and retirement particularly at either end of the working population aged 16-64. The diminishing number of housewives covered by flat-rate sickness cash benefits is also shown in graph 30, this being mainly an indication of the growing employment participation among adult females.

In the case of unemployment, the situation is rather different. Unemployment insurance was originally linked to membership of an industrial trade union. Today, it is still voluntary and closely connected to unions, but it covers most of the full-time working population. As seen in *Graph 31*, the curve showing the insured as a percentage of the labor force moves from just under 40 percent in 1950 to almost 80 percent in the late 1970s. The rapid growth of

Table 4 Social security coverage: extension by social category

Year	Pensions	Health	Family and maternity	Unemployment	Housing	Year
1945(a)	Universal but mainly income-tested	Occupational injury insurance for all employees; state subsidies for voluntary sickness insurance	Income-tested maternity grants and voluntary insurance for maternity allowances	Voluntary and state subsidized insurance for unionized workers	Various state supported municipal programes for families and pensioners	1945
1948	Universal flat-rate old-age and invalidity pensions (survivors' pensions still income-tested)		General child allowances		Income-tested allowances for families	1948
1954					Income-tested all. for pensioners	1954
1955		Compulsory earnings-related sickness insurance for all citizens and residents	Earnings-related maternity allowances for all female citizens and residents			1955
1957	Universal flat-rate survivors' pensions					1957
1960	Earnings-related supplementary (old-age, invalidity and survivors') pensions for all employees					1960
1964			Educational allowances			1964
1968				Duration extended and special allowances for elderly members		1968
1970	Invalidity pensions for 'socially weak groups' (unemployed in particular)					1970
1972					General income-tested allowances	1972
1974		Universal dental insurance	Universal parent's insurance	General unemployment assistance		1974
1976	Part-time pensions for economically active persons aged 60 to 65					1976

(a) Regulations existing in 1945

151

unemployment insurance in the late 1960s and early 1970s reflects the changes in the composition of the labor force and the increased unionization among women and salaried employees.

Table 5 and *Graph 32* give a picture of the growth in the number of beneficiaries. The table reports the number of recipients in each income maintenance program and the percentages of beneficiaries in relation to each target group. *Graph 32* allows comparisons across the schemes in relation to total population. But before entering the gardens of welfare, just a quick walk in the bruschwood of official statistics.

It is difficult to quantify precisely the number of beneficiaries covered by each scheme. Official statistics usually report the number of benefits paid or cases which overestimates the number of beneficiaries, because an individual recipient may make more than one application for benefit in a year (e.g. sickness cash benefits, unemployment insurance, social assistance etc.) or may be in receipt of more than one benefit simultaneously (this applies particularly to pensioners). The data given in *Table 5* and *Graph 32* do, however, permit an approximate assessment of the quantitative growth of the various categories of beneficiaries, both absolutely (as actual numbers of, for example, pensioners) and as a percentage of the relevant risk group, and total population.

Recipients of sickness cash benefits are by far the largest group of beneficiaries. The effects of the abolition of waiting days in 1967 is visible both in the figures given and in the graph. The recipients almost doubled during the years for which we have data (1965-1980) and nowadays more than half of the population aged 16-64 get a sickness cash benefit at least once a year. Of course, for the great majority these benefits are only temporary and are thus not an important part of the recipient's income.

Pensioners are a key welfare clientele. Over all, their number has more than doubled in the postwar period from almost 800 000 in 1950 to just over two millions thirty years later, i.e. a quarter of the population. Today pensioners of all kinds add up to over 100 percent of the population aged over 60; (a common reference point in the international literature on the development of this group). There are various subgroups, the largest being the oldage retirement pensioners, whose number rose from 600 000 in 1950 to over 1,3 millions in 1980. For a long time this group made up around

Table 5   The clienteles of the major welfare schemes

		1950	1955	1960	1965	1970	1975	1980
Basic Pensioners								
Old-age pensioners:	In thousands	603	664	739	827	947	1062	1363
	As % of pop. over 60	58	59	59	59	61	62	76
Invalidity pensioners:	In thousands	130	140	143	151	188	289	293
	As % of labour force	4	4	4	4	5	7	7
Survivors' pensioners:	In thousands	45	44	50	120	135	151	127
	As % of pop. over 60	4	4	4	9	9	9	7
Recipients of wife supplements:	In thousands	17	24	34	42	54	68	56
	As % of women 60–65	10	13	17	19	22	27	24
Supplementary Pensioners								
Old-age pensioners:	In thousands				51	225	420	757
	As % of pop. over 60				4	15	26	42
Invalidity pensioners:	In thousands				18	70	174	209
	As % of labour force				.5	2	4	5
Survivors' pensioners:	In thousands				32	98	176	261
	As % of pop. over 60				2	6	10	14
Part-time Pensioners	In thousands							67
	As % of pop. 60–64							14
All Pensioners	In thousands	801	882	969	1140	1324	1595	2040
	As % of pop. over 60	77	78	77	82	85	93	113
Sickness Insurance								
Recipients of daily allowances:	In thousands				1744	2487	2787	2861
	As % of pop. 15–64				34	47	52	54
Unemployment								
Recipients of insurance benefits:	In thousands	22	25	19	17	30	37	44
	As % of labour force	.7	.8	.5	.5	.8	.9	1
Recipients of assistance benefits:	In thousands						41	101
	As % of labour force						1	2
Families and Children								
Child allowances:								
receiving families	In thousands						1058	1047
supported children	In thousands	1700	1812	1816	1734	1790	1791	1739
Advance payments:								
recipients	In thousands		40					166
supported children	In thousands	38	52	74	104	127	221	232
Maternity all./parents' ins.:								
recipients	In thousands		106	105	134	136	158	146
Social Assistance								
Recipients of social assistance:	In thousands	293	275	292	275	445	417	343
	As % of total population	4.2	3.8	3.9	3.5	5.5	5.1	4.1
Housing								
Households receiving housing allowances:	In thousands			128	174	452	661	472
	As % of all households			5	6	15	20	13
Education								
Recipients of study allowances:	In thousands				209	223	219	277
	As % of pop. 16–19				41	50	51	64
Recipients of study grants:	In thousands				67	107	78	92
	As % of all students				74	69	59	58

153

60 percent of total population aged over 60, but by 1980 its share had risen to 75 percent as a result of the lowering of the general retirement age from 67 to 65 in 1976, together with the introduction of a flexible system permitting retirement from 60 onwards, both fulltime and on a special parttime retirement program for those in full- or part-time employment. Many old age pensioners also receive a superannuation pension and appear under the heading of old age supplementary pensions. During the period 1963-80, there was a rapid growth in the number of recipients of old age supplementary pensions, and at the end of the period more than 60 percent of the population aged over 60 were in receipt of this type of pension, not including invalidity pensioners over the age of 60. The number of recipients of invalidity pensions has been more or less constant up to the late 1960s, when there was a marked increase, while the number of recipients of basic suvivors' pension (widows and orphans) reached a peak between 1965 and 1975, probably as a consequence of the withdrawal of the income-test in around 1960. The numbers of both invalidity and survivor pensioners have also increased under the national supplementary scheme, too.

Besides retired persons, a notable group with an additional income from transfers is families and children. All Swedish households with children under 16 receive child allowance and since the mid-1960s a majority of those with children aged 16-19 receive study allowances. In 1980 over one million guardians (generally the mother) received child allowances, and half a million housing allowances were paid out to families with children in particular (some low-income earners are also entitled to these).

Of the remaining categories, the number of social assistance recipients has been fairly constant throughout the period, while the number of children supported by advance payments increased dramatically towards the end of the period due to changing family patterns. Finally, *Graph 32* gives a comparative picture of the programs; the curves on the whole, with the exception of housing allowance and social assistance recipients, pointing upwards in the latter part of the period.

2.7 The Development of Benefits

To what extent has the apparent extension of the social security programs resulted in a corresponding improvement of the economic status of beneficiaries?

In this respect there have been two particularly important changes in institutional regulations. First, the replacement of flat-rate benefits with earnings-related benefits which has tended to stabilize replacement ratios, provided that the earnings/benefit relation is not altered to the detriment of the beneficiary (the postwar period being characterized by alteration). Secondly, the indexation of benefits has afforded protection in times of inflation. Other institutional changes affecting the value of benefits are the abolition of waiting days (in sickness insurance, not unemployment), and the extension of benefit duration to 365 days or more (with no upper limit in sickness insurance).

The main reference point in the Swedish social security system is the base amount, constructed in the late 1950s in conjunction with the supplementary pension, and linked to the consumer price index. It can be seen as a kind of subsistence level. Today pensions, sickness, parents and occupational injury insurance and study loans are in various ways linked to the base amount. This not only determine the level of benefits, but also acts as an income ceiling in the supplementary pension system and sickness, parental and occupational injury insurances (income exceeding 7.5 times the base amount is excluded in the calculation of benefits).

As seen in *Table 6*, sickness cash benefits have been augmented on at least three occasions during the postwar period. Initially a system comprising different replacement classes without an explicit goal it compensated up to 60 percent of *net* income from 1963. In the late 1960s the level was augmented to 80 percent, still of net income, while in mid-1970s the level was changed to 90 percent of *gross* earnings (this probably did not augment the benefit). The replacement rates for sickness insurance also apply in general to the maternity shelter, though the minimum flat-rate benefit has been higher in the latter part of the period. When the gross income base was introduced, maternity benefits were replaced by parental insurance and the number of days for which this benefit could be claimed was considerably increased.

In contrast to these apparent improvements, the unemployment insurance benefits have fluctuated around 50-60 percent of lost earnings, though a substantial increase was achieved in 1974, when also a goal (never reached) was set at 90 percent. For most years, the majority of full-time wage-earners and salaried employees have been entitled to maximum daily allowances.

Of all the above mentioned benefits, the occupational injury insurance's life annuities at the maximum rate are the highest. In the case of permanent incapacity, they amount to 100 percent of gross earnings.

Basic pensions have been indexed since the early 1950s, but it was not until 1967 that they were tied to the base amount, originally at 90 percent for single pensioners and 140 percent for couples. In 1975, the fixed point was upgraded to 95 percent, while from 1969 there has been a special pension supplement, linked to the basic pension and paid to all those with little or no supplementary pension. This supplement was augmented annually by three percentage points of the base amount up to 1976, when the increment was raised to four percentage points, thus giving a single pensioner a "minimum pension" at 142 percent of the base amount in 1982 (95+47, in 1983 again raised to 96+48=144). Thus, besides the indexed basic pension, a considerable increase has been achieved by adding percentage points to the likewise base amount-related pension supplement.

With respect of the real value of the benefits, *Table 7* monitors the development of average benefits at 1975 prices. It shows that the real value of pensions has improved continously, particularly since the payout from the supplementary pensions started, while child allowances have changed less and thus reflect the absence of indexation. From the early 1960s social assistance and housing allowances has been fairly stable.

3. Achievements and Shortcomings: Evaluations

In the 1960s and 1970s, Sweden was often regarded as the model of the Welfare State. It was either celebrated by its supporters or refuted by those who only saw threats to freedom, too far-reaching nivellation or even new modes of totalitarianism.[53] The aim of this

Table 6   R e p l a c e m e n t   r a t i o s   a n d   s t a n d a r d   b e n e f i t s

Year	Base amount (BA) (in SKR)	Basic pension (a) as % of BA (incl. pension suppl.) Single	Couples	Basic pension (a) annual benefits at 1975 prices Single	Couples	Univ. study grants/loans as % of BA	% grants	Child allowance at 1975 prices	Sickness and maternity/parent's insurance % of earnings	daily allowance at 1975 prices min.	max.(d)	Maternity/parents no. of days(f)	Unemployment ins. benefits at 1975 prices min.	max.	days (g)	Average gross wage of industrial workers at current prices	at 1975 prices	Year
1950				3 608	5 773			893					7	7½	120	5 990	20 594	1950
1955	4 000			4 700	7 520			753		8	44	90	52		138	10 109	26 394	1955
1957				5 144	8 230			694								12 823	27 998	1957
1960	4 200	(60)(b)	(95)(b)	5 458	8 774			986	60% (net)				45	44	156			1960
1961	4 300			5 957	9 532			957										1961
1962	4 500			5 918	9 469			1 122		10	46							1962
1963	4 700			6 746	10 794			1 091				180						1963
1964	4 800			6 657	10 651			1 341										1964
1965	5 000	(77)(b)	(120)(b)	7 064	11 046	140	25	1 651	80% (net)				22	73	150	18 814	34 521	1965
1966	5 300			7 294	11 392		24	1 546										1966
1967	5 500	90	140	7 984	12 419		23	1 480		10	76				150/300			1967
1968	5 700			8 438	12 527		22	1 452										1968
1969	5 800	93(c)	146(c)	8 468	13 294		22	1 413					26	7½		23 849	37 440	1969
1970	6 000	96	152	8 471	13 412		20	1 324								26 579	39 087	1970
1971	6 400	99	158	8 656	13 814		19	1 639								27 955	38 190	1971
1972	7 100	102	164	9 345	15 025		18	1 548								31 179	40 231	1972
1973	7 300	105	170	9 268	15 006		17	1 596								33 883	40 971	1973
1974	8 100	108	176	9 603	15 649		16	1 647	90% (gr.)	9 (4.1)(e)		210				38 043	41 760	1974
1975	9 000	116(95)	197(155)	10 440	17 730		17	1 800					40	130	300/450	44 595	44 595	1975
1976	9 700	120	205	10 572	18 061		15	1 635								50 773	46 115	1976
1977	10 700	124	213	10 805	18 559		14	1 710					57	147		54 600	44 462	1977
1978	11 800	128	221	11 172	19 288		13	1 672								58 614	43 745	1978
1979	13 100	132	229	11 950	20 732		12	1 728								63 419	43 828	1979
1980	13 900	136	237	11 949	20 734		11	1 823					43	128		70 075	42 572	1980
1981	16 100	140	245	12 223	21 391		10	1 627								77 800	42 991	1981
1982	17 800	142	249	12 619	21 772	142	9	1 648								84 600	42 237	1982

(a) From 1948 old age pension and invalidity pension were the same, as was widows' pension from 1960 (if the widow is over age 50); from 1976 invalidity pensioners received an extra pension supplement; (b) calculated from standard benefits, indexed to base amount of 1967; (c) pension supplement introduced for pensioners with no or low supplementary pension; the figures in brackets for 1975 give the basic pension without pension supplement; (d) income ceiling for sickness cash benefits set at 7,5 times the base amount of 1974; (e) figures in brackets are the flat-rate minimum for parental cash benefits, otherwise the same as for earnings-related sickness insurance; (f) there is no limit for sickness cash benefits; (g) up to 1964 benefits were paid for six days a week, from 1965 for five days only; from 1968 persons over age 60 (in special cases 55) could draw unemployment benefits for 330 days, extended to 450 days in 1974.

Table 7   A v e r a g e   b e n e f i t s

	1950	1955	1960	1965	1970	1975	1980
BASIC PENSIONS							
Old-age							
at constant (1975) prices		4384	4969	6543	8405	8983	8930
as % of aver. gross ind. wage		16.6	17.7	19.0	21.5	20.1	21.0
Invalidity							
at constant (1975) prices		4115	4672	6703	8362	8665	9718
as % of aver. gross ind. wage		15.6	16.7	19.4	21.4	19.4	22.8
Survivors							
at constant (1975) prices		2611	3694	5015	6001	6556	5836
as % of aver. gross ind. wage		9.9	13.2	14.5	15.4	14.7	13.7
SUPPLEMENTARY PENSIONS							
Old-age							
at constant (1975) prices				1440	3081	5306	8735
as % of aver. gross ind. wage				4.2	7.9	11.9	20.5
Invalidity							
at constant (1975) prices				3850	6521	9751	12143
as % of aver. gross ind. wage				11.2	16.7	21.9	28.5
Survivors							
at constant (1975) prices				2809	3342	3758	4259
as % of aver. gross ind. wage				8.1	8.6	8.4	10.0
PART-TIME PENSIONS							
at constant (1975) prices							11015
as % of aver. gross ind. wage							25.9
ALL PENSIONS							
Old-age							
at constant (1975) prices				6619	8244	11078	13780
as % of aver. gross ind. wage				19.2	21.1	24.8	32.4
Invalidity							
at constant (1975) prices				7119	9910	14522	18372
as % of aver. gross ind. wage				20.6	25.4	32.6	43.2
Survivors							
at constant (1975) prices				5750	8452	11185	7100
as % of aver. gross ind. wage				16.7	21.6	25.1	16.7
Housing allowances							
at constant (1975) prices				1353	1825	2095	1946
as % of aver. gross ind. wage				3.9	4.7	4.7	4.6
CHILD ALLOWANCES							
at constant (1975) prices	920	761	980	1464	1315	1579	1745
as % of aver. gross ind. wage	4.5	2.9	3.5	4.2	3.4	3.5	4.1
FAMILY HOUSING ALLOWANCES							
at constant (1975) prices			1977	2213	1805	2874	3261
as % of aver. gross ind. wage			7.1	6.4	4.6	6.4	7.7
SOCIAL ASSISTANCE							
at constant (1975) prices	1468	1785	1151	1200	1326	1544	1673
as % of aver. gross ind. wage	7.1	6.8	4.1	3.5	3.4	3.5	3.9
STUDY GRANTS AND LOANS(a)							
at constant (1975) prices				12844	12662	12250	11823
as % of aver. gross ind. wage				37.2	32.4	27.5	27.8
UNEMPLOYMENT BENEFITS							
at constant (1975) prices	10721	16292	13624	19083	19118	33800	33171
as % of aver. gross ind. wage	52.1	61.7	48.7	55.3	48.9	75.8	77.9

(a) Standard benefits

158

section, however, is to evaluate the success of the Swedish welfare state by its own standards rather than in the terms of the ideological debate at home and abroad. This is a risky task because the welfare state defines goals in a way which leads to a preoccupation with the application of resources to individual needs. In the last instance, it is impossible to give definitions of medical, social and educational needs which are not controversial. Nevertheless, in the political process some of them become institutionalized. Even if each programme does not have one single objective to be used as a yardstick, we will try to evaluate the results of various programmes in terms of the resources of the respective beneficiary groups.[54] Thus, we shall examine the extent to which the Welfare State has succeeded in attaining the following objectives: improved social security among the total population; greater equality between the social classes and between single persons and families as well as between retired people and the labour force; and a reduction or elimination of poverty.

3.1 Social Security

Pension Schemes

The impression from the preceding section is that the general improvement of eligibility and benefits was particularly strong for pensioners. There is a widespread consensus that oldage pensioners are adequately catered for by the welfare state. *Table 8* shows that the real value of the basic pension (including general supplements but excluding housing allowances) has more than trebled during the 35 years the system has been in operation.

However, this gives only an imperfect impression of pensioner income because one should also take into account other sources of income, specially the national supplementary pension scheme. According to the level-of-living investigation, the average income of *individual* pensioners in the age-group 65-74 increased from 23 100 to 40 100 SEK (at constant 1980 prices) in the period 1967-1980, of which the pension share grew from 82 to 85 percent.

In 1967, 76 percent of the pensioners aged 65-74 said that they could raise 5 000 SEK cash at a week's notice; by 1980 this percentage had risen to 89 percent.[55] Financial resources and material standards among the elderly seem to have improved in general.[56] Furthermore, they have improved more quickly than for economically active persons. While pension income grew by 79 percent during the period 1967-80, annual full-time earnings rose only 19 percent.

When comparing income and consumption levels, however, the household is in some respect a more adequate unit of analysis. In

Table 8   Basic flat-rate annual pensions

Year	Basic pension for single person (in SKR at current prices)	Index of basic pension	Consumer price index	Real value index of basic pension
1949	1 050	100	100	100
1954	1 750	167	129	129
1959	2 450	233	153	152
1964	3 400	324	181	179
1969	5 400	514	221	233
1974	8 748	833	301	278
1979	16 768	1 597	502	318
1984	29 232	2 784	796	350

1980, a pensioner household comprising a married couple (ca 40 percent of all old-age pensioners) in receipt of a basic pension, the general supplement *and* an average housing allowance but without other forms of income received around 40 000 SEK (tax free). This was 76 percent of the average income for a married worker with two children (52 600 SEK net) in 1980, which makes a *per-capita* income considerably lower for worker households.[57] It should be added that today this family is no longer typical as most women in this kind of household now work at least part-time. In 1957, when this family was more typical, the basic pension for a couple, including housing allowances, reached somewhat more than 40 percent of an industrial worker's net wage.[58]

Table 9 allows us to compare the total household income of pensioners with a few other, partly overlapping household types. As 'pensioner households' is not a separate category in the official income survey, households where the main earner is over 65 have been taken as the closest equivalent.[59] Transfer income is, of course, particularly important for these households, and they may pay less direct taxes in absolute terms than any other type of household.

160

This is mainly a consequence of the tax exemption for old people whose only source of income is the basic flat-rate pension (including the general supplement and a housing allowance). This situation will change, however, with the increasing number of retired people who are entitled to a supplementary pension which is taxable.

The average old age pensioner household's total *disposable* income is below the mean for all households and slightly higher than for pensioners below 65. Disposable household income is highest in the "typical" family with children, closely followed by married without children or, more accurately, couples where the children are over 20 and no longer live at home, while skilled industrial workers fall between these two groups.

Table 9   Sources of income by household type in 1981 (in 1,000 SKR)

	Age group 65+, all households	Pensioners 20-64(a)	Industrial skilled workers(b)	Families	Married couples without children	All house-holds
Factor income	17.4	8.8	103.5	127.6	123.7	72.8
Direct taxes	15.0	14.4	32.5	37.4	45.0	26.2
Pensions transfers	46.6	45.3	2.0	2.5	16.0	16.2
Family transfers	2.8	5.1	5.0	12.0	.5	4.1
Health transfers	.4	4.4	6.4	4.1	6.2	3.2
Other transfers	.2	1.5	3.7	3.9	1.9	3.2
Disposable income	52.4	50.7	88.0	112.7	103.3	73.3
Disposable income per capita	38.4	38.5	42.7	32.7	51.7	42.0
Number of households (1,000s)	1 139	234	438	1 033	692(c)	4 364
As % of all households (d)	26.0	5.4	10.0	23.7	15.9	100.0

(a) Calculated only where pension transfers exceed factor income; mainly invalidity pensioners; for technical reason it is impossible to calculate the group as a whole; (b) calculations for blue-collar workers give lower figures for all items, but per capita income is almost the same (41 900); (c) 43,000 households with no income earner are excluded (no factor income); (d) the categories used in the table do not include all households and partly overlap (no overlapping for the age group 65+ and other categories).

Looking at disposable *per-capita* household income, taking into consideration the number of dependents (but without weighting adults, couples, singles and children differently according to an assumed consumption pattern) reveals a new and probably more important pattern: marrieds without children are now at the top, followed by skilled industrial workers, who are just above the *per-capita* mean for all households. The two types of pensioner households are just below the mean, while families with children at the bottom are almost as far from the mean as marrieds without children at the other side on the scale.

161

Statistics for invalidity pensioner households are scarcer and not directly available from the household income survey. Our constructed pensioner household under 65 consists of both invalidity and survivor pensioners (see footnote, *Table 9*) and is thus not completely satisfying. In a recent elaboration of other official statistics, average households income in 1981 was slightly lower for severely disabled with just an invalidity pension than for households aged 20-64 with no handicapped members. But taking the number of household members into account, the *per-capita* income pattern is reversed. The overall impression of average household is that, in *per-capita* terms both invalidity and old age pensioners are favoured.[60]

In examining differences between pensioner groups, we have to rely again on data of individual incomes, taken from tax statistics.[61] Pensioner incomes vary greatly according to scheme membership, previous economic activity, age, and sex.

Long before the introduction of the national supplementary pension scheme (ATP) in the early 1960s, private white-collar employees and public employees had various earnings-related occupational pension schemes. These have been renewed and partly brought into line with the statutory system. New occupational pension schemes have been created through collective agreements, especially for industrial workers and lower white-collar employees. *Table 10* shows the percentages of old age pensioners who have a national supplementary pension and/or a pension from an occupational pension scheme.

Benefit levels vary between schemes. Private sector white-collar employees receive the highest pensions, followed by central government employees, private sector workers and local authorities employees. Those receiving the combined supplementary/basic pension are second lowest group, the worst off being those receiving only a basic pension.

Pensioners' disposable income varies by sex and age (see *Table 11*). In 1981, the income differences between men and women over 75 were relatively small, although men had somewhat higher average income and a more unequal distribution of income. With decreasing age of pensioners, however, income inequality has increased, above all between men and women, but also within these two groups. In general, discrepancies are closely related to the introduction of the supplementary pension scheme, where pension benefits are determined by previous earnings, hence initially favouring men and white-collar employees. It is debatable as to whether the income ceiling in the supplementary pension scheme, together with the increasing number of women in employment will do much to change this pattern of inequality, given the growing importance of private pension schemes. The "long arm of the job" is also pertinent for retirement.

Table 10 — Percentages of old age pensioners in receipt of national supplementary and occupational pensions, 1981

Age-group	National suppl. pension	Occupational pensions					
		Total	STP	ITP	SPV	KPA	Other
Men							
66–69	95	76	36	13	13	6	8
70–74	93	71	33	10	13	6	9
75–79	89	35	1	9	12	4	9
80+	56	37	0	7	13	4	13
Women							
66–69	65	44	12	5	9	12	6
70–74	59	37	7	5	11	7	7
75–79	52	30	0	5	12	5	8
80+	23	36	0	5	15	5	11

STP — occupational pension scheme for workers
ITP — occupational pension scheme for white-collar employees
SPV — occupational pension scheme for central government employees
KPA — occupational pension scheme for local authority employees
Other — mainly old semi-state and private schemes, few municipal

Table 11 — Disposable income of old people by age group and sex, 1981 (in 1,000 SKR)

Income decile	Men				Women			
	66–69	70–74	75–79	80+	66–69	70–74	75–79	80+
1	28.8	26.4	24.8	24.8	21.4	21.7	22.3	22.3
2	34.1	29.3	26.0	25.4	21.2	21.6	22.1	27.6
3	38.1	30.9	27.8	26.0	21.9	21.9	24.1	28.6
4	40.1	32.8	29.3	27.9	24.7	25.0	29.7	28.7
5	41.9	34.6	29.3	28.1	29.7	30.0	30.1	28.7
6	43.7	36.5	30.6	29.3	30.0	31.9	31.8	29.5
7	46.0	38.7	32.4	29.7	32.4	31.3	31.8	30.8
8	49.4	41.9	36.4	32.4	36.0	33.6	32.8	31.9
9	56.7	48.0	41.8	39.4	40.7	37.4	36.1	53.3
10	76.1	67.0	59.5	54.9	51.4	47.5	45.9	45.2
Average	45.5	38.6	33.8	31.8	30.9	30.2	30.7	30.9
No. of persons (in 1,000s)	164	174	116	98	185	211	163	174

In the early 1950s, public services to pensioners were restricted to special arrangements for the disabled, and homes for the elderly. During the last two decades, however, the services for the disabled, handicapped and mentally ill have increased considerably. The emphasis have been to avoid special housing solutions for these groups, which would separate them from society. Thus, during the last decade the trend has been away from long-term care in large institutions to smaller units integrated in normal surroundings.[62]

Despite the ageing of the Swedish population, the number of places in homes for the old has not increased; in the 1970s, it actually decreased and was about 55 000 in the early 1980s. Of those aged 80+ only seven percent lived in residential homes in 1983. This is partly due to the increase in the number of hospital beds and places in nursing homes, but mainly the result of the shift away from municipal institutional care.

In line with this policy, the number of old people staying at home and receiving assistance from municipal domiciliary services has grown from 7 percent in 1960 to more than one-quarter of the population 65+ in early 1980s.[63] There are a variety of municipal housing provision for the old and disabled. Nevertheless, the great majority of old people (90 percent) still live in their own homes. This fact is also due to the higher availability of subsidized housing loans for pensioners.

Beside the obvious financial reason behind the move from the expensive large-scale institutions to less expensive measures such as home help services and supported housing, an ideological factor is also involved in this process: it is supposed to enable pensioners to continue their normal style of life and preserve their traditional social relations.[64] It is a matter of dispute as to whether the latter has been achieved. According to one survey, the number of pensioners below the age of 76 with limited social relations is small (some 3 percent with no relations with relatives or friends and 13 percent defective relations) and these percentages do not seem to have changed between 1967 and 1981. Another survey with slightly different questions reports somewhat higher figures: 5 percent of old age pensioners and 11 percent of the invalidity pensioners live alone and have no regular social contacts.[65] However, when the level-of-living perspective is widened to include such aspects as loneliness, there are no recognized indicators to grasp the intrinsic nature of love, hate, friendship and human isolation.[66] In order to facilitate social contacts the municipal authorities also provide a health- and means-tested on-call transport service, especially for those aged 80+ and the severely disabled. In 1981, over 300 000 were entitled to this service.

Table 12	Services for the elderly and disabled						
	1950	1955	1960	1965	1970	1975	1980
Beds in homes for the old	22 888	33 492	37 098	43 216	55 738	57 233	56 815
as % of population 65+	3.2	4.2	3.7	4.4	5.1	4.6	4.2
Persons receiving domiciliary services			61 000(a)	143 900	251 600	328 600	348 100
as % of population 65+			7	15	23	27	26
Persons entitled to transport services						159 324(b)	287 158
as % of population 65+						13	21

(a) Figures also include home nursing; (b) available in 265 of the 280 municipalities; figures from Malmö – Sweden's third biggest town not reported; aggregated figure for 1976 was 195, 605 or 16%; no figures reported before the mid-1970s; service built up in the early 1970s and available in all municipalities from 1976.

Health Insurance

The objective of sickness insurance is to protect against loss of income and promote the use of health services according to need. Starting with cash benefits, the most widely used welfare scheme, all wage-earners are entitled to 90 percent of normal earnings.[67] In practice some receive more, as a result of collective bargaining agreements. Unlike almost two million publicsector and private white-collar employees, the more than 1.2 million private-sector blue-collar workers still do not have a collective agreement for sick pay. For private white-collar employees, these agreements cover up to 100 percent of income lost through illness. Public employees – both blue and white collar – do not have such extensive reimbursements, but in general they have better compensation than Social Insurance affords.[68] Consequently, among the gainfully employed, the protection against loss of income during illness is fairly adequate, particularly as the duration is unlimited and, if the illness is occupational, the replacement rate goes up to 100 percent of gross income after three months. But the system is constructed for fulltime employees, thus making the situation of the growing number of particularly female part-time employees less protected and more unsecure. Depending on which day sickness occurs a part-timer may receive a full, partial or no benefit at all. Even harder is the position for housewives receiving only the flat-rate benefit from the insurance system: since 1974 the same small amount (8 SEK) has been paid out, providing no compensating for inflation and rising costs of living. As it is still the policy to promote female participation in the labour market, there was a proposal in early 1984 to remove this protection from compulsory insurance altogether.[69] If this proposal had gone through, it should not be seen as an indicator of financial savings (the current fashion is most analyses of the social sector today), as in this respect it is negligible.

The fears and hopes for compulsory sickness insurance were rather mixed prior to its introduction. One of the hoped-for returns was a reduction in the number of work-days lost from sickness absenteeism. In retrospect this seems rather naive, considering the low level of earnings-replacement initially. More recently, increasing benefit rates have created fears, particularly among employers, that absenteeism might be encouraged. Up to the early 1960s, the average annual number of benefit-days for sickness was below 15; during the next ten-years period the figure leapt up after every reform with a peak of 23.5 in 1976. Since then it has moved down to under 20 in 1981.[70]

The pattern of sickness absenteeism does not suggest that the health status of the population has improved since the insurance system came into operation, nevertheless 40 percent of the beneficiaries do not use a single benefit day in any one year. The frequency of sickness cash benefits is related to the work environment, i.e. health hazard differentials. There is a clear connection between low sickness absenteeism and high salaries on the one hand, and high absenteeism and low (but still full-time) wages on the other. The highest incidence of sickness absenteeism is found in poor working-class areas with a large immigrant population.

Occupations with a high level of sickness absenteeism are blue-collar jobs in steel mills, mines, pulp and paper mills, the heavy engineering industry and the food-processing industry (much piece-work in the latter two)[71] In the white-collar sector, managers, professionals, etc. had three times fewer benefit days than white-collar workers with the most routine type of work. The number of sickness benefit days was at least three times greater among employees exposed to stress, monotony and physical load factors (such as heavy lifting, inappropriate work positions, jolting, vibration and daily sweating during work) than among those not exposed to such conditions.[72] The differentiation of sickness benefit days highlights where poor health conditions are still to be found, while the rising costs of sickness insurance might be attributed to the overall development of wages.

Health Services

At the beginning of this century access to medical services was least where morbidity was highest. Despite their higher mobidity rates, the badly paid and weaker social groups used the public facilities less than the stronger and better off. The late 1960s saw the first level-of-living investigation was carried out and produced evidence of medical hardship among large low-income families, the elderly and the chronically sick – these groups were also found to use medical services less. Since then many of the disparities have been eliminated. Using visits to a doctor as an indicator of health service utilisation, according to the latest survey, workers and low-income earners, including retired households of this kind, have increased their percentage of visits considerably and now outdo the upper classes.[73] To some degree this is because their health status is poorer – and their jobs expose them to more illness and accidents.

The increasing rate of health service utilization among lower social groups is also explained by the growing access to these services (see *Table 13*). The growing number of inpatient treatments and the number of beds indicate that hospitals have greatly expanded their capacity.[74] This expansion, which is nationwide, has not been without problems, particularly given the shortage of trained medical personnel up to the 1970s. There is still a shortage of doctors, particularly in general practice, psychiatry, and long-term medical care. The situation is expected to improve quite soon as the growing number of trainees get their certificates, and recently, the number of students admitted to these courses have been cut down.

Of all those receiving hospital care, the elderly are in a special situation. The estimated proportion of persons with a long-term

167

illness increases from 18 percent in the age group 16-24 years to 68 percent in the oldest group studied (65-74). Biological ageing obviously contributes to the even higher figure in the age-group above this.[75] In general, services for the elderly and disabled belong to the municipalities (see above), but the county councils are also involved and some pensioners receive regular support from sickness insurance (part of the inpatient hospital treatment costs, travel costs to hospitals and out-patient centers, reimbursements for pharmaceutical outlays etc). As discussed earlier, it is the long-term institutional care of the elderly that the health administrators are trying to restructure. Today, county councils actively supply pensioners with visiting nurses in order to avoid hospital treatment. According to a recent investigation, 26 000 persons received this new type of old-age health service in 1981, and this number is projected to increase rapidly. As public expenditure on long-term care amounts to a third of total health service costs, the interest in financial savings here goes without saying.[76]

Table 13   Indicators of health service growth

	1950	1960	1970	1975	1980
No. of hospital beds	99 232	116 681	133 644	136 393	134 187
– per 1,000 population	14.1	15.6	16.5	16.6	16.2
No. of hospital in-patient treatments	849 960	1 001 200	1 341 077	1 483 238	1 535 714
– per 1,000 population	12.1	13.4	16.6	18.1	18.5
Doctors	4 890	7 200	10 560 (a)	14 050	16 900
– per 1,000 population	0.7	1.0	1.3	1.7	2.0
Medical students	304	431	956	1 026	1 002 (b)
Nurses	12 810	22 050	34 240	48 380	58 500
– per 1,000 population	1.8	2.9	4.2	5.9	7.0
Student nurses	1 382	1 872	3 084	2 899	3 747 (b)
Paramedical staff	21 520	32 860	53 960	54 400 (a)	64 860
– per 1,000 population	3.1	4.4	6.7	6.6	7.8
Dentists	3 430	5 090	6 720 (a)	7 060	8 320
– per 1,000 population	0.5	0.7	0.8	0.9	1.0
Pharmacists	906	773	812	737	715
Pharmacies	493	558	665	674	732

(a) Indicates changes in the method of calculation; (b) students admitted to courses in 1978.

Pharmaceutical services are generally heavily subsidised and certain life-saving drugs are obtainable free of charge. Expenditure on drugs has risen faster than any other item of medical care, with the number of prescriptions more than doubling since the introduction of compulsory sickness insurance. Pharmacies have been tightly controlled as regards profits and type of drugs sold and were nationalized in the early 1970s.[77]

As shown in *Table 13*, the number of dentists has almost trebled in the postwar period. Today, there seems to be an overproduction of dentists and two training centers will probably be closed in 1985. The change reflects an improvement in the health status of the population and an increasing utilisation of services provided with the support of dental insurance, introduced in 1974. Prior to that, free treatment was given only to preschool and school children and subsidised treatment for pregnant women and mothers of young infants, who were refunded with about three-quarters of the costs. Dental insurance today covers 40 percent of the costs of treatment. Between 1968 and 1981, the proportion of all those aged 15-75 who annually visit a dentist rose from 55 to 67 percent. The increase is greatest among workers and low-income-earners; from 46 to 61 percent. Persons reporting good teeth have increased from 63 to 75% of the total population.[78]

Although we are not in a position to evaulate all the effects of the tremendous growth of health transfers and services on health, we can indicate some areas of general improvement in the postwar era. Judged by one of the most commonly used health indicators infant mortality rates – very substantial improvements are obvious. Deaths of infants under age one per thousand live births fell from 18 in the period 1951-60 to the extremely low figure of 7 in 1980. Age-specific mortality rates fell continuously over the same period for every age group except for middle-aged men. Another common indicator, life expectancy, improved for both sexes up to the beginning of the postwar era, but since then it has increased for women in particular (from 70 in the early postwar period up to 79 forty years later). Among men, life expectancy shows only a small increase in the postwar period. However, these are trends started long before the advent of the welfare state, and only in one case, life expectancy for men, we can talk of a break in the trend or at least a levelling off.[79]

Health economists have advocated that the correlation between medical costs and health does not hold in the late 20th century.[80] The massive increase in health expenditure has no bearing on the quality of life among the population today, unlike the earlier introduction of anti-infectious drugs. High standards of cleanliness and nutrition, improvements in housing and environmental conditions and a high standard of health-consciousness, might be credited for the health status. The increase in medical care today is directed towards more trivial complaints, as need in unlimited. On the other hand, the practitioners' monopoly of information can direct investments in the health sector to extremely specialized and expensive procedures with small apparent returns, except perhaps for research. The criticisms of "medicalization of health" and "professionalization of medicine" are heard in Sweden, too, but it would be speculative to apply them to the overall development so far.

Transfers and Services to Families with Children

Besides the general child allowance other measures taken at the inauguration of family policy in the 1940s had clear effects in the first decades of the postwar period. With the introduction of the new 9-year comprehensive school, free school meals and free school health, including dental care, became available to a larger number for a longer period of time.[81] However, in the early 1980's free school meals have again become a symbol of the welfare state, as the measure has been contested by stingy local politicians in an effort to cut municipal spending. So far, very few municipalities have taken this step. Another universal benefit that has grown in duration, eligibility and importance for families is the maternity allowance, more recently the cash benefit from parental insurance. In general, compensation is the same as the earnings-related sickness insurance. The number of days for which the benefit is claimable has been increased several times and also includes temporary absence from work during the child's pre-school years.[82] Young parents, females in particular and students in general, with bad employment records are, however, still disfavoured and have more often to rely on the much lower flat-rate benefit (48 SEK in 1985).

The expansion of the welfare state has coincided with rapid changes in lifestyles and other social and economic patterns of family life. The number of divorces per 1 000 married women in Sweden was 5.04 in the 1950s, reached 6.85 in 1970, peaked at 14.27

in 1974, when a new law made separations easier, and has stabilized just above 11 at the turn of the last decade. Also the proportion of extra-martial births has grown markedly, from an average of about 10 percent in the early postwar years to over 40 percent in the early 1980s. This is mainly explained by the widely accepted and growing number of persons cohabiting without marrying. About 60 percent of those aged 20-24 living together with a person of the opposite sex are not married and the average age at the first marriage has increased by three years for both sexes between the late 1960s and the early 1980s. In relative terms, the annual number of marriges per 1 000 persons decreased from above nine to below five between 1950 and 1980. Since the introduction of free abortion in 1974 the number of legal abortions has doubled and is now more than a third of all live births.[83]

These developments point towards a looser partner relationship and an increasing number of children in more insecure families. This is one reason behind the growing demand for changes in family policy and state support to children. It has also frequently been argued that the level of economic support to families is inadequate and that there is a great need for new family services.

Table 14 — Sources of income by type of households with children, 1981 (a)

	Married couples with 1 child	Married couples with 2 children	Married couples with 3 children	Married couples with 4+ children	Singles with 1 child	Singles with 2+ children	All households with children
Factor income	142.1	144.8	146.7	120.0	57.7	50.8	127.6
Direct taxes	43.1	40.8	42.9	34.1	18.3	14.4	37.4
Family policy transfers	7.8	11.1	16.9	28.9	12.1	25.1	12.0
Health policy transfers	4.2	4.2	4.7	3.4	3.9	3.0	4.1
Pensions	3.0	0.8	2.0	3.4	4.0	6.2	2.5
Other transfers	3.7	4.1	3.6	2.7	4.5	4.1	3.9
Disposable income	117.7	124.2	131.0	124.3	63.9	74.8	112.7
Disposable income per capita	39.2	31.1	26.2	20.2	32.0	23.4	32.7
Number of households	362	376	118	20	108	49	1 033

(a) Households with head of household aged 20-64, thus excluding pensioners' households.

Table 14 shows quite considerable variations in average disposable per capita income between families with different numbers of children and households without children. Married couples with two children – the better off than singles with one child if looking only at per capita-income. Particularly young couples (aged 18-25)

171

with children tend to be in a tight economic situation.[84] For singles
with two children, family policy transfers – general child allowance, housing allowance, advanced maintenance payment, parental
benefit, etc – amounted to a third of average disposable income in
1981, as compared with 10 percent for all households with children. Transfer payments are also of considerable importance for the
large families with two adults (almost one-fourth of disposable
income) and for single parents with one child (almost one-fifth of
average disposable income), while they are less important for the
main types of family households. It is difficult to get a clear picture
of the redistributive effects of the welfare state, but *Table 14* does
indicate that transfers and taxes tend to equalize the economic
burdens for child-rearing, favouring single-parent families in particular. Maintenance advances, for example, have been of growing
importance for divorced and remarried parents in recent decades.[85]

The growing number of two-earner families and the steadily
falling birth rate in recent decades are reasons behind the rapid
development of public or semi-public child minding since the
mid-1960s, when central government support for municipal nurseries was increased. The numbers of places in different kinds of
recognized child minding are given in *Table 15*. In the early 1980s
almost 40 percent of all children below the age of seven were
enroled in these services. Despite the increased number of places,
demand is by no means met. A recent official investigation concluded that 32 percent of all pre-school children want a place at a
municipal day care center, while another 19 percent asked for
family day care. There is also strong demand for care of young
school children (aged 7-10) after school hours.[86] In the big cities
and other larger municipalities the services are most adequate and
there it is quite uncommon that one of the parents stays at home.
According to *Table 16*, over 40 percent of all children under seven
were cared for by their mothers at home; about 10 percent attended
private nurseries, including cooperatives run by the parents involved, or private child-minders. The last type is unregistered and
has even been described as a "black market", (i.e. non-taxed income) estimated by Sweden's largest private bank to be almost two
billion Skr or one-fifth of public spending on day care.[87] About five
percent of all children under 7 were reared by relatives or other
non-paid persons.

172

Table 15   The development of public day care

Year	Day nurseries	Family day care	Part-time pre-school	Children aged 0-6
1950	9 700		18 700	879 000
1955	10 000		27 800	781 000
1960	10 300	3 700	34 800	734 000
1965	11 700	13 800	47 000	752 000
1970	33 800	36 600	72 000	823 000
1975	66 000	49 800	112 000	774 000
1980	135 200	90 200	104 700	714 000

Table 16   Child care arrangements for pre-school children and young school children as percentage of all children, 1982

	Pre-school children (below 7)	Young school children (aged 7-10)
Municipal day care or leisure centres	23	10
Municipal family day care	15	15
Parent also employed as a municipal or private nurse	4	4
Parent stays at home	41	32
Part-time care only outside home; one parent away/working during school or day care hours	3	12
Paid private day care	10	7
Non-paid private day care	5	8
School children without care after school hours		12

Unemployment Insurance and Employment Services

Unemployment has been a major political issue but a minor social problem in postwar Sweden. Up to the early 1970s, unemployment has usually been below two percent of the total labor force and was mainly seasonal and/or regional. Even in the last decade, when most capitalist democracies, particularly in Western Europe but also in neighbouring Denmark and Finland, were experiencing sharp increases in the unemployment rate, Sweden has managed to avoid open unemployment of continental dimensions (see *Table 17*). However, regional variations have been considerable and unemployment has hit the sparsely-populated areas in Northern

173

Sweden severely. The generally good Swedish employment records explain the comparatively bad economic security offered by unemployment insurance: cash benefits are considerably lower than in sickness insurance, waiting-days have not been abolished as in the other social insurance schemes, and duaration is limited to one year; one and a half for those over age 55. But forces acting for change have been absent or rather uninterested until recently.[88]

Table 17	The development of unemployment (a)			
	Annual average rates			Whole period
	1960–67	1968–73	1974–81	1960–1981
Sweden	1.6	2.2	2.2	1.9
Nordic countries (average)	1.5	2.0	4.2	2.6
Smaller European (average)	3.8	4.5	7.2	5.2
Major OECD countries (b) (average)	2.9	3.2	5.2	3.8

(a) As a percentage of total labour force; (b) United States, Japan, West Germany, France, United Kingdom, Italy and Canada.

The favourable employment situation is stressed by the development of the labour force which grew by 7 percent between 1970 and 1980 (*Table 17*). As the increase consisted almost entirely of people who obtained or sought part-time jobs, the volume of hours worked rose less strongly. Even if the expansion was most visible in the boom of 1973-75, the annual increase averaged roughly 30 000 persons during the recession in the second half of the decade. In Southern Sweden, where unemployment was extremely low, the high labour demand from industry was met both by the rural population (the number of farmers decreased rapidly, and with few protests, in the 1950s and 1960s) and by northeners. In the reallocation of people from north to south, the Public Employment Service took an active part, which caused criticisms among those exposed to labour force mobility.[89] In 1954, the Nordic countries set up a common labour market and many Finns have since then crossed the Baltic.[90] A considerable number of workers also migrated from Southern Europe, and in this recruitment process industry and the Public Employment Service cooperated in this recruitment process. Although men have dominated these groups,

174

male participation in the labour force has deteriorated. Virtually the entire growth was made up of women; many of them found jobs in the public welfare sector.[91] The pattern of labour force growth and female employment differs from the continental picture, but is fairly close to general development in the Nordic countries.

Table 18   Total labour force by sex as a percentage of population aged 15–64

	1960	1970	1980
Total labour force			
Sweden	74.3	74.3	81.0
Nordic countries	72.0	71.3	77.3
European community	68.9	66.6	66.4
Male labour force			
Sweden	98.5	88.8	87.8
Nordic countries	95.3	88.2	85.6
European community	95.5	90.2	84.2
Female labour force			
Sweden	50.1	59.4	74.1
Nordic countries	49.0	54.4	68.9
European community	43.8	43.6	48.7

However, the difficulties in maintaining employment has been growing in the late 1970s and early 1980s. While women have strengthened their position on the labor market, youth, for example, has not.[92] Since the mid-1970s youth unemployment has been considered a serious problem in Sweden with persons under 25 accounting for over a third of the total registered unemployed in late 1982. This group has benefitted little from general improvements in the economic situation, and has been affected adversely by industrial rationalization, e.g. traditional sources of youth employment, such as apprenticeships and unspecialized work not requiring particular qualifications, have largely vanished. Especially those aged 16-19 have experienced a continuous deterioration in their employment situation.

In an attempt to alleviate this situation the government in the 1970s introduced a series of measures and legislation.[93] Youth officers have been appointed to local employment services. In 1974, general unemployment cash assistance was introduced which also benefitted young people who did not qualify for insurance benefits; the amount of this assistance, however, is not comparable with

175

unemployment insurance, being far lower. Since the mid-1970s the Public Employment Service and schools have had joint responsibility for unemployed school leavers: starting in 1977, all municipalities have established councils to improve cooperation between schools and working life (unions, employers, etc). In 1980 an Act made schools responsible for ensuring that all those aged 16-17 are either in education or employed. Special youth centres have been set up to cope with those who have not reached a certain educational standard after having completed the period of compulsory schooling. All these measures are parts of the governing principle of full employment which emphasis job creation and partly is responsible for the weakness of direct economic support in Swedish employment policy.

Housing Services and Allowances

To what extent has Swedish housing policy coped with the post-war growth of housing demand caused by rural redeployment, the urbanization of the rapidly expanding areas of secondary and tertiary production mainly in the Stockholm and the Southwest, and immigration? And, secondly, how have housing standards been improved during this period?

The population shift from rural to urban settings (in 1900 28 percent of the population lived in urban areas as compared with 60 percent in 1950 and 80 percent in the early 1980s) stimulated by agricultural rationalization, and the settlement of immigrant industrial workers in the 1960 and 1970s, created considerable pressure for increased state supported production of housing.[94]

In the period 1945-60, a total of 900 000 new dwellings were constructed, and during the 1960s Sweden vied with West Germany for the highest per capita volume of housing production in the world. Despite this there was still a housing shortage in the mid-1960s. This was influential in the defeat of the Social Democrats in the 1966 municipal elections and led to the government formulating a new housing policy (increased state guaranteed loans and interest subsidies), which planned to, and succeeded in, the construction of one million new apartments in a decade.

In an attempt to avoid segregation and the development of social ghettos, there is no provision for state-subsidized housing for poor

176

people. Instead these groups are entitled to housing allowances under the normal system, i.e. as pensioners, low-income singles and childless couples, families with children. However, this has not been fully successful, as low-income groups, especially immigrants, tend to be concentrated in municipally owned multidwelling housing, as private landlords are unwilling to rent to them.[95]

Housing allowances were particularly important source of income for pensioners, between the mid-1950s and mid-1970s but with increasing supplementary pensions the proportion of pensioners receiving these allowances has declined from 57 to 44 percent. Allowances for families with children became important in the late 1960s and early 1970s, when over 50 percent of this group were in receipt of this benefit. In the late 1970s the proportion declined, after changes in income-limits, and it is now below 40 percent of all households with children. The decrease among single-parent families has been smaller.[96] Allowances to singles and childless couples with low incomes, introduced in the mid-1970s, benefitted at most five percent of such households, falling to three percent in the early 1980s. Tax-deductions for owner-occupiers, on the other hand, have increased in recent years and constitute in the 1980s the main item of housing "expenditure", to the benefit of the richer half of the population.[97]

This conclusion also reflected in the findings of the latest level-of-living study. According to this, in the late 1970s and early 1980s the pattern of home ownership have been much closer related to social class than was previously the case. As regards the postwar pattern of housing construction and housing ownership, from the mid-1970s the construction of owner-occupied single family housing rose considerably, whilst that of multi-dwelling housing almost ceased. The figures for house ownership in 1968 were 31 percent owner-occupiers, 13 percent tenant owners, 48 percent tenants protected by the housing legislation and 8 percent tenants without security rights. The respective figures for 1981 were 41, 14, 43 and 3. White-collar employees have benefitted from the expansion in housing production in the last decade moving into owner-occupier dwellings, whilst there has been virtually no change in the housing pattern of working class families.[98]

Consumer expenditure for housing is quite high, particularly in modern dwellings, though development has been reasonably stable

177

in the last fifteen years. The average is between a fourth and a fifth of disposable income excluding public transfers.[99] Housing standards have improved in the postwar period, and particularly in the last 20 years. In 1945 about a fifth of the population lived under circumstances described by the contemporary State Commission on Housing as overcrowded, i.e. more than two persons per room excluding the kitchen. Given today's official norm, i.e. no more than two persons per room excluding kitchen *and* living room, housing standards have improved tremendously: less than 5 percent of households were overcrowded in the early 1980s as compared to almost 40 percent in 1966. Nevertheless, there is still a pattern of overcrowding with married or cohabiting couples aged 16-24, young families, and households with three or more children being more likely to live in overcrowding housing.[100] Overcrowding might be a problem for the growing number of divorced and/or remarried parents with a joint responsibility for their children.

Another consequence of the forceful production of new houses is the great improvements in modern housing facilities. This is evidenced by the increase in number of houses with running water and drains, sanitation, own bathroom and central heating. In 1960, 40 percent of the adult population lived in houses lacking at least one of these facilities, whereas in the 1980s it is hard to find an apartment of this kind.[101] The level of living survey distinguishes between the following three standards of housing: modern – households with a modern cooker and refrigerator in addition to the four above mentioned facilities; semi-modern – lacking one to three of the above mentioned facilities; and inadequate – all other housing (see *Table 19*).

Table 19   Housing standards by type of household
percent distribution

| Type of household | Housing standard | | | | | |
| | modern | | semi-modern | | inadequate | |
	1968	1981	1968	1981	1968	1981
All households	76	95	15	4	9	1
Households without children	68	93	29	6	12	1
Households with 1 child	86	98	9	2	5	–
Households with 2 children	88	98	8	2	4	–
Households with 3+ children	87	98	9	2	4	–

Summarizing housing standards of various kinds, less than 10 percent of all households lack what might be termed acceptable housing, i.e. a dwelling with modern conveniences and a sufficient number of rooms.

Education

There has been a tremendous growth of public education at all levels during the postwar period. The extension of formal education has been considerable. In 1981 the proportion of different age-groups with only primary schooling ranged from 71 percent of those aged 65-76 to just below 12 percent of those aged 25-34. In addition, the maximum duration of primary education was six years for the oldest group as compared with eight years for the youngest.[102] A notable change has occured since the mid-1960s. In 1968 65 percent of the population aged 15-75 had primary schooling only, compared to 40 percent in 1981.[103] *Graph 33* gives the average years of school attendance for five-year birth groups between 1892 and 1956. Seven years is the norm for the oldest gener-

Graph 33

Average years of schooling by age cohort (a)

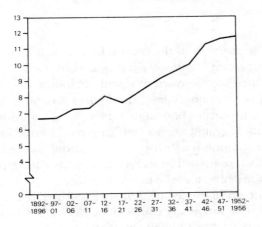

(a) Population aged 15–75, excluding students

ation. There was a slight increase for those born after the World War I, but the great leap forwards was taken by those born in the late 1930s. The generations born from the mid-1940s onwards has average of twelve years education (see *Graph 33*). It is likely that the upper limit has not yet been reached, as employment (re)training will increase the average number of education-years for a growing number of people.

Although the introduction of comprehensive education throughout Sweden, together with the decentralization of higher academic education, have reduced the marked disparities between large urban and remote rural areas, access to educational facilities and academically-oriented employment is still to a great extent determined by geographical settings. But regional differences, however, as measured by number of school years, tend to diminish in the younger age cohorts (see *Table 20*).

Table 20   Years of schooling by childhood residence and present age (a)

Childhood residence	Age					
	25–34	35–44	45–54	55–64	65–75	25–75
Rural areas	11.0	9.4	8.4	7.2	6.8	8.4
Small towns	11.8	10.6	9.2	8.2	7.8	9.8
Bigger towns	12.1	12.0	11.3	8.8	8.8	11.0
Stockholm, Gothenburg, Malmö	12.2	12.0	10.8	9.8	9.8	11.2

(a) Population aged 25–75, excluding students

With the introduction of the comprehensive school system, the limited number of girls' schools disappeared in the late 1960s and classes everywhere became co-educational, including physical training. At the upper secondary level differences according to sex are still visible, with pupils choosing courses along traditional lines. Boys take technology and science, whilst girls take nursing and, to a lesser extent, economics. In higher education, women are consequently badly represented in technical subjects and heavily over-represented in teaching and the medical sector.

Developments in higher education are indicated by the numbers attending full-time university courses (100 000 – see *Table 21*), and other university courses (30 000), in 1980, in comparison with a combined total of less than 20 000 in 1950. This expansion has mainly taken place in the old university towns, although there has

180

been some decentralization with the establishment in the mid- and late 1960s of two new universities and several satellite colleges offering a wide range of undergraduate courses.

Adult education has also undergone a marked expansion in the last twenty years in an effort to bridge the generation gap resulting from the extension of the regular school system. In 1979 almost 40 percent of the population aged 16-74 participated in some form of adult education, but it appears that the take-up rate was far greater among those with a good general education than among those with only primary schooling.[104] In particular, the study circles (organized by popular education organizations, but heavily state subsidized) attract all those with little formal training, Sweden disfavoured by the old school system as well as immigrants (the latter being entitled to 200 hours free education in Swedish). In addition, a 1974 law gave working adults the right to temporary leave from work in order to attend courses of further education, and entitled them to a special adult educational allowance whilst doing so.

Table 21   Distribution of students in tertiary education by sex, 1980

Sector	Total enrolment	% women
Technical	23 451	17
Administrative, economic and social welfare	25 700	50
Medical and nursing	22 433	73
Teaching	24 194	75
Cultural and information	4 592	56
Full-time academic education, total	100 370	54

3.2 Equality and Inequality

Income Inequalities

What has been the overall redistributional effect of welfare policies in Sweden in the postwar period, and to what extent has there been a reduction of income inequalities and inequality in the access to services, between and within groups?

The pattern of income inequality was one of considerable change in the 1930s and 1940s, this particularly affected the lower income groups and was mainly due to the fall in the unemployment rate and rural redeployment, followed by a levelling off of this trend in the 1950s and 1960s, and a further reduction of inequalities from the mid-1960s until the early 1980s.[105] *Graph 34* shows the development of the maximum equalization percentages in the postwar period based on two studies using slightly different methods but with the same general trend. During the latter part of the period there was an overall equalization attributable to the rise in female employment, increased taxes and social transfers, and to a lesser extent, unions wage solidarity, the main counteracting force during this period being "wage drift".

Graph 34

The development of
maximum equalization percentages

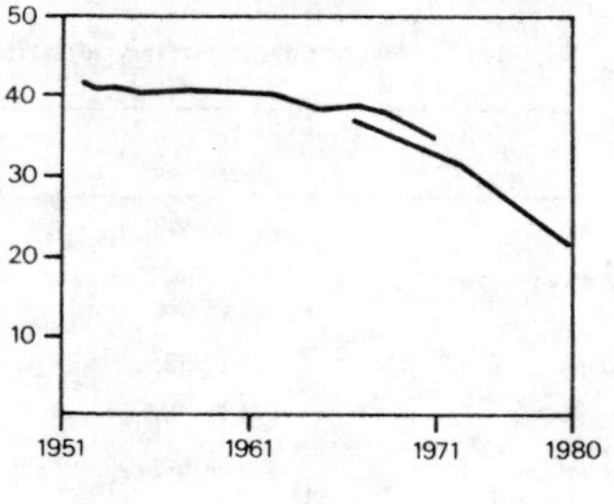

Table 22 gives the distribution of individual income by occupational groups and socio-economic categories. Firstly, the gap between the top and the bottom for full-time working income earners has been reduced. Secondly, the only groups that have experienced a drop in real wages are the upper echelons; i.e. private managers and senior salaried employees. At the same time, these groups were favoured by tax deductions. Thirdly, all other groups have increased their absolute income. Fourthly, although the pattern of relative earning is largely stable among the major occupational groups, technical and office white-collar workers as well as smallholders,

forestry workers and blue-collar workers in the service sector have gained, whilst supervisors, construction workers and public sector blue-collar workers, have lost. Fifthly, wage differentials within groups have declined and full-time female wages as a percentage of full-time male wages have increased for most groups (see *Table 22*). The equalization of earned income between men and women was accepted in principle by the trade union movement in 1960, but as many women work part-time, the earnings gap is still considerable. In 1979, when average total taxable income before deductions and taxes was 60 000 SEK for men and 36 000 SEK for women, only one percent of women had an income of more than 100 000 SEK as compared with ten percent of men.[106] The general pattern for individual income is similar to that for the development of household income for socio-economic and occupational groups.[107]

Table 22 — Individual full-time earnings by occupation and sex

	In 1,000 SKR, at 1980 prices			As a % of average earnings			Female wages as a % of male wages		
	1967	1973	1980	1967	1973	1980	1967	1973	1980
Private sector managers	153	146	137	238	199	179	60	72	80
Senior civil servants	142	132	115	220	179	150	91	81	81
Socio-economic group I, total	147	137	124	228	185	161	81	75	76
Entrepreneurs/farmers	53	57	69	82	77	90			
Supervisors in private industry	75	85	85	117	115	110	78	96	71
Technical and office white collar	63	73	80	98	99	104	63	69	79
Junior civil servants	68	74	74	105	100	97	74	82	84
Socio-economic group II, total	66	74	77	102	101	100	71	76	81
Smallholders, forestry workers, etc.	36	55	56	55	75	72			
Metall workers	56	65	66	87	88	85	77	74	84
Other industrial workers	53	62	64	82	84	84	71	78	82
Construction workers	65	70	73	101	94	96	-	-	-
Manufacturing workers, total	57	65	67	88	88	87	69	75	81
Trade, hotel, restaurant workers	45	53	58	70	72	75	52	47	80
Other service workers	45	53	66	70	72	86	52	47	80
Service workers, total	45	53	62	70	72	81	64	64	80
Municipal blue-collar	54	62	66	84	84	85	66	80	82
State blue-collar	62	71	71	96	97	93	81	93	100
Total public sector blue collar	58	66	67	90	89	88	70	80	85
Socio-economic group III, total	53	62	65	82	84	85	67	73	83
Total average earnings	64	74	78	100	100	100	68	73	79

Table 23 reveals changes in the distribution of household income by deciles for the second half of the 1970s and the two first years in

Table 23   Redistribution of household incomes by deciles of factor income
(percentage distributions)

Decile	Factor income							Disposable income						
	1975	1976	1977	1978	1979	1980	1981	1975	1976	1977	1978	1979	1980	1981
1st	-0.1	-0.1	-0.1	-0.2	-0.1	0.0	-0.1	3.7	4.0	3.8	4.0	4.3	4.6	4.6
2nd	0.5	0.5	0.4	0.3	0.5	0.6	0.7	4.8	5.0	5.1	5.4	5.3	5.3	5.3
3rd	2.0	1.8	1.7	1.4	1.6	2.0	1.9	5.7	5.7	6.0	5.7	6.0	6.1	6.0
4th	4.5	4.1	4.1	4.1	4.1	4.3	4.0	6.7	6.6	6.7	6.8	6.9	6.8	7.2
5th	7.4	7.3	7.3	7.4	7.2	7.2	6.8	8.0	8.0	7.8	7.9	7.6	7.7	7.8
6th	9.7	9.7	9.6	9.8	9.6	9.5	9.2	9.3	8.9	8.8	9.1	8.7	8.5	8.1
7th	12.0	12.2	12.2	12.1	11.9	11.7	11.8	10.9	10.7	10.8	10.8	10.4	10.0	10.4
8th	15.0	15.3	15.2	15.4	15.4	15.1	15.5	13.4	13.5	13.2	13.1	13.3	13.2	13.0
9th	18.9	19.4	19.4	19.7	19.8	19.7	19.9	15.9	16.1	16.0	16.0	16.1	16.0	15.9
10th	30.1	29.9	30.1	30.0	29.9	30.1	30.3	21.8	21.6	21.8	21.3	21.4	21.8	21.8
Total	100.0	100.0	100.0	100.0	100.0	100.0	100.0	100.0	100.0	100.0	100.0	100.0	100.0	100.0
Maximum equalization percentage	35.7	36.4	36.6	37.0	36.7	35.9	36.7	21.1	20.7	20.6	20.2	19.9	19.5	19.1

the 1980s. The pattern for both factor and disposable income is quite stable, although the small changes in the latter type of income are more pronounced with the trend being towards equalization. In the early 1980s, the distribution of disposable income was less than half as unequal as that of pretax income. The considerable differences between factor and disposable income illustrates the combined effects of social transfers and taxes on overall income distribution. In 1981, the richest half of all households obtained 69 percent of total disposable income as compared with 71 percent seven years earlier. The top incomes have maintained their relative position; in 1981, the upper 2.5 percent received 7.5 percent of total disposable income, with an average of 218 000 SEK for this tiny minority or three times that of all households.[108] However, the overall trend towards the equalization of disposable income is much stronger among households with members aged 65+, this being mainly attributable to the increasing welfare state support for pensioners. Changes seem to be smaller or even negative among other types of households. For all heads of household aged 20-64 the maximum equalization rose from 21 to 22 from 1975 to 1981; in particular it was the third to fifth lowest deciles that decreased their relative share of total disposable income during these years.[109]

184

The trend in income distribution in Sweden is thus similar to that of other industrialized European nations.[110] However, the level of redistribution achieved by Sweden in the mid-1970s was one of the highest among all Western societies. This must certainly be understood in the light of the longstanding pattern of equality. The Swedish pattern of equalization is underlined when groups such as business executives and members of government are compared to workers.

Utility of Services

There seem to be no apparent inequalities in the utilization of the main public services such as old-age, invalidity and general health care services.[111] One exceptions is dental insurance which is utilized more by the better educated groups although the gap between this group and the less educated is narrowing. The two areas where utilization reveals a noticable pattern of inequality are child care and education.

The most important family service, child care, is not universal and demand is greater than supply, as noted earlier. Care is means-tested, favouring thus single parents. Salaried employees are more likely than workers to have their children in public day care. This is partly attributable to the fees charged for public day care, but it seems that the queueing system makes access far easier for nimble lobbiers and the bureaucratically minded than for the less well educated.[112]

Large class differences still persist in the utilization of educational services, despite the equality of access to basic education and a narrowing of class differentials generally. Social class remains a key factor in the choise of subject studied, and the length of education: 90 percent of children with university educated parents attended voluntary upper secondary school, as against 70 percent for unskilled workers; 74 percent of the first group were enrolled in three- or four-year theoretical courses, as against only 15 percent for the children of unskilled workers. These differences are sometimes accentuated by the low level of social heterogeneity during the period of compulsory schooling, as neighbourhoods tend to be socially homogeneous.[113] A new area unequal utilization of publicly provided services is leisure and sparetime activities.[114]

185

Property Inequality

The case of wealth distribution is far less equitable than that of income distribution, but although markedly uneven, the overall pattern of ownership has changed in important respects throughout the twentieth century.[115] In 1920, the richest one percent of all households owned half of all wealth, as against a fifth in 1975. Just after the World War I, this group, together with the next 19 percent of all households, owned all total declared property, whereas in the mid-1970s, 20 percent of the total wealth belonged to other households. Those in the highest brackets, the "superrich" have lost the relative most, whilst the groups just below have done better. The 95 percent of households (half of which reported no wealth at all) increased their share of total net wealth from 23 percent in 1920 to 56 percent in 1975. In addition, only 13 percent of all adults had received a legacy or gift exceeding 10 000 SEK in the 1970s; among the recipients, farmers, senior salaried employees and entrepreneurs were overrepresented.[116]

Table 24   The development of the distribution of wealth
Percentage of total taxed net wealth owned by the richest households(a)

Year	Richest households as of all households				
	1%	2%	5%	10%	20%
1920	50	60	77	91	100
1930	47	58	74	88	98
1935	42	53	70	84	97
1945	38	48	66	82	96
1951	33	43	60	76	92
1966	24	32	48	64	82
1970	23	31	46	62	84
1975	21	28	44	60	80
1975	17	24	38	54	75
1979	13	19	33	51	75
No. of households in 1975 (in 1,000s)	41	82	205	410	820

(a) Evaluated of market prices in 1975 and 1979

This redistribution of wealth is attributable to the increase in total wealth and to relative changes between the importance of various kinds of property. Traditional forms of wealth, such as landed property and stocks, etc. have decreased as a proportion of total net wealth whilst durable goods such as owneroccupied and other forms of owned housing have increased their share from 17 percent of total wealth in 1945 to 45 percent thirty years later. *Table 25* shows the changes between 1968 and 1981 for durable goods, as reported in the latest level-of-living survey: only four percent of all adults aged 15-75 had all six types of asset as compared to two percent fourteen years earlier. In contrast, those with only one asset have decreased from 13 percent in 1968 to 8 percent in 1981.[117]

Table 25	Distribution of assets		
Percentage of population aged 15-75 owning assets (a)			
Number of assets	1968	1974	1981
6	2	3	4
5	7	11	15
4	19	24	28
3	29	28	25
2	25	20	17
1	13	10	8
of which:			
car	(1.6)	(1.2)	(1.1)
boat	(0.2)	-	-
summer cottage/caravan	(0.1)	(0.1)	-
holiday trip	(2.6)	(2.3)	(2.1)
cash margin	(6.9)	(5.3)	(3.9)
dwelling	(1.8)	(0.7)	(0.6)
0	5	4	3

(a) The following items are counted: "owns a car", "owns a boat", "owns a summer cottage or caravan", "had a holiday trip last year", "has a cash margin" and "owns a house or apartment".

Another important development has been the stock market boom in around 1980 and the growth of Swedish multinationals in recent decades.[118] Of the fifteen families who dominated Swedish industry in the 1950s and 1960s, only five have survived. However, new major industrial financiers have emerged in recent years.[119]

Table 26, based on a survey by Statistics Sweden gives a more detailed picture of the development of wealth distribution in the period of inflation and economic recession by major socio-economic groups at the turn of the last decade. Pensioners and senior white-collar employees are the winners together with married couples with one child and single persons without children (the latter groups not shown in the table). Losers include workers and low-income employees and young households in particular. Overall, there is a clear connection between income and wealth. Accord-

187

ing to the survey, all married couples aged 20-64 and pensioner households had net wealth in excess of disposable income, whereas for single people wealth only exceeds income in the 9th and 10th deciles. All housholds in the 10th decile had net wealth of between 2.3 and 4.5 of disposable income.[120]

Table 26   Average net wealth of households (in 1,000 SKR) by socio-economic group (a)

	Number of households	Average net wealth at current prices 1978	Average net wealth at current prices 1981	Changes 1978–1981 at constant prices in 1,000 SKR	Net wealth as % of annual disp. income 1978	Net wealth as % of annual disp. income 1981
Total employees (b)	2 519	98.8	130.6	− 3.8	1.61	1.52
workers	1 307	73.8	89.6	−10.8	1.36	1.18
junior white-collar	853	118.1	157.4	− 3.2	1.74	1.66
senior white-collar	258	173.2	266.3	+30.7	2.06	2.10
Non-farm entrepreneurs (c)	236	174.5	238.4	+ 1.1	–	–
Pensioners 65-74	547	94.2	185.2	+57.1	2.42	3.33
Pensioners 75+	508	54.2	117.7	+44.0	2.03	2.74

(a) Farmers are excluded because figures are not comparable.
(b) Including those not classified according to socio-economic group (ca. 100,000 persons).
(c) Figures for disposable income not given in the sources.

3.3 Poverty in the Welfare State

Poverty is foreign to most ideas of a welfare state, understood as a safety net for the individual from the cradle to the grave.[121] Although recognized, poverty has never been officially defined in Sweden either before or after the World War II. Its persistence in the postwar era, is a matter of dispute. First, measures of inequality will be used as indicators of poverty.

In the last decade a number of studies have focussed on low-income earners and families below the subsistence level.[122] Defined in this way, poverty is relative to the overall development of wages and salaries. In 1979 there were 100 000 full-time employees who were extremely low-paid in Sweden. Their annual income was less than 38 000 SEK, which is equal to the wage level at the top of the lowest paid five percent of all full-time employees and far below the lowest tariff of pay negotiated by the trade union movement at that time (also very close to the basic pension for a couple in 1980). Of all full-time, unskilled workers, 16 percent belonged to this group.[123]

188

Graph 35 shows the development of the number of meanstested
social assistance beneficiaries in the 20th century. The curve reflects
of course business cycles and employment levels (with the peak
during the Great Depression). The reduction in the early postwar
years was also connected with the introduction of substantially
augmented national basic pensions, a general child allowance
(1948), and universal sickness insurance (1955). One must be very
cautious however when using recipients of social assistance as an
indicator of poverty.

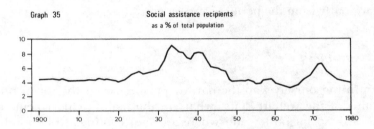

Graph 35   Social assistance recipients
as a % of total population

The increase of recipients in the most recent decades has been
affected by augmented housing allowances and an extended right
to invalidity pensions in the early 1970s. Given the extended safety
net of social security, an increasing proportion of assistance recipients are single men and women in the "productive" age groups
rather than large families and the elderly. At least one of Rowntree's famous phases of poverty – old age – has virtually disappeared.[124] Annual variations in the number of recipients are to
some degree related inversely to economic growth and directly to
the rate of unemployment.[125]

There are no available nation-wide statistics which give information of the reasons for claiming social assistence, but it seems that
unemployment, drug abuse, a large number of children and low
socio-economic status are the main grounds. Sickness seems to have
disappeared as a major ground for claiming social assistance.[126]

Another indicator of poverty is the number of tenants actually
evicted from private or municipal multi-dwellings. This has more
than doubled from 1970 to 1983, the absolute number increasing
from 2 014 to 4 754 in the respective years or from 11 to 24 per

189

10000 apartments.[127] The problem of interpreting poverty today is that in the public perception it has remained related to the average standard of living.[128] While the standard of living has increased tremendously in the postwar era for lower income groups, at the political level their conditions are still defined, in terms of poverty. In Sweden, the close relationship between low earnings and other dimensions of welfare, in particular education and working environment, has been stressed by the social report on inequality, while other Sandinavian level-of-living surveys tend to argue that the welfare profile of the low-income group often differs only marginally from the population average.[129]

3.4 Summary

Confining ourselves to the narrow perspective of the social programs of the welfare state, what are the major achievements of Swedish social policy and where are shortcomings to be found? The income maintenance schemes for the quarter of the population who are either old or disabled and the health system, with its benefits in cash and kind for both long- and short-term illness, must without doubt be seen as success. Although much debated during the last decade and quite controversial from a regional point of view, the efforts to keep up employment during years of recession and industrial renewal have been in line with the objectives of the official manpower policy.[130]

The levels of security and opportunity achieved in housing and education are much more open to question. Although the improvements in housing conditions have been tremendous, many newly developed residential areas have been heavily criticized. The old elitist and authoritarian school system has been replaced by an extended, uniform system. The general level of education has increased considerably. To what extent though is this a consequence of conscious efforts as opposed at least in more recent years to a worsening labor market for those aged under 20s? And how far does the comprehensive system still favour the same old guard?

This and other criticisms may be levelled at the present welfare system. Inequalities do persist especially as regards income, but the gap exposed by inequality is one of the narrowest among the capitalist democracies. Taxes and social transfers are obviously not so much of a roundabout, as is sometimes argued, as a redistribution takes place over the lifecycle and between households of differing size and with different needs thus, reducing inequalities in purchasing power and access to amenities. Of course, there are threshold effects in the combination of direct taxes and social benefits which may have an impact on work incentives, which should not, however, be exaggerated. Social services are often available more or less free of charge, but are more often utilized by the upper classes. Wealth distribution is still extremely uneven and in recent years tax deductions have tended to increase inequalities in the housing sphere. Poverty, whether measured by the size of the low-income group, the number of social assistance recipients, or the number of evicted tenants, still persists, but this is partly a consequence of the relative character of these estimates.

Let us now return briefly to the level-of-living survey. *Table 27* gives percentages of respondents reporting "problems", "difficulties" or bad "conditions" in various fields.

Table 27   Individuals with "problems" on level of living components (a)

| Components | As % of total population | | | As % of labour force | | |
	1968	1974	1981	1968	1974	1981
Economic resources	19	13	11	14	9	7
Health	24	25	24	18	19	18
Housing	48	27	11	46	25	11
Leisure activities	20	12	10	16	10	8
Political resources	44	36	26	32	25	16
Social relations	6	6	7	6	5	5
Working conditions	–	–	–	9	9	10
Total number of respondents	5 711	5 900	6 041	3 647	3 985	4 191

(a) Of the nine components in the level of living survey, education is excluded here because the only really problematic group with less than six years of formal education is extremely small. Another component, security of life and property, was not included in the 1968 survey and is therefore absent here.

The overall pattern of progress is evident from the table, with a general decrease in the proportion of individuals reporting "problems" for one or more of the components. This is especially true for the housing component, where almost half of the population reported some kind of "problem" in 1968. But there are also signs of a stand-still. As mentioned earlier, no change has occurred in the

191

size of the group having no contacts with relatives or no friends, i.e. the "social-relation" component. Nor is there any progress in the much larger group reporting health problems – either for total population or for the active labour force. In particular the group reporting "physical ill-being" that has not changed in size, while the group reporting "psychiatric ill-being" has decreased slightly. In the labour force, the group with a difficult working environment has not decreased. If we combine the number of "problems", the pattern of progress remains the same (see *Table 28*). The group reporting "no problem" on any component has doubled for both in total population and among working people. Even the worst-off group, individuals with problems on three or more components, has diminished greatly since the mid-1960s, being two thirds smaller in the early 1980s.

Finally, the level-of-living survey indicates that connections between the components are the same for the three years investigated.[131] The central component is economic resources: those with low income and other scarce resources are more inclined to report "problems" on other components. No "problem" is completely isolated from the others, but there are nevertheless three identifiable clusters for the total population (see *Graph 36*).

1. Economic resources – social relations – health – leisure activities.
2. Economic resources – political resources – leisure activities.
3. Economic resources – social relations – housing.

Table 28   The cumulation of "problems". Percentage distribution of respondents by number of "problems"

	Total population			labour force		
	1968	1974	1981	1968	1974	1981
No problems	21	33	45	26	39	52
1–2 problems	57	54	47	58	52	42
3+ problems	22	13	8	16	9	6

The clusters are linked to certain population groups. The first pattern is most often found among the elderly – health is a central component. The second configuration is especially frequent among females and points to limited communication possibilities (wich may be related to level of education, not included here in the component analysis) as an obstacle to political and cultural participation. These two clusters are less relevant for the labour force, which in general has less "problem". In the third cluster it is economic resources themselves that constitute the most important component, and the constellation "economic resources social relations-housing" is also more closely related to the socio-economic structure than the first two clusters. This indicates that although the overall number of social contingencies is diminishing, signs of a class society are still visible in Sweden. The postwar decades of rapid economic growth and structural change were accompanied by substantial improvements in the population's standard of living, but to see these years solely as an era of progress, as was often done in the mid-1960s, would be an oversimplification, as the transformation involved both the emergence of new social pathologies and the rediscover older ones.[132]

Graph 36

Clusters of problems

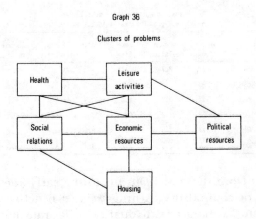

4. Correlates and Causes: Explanations

From the post-Napoleonic era onwards, Sweden has had the good fortune of remaining outside all the wars that have shaken the European continent. The construction of a welfare state in the postwar period is part of this pattern of peaceful evolution and remarkable stability. The second half of the 1940s and early 1950s

193

was a period of adaptation to the new international economic and political order, characterized in Sweden by problems of inflation and the external economic balance. Internally, it was a period marked by the outbreak of conflicts caused by the forced cooperation during the war. A major clash over the "plan or market" question developed between private industry and the Conservative-Liberal parties, on the one hand, and the ruling Social Democrats with the support of the trade union movement on the other, culminating in the 1948 election.[133] The result was narrow victory for the left parties which laid the base for the long period of Social Democratic dominance over welfare state developments. Social expenditure growth was rapid but uneven during this period (see *Table 29*) This was largely the result of the pension and child allowance reforms in 1948, which more than doubled social security costs immediately after the war.

Table 29   Phases in welfare state development
Annual real growth rates of social expenditure

Period	Average	Standard deviation	Education	Health	Social security	Income maint.
1946–1954	12.7	8.7				
1950–1954			8.5	7.2	5.4	5.6
1955–1962	7.3	0.7	8.0	10.9	9.5	4.8
1963–1970	11.7	2.2	10.5	13.8	15.9	9.3
1971–1976	7.7	1.5	2.4	6.6	10.7	11.2
1977–1980	4.4	2.0	2.2	3.5	8.5	5.0

The period from the mid-1950s up to the early 1960s saw the introduction of compulsory earnings-related benefits giving the Swedish system its characteristic duality of flat-rate and earnings-related benefits. Social expenditure growth was still quite considerable in this period and much more uniform than earlier. The GDP share of welfare grew continuously, from below 13 percent to over 15 percent. The composition of welfare expenditure changed slowly: the predominance of income maintenance decreased gradually, while education maintained its rank as second, and both health and social services crept up from a low level.

The 1960s form a third phase of rapid expansion in almost all fields of welfare provisions, however with notable variations between the years. The main expansion took place outside the in-

194

come maintenance system, which actually decreased to its lowest share in the entire postwar period (35 percent of all social expenditure in 1970). Generally, it was public consumption that expanded during this period as various public services were built up. Educational reforms were initiated, from compulsory schooling to the universities and in adult education. New hospitals were built in all counties and the low uniform tariff for visits to the doctor resulted in a tremendous increase in the numbers of patients. The highest growth rates were noted for the social services: social outlays for homes for the aged, family services (child day care centers in particular), and employment services such as vocational guidance and retraining programs, more than doubled during the period. Total social expenditure as a share of GDP increased from 16 percent in 1962 to 26 percent in 1970.

The pattern of the fourth period, the early 1970s, is closer to that of the late 1950s than to the immediately preceeding period. Welfare's share of GDP grew but its share of total public expenditure stagnated. The growth in educational expenditure levelled off after three decades of uninterrupted, rapid expansion. There was also a slowdown in the expansion of the health sector and the social services, while income maintenance expanded more steadily. To some extent this was an artificial growth because several earnings-related cash benefits, such as sickness and unemployment reimbursements, were raised when they became taxable income in 1974.

The late 1970s, will be reviewed later on in the light of the 1980s (see Section V). Briefly stated it was a period with no major reform in any area of welfare policy, but with a strong emphasis on full employment, also reflected in the relatively strong growth expansion of social services. Due to the slow growth of GDP and rapid inflation, indexed income maintenance programs enlarged welfare's share of GDP. The relative growth of social expenditure was, however, not matched by a similar growth in public revenues (which actually decreased as a share of GDP) and the rapidly increasing public debt formed the background to the first proposals for welfare cuts in 1980.

With this preliminary periodization in mind, we will dedicate the coming pages an identification of the demographic, economic and political factors which have influenced the making of the Swedish welfare state.

4.1 Demografic Components

Population growth has been very low for many decades and comes largely from immigration. The demographic transition in Sweden had already started in the first part of 19th century with a decline in mortality rates, followed by a falling birth rate in the 1870s. At this time the wave of overseas emigration started and continued up to the 1920s. By the 1930s Sweden had reached one of the lowest levels of population growth in Europe. In the aftermath of the war-time baby boom fertility declined again in the 1950s. There was a smaller wave in the mid-1960s, followed by even lower reproduction rates in the 1970s.[134] As a consequence, the age structure of the population has altered: the share of the population under 16 diminished from 23.4 percent in 1950 to 19.4 percent in 1980, accompanied by an increase in the over-65s from 10.3 to 16.4 percent. In a comparative perspective, the economically active population is still large and the dependency ratio thus remarkably unaltered. Immigration helped to maintain this balance up to the early 1970s (see *Graph 37*).

Graph 37

Demographic changes

Rates per 1,000 population

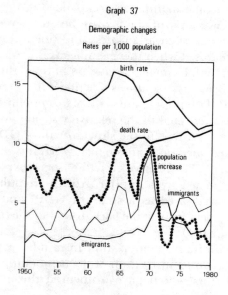

In order to assess impact of these demographic changes on welfare state development, we shall look in some detail at two relevant public expenditure items – basic pensions and child allowances – using a component analysis developed by the OECD. Briefly, this method distinguishes between three types of components or ratios:

– the demographic ratio, which is the target group as a proportion of the total population;

– the eligibility ratio, which is the actual number of beneficiaries relative to the relevant target group.(However, given the universal character of welfare policy in Sweden, this ratio generally is of minor importance for the analysis.);

– the transfer ratio, which is the average payment per beneficiary as a proportion of per capita GDP.

The OECD method is explained more fully in the general introduction to this volume. Here, the method is applied first to the relative expenditure growth and then these ratios are expressed in index form in order to facilitate direct comparisons between them. Thus, looking at change over time in the share of GDP absorbed by a given programme, we can discover the relative influence of demographic change on expenditure growth.

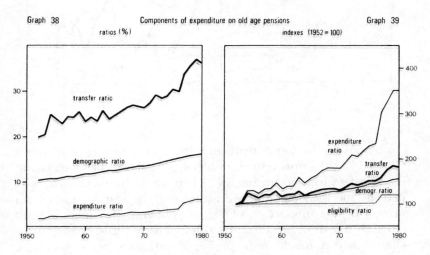

Graph 38   Components of expenditure on old age pensions   Graph 39
          ratios (%)   indexes (1952 = 100)

197

Old Age Pensions

In relation to GDP, old age pension expenditure more than trebled increasing from 1.7 percent in the early 1950s to 6 percent three decades later (see *Graph 38*). During the first two postwar decades social outlays for pensions increased rather slowly (roughly doubling over the period), as compared to the subsequent rapid expansion especially in the second half of the 1970s. The demographic ratio – the proportion of people in the over-65 age group – has risen gradually. As noted earlier, general retirement age was 67 up to 1976 and 65. Thus, the eligibility ratio (not shown in the graph) varied around 85 percent for 25 years, and thereafter rose to 100 percent in the second half of the 1970s. The transfer ratio, i.e. the average pension as a proportion of GDP per capita, gradually improved from a fifth in the early 1950s to a third thirty years later.

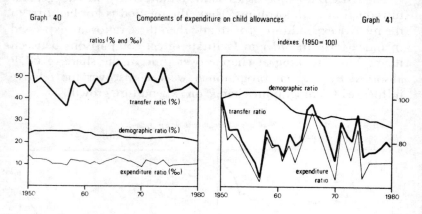

Graph 40   Components of expenditure on child allowances   Graph 41

Comparing the components in relative expenditure growth (see *Graph 39*), the improvement in benefits has been the main factor, the transfer ratio accounting for 39 percent as compared to only 14 percent for the demographic ratio, and the rest accounted for mainly by the interaction of the components. But there are differences over time. For the late 1950s and early 1960s, demographic change had a much more profound influence on expenditure developments, while the benefit level even had a negative impact (see *Table 30*).

198

Table 30   Phases in development of old age pensions (a)

Period (b)	% change in share of GDP	Due to demographic change	eligibility change	transfer ratio change
1952–1954 (b)	0.4	0.03	0.001	0.49
1954–1962	0.2	0.13	0.007	-0.15
1962–1970	0.7	0.16	0.023	0.29
1971–1976	0.9	0.16	-0.005	0.38
1976–1980	2.0	0.10	0.145	0.62
1952–1980	4.2	0.58	0.171	1.63

(a) Ratio of end-year to initial year.
(b) Figures on old age pension are not available prior to 1952.

Table 31   Phases in the development of child allowances (a)

Period	% change in share of GDP	Due to demographic change	eligibility (b) change	transfer ratio change
1950–1954	-0.3	0.07	-	-0.14
1954–1962	0.0	-0.19	-	0.05
1962–1970	-0.2	-0.07	-	-0.07
1970–1976	0.1	-0.05	-	0.02
1976–1980	0.0	-0.07	-	0.01
1950–1980	-0.4	-0.31	-	-0.13

(a) Ratio of end-year to initial year.
(b) All children below age 16 eligible throughout the period.

Child Allowances

The factors influencing changes in expenditure have operated somewhat differently as regards child allowance. Public spending on this item relative to GDP has been almost constant throughout the period oscillating around one percent (see *Graph 40*). With 1.4 percent the peak had already been reached in 1950. The proportion of people in the age group below age 16 has declined from a fourth of the total population in the early 1950s to a fifth thirty years later. There are many ups and downs during the three decades, but

199

the trend is downwards. Contrary to old age pension, the child allowance has not improved in value relative to per capita GDP. The transfer ratio has oscillated between four and six percent. Comparing the transfer and the demographic ratio change rates for the whole period, the latter one is the main contributor to the relative fall in expenditure (see *Graph 41*). It accounts for 77 percent as compared to 33 percent for the transfer ratio – the overproduction being caused by the negative interaction effects. But there are differences between the decades. The transfer ratio was the sole factor behind the fall in the expenditure ratio in the early 1950s. When expenditure fell again in the 1960s, both components were of equal importance, while the relative expenditure growth in the early 1970s was caused by the combined effect of negative demographic change and positive developments in the transfer ratio (see *Table 31*).

The component analysis of social expenditure growth indicates that demographic changes are not the major cause behind the cost explosion, and that their impact varies. It is relatively small for the increase of pension expenditure, but more important for the relative decline of expenditure on child allowances. Concerning eligibility, universal child allowances had already been introduced in 1948, while a minor extension of the pension programme in 1976 had some influence on expenditure developments. Finally, the relative improvement of benefits has had a major impact on the growth of pension expenditure from the 1960s onwards, but has been rather insignificant as regards child allowance costs.

4.2 Economic Correlates

Sweden, one of the poorest countries in early 19th Europe, became one of the most prosperous in the world in the middle of the 20th century. Industrialization began comparatively late, in the last quarter of the 19th century, but at the outbreak of World War II only some fifty years later, Sweden vied with Great Britain for the highest per-capita income in Europe.

The strong economic growth has continued on a relatively high and stable level. The 1950s and 1960s, were the optimistic era of the affluent society. With the exception of one year (1951), annual real

GDP growth rates never fell below two percent. In particular, the early 1960s was a time of rapid expansion with no year below three percent and an average rate of five percent. The variations in annual growth rates have increased since the mid 1960s, in particular in the second half of the 1970s (see *Table 32*). Although the country has experienced slow and even negative growth in the late 1970s and early 1980s, prosperity has not faded away. According to a recently published estimation by an economic historian, GDP per-capita is more than 15 times as high as it was over hundred years ago.[135]

Table 32   Annual real growth rates of GDP

Period	Average	Standard deviation
1950–55	3.4	1.40
1954–60	3.4	1.04
1961–65	5.0	1.07
1966–70	4.0	1.21
1971–75	2.7	1.57
1976–80	1.2	3.74

Table 33   Sectoral change of gross domestic product and employment
Percent distributions

Year	Gross domestic product (a)			Employment		
	Agri-culture	Industry	Services	Agri-culture	Industry	Services
1950	11	48	40	20	39	39
1960	10	47	44	13	45	41
1965	7	44	49			
1970	5	40	52	8	40	52
1975	5	40	54			
1980	4	35	60	5	36	59

(a) Figures do not add up to 100 percent for all years.

In 1980, the gross domestic product (at 1975 prices) was 2.7 times higher than in 1950. This enormous economic growth was accompanied by a market shift in the origin of GDP as well as the structure of employment (see *Table 33*). Although food production shows impressive records in absolute terms, the relative importance of agriculture has diminished, farm labour has declined to below five percent of the total labor force. From the turn of the century, industrial production outstripped agriculture in GDP-terms and from the 1930s also in employment figures. Iron, mines and forests have always played a decisive role in the Swedish economy, and technologically advanced products were the basis for the first companies competing on the world market. The importance of manufactured goods for Swedish export and industrial production has further increased in the postwar period. Industrial employment increased up to the mid 1960s, but has since declined, surpassed by the tertiary sector in both employment and GDP-terms. Growth has been more concentrated in social services, financial, insurance, real estate and other services for private business, while it has been modest in traditional services, transport and trade.

Thus, postwar Sweden is characterized by simultaneous processes of rapid economic transformation and extensive welfare state developments. From World War II onwards, a typical feature of Swedish society was social reform based on an increase in material wealth. *Graph 42* shows the annual real growth rates of GDP and social expenditure. With the exception of one year, 1979, social expenditure has grown more rapidly than GDP, and in no year has social expenditure turned negative. Despite the general pattern of consistent and relatively high growth rates for both intems, there have been substantial variations. On average the difference was just above 4 percent. However, in two years, 1967 and 1968, with economic growth rates slightly above the average, the differences climbed to over 10 percent (see *Graph 43*). And in 1976 and 1977, two years with bad economic growth records, the annual differentials came also very close to the peak.

Table 34 gives the correlation coefficients for the annual changes in GDP and the major social expenditure items. Most coefficients are rather weak. Thus, although the unprecedented economic growth of the postwar period was a necessary precondition for the expansion of the welfare state, the short-term relationship between these processes were rather loose. The explanation for this is given by *Graph 44* which shows various time-specific clusters of annual growth rates of GDP and social expenditure.

Graph 44 shows that of out of 30 years, 10 are located in the upper right high growth quadrant, and 8 in the opposite lower left low growth field. There are two clusters, one of modest or low social expenditure growth and high or modest economic growth in

Graph 42

Real annual growth rates of GDP
and social expenditure

Graph 43

Annual differences between GDP and
social expenditure growth rates

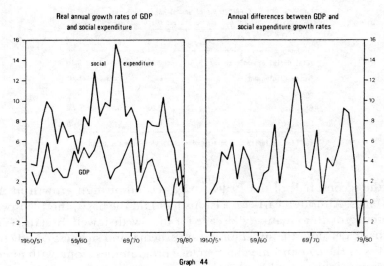

Graph 44

Relationships of GDP and social expenditure
annual real growth rates

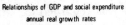

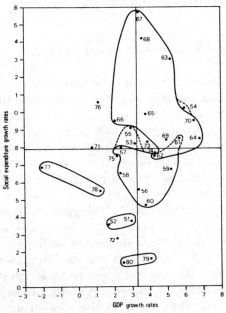

203

Table 34   Correlations of annual real growth rates
                  of GDP and social expenditure items

	Lag 0	Lag 1	Lag 2	Lag 3
Total social expenditure (a)	0.20	0.26	0.31	0.29
Income maintenance	0.06	0.21	0.08	0.03
Health	0.19	0.32	0.20	0.05
Education (a)	0.19	0.06	0.28	0.52
Social services	0.04	0.02	0.35	0.25

(a) Figures for education expenditure are on a biannual basis.

the second half of the 1950s, and a second of high growth in the 1960s. Although earlier decisions had laid the basis, the 1960s was the 'growth to maturity' decade for the Swedish welfare state, with basic pension, the superannuation scheme, and sickness cash benefits as the core income maintenance programmes along with major expansions in health and schooling. This is also the decade when public sector growth was regarded as a necessary correlate to an even more perfect market economy.[136]

4.3 The Welfare State in a Political Context

As in the other Nordic countries, the gospels of evangelism, nationalism, ethnicism and regional matters have had little impact on 20th century Swedish politics. The Lutheran state church has always been subjected to central state power and small Finnish and Samian minorities in the far North have never been a threat to the socio-political order. The power structure of Swedish society has primarily been rooted in the institutionalized class divisions and interests generated by the advent of capitalism in the late 19th century. Political cleavages, and ideological and economic interest articulation, follow this pattern.[137] The parties have remained almost the same since the introduction of parliamentary democracy after World War I.[138] This pattern was reinforced in the 1930s with the advent of majority governments, and the defeat of the small Nazi current.[139] Table 35 shows the major actors on the socio-political scene and their basis in the socio-economic structure.

204

Table 35   Social structure and interest articulation

Socio-economic class	% of economically active population 1950	% of economically active population 1980	Major representative political parties	Major representative labour market/economic interest organization
Workers and lower salaried employees	56	52	Social Democrats	Trade Union Confederation (LO)
Middle level and upper salaried employees	22	39	Electoral support divided between the four major parties, upper white collar mainly Conservative	Central Organization of Salaried Employees (TCO; mainly middle level) and Confederation of Professional Associations (SACO/SR; mainly upper level)
Farmers	10	4	Center/Farmers' Party	Federation of Swedish Farmers (LRF)
Propertied middle class	8	3	Divided between non-socialist parties	Federation of Trades, Industries and Family enterprises (SHIO)
Propertied upper class	1	1	Moderates (Conservatives)	Swedish Employers' Confederation (SAF) Federation of Swedish Industries (SI)

Only the four parties listed in the table and the Left Communist Party have been represented in Parliament in the postwar period and since the 1920s these five have always obtained more than 90 percent of the vote.

In general, party identification is anchored in the social stratification of Swedish society. *Graph 45* gives the percentages voting socialist (Social Democratic and Communist Parties) among workers and all other socio-economic groups in elections during the period 1956-1982. The difference narrowed from over 50 percent in the first elections to just below 35 percent in the 1982 election.[140] This primarily reflects the growing proportion of white-collar employees: about 40 percent have voted for the left in the postwar elections and the other 60 percent distributed their votes among the non-socialist parties. The Social Democrats have stronger white-collar support in the public than the private sector. The white-collar unions (TCO and SACO) are less politically partisan than the blue-collar Trade Union Confederation (LO).

205

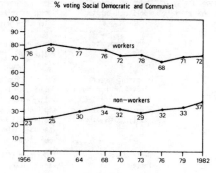

Graph 45

The social basis of socialist voting

% voting Social Democratic and Communist

Parties and Governments

A distinctive characteristic of interest representation is the extremely close tie which exists between the Social Democratic Party (SAP) and the LO. Throughout the 20th century Social Democratic trade unionists have dominated the LO.[141] The local branches of the unions have often been collective members of local party organizations, which has given the working class movement a tremendously strong infra-structure in political strife.[142]

The Social Democratic Party has for a long time been the leading political party, advocating increased state intervention in the economy and labor market, although in the postwar period quite sceptical about the nationalization of private industry. It favoured a "social market" model which meant a competitive market economy in an international free-trade system, combined with social reforms to redistribute the fruits of production. There has been a distribution of functions between the two pillars of the working class movement: while the trade unions have sought to increase the prosperity of their members through wage bargaining, the party has tried to improve the situation of the whole population through welfare state action. This strategy was reinforced in the 1970s by the growing influence of public sector unions inside both the LO and TCO.

Another major characteristic of Scandinavian politics is the existence of agrarian parties.[143] Swedish agriculture has been dominated by family farms, and their proprietors have for centuries belonged to the political core of the country, first as an Estate in the old Parliament and then as the majority in the lower chamber in the second half of the 19th century. Following an agricultural crisis after World War I the farmers reemerged as an independant political force and for a long time their political profile was quite distinct from the other non-socialist parties.

Since the 1920s overproduction and price regulation have created a special relationship between farmers and the state. Agricultural policy should be seen as a special form of social policy, almost a Bismarckian model of class politics aimed at maintaining a particular social category.[144] The Federation of Swedish Farmers (LRF) organizes almost all farmers and represents the interests of farmers as producers in negotiations with the state. As with the working class movement, the ties between the LRF and its political wing are very close. The Centre/Agrarian Party has traditionally received approximately two-thirds of the farmers' vote. From the 1930s up to the end of the 1950s it was the Social Democrats' coalition partner and it was only the 1970s that it rallied in a more determined way with the Liberal and Conservative parties. The coalition of workers and farmers forms the basis of much of the all-embracing nature of the Swedish welfare state.

The political support of the rest of the middle classes has been divided, as in the other Nordic countries, between the Liberal and Conservative parties. In the early postwar period the liberal Peoples' Party under the leadership of the keynesian economist Bertil Ohlin, regained much of its popular influence from the struggle for universal suffrage in the early 20th century, and was for a long time the leading opposition party (see *Graph 46*). In the mid-1960s, the Liberals, together with the Centre/Agrarian Party, formed an alternative in the "middle", opposing both anti-welfare conservatism and socialist extravagance concern ingequality and social security. In comparison with the Conservative Party, the Liberals have always been much more reform-minded and participated in most welfare decisions.

Although they endorsed the introduction of child allowance and of a pension reform in 1948, the Conservatives had a much harder time in influencing domestic politics in the first postwar decades. It was only in the early 1980s that the party regained its former position as the leading bourgeois party. The Conservatice Party was for long regarded as solely a representative of upper-class interests, being notoriously sceptical of state intervention in social welfare. In the period 1965-1975 the party had to operate in the shadow of the "middle alternative", but the Moderates (as they call themselves since 1969) consistently criticized the high rates of taxation.

Graph 46

Parliamentary seats by party

percent distribution

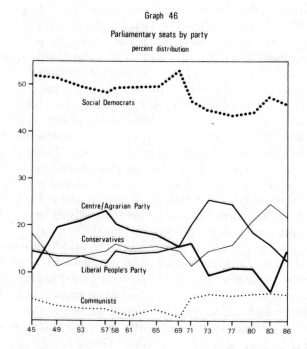

Graph 45 indicates that the affiliation between class och party became somewhat looser in the 1960s and 1970s, but compared to the major changes in the socio-economic structure, the distribution of votes between the two political blocs remained extraordinarily stable. In particular, the Centre/Agrarian Party was for a long time extremely successful in obtaining support outside its diminishing group of traditional supporters, a factor contributing to its eventual break with the Social Democrats in the early 1970s. Unlike in

the other Scandinavian countries, the Social Democrats in Sweden maintained a fairly stable level of support, around 45 percent. Together with the Communists, they hold a majority most of the time up to the mid-1970s. Formed after the Referendum on Nuclear Energy in 1980, a new green ecologist party has participated in elections in the 1980s, but so far has not surpassed the 4-percent required to enter Parliament. The Social Democrats governed the country – alone or in coalitions but always heading the executive – almost continuously from 1932 to 1976, and returned to power in 1982. From 1946 to 1969 Sweden had the same Prime Minister, Tage Erlander, who was then succeeded by Olof Palme. Up to 1951 Erlander headed a one-party government that replaced the four-party wartime coalition. In that year a new coalition was formed between the Social Democrats and the Agrarian Party. It lasted until 1957, when it broke up under the pressure of the supplementary pension question. After the introduction of the unicameral system a minority government, the Social Democrats then governed alone until 1976, mainly relying on support from the Left Communist Party (VPK). In 1976 the political Left was defeated by a centerright coalition and Thorbjörn Fälldin, leader of the Centre/Agrarian Party, served as Prime Minister in 1976-78 and 1979-82. In the intervening year, a liberal minority government held office after the first non-socialist coalition had dissolved over the nuclear energy question. In 1981, the Conservatives left the second non-socialist coalition over a tax agreement with the Social Democrats.

Labour market organizations

The interest organizations play a crucial role in Swedish society.[145] From the mid-1950s onwards, the voluntary central bargaining agreements between employers in private industry (SAF) and the LO were as important for economic policy as income policy and tripartite agreements were in other countries. In the late 1960s and first half of the 1970s, the close cooperation between the blue-collar unions (LO) and the main white-collar unions (TCO) was almost as decisive as Parliamentary support for the Social Democratic minority government.

The intimate relationship between the Social Democrats and the LO goes back to the breakthrough of the working class movement

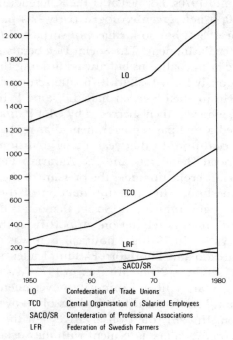

Graph 47

Membership in central interest organisations

in 1,000s

LO	Confederation of Trade Unions
TCO	Central Organisation of Salaried Employees
SACO/SR	Confederation of Professional Associations
LFR	Federation of Swedish Farmers

in late 19th century. With the exception of the defeated general strike in 1909, the trade union movement has grown almost continuously in absolute as well as in relative numbers, even though the expansion of industrial employment almost stopped in the late 1960s.[146] At the time of World War II, apart from an insignificant number of syndicalists, all organized workers belonged to the LO. The industrial principle of unionization was predominant. In the public sector there are two blue-collar unions (the Municipal Workers Union and the State Employees' Union – both affiliated to the LO), which increased considerably in the postwar years.

Of the entire adult population aged 15-75 60 percent belonged to one of the major interest organizations in 1980 as compared to 73 percent in 1968 according to the level-of-living survey. For the working population the respective figures were 60 percent in 1981 and 45 percent in 1967. *Graph 47* gives membership figures for the major central interest organizations with the exception of employers (and pensioners; see below). The LO has doubled in the postwar period from little more than one million in 1945 to over two million in the mid-1980s. Roughly 90 percent of all blue-collar workers belong to the LO in the 1980s.[147]

White-collar employees started to organize relatively late, althoug they were quite advanced in an international perspective.[148] Since the mid-1940s these unions have merged into two confederations with rather different profiles. The Central Organization of Salaried Employees (TCO) now represents more than one million members, mainly low- and middle-level white-collar workers. The Confederation of Professional Associations (SACO/SR) mostly organizes academically trained employees in the higher income brackets. Despite some boundary disputes in public sector recruitment, the two white-collar unions coordinated their negotiations with management in the private sector, and in some years jointly with the LO. Over 80 percent of all white-collar employees belonged to a union in the early 1980s, an increase of more than ten percent since the mid-1960s.[149]

Union development reflects, at least partly, changes in the socioeconomic structure. The LO today organizes lower income salaried employees in the public sector and unionization has increased among white-collar employees in general and strengthened the TCO in particular. Membership of the Federation of Swedish Farmers declined in the late 1950s and 1960s with the diminishing size of the agricultural population, but over 75 percent of all farmers belonged to this organization in 1981.[150]

A vital role is also played by the SAF, which organizes most private employers, including the smaller ones, in industry, trade and the services. While the non-socialist parties have been divided in the postwar period, the Swedish right has been strong and united on the industrial front.[151] The SAF has always been dominated by big business and extremely centralized. In 1938, after four decades of industrial disputes, a basic agreement on periodical national negotiations (the *Saltsjöbaden Agreement*) was reached between the SAF and the LO under the threat of legislation restricting the independence of collective bargaining.[152] From the mid-1950s up to 1981 central negotiations dealing with wage policy were conducted by the SAF and the LO almost every second years. For 25 years, no labour conflict occurred between the two, although there were some important wildcat strikes. The state gave its tacit approval to the outcome of negotiations on wage policy and occasionally cabinet-appointed mediators proposed mutually acceptable solutions. Through selective labour market measures, the state could intervene in areas were the negotiations created unemployment or other disruptions.

The policy of wage solidarity, pursued by the LO since the early 1950s, meant that wage differentiation should be based on the nature of and demands for jobs, and not on the profitability of individual firms. Both the LO and the white-collar unions in the private and public sections have given high priority to raising the relative earnings of low-income groups, including women since the 1960s, thereby gradually narrowing the income gaps between different occupations. In addition to the wage contracts, labour market organizations have also concluded contracts dealing with, for example, a reduction of the working week (the 40-hour week agreement was settled in 1966 and gradually implemented up to 1971), and a second supplementary pension "on top" of the mandatory one (this was extended to workers and lower-income white-collar employees in the early 1970s). Other issues, however could not be settled in this way, and the LO turned to the political wing of the labour movement to enact legislation. This was the case with the national supplementary pension system in the 1950s and with job security and industrial democracy in the 1970s. In the latter decade wage negotiations became increasingly complicated and affected by state economic policy. Government proposals to change taxes, benefit or subsidies often being a requisite for labour market settlements. This probably explains the far greater extent to which the Employers Confederation (SAF) since the mid-1970s intervenes in general political issues, in close cooperation with the Swedish Federation of Industry.[153] After a general strike in 1980, the system of centralized bargaining began to show signs of breakdown.

Other pressure groups[154]

In the postwar period, the process of interest articulation has gone beyond pure party politics, the labour market, and the old popular movements. Today, the logic of collective action is applicable to most sectors of contemporary Swedish society. Pressure groups, primarily in the form of voluntary, national associations with local and regional branches, have mushroomed. In many respects they can be regarded as responses to welfare state developments. Most of them enjoy financial support from the state, but they ought to be seen as independent social forces. Most associations participate in one way or the other in the making och implementation of social policy, but the present-day interaction between organized interests and the welfare state is far from the traditional corporatist mode of societal representation.

There is a mixture between old and new institutional representation. For instance in the field of education, besides the trade unions for teachers and other public employees in that sector, university students have long been forced by law to join the local student union, and thereby often collectively the national student organization. Secondary school pupils, on the other hand, have in the postwar period created their own voluntary interest organizations both on the local and national levels. Finally, there are the parents' organizations, which have been active on the local level in pre-school activities such as day care and on the national and local level in compulsory education.

In the field as housing, savings cooperatives and tenants' organizations work intimately together against private houseowners and their associations as well as with local authorities responsible for social housing. The tenants' organizations' bargaining power was strengthened, not only through increased membership but also through legislative measures, in the late 1960s and early 1970s. In recent years, the organizations of single-family homeowners have gained some influence on public opinion after ten years of constant increase in this part of the housing stock.

Also regarding pensioners, organizational efforts have proved successful. A third of all old-age pensioners belong to a national union. But pensioners are split between two national associations broadly along political lines: the more social democratic **PRO**

(*Pensionärernas riksorganisation*) is the major one, with some 370 000 members in 1981 or more than a fourth of all old-age pensioners, while the non-socialist SFRF (*Sveriges folkpensionärers riksförbund*) is distinctly smaller, with some 75 000 members.

The Swedish organizations for the handicapped are to a large extent dominated by the handicapped themselves, and are generally sceptical towards charity. At a national level there are about 25 associations representing some 300 000 members with different handicaps. The majority of these cooperate within the Central Committee of National Associations of the Handicapped, HCK (*Handikappförbundens centralkommitté*). DHR (*De handikappades riksförbund*), is outside the HCK and represents some 40 000 motor-handicapped.

In the health sector, combined professional and trade union organizations of physicians, dentists, and pharmacists are very influential and form the core of the earlier mentioned national association of professionals (SACO/SR). Patient associations are weak, but some groups with long-term illnesses have succeeded in organizing themselves rather well.

In the social welfare sector, *Försäkringskasseförbundet* (FKF) and *Arbetslöshetskassornas samorganisation* are remnants from the period of voluntary insurance and nowdays act in close co-operation with the state authorities in these fields (National Insurance Board and National Labour Market Board; see *Table 2*). The unemployed outside the trade unions are comparatively ill-organized.

In the social welfare sector, various client organizations in the 1970s successfully defended the interests of former alcoholics, drug-addicts, mentally disturbed, etc. They also cooperated with lobby organization of welfare bureaucrats and activists (*Samarbetskommittén för socialvårdens målfrågor*) with several of the most important social politicians among its members, acting as a "shadow commission" from the late 1960s and throughout the 1970s to put pressure on the official State Commission on Social Welfare. In particular the national organization of municipal social welfare directors played a crucial role in these efforts to influence social legislation. These lobbyists have in recent years reorganized themselves, and formed their own journal, conferences etc with the support of the handicap, client and trade union movement with the openly declared aim of defending the welfare state against cuts and other threats.

4.4 Welfare Reforms: Three Case Studies

Turning to a more detailed investigation of the complex relation between welfare and the political process, three main decisions will be singled out: the introduction of child allowances in 1948; the basic pension reform in the same year and the clash over the supplementary pension reform in the late 1950s.

The General Child Allowance act[155]

The present system of child allowances has been in force since 1948. From 1917 up to 1950, parents were entitled to a tax deduction for children. Up to the 1920s, employers frequently paid family supplements as part of the wage bill, but with the growth of collective bargaining the trade unions successfully stopped this practice.[156] The 1933 pact between the Social Democratic and Agrarian parties included state support to improved housing conditions for families with children. Under the new political majority, earlier proposals for family welfare were combined with concern about the extremely low birth rates in the early 1930s. The symbol of the new mix was Alva and Gunnar Myrdal's *Crisis in the Population Question*, published in 1934, which combined far-reaching social democratic social and sexual policy proposals with what was regarded as the conservative theme of the national destiny. The Myrdals' book influenced the non-socialist parties to propose the introduction of cash benefits for families with children in 1935. A Government-appointed Population Committee was set up in the same year with representatives from the four major parties (Gunnar Myrdal was one of the Social Democrats). The Committee presented a number of recommendations for extensive social reforms for families, women and children, including a general child allowance, but only a few inexpensive reforms were adopted in 1937 (e.g. child allowances to widows and maternity allowances). Questions as to the realism of the Committee's other recommendations, together with the worsening international situation resulted in an offically proclaimed reform "pause".[157]

However, the issue was revived in the early war years when the birth rate once again started to decline, and a State *Commission* on Population was set up (under Tage Erlander, at that time the Undersecretary of State for Social Affairs). During this period nationalistic arguments were frequently used. Conservatives proposed that family salaries should be introduced. In the meantime, initially meanstested "war supplements" were paid to families where the breadwinner had been conscripted (in 1943, almost half a million men). These were administered by the municipal poor relief system and financed by the Ministry of Defence. Gradually this developed into a general earnings-related system and became an important forerunner of the mixed local-central systems of income support (housing allowances etc).[158]

Thus, during the 1930s and 1940s there was a growing political consensus that families should be compensated by the state for the economic burdens of child-raising. Towards the end of the war this consensus among the parties was extended, with the idea that a great deal more money should be spent on postwar socio-political reforms. When the Government following the recommendations of the State Commission, proposed the introduction of general child allowances, it obtained unanimous parliamentary support.[159] Within the politically influential Commission a compromise had been reached: the Social Democrats approved non-socialist proposals that the allowance should be paid irrespective of the family's economic status and number of children (although some large trade unions opposed this unfair advantage to high-income families), while the Conservative and Liberal parties abandoned their support for a system with tax deductions, which obviously favoured those with high incomes.

The Basic pension reform[160]

Two bills introducing a general child allowances and a fundamental revision of the basic pension system were unanimously passed in 1946 and implemented in 1948. At this time parliament was almost as united as it had been in 1913 when Sweden introduced the world's first universal old age pension system: a combination of a contributory universal insurance-based system and

216

meanstested supplements for the poor and needy. The latter was the significant component up to the mid-1930s. Despite a serious decline in the real value of pensions and a number of suggestions from MPs, the old system was not reformed until 1935. The means-tested supplement was then transformed into a "supplementary pension to all low-income earners" and the pure insurance system moved towards a pay-as-you-go system favouring those who had contributed little. Nevertheless pensions were still rather low and the Social Democrats' proposals for higher benefits in the big cities and other high cost-of-living areas was turned down by the non-socialist majority in 1936.[161]

The Social Democrats tactically resigned and fought a successful election in the summer of that year mainly over pension policy – "Remember the Poor and Old" was their slogan – obtaining the party's first majority ever in the lower chamber. A formal coalition was formed with the Agrarian Party and the pension proposal was also supported in both chambers by the Liberals. Finally in 1938 a State Social Welfare Committee with strong political backing, (similar to the Population Committee and Commission), was established and soon after the war it submitted a plan for a sweeping reform of the pension scheme.

Two of the Commission's three alternatives were seriously considered by both the government and the opposition. Most Social Democratic commissioners, together with one liberal MP and a civil servant, had favoured the lower flat-rate alternative combined with a meanstested supplement to the most needy. But this was not subsequently accepted as a Government proposal. The Conservative party, supported by the Agrarian Party, favoured the higher flat-rate alternative without meanstesting, except for housing allowances.

Although the Social Democratic leadership with the exception of the Minister of Social Affairs, feared that an immediate increase in pension expenditure would contribute to a postwar economic crisis, pressure from inside the party, from the labour press and trade unions, together with fears of a Conservative breakthrough, paved the way for a pension bill along the lines of the more generous alternative.[162] The background to the new Conservative attitude was both strategic and ideological. The Conservatives tried to wrest the initiative in welfare reform from the Social Democrats and as the former had always been critical of meanstested relief programs a flat-rate pension was an easy choice at a time when the Conservatives were calling for lower taxes (after considerable increases for defence purposes during the war). Another important factor was the emergence of organized pressure groups among pensioners.

The Struggle over Earnings-related Pensions[163]

Prior to World War II only Central State employees were entitled to public occupational pensions, and voluntary occupational pensions had been introduced mainly for salaried employees in private industry. As part of the debate leading to the basic pension reform in 1946, there were also proposals for a work-related superannuation pension. Conservative MPs had argued in favour of guarantees for private pension insurance and an individual Liberal MP had also submitted a proposal neither of which gained parliamentary approval.

The LO acted as the major pressure group, demanding earnings-related pensions. In the mid-1940s, a third of the blue-collar trade union members in the export industry were entitled to such pensions, while the corresponding figure for the "home-market" industry was below 15 percent.[164] However, the SAF rejected all legislative attempts and tentatively suggested pension agreements through collective bargaining. The Agrarian Party opted most consistently for substantial improvements of the basic pension system but against superanuation. It also made suggestions concerning protection for the selfemployed during old age. The Liberal leader in Parliament submitted a complex plan for a state-guaranteed voluntary superannuation scheme based on a redistributory system coordinated with the basic pension. The Conservative, as well as the Social Democratic leadership, were initially rather silent on this issue.

An agreement to set up a State Commission – the typical Swedish policy "solution" – had been reached in Parliament in 1944. It was headed by the Director-General of the State Insurance Inspectorate and consisted of representatives for the major interest organizations. It presented a unanimous proposal concerning the principles for a compulsory earnings-related pension, based on a modified redistributory social insurance system (pay-as-you-go but with some funding in the initial period). This proposal was received critically by most social agencies.

A second State Commission was appointed in 1951 with the same civil servant as chairman but with a broader representation, including some politicians. In the same year a new coalition was formed between the Social Democrats and the Agrarian Party, the pension issue not yet being a divisive factor.[165]

Although the SAF representative had approved a compulsory supplementary pension system in the first State Commission, internal conflicts forced the organization to reopen negotiations with the LO over a proposal for a private earnings-related pension scheme worked out by SAF experts.[166] In 1954 the LO rejected this after consultations with the Social Democratic party, and the labour movement was now united behind a legislative solution.

In September 1955 the second Commission presented a proposal that for the most part followed the system suggested in 1950. But the unity which had characterized the first Commission had vanished, leaving the LO trade unionists and the chairman to form a slim majority. A Conservative MP representing the supervisors union (member of the TCO) and SAF's representative put forward minority proposals for increased basic pensions and voluntary negotiated pensions respectively. The Agrarian Party representative was surprisingly positive towards superannuation and until the Coalition cabinet dissolved after the referendum the Agrarians never united with the other non-socialist parties in political actions. The Commission's Report was sharply criticized by most interest organizations except the LO and by the non-socialist parties.

Thus, the Government had to appoint a third Commission with representatives from all parties except the Communists and from the major labour market interest organizations (LO, TCO and SAF). The coalition cabinet also presented a bill for successively increased basic pensions, which was approved unanimously by Parliament. The election that followed these decisions was another setback for the government parties, and created hopes of breaking the Social Democrats' dominance, especially among the Liberals. Although the Liberals had been fairly positive since the 1940s as regards a legislative solution to the supplementary pension question, they now tried to lead the centerright opposition to compulsory insurance by setting up an alternative. The third State Commission presented three alternatives and disunity between the coalition parties led the Government to submit these to the electorate in the third consultative referendum in Swedish history. The three proposals were:

1. Compulsory insurance for all economically active persons, financed by employers and administered by a State fund. This was the position of the representatives of the Social Democratic Party and the trade union confederations LO and TCO (the latter, white-collar organization had to withdraw in the referendum campaign after serious internal divisions).

2. Government-administered voluntary supplementary pension insurance. The alternative suggested by the Centre/Agrarian Party.

3. A voluntary pension system, administered by a private fund with a board chosen by employers and employees, and rules to be laid down through collective bargaining. This was the united position of the Liberal and Conservative parties and the Employers Confederation.

There was an intense campaign, not directly between the political parties but between committees including representatives from a broader social spectrum. An essential aspect of the campaign was the fear and/or hope that large funds would result in greater state control over private industry. In the referendum 72 percent of the electorate voted, somewhat less than in general elections in the 1950s (in particular Liberal voters abstained): 46 percent supported the labour proposal, 15 percent the Agrarian proposal (6 percent more than in the 1956 election), and 35 percent voted for alternative 3; 4 percent voted blank as proposal by the white-collar trade union SACO/SR.

The result was interpreted in diverse ways. The labour movement took it as a mandate for their original ideas, while the non-socialist parties claimed that a majority had rejected compulsory insurance and voted for voluntary solutions. The coalition government resigned after a week. As the Centre/Agrarian Party refused to consider a non-socialist coalition, the way was open for a Social Democratic minority cabinet. The Liberals, tried to persuade the Conservative and Centre/Agrarian parties to submit a united alternative. As no compromise could be achived on the pension question, the Government tabled a bill launched by the fourth State Commission (only Social Democrats and experts appointed by the new minority government). This was rejected in the Lower Chamber by the non-socialist majority, and the Lower Chamber was dissolved. The Liberals lost considerably in the following election, while the Conservatives, the Centre/Agrarians and the Social Democrats gained. In the new lower chamber the vote on a compulsory system was likely to be 115-115.

In January 1959, when the bill was almost ready with no compromise in sight, a Liberal MP (the only Liberal Christian worker) announced that he would abstain. The bill was passed by 115-114 in the lower chamber, the Social Democrats had a majority in the upper, and the abstaining Liberal was expelled by his local party branch in the aftermath. In January 1960 employers started to pay contributions to the new State funds but in the September election to the lower chamber the pension issue still dominated the campaign as the Centre/Agrarian and Conservative parties both fought for abolition. The Liberals, however, joined the Social Democrats in defence of the new social right. This explicitly welfare election was a success for the Social Democratic Party, which obtained a majority in the lower chamber. After the elections the opposition parties officially declared their acceptance of the supplementary pension system. In 1965, when some influential young industrialists in pursuit of the Conservative leadership again tried to abolish the system, the party's welfare profile was seriously damaged once again.

Summing up, to study the intricate pattern of consent and conflict in political decision-making is only one way to explain the growth of the Swedish welfare state. The whole spectrum of social and political organizations and their roots in the class structure of Swedish society has to be analysed in the context of long-term demographic changes, social transformation and economic growth in order to understand the complex nature of a welfare state generally so closely linked to one party or movement: the Social Democratic party and the trade unions.

5. The Crisis of and Prospects for the Welfare State

5.1 Recent Adjustments and Social Policy Alternatives

Despite the early 1970s backlash in nearby Denmark, echoes of the crisis of the welfare state reached its Nordic heartland relatively late, in the first half of the 1980s. Already in the 1970s there were signs of uncertainty. In 1976, the first bourgeois, Center-Right coalition government in almost half a century came to power. Initially the political issues were nuclear energy, economic democracy (wage-earners funds) and abuse of power. In the wake of the international economic crisis, however, growth became sluggish, and was even negative for one crucial year, the first of the new cabinet. All of a sudden, public income was clearly insufficient to meet public spending. Tremendous problems occurred also in the private sector; basic industries was regarded as the backbone of Swedish industry and technology – steel, shipyards, etc – which threatened to fold had to be heavily subsidized by central government in an effort to rescue employment. Since the new government was not inclined to increase taxation, public borrowing, in particular foreign loans, soon created a major public deficit problem. Inflation became worse each year, and finally went above the OECD-average. The Social Democratic opposition kept a careful eye on existing achievements in social policy, and the new cabinet was as eager as its predecessor to maintain what had become the welfare norm in a prosperous society. Especially the maintenance of full employment by an active labour market policy was regarded as holy and untouchable by both government and opposition in an employment situation more strained than ever before in the post-war epoch. Some social reforms were introduced but were in principle not allowed to augment central government expenditure.[167]

After the September election of 1979, and after the Referendum on nuclear energy in early 1980, things slowly changed: public spending and welfare policy finally became controversial. Part of the background was the deterioration of the economy after a brief economic upswing in 1979. A major ideological onslaught on the welfare state was conducted outside Parliament by one of the chief partners in Sweden's "historical compromise" – the Employers' Confederation. In the preparatory documents for its Congress in late 1980, radical solutions at least in the Swedish context like privatization of sickness insurance, and competition in such protected areas as child daycare, health services etc, were presented.[168]

The state budget deficit became a major political issue during this second term of bourgeois governments. During the first term it had grown from 1 to over 10 percent of GDP (see *Graph 48*). The cabinet still refused to increase taxes. Instead from mid-1980, all major state agencies were subject to an annual 2 percent cut in outlays after compensation for inflation.[169] Although this method was applied in the three consecutive years of non-socialist governments, the impact on the budget deficit remained negligible.

Towards the end of 1980, the government presented its first clear-cut austerity bill: Savings in state activities (*Besparingar i statsverksamheten*). It suggested changes in the indexation of the crucial base amount, and some direct cuts in social programs. Out of a central government budget of 200 billion SEK, 6 should be cut, 4 of which being transfers and benefits in kind to households, and the rest being mainly transfers from central to local authorities. These arrangements, affecting the general income-earner, were "compensated" for by efforts to limit the upper echelons' possibilities of tax evasion and "speculative" housing profits. The government announced its adherence to the traditional redistributive policy, but saw the public sector as being too big and an obstacle to industrial growth.[170]

Moreover, unemployment and active manpower policy became a more controversial issue in the closing years of the bourgeois governments. In a situation where the budget deficit had top priority, the government began to consider of new approaches to unemployment policy. It emphasized the importance of exhausting every possibility for offering jobs on the open labour market before putting the unemployed into government-run programmes. In early 1982, unemployment rose to and stayed at a level of over 3.5 percent, and became a major election issue.

A second important austerity bill was presented half a year before the September election in 1982 by the fourth bourgeois cabinet (the Conservatives had left in May 1981 because of a controversy over taxation). It proposed a reintroduction of two waiting days and a

Graph 48

The growth of public debt

as % of GDP

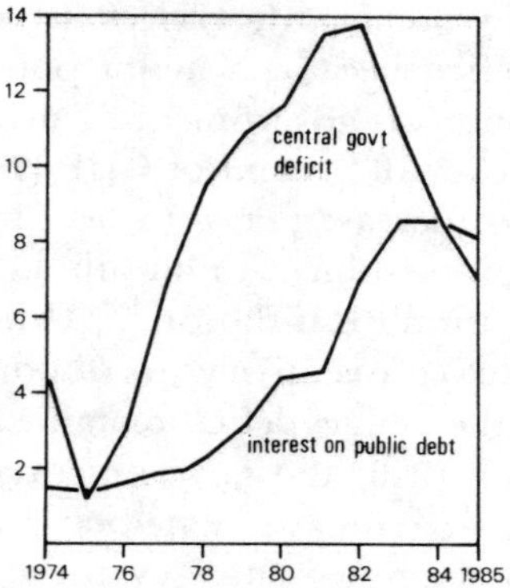

decrease in earnings-replacement from 90 to 87 percent in sickness cash benefits, thereby saving an estimated 1.5 billion SEK. The austerity measures directed at central government transfers to the municipalities, as well as increased contributions from the insured in unemployment insurance, resulted in an estimated savings amounted to almost 10 billion SEK or 4 percent of the 1982/83 central government budget.[171]

Changes in sickness cash benefits were approved by Parliament in May 1982 by the smallest possible majority and were due to be effective as of 1983. The proposal would in particular have hit private sector blue collar workers who, unlike all public employees as well as all private sector white collars employees, had no collective agreement with their employers concerning sick pay. The withdrawal of the new law became one of four specific election promises by the Social Democrats in addition to increased unemployment benefits, continued central transfers to municipalities engaged in building child daycare centers, and, full value qurantee of pensions. The blue collar Trade Union Confederation, more determined than for many years, rallied behind the Social Democrats and succeeded in bringing them back into power. At least three of the four election promises were fulfilled (a 16 percent devaluation of the Krona in October 1982, made the pension guarantee rather obsolete).[172]

Table 36   Austerity measures 1980–1985 (a)
_____

Social Transfers

1981/   Change in general indexation: the base amount, previously linked to the consumer price index and
1982   adjusted with a two-month lag each time the index had moved up by 3 percent, is changed only once
        a year as of 1982 and is no longer influenced by changes in energy prices (1981 and 1982), indirect
        taxes and food subsidies (from 1981). This affects basic and supplementary pension, advance maintenance
        allowance and the combined study loan/grant.

Pensions

1981   Reduction of benefit level of part-time pensions from 65 to 50 percent of previous wage (from 1980 to
        1983 the percentage of those eligible decreased from 27 to 20 percent).

Health

1981   Introduction of income-related hospital fees for chronically ill (with variations among counties);
        increased individual fees for dental, hospital and pharmaceutical services, but with a price ceiling
        for multi-users.

Housing

1981   Tightening of eligibility criteria (such as lowering of income ceiling and new methods for calculating
        income); cuts in housing allowances and gradual reduction in interest subsidies to home-owners.
1982   Abolition of a minor, complementary housing allowance programme for pensioners.

Social services and education

1981   Reduction of general and special central government transfers to local authorities leading to frequent
        increases in municipal fees for day care and short-time vacancies not filled in schools.
_____

(a) No clear-cut retrenchment measures were introduced prior to 1980.

Minor changes in the welfare system have continued since the return to office of the Social Democrats.[173] One important difference is that they came to power during an economic upswing and after two major devaluations in 1981-82, temporarily diminishing the pressure of the huge public deficit. Neverthelsess, the Social Democrats have tried to adjust the welfare programs to the tighter economic conditions (see *Table 36*).

However, some improvements in social benefits have also occurred during the period (see *Table 37*). As of 1982, and further improved in 1983, general child allowance supplements were paid to families with 3 or more children. Unemployment cash benefits

225

Table 37

Changes in annual cash benefits 1980-1985, at constant (1975) prices (in SKR)

Year (January)	Base amount (January)	Basic pension incl. pension supplement As % of base amount		Annual benefit		Child allowance(c)			Max. advance maintenance allowance	Max. unemp. daily allowance	Consumer price index(h)	Year
		Single	Couple	Single	Couple	1 child	2 children	3 children				
1980	13 900(a)	136	237	11 485	20 014	1 701	5 103	6 804	3 378	118	164.6	1980
1981	16 100(a)	140	245	12 223	21 391	1 627	4 881	6 508	3 492	106	184.4	1981
1982	17 800	142	249	12 619	22 128	1 498	4 868	7 114	3 644(d)	105	200.3	1982
1983	19 700(b)	142	249	12 820	22 481	1 512	5 270	8 318	3 645(f)	128	218.2	1983
1984	20 300	144	253	12 407	21 799	1 401	4 881	7 704	3 533	127	235.6	1984
1985	21 800(e)	144	253	12 751(e)	22 402(e)	1 950(e)	6 824(e)	10 723(e)	3 630(e)	122(g)	246.2	1985

(a) Figures for January; in 1980 and 1981 the base amount was adjusted each time the consumer price index had moved up by 3 percent; for the rest of 1980 the base amount was 14,400 (February), 14,900 (March–June), 15,400 (July–October), and 16,100 (November–December); for the remainder of 1981 it was 16,700 (March–May), and 17,300 (June–December).

(b) Including a special supplement of 300 SKR.

(c) From 1982 supplements have been paid to families with 3 children (1/4 allowance in 1983, 1/2 allowance from 1983) and with 4 or more children (1/2 allowance for each child in 1982, a full allowance since 1983).

(d) The maximum advance maintenance allowance was 40 percent of the base amount up to 1981; since then it is 41 percent.

(e) Benefits in 1985 calculated on the basis of the January 1985 consumer price index (otherwise on yearly average), i.e. the value is overestimated.

(f) Advance maintenance allowance calculated on the basis of the formal base amount of 19,400 SKR, i.e. excluding the special supplement.

(g) Changed to ca 127 as of July 1985.

(h) 1975 = 100; yearly averages 1980–1984; January figure for 1985 (see Appendix Table 1).

in particular have been raised since the return of the Social Democrats. In the autumn of 1983, the Minister of Social Affairs and representatives from the organizations of pensioners' and the handicapped negotiated the first agreement on some extra funds to their groups.

There are also examples of Social Democratic austerity measures that have failed. For instance, the Government tried to replace separate widows' pensions with meanstested benefits.[174] Both within the Social Democratic party and the opposition there were strong feelings against this proposal. It was withdrawn before it came up for vote in Parliament. Another unsuccessful attempt by the cabinet concerned introductions of fees for hospital stay in connection with childbirth. The Centre-Right parties, together with the Left Party Communists, voted this down in Parliament in late 1984.

In the vocabulary of the Left, "consolidation" versus "dismantling" represent the two main alternatives in the current controversy over the welfare state. In the 1980s, consolidation of what has been achieved has become the new motto of the Social Democrats.[175] "Irresponsible", expansionist policies are relegated to their junior partner to the Left, the Communists.[176] The growth of the Conservative Party has brought alternative in social policy and full employment to the fore.[177] During the 1982-85 parliamentary period, this party became the undisputed leader of the non-socialist opposition, with over 30 percent in opinion polls during 1984-85 and with a new program containing clearly neo-liberal elements. Since the early 1980s, the Centre-Right parties have suggested cuts in sickness insurance and increased contributions from the insured in unemployment insurance. They have also opted for a deliberately more market oriented manpower policy, making the unions responsible for unemployment costs when wages exceed the level acceptable to the national economy. Other promises by the Conservatives include a reduced income tax and lower earnings-replacement ratio in sickness cash benefits. Whereas the Conservatives favour a reduction from 90 to 60 percent, the Liberals and the Centre Party, suggest a more moderate reduction from 90 to 80 percent.[178]

The 1985 election was a clearcut defeat for a 'policy of social dimantling', the main charge levelled against the Conservatives by

Prime Minister Olof Palme during the election campaign. The radical 'change-of-system' advocated by some neo-liberal hotheads within the conservative leaderhip and inside the Employers' Confederation was received unenthusiastically by the voters and was even silently contested by a number of strong county council and municipal politicians within the party. Not even their anti-tax campaign attracted widespread attention. The Conservative/Moderate Party never achieved the success forecasted in opinion polls before the election and failed to get a majority position within the bloc of non-socialist parties. Also the Centre Party lost considerably, especially in the towns. The main winner was the Liberal People's Party. Under the banner of 'social responsibility without socialism' and with a clear commitment to both free enterprise and social welfare, the party made a dramatic comeback and almost trebled its electoral and parliamentary strength (See *Graph 46* above).

The 1985 election was only a narrow victory for the welfare state consolidation policy as presented by the Social Democrats. The new liberal mood and the setback suffered by the Conservatives may herald a restructuring of Swedish politics, but very probably the Social Democrats will be forced to get the active support of the Left Party Communists. The latter party scored some spectacular parliamentary victories during the 1982-85 Social Democratic reign, but it is seriously split between euro-communist reformists and orthodox revolutionaries over the issue of governmental support. More important, however, there have been major disagreements on expansionist versus restrictive economic policies inside the labour movement, between the Social Democratic party and the unions in particular. The devaluation policy adopted in 1982 worked reasonably smoothly during the economic upswing of 1983-85, although wage negotiations were as troublesome as under the previous non-socialist governments. The unity of the labour movement has been under a pressure that lacks precedence in the postwar period. The ambitions of the Minister of Finance to reduce the budget deficit was openly criticized as an austerity measure by the new chairman of the Trade Union Confederation. In earlier days, such conflicts at the leadership level were solved behind closed doors. The period up to the next election in 1988 will without doubt be a major test for the Social Democratic social policy alternative.

Although the party even promised to increase some social benefits, the threat to public welfare has definitely not faded away. In view of the central budget deficit, an inflation rate above the OECD average, and the expectation of a recession in the second half of the 1980s, the consolidation policy will meet serious obstacles. Of course, there are several roads to choose from. Cuts and adjustments may be made, whatever the colour of the cabinet. But in most cases, they will cause severe social and political difficulties.

5.2 Forecasting Social Expenditure

As the survey of recent developments in social policy indicates, it would be an exaggeration to talk about a fiscal crisis for the Swedish welfare state in the mid-1980s. What is the outlook for the coming decades? No overall projections exists for Swedish social expenditure,[179] apart from a recent OECD-survey for the period up to 1990, which suggests a slight increase for the rest of the 1980s.[180] However, a more detailed forecast concerning pension and health costs from 1985 to 2025 has been developed, based on information provided by the National Social Insurance Borad. [181]

These projections are based upon certain assumptions with regard to demographic developments, economic growth and legal entitlements. The demographic scenario assumes a long-term rising trend in the share of the population aged 65 and over, but with a temporary break from 1990 up to 2010 at which point the post World War II baby boom reaches retirement age. Although the overall dependency ratio will change only marginally, the relationship between the economically active population and the elderly will be altered considerably.[182]

These demographic changes would lead to a development of pension expenditure as shown in *Table 38,* assuming that no changes will occur in existing entitlements. This means that a single basic pension remains 0.96 of the base amount while a couple receives 1.57 (both figures as of 1984). On top of this comes a pension supplement and/or a supplementary pension (see the Institutional Synopsis in the Appendix Volume – Flora 1987).

Table 38 shows that, except in the middle of the period, pay-outs from the basic pension scheme will increase. Pension supplements

Table 38

Projected old-age and invalidity pension expenditure 1985-2025

Base amounts in thousands (a)

Year	Basic pension (1)	Pension supplements (2)	Old-age housing allow. (3)	Sub-total (1-3)	Supplementary pensions alternatives		Total pension expenditure alternatives		As % of GDP alternatives		Year
					1	2	1	2	1	2	
1985	1 584	360	180	2 124	1 840	1 840	3 964	3 964	11.3	11.0	1985
1986	1 601	347	173	2 121	1 965	1 968	4 086	4 089	11.6	11.1	1986
1987	1 612	334	167	2 113	2 071	2 074	4 148	4 187	11.6	11.1	1987
1988	1 621	321	161	2 103	2 172	2 178	4 275	4 281	11.8	11.0	1988
1989	1 626	309	155	2 090	2 273	2 279	4 363	4 369	11.7	11.0	1989
1990	1 628	296	148	2 072	2 363	2 371	4 435	4 443	11.7	10.8	1990
1995	1 617	240	120	1 977	2 764	2 804	4 741	4 781	11.1	9.9	1995
2000	1 591	188	92	1 871	3 131	3 220	5 002	5 091	10.6	9.0	2000
2005	1 599	151	73	1 823	3 587	3 757	5 410	5 580	10.2	8.4	2005
2010	1 682	128	61	1 871	4 248	4 538	6 119	6 409	10.4	8.3	2010
2015	1 768	119	57	1 944	4 834	5 265	6 778	7 209	10.3	7.9	2015
2020	1 806	111	53	1 970	5 238	5 777	7 208	7 747	9.8	7.2	2020
2025	1 807	105	50	1 962	5 533	6 154	7 495	8 116	9.1	6.5	2025

(a) The projections are based on the assumption of a stable 'base amount', which is the index regulator in Swedish social security (see Institutional Synopsis).
In January 1985, the base amount was 21,800 SKR.

and housing allowances will automatically decrease as a result of increasing supplementary pension payments. The supplementary pension scheme will grow throughout the period due to the maturation of the system (in 1990 the first full pensions will be paid out) and due to an increasing number of persons (women in particular) with earnings-related pension rights.

Of course, expenditure on earnings-related supplementary pensions is also dependent upon the development of real wages. Two alternative assumptions have been made: a first assumption of zero-growth up to 1990, followed by an annual increase of 1 percent (alternative 1); and a second assumption of an annual increase of 1 percent up to 1990 with a 2 percent thereafter (alternative 2).[183] The table also shows expected pension expenditure as a share of GDP. Two corresponding alternative assumptions have been made: a GDP growth rate of just below 2 percent up to 1990, then rising to 2.5 percent (alternative 1) or first 3 percent and then 3.5 percent (alternative 2).

Up to 1990, pension expenditure rises faster than GDP, but later the relationship is reversed. Note that the GDP-share is larger in the scenario with a slower pace for both real wage and GDP growth. Slow or zero economic growth will create problems for a smooth functioning of the system.

Table 39 gives the projected figures for health service and municipal care costs, for the population aged 65s and over. In the early 1980s, this group's share of total public health costs was estimated at roughly 60 percent.[184] All the major subitems develop in the same direction. The general trend is the same as for basic pension in the foregoing table, although the decrease occurs a decade later. Between 1990 and 2025 the projected GDP-share will be cut practically in half. Thus, in 2025, gross pension and health expenditure are projected to be either 10 or 7.7 percent of GDP, as compared to almost 14 percent in the mid-1980s.

No comparable projections exist for other social expenditure items.[185] A decreasing number of children indicates lower family and educational outlays, although this might be counteracted by changing family patterns and longer average years of schooling. The future of employment and housing subsidies is uncertain. Fees in general will probably be higher and more widely used in the public sector. This also implies a shift in the mode of financing the

Table 39   Projected expenditure on health services and municipal care for old-age pensioners 1985–2025 (a)

Base amounts in thousands (b)

Year	Longterm care	Homes for the aged	Residence hotels	Domestic services	Home health services professional care	family grant	Somatic emergency care	Psychiatric care	Total	As % of GDP alternatives 1	2	Year
1985	570	374	70	228	27	10	368	232	1 839	5.3	5.1	1985
1986	583	343	71	232	28	10	373	235	1 876	5.3	5.1	1986
1987	597	351	73	236	28	10	378	238	1 911	5.3	5.1	1987
1988	608	358	74	239	29	10	381	241	1 940	5.3	5.0	1988
1989	619	366	75	242	29	10	384	242	1 967	5.3	4.9	1989
1990	630	373	75	245	29	11	386	244	1 993	5.3	4.9	1990
1995	667	397	77	252	30	11	386	245	2 064	4.9	4.8	1995
2000	673	403	77	249	30	10	375	238	2 055	4.4	4.3	2000
2005	662	397	75	241	29	10	365	232	2 012	3.8	3.7	2005
2010	646	383	74	237	30	10	376	238	1 994	3.4	3.3	2010
2015	634	371	75	243	30	11	308	251	2 014	3.1	2.9	2015
2020	652	380	80	260	31	12	416	263	2 092	2.8	2.7	2020
2025	703	417	85	276	33	12	430	272	2 225	2.7	2.5	2025

(a) Under the assumption of an unchanged 'standard of care'.
(b) Base amount in January 1985: 21,800 SKR. For further explanation, see Table 38.

welfare state: from employers' contributions and taxes towards direct outlays from the user's and consumer's own pockets. Increased contributions from the insured have in recent years been presented as an alternative for financing social insurance. Both model calculations and predictions based on more arbitrary observations, have shakey foundations. Taken together, however, there is no reason to believe that social expenditure will grow as previously in the postwar epoch.

When forecasting social expenditure forty years ahead in the second quarter of the next century, it is worth remembering that approximately 40 years ago at the end of World War II child allowances and basic pensions of the present type. Many other core welfare programs were being considered at that time, but had not yet been decided upon. Although people were at least partly aware of the far-reaching financial consequences of the reforms, noone dreamt of a public sector consuming and redistributing two-thirds of GDP. In 1945 such a figure would have seemed absurd. Social benefits had been upgraded, but were still fairly low by today's standards. In general, there has been no considerable improvement in benefits since 1980. It is to early to predict whether this levelling-off will prove to be a break in the trend or just a pause. Considering the entire postwar period as the basis for projections, social benefits will continue to improve.

The role of the state as a redistributor has changed drastically in the 1970s and 1980s. Redistribution occurs not only through taxes, social benefits and various services, but also through "tax expenditure", such as tax deductions on housing loans, not to mention the rising interest on the public debt (on a par with the social budget in the 1980s). Tax deductions have been limited somewhat in the mid-1980s, but will continue to be the largest form of housing subsidy for the rest of the decade. Over a longer time-span, the whole relationship between social allowances, social services, direct taxes, social security contributions, tax deductions, national debt interests, etc. may be completely reconsidered. The present system is probably too intricate for a single sweeping reform, but here and there changes will be made, that will affect the future of the whole welfare system. From the perspective of the mid-1980s, it is the importance of the "market wage", and not the "social wage", that is emphasized by most leading social actors. In the attempt to restore national price competitiveness, the spending power of pensioners and employees in the public sector ought to be subordinated to those producing export goods. Exactly what kind of social and political responses this will elicit in the next century is an open question hard to predict.

5.3 The Legitimacy of the Welfare State

There is widespread concern in all industrialized Western nations about the legitimacy of public policy, i.e. that citizens have lost their confidence in state redistributory policies. The system of representation is supposed to have been weakened and there has even been talk of a crisis of democracy. A common assumption is that things used to be better, or that there was a consensus on social policy in the affluent societies of the 1960s.[186]

Is Swedish welfare state it facing a crisis of legitimacy? First it should be said that the concept of legitimacy is as ambiguous as the survey data often used to discuss it. Second, that electoral apathy is absent in Sweden: participation in elections has remained high and stable even during the recession.

Concerning the absolute support for the welfare state, very little can be said on the basis of opinion polls. Let us start with an international comparison. In 1983, a survey was made among young people (18-24) in a number of western countries: when asked "What do you think that your country can be proud of?", 62 percent of the young Swedes answered their country's social welfare as compared to 42 percent in Great Britain, 31 percent in Germany and 23 percent in Switzerland. In contrast, French, American and Japanese youngsters were proud of their country's history and cultural heritage, Americans and Japanese also of their science and technology, while Germans held their standard of living in high esteem.[187]

The Statistics Sweden election survey yield a fairly long time-series on the attitude toward "social reforms" (see *Table 40*). Unfortunately, the phrasing and response alternatives were altered after 1979, and the subsequent data underline the methodological problems involved in inquires of this kind. The only point in time (1968) when a majority disagreed with the statement that social reforms have gone too far, coincided with an election in which the Social Democrats, fighting more decisively than ever for "equality", won their highest postwar vote. Since then, the pro-welfare majority has diminished into a minority, which could be interpreted as supporting the thesis of a crisis of legitimacy. On the other hand, 1979 is the only year, in which we find a greater number of opponents than in 1964.

Table 40   Opinions on social reforms in Sweden 1960–1982
                                            Percent distribution

Question:	1964(a)	1968	1970	1973	1976	1979	1980(b)	1982(b)
"Social reforms have gone so far in this country that·in the future the government ought to reduce rather than increase allowances and assistance to citizens."								
Agree	63	42	58	60	61	67	49	45
Disagree	33	51	36	33	32	27	37	40
Don't know	4	7	6	7	7	6	14	15

(a) The original question had also been posed in 1960, but the response alternatives were slightly different. Still the agree/disagree relationship was roughly 60/40 percent.
(b) The question was changed in 1980 (the Referendum survey) and 1982. In those years the respondents had to answer if it was 'very important', 'rather important', 'rather unimportant', or 'very unimportant' for the government to decrease social benefits. Important=agree and unimportant=disagree; 'No matter' and 'no answer' = Don't know.

Similar questions, have also been asked in polls conducted by the leading private opinion institutet (see *Table 41*). Here, too, the stability in response behaviour is remarkable, particularly as one question deals directly with the costs of social programs and the necessity of cuts. Although the gap is only half as big as in 1967, almost half of the respondents still think that existing social programs are not too expensive and should not be cut. Usually, the more specific the questions are about increase and decrease of well-defined social programs, the more support for them. But as long as survey questions are fairly general, selective benefits (as opposed to the universal Swedish system) have a strong backing in opinion polls throughout the postwar era.

From the level-of-living survey (see Section III) there is also a time-series which indicates changes in actions and attitudes towards the welfare system, through both actual attempts to reverse

235

decisions and feelings of unfavourable or unjust treatment. The proportion who actually appealed (in verbal or written forms) almost doubled between 1968 and 1981, (from 16 to 30 percent). It seems, that a growing number of previously regimented Swedes are taking issue with institutions of social control, i.e. that the citizen's "political resources" have increased.[188]

Reported feelings of injustice can be disaggregated and spread over various public welfare authorities (as a reference-point, the police is added). As shown in *Table 44*, the proportion expressing protests is generally very low. However, some increase over the years can be noted. The tax authorities are in a class of their own, with a level above 10 percent for the three years under investigation and growing between 1968 and 1981 from 10 to 16 percent. Second in line come hard feelings created by the social insurance office. Thus, the two most important welfare authorities are most vulnerable to public criticisms. The tax/benefit package is evidently scrutinized from both ends of the welfare state.

Table 41   Swedish attitudes towards social policy, 1955-1978

Percent distribution

	1955(a)	1964	1967	1978
Question:				
"Sweden is known for its social policy. Is there some aspect of this social policy which you dislike or do you generally like it? Which of the following statements comes closest to your opinion?"				
Social policy is generally worth what it costs, but certain features ought to be expanded.	17	19		14
Social policy is generally satisfactory as it is, but means-test ought to apply to more benefits.	46	45		45
Social policy has gone too far; reliance on welfare and a poor sense of responsibility follow in its tracks.	31	33		36
Hesitant, don't know	6	2		6
Question:				
"Do you think that our current social programmes are too expensive and therefore ought to be reduced?"				
Yes			34	39
No			50	47
Don't know			16	14

(a) Approximations of fairly similar questions.

236

Table 42

Attitudes towards the welfare state in Sweden, 1984,
by party affiliation and trade union membership

Percent distribution

Statements:	Party affiliation					Union membership		Total
	Cons.	Lib.	Cent.	SD	Comm.	LO	TCO	
(1) "The public sector is too costly and a threat to the national economy."								
Agree	74	64	69	33	25	48	5	52
Disagree	23	33	30	64	72	47	48	43
Don't know	3	3	1	4	4	5	1	5
(2) "The public sector must be retained at its present level and even expanded."								
Agree	36	52	35	82	87	74	54	62
Disagree	62	46	64	15	14	21	43	35
Don't know	2	3	0	3	0	5	3	3
(3) "Sweden can afford as large a public sector as at present."								
Agree	22	37	29	73	85	56	49	48
Disagree	74	58	69	20	4	30	47	44
Don't know	4	5	2	7	12	14	4	9
(4) "The state is needed to equalize injustices that reproduce themselves in a society like ours."								
Agree	56	73	87	90	79	80	80	75
Disagree	40	23	12	6	17	12	16	19
Don't know	4	5	1	5	4	8	4	7
(5) "Tax pressure today is so high that the individual doesn't feel inclined to work."								
Agree	93	85	77	49	28	67	69	72
Disagree	7	14	22	50	68	31	31	27
Don't know	0	0	0	1	4	2	0	1
(6) "The state has become increasingly despotic at the expense of individual rights."								
Agree	97	92	93	63	64	78	76	81
Disagree	2	7	6	31	34	17	24	15
Don't know	1	0	2	5	2	5	0	4

Characteristic for all the reported time-series on welfare attitudes is that people seems to be slightly less satisfied with the workings of the welfare state in the late 1970s and early 1980s.[189] However, the election survey emphasizes, that the waiting days in sickness insurance were crucial for the Social Democratic victory in 1982. Overall, the relative stability in opinions expressed over the years is palpable. Although not the only aspect of such a far-reaching concept, this might indicate that the crisis of legitimacy either does not exist or is not a new phenomenon. From *Tables 40* and *41* it follows that between a third and two-thirds of the respondents seem to subscribe to the present social programs and regard them as worthwhile.

Is the division between pros and cons a reflection of socio-economic and political cleavages? *Table 43* gives a breakdown of responses to the statement 'social reforms have gone too far' by social group and party affiliation in 1976 and 1979. The anti-welfare trend in the late 1970s is clearly visible. The general support for social reform declined in all social strata, except among farmers where it had already been lowest. The entrepreneurial categories converged in their anti-welfare opinion, and the attitudes among wage earners became more similar as workers' support for social reforms diminished. There is still a clear difference between wage earners and the propertied classes. This cleavage becomes even more evident if a distinction is made between the public and private sector. A recent elaboration of the same data has shown that nowadays it is not the working class but the public white collar employees who constitute the stronghold of welfare state support.[190] This finding has been disputed, however, other analyses emphasizing that differences among wage earners are still fairly small.[191]

The relationships between party preferences and attitudes towards the welfare state seem to be more consistent and obvious. *Table 42* summarizes some results from a Gallup opinion poll in 1984. The figures demonstrate a clear division between the two political blocks of the 1970s and 1980s, the Social Democrats and Communists on the one hand, and the Conservatives, the Liberals and the Center Party on the other. An overwhelming majority of Socialist voters are convinced that Sweden can indeed afford a large public sector and that the present level must be retained or even expanded. In contrast, a great majority of bourgeois voters perceives the public sector as too costly and a threat to the national economy, and believes that tax pressure is so high that the individual doesn't feel inclined to work.

In the Socialist camp, attitudes are more homogeneous than among the three bourgeois parties. The only marked difference between the Social Democrats and Communists is seen in their opinions on tax pressure. The Social Democrats are also somewhat less convinced that Sweden can afford as large a public sector as at

238

Table 43   Responses to the statement that social reforms have gone too far, 1976 and 1979 (a)

(1) by social group (percent distribution)

	Workers		Social group II Salaried employees		Small businessman		Farmers		Social group I (b)	
	1976	1979	1976	1979	1976	1979	1976	1979	1976	1979
Agree	56	64	62	65	72	83	85	81	65	75
Disagree	36	28	32	31	21	14	8	8	31	23
Don't know	8	8	6	4	7	3	7	11	4	2

(2) by party affiliation (percent distribution)

	Communists		Social Democrats		Liberals		Centre Party		Conservatives	
	1976	1979	1976	1979	1976	1979	1976	1979	1976	1979
Agree	27	25	44	53	73	77	78	83	84	90
Disagree	69	70	49	40	23	19	16	11	13	6
Don't know	4	5	8	8	4	2	7	5	3	4

(a) See Table 40.
(b) Persons in managerial positions in private companies and senior civil servants.

present. In the bourgeois camp, the Conservatives clearly have the least favourable attitudes towards the welfare state. This is true in particular with respect to the fourth question which touches the central ideology of the welfare state. Even among the Conservatives, however, a majority shares the opinion that the state is needed to equalize injustices that reproduce themselves in a society like Sweden. In this respect, the Centrists (farmers) are almost as pro as the Social Democrats, and the Liberals have a much more favourable attitude towards an extended public sector than the supporters of the other two bourgeois parties.

On the whole, trade union members position themselves between the two political blocks. This may not be too surprising given the high union density in Sweden. In general, the differences in attitude between the members of the LO (blue collar workers) and the TCO (white collar employees) are small, except that the former support an expanded public sector much more strongly than the latter.

Beyond all these differences, the figures given in *Table 42* also

239

Table 44   Relations between citizens and public authorities, 1968-1981

Question:	1968	1974	1981
Have you once been treated wrongly or unjustly by the:		% answering "Agree"	
Social insurance office	3.5	4.3	5.9
Unemployment insurance	0.5	0.7	0.8
Employment exchange	-	2.1	2.5
Municipal social welfare board	1.9	2.1	2.3
Housing allowance board	-	-	2.7
Hospital or doctor	2.9	5.6	5.5
School	3.2	4.1	3.9
Tax authorities	10.3	14.2	16.1
Immigration office	-	-	0.2
Police	2.5	2.8	3.5

reflect a basic ambivalence in the attitudes of the great population majority towards the welfare state. Three fourths of the population think that the state is needed to equalize injusticies; however, similar majorities not only complain about an excessively high tax pressure, but also agree with the statement that the state has become increasingly despotic at the expense of individual rights. Even among the usually much more defensive supporters of the Socialist parties, this opinion is shared by a majority of almost two thirds.

Public approval of social policy is obviously not as strong as it was a decade or two ago. In particular, it is more questioned among Centre-Rightists. The data in this section, however, do not support the thesis that the general credibility of the welfare state has eroded in recent years (at least not among its old friends, although even former convicts show signs of reluctance). The impertinent question 'who loves the social engineers of the welfare state?' is posed nowadays in the midst of the etatist party. There are also signs that point towards a growing cleavage between persons dependent upon the private and the public sector. More important, however, is that survey results bring to the fore the longstanding differences between various ideological camps, which may have been rather silently expressed in Parliament and by the major interest organizations at the high-tide of economic growth and welfare state expansion from the mid-1960s to early 1970s. In the mid-1980s, the Social Democrats are consciously backing the theme

240

of consolidation of the public sector. In general, differences between parties and interest organizations have increased and what seemed to be a consensus on the Swedish model has partly withered away in the 1980s. But do the present conflicts over welfare state developments really indicate that the model is outdated and will go through a metamorphosis?

5.4 The Future of the Welfare State

There can be no doubt that the welfare state has contributed a great deal in terms of the abolition of extreme poverty and starvation, the creation of a safetynet to alleviate sufferings caused by economic downturns, personal misfortunes and impecunious old age, and the promotion of equality, dignity and self-respect among the great majority of the population. Like most utopias that set out to create happiness and human well-being, however, it has built-in discords that sooner or later reach the audience.

The welfare state as a unified system has lost part of its grandeur and attraction, even among its former adherents. Central planning and the rationality of social engineering are less valued the early 1980s than some decades ago. Concerns about the individual's social rights are now much more widespread and part of a suspiciousness against the likelihood of just bureaucratic rule. Many themes in this controversy are a familiar ingredient of the contemporary debate in most western countries about the individual's opportunities in an increasingly technocratic and bureaucratic society. While most of those leaning towards the Left tend to emphasize security as an important aspect of freedom – freedom from unemployment and other economic risks – those drifting in the opposite direction often stress the intrinsic value of liberty, maintaining that without liberty there can be no security.[192] But also many intellectuals from the New Left of the 1960s underline the necessity of freedom from the authoritarian state.[193]

Public reorganization and revitalization are on the agenda in Sweden in the 1980s. The present government is actively promoting decentralization and freedom for local initiatives in the public sector, in contrast to earlier centralist tendencies. In 1983 Parliament declared several municipalities and a few county councils as

"free zones for administrative experimentation".[194] Deprofessionaliz-
ation is cautiously being encouraged. Still, the steps taken are not
uncontroversial. To the mainstream Left, liberty often means a
choice between various public alternatives available to the individual, whereas neo-Liberals of the 1980s argue for genuinely
private alternatives to public services.

In the 1980s, social reform has been halted in the light of weak
economic growth and the public deficit. Even with a variety of
"automatic" increases in pension, health and unemployment expenditures, the increase in social expenditure is no longer accelerating.
Any reforms must be financed "from within", by reconstructing
existing programs as there is no new money for social reforms. Still
the social budget is voluminous, and a sizeable proportion of the
GDP, whichever way it is calculated, is spent by the welfare state.
There may be talk of and even proposals for social dismantling,
but whether the welfare state is measured in fiscal terms or in
numbers of clients, providers and beneficiaries, it remains a corner-
stone of Swedish society.

The "welfare classes" (public employees, pensioners, etc.) make
up the majority of the electorate in the mid-1980s. The present
universal system is likely to be defended, in one way or another, by
most of its beneficiaries. On the other hand, some opportunities
will surely arise for those who would like to split the system up,
and one can hardly expect there to be a united front on all the
borders of the welfare state.

Although the comprehensive features of the welfare state are not
seriously questioned, even small adjustments, such as cuts and
reduced social benefits may, taken together, have important repercussions on the overall structure in the long run. The tolerated
limit of unemployment might be upgraded not only from 2 to 3
percent, as has happened in the 1980s, but higher, even much
higher, resulting in a much less active manpower policy. Selectivity may be introduced here and there, and finally become a governing principle in the whole income maintenance system. Decentralization may be promoted to the extent that it endangers the nation-
wide, unifying elements. The present model might be consolidated,
in either a creative or a petrifying manner. Ways may be found,
and some are already trodden, whereby welfare implies more freedom of choice and less of standardized, "despotic" rules.[195] More

242

radical alternatives may also see the light of day. The green alternative may again shine more brightly than at present,[196] and some form of feminist alternatives is not wholly unlikely in a welfare system, where a majority of the employees are subordinated, but unionized women. The future is open, but one can be certain that the process of change will involve conflicts over the alternatives. The outcomes and compromises over various small issues, will be determined by the possible coalitions and power structures of the day, and this in turn will affect the future distribution of power as well as the distribution of equality, security and even poverty.

From the start of this chapter, the historical dimensions of the Swedish welfare state have been emphasized. In his maiden speech in Parliament in 1987, Hjalmar Branting, the founding father of Swedish Social Democracy and later Nobel Peace Prize winner, announced a coupling of military and social reforms.[197] A few years later, the restructuring of the old conscript army was accepted in exchange for the first steps towards social and political rights in the modern sense. Almost a century later, defence and social reform might again become a battleground for new coalitions and compromises in a situation where pressure for increased military expenditure is excerted against the background of a changing military-political set-up in Northern Europe. It is not the most likely scenario, but worth considering in order to dispell the impression that only international economic developments and export prices influence the future of the Swedish welfare state.

As noted earlier, developments associated with World War II launched the postwar model of the welfare state. Industrial and technological improvements were getting underway just at a time when Sweden was virtually the only European country with an intact production structure. The strategies of the Employers' Confederation, the Labour Movement and the farmers largely coincided. This "historical compromise" was a unique constellation and an unbeatable combination for the years ahead in which Sweden became one of the world's leading export countries. Some of the advantages of the "historical compromise" have disappeared, others are still at work today. In the mid-1980s, both the political blocks aim to renew the exportled growth strategy, but it has proved difficult to unite various social forces behind this goal. However, the role of the welfare state is rather different in the two strategies:

243

metaphorically, it has been described as the difference between a leaky bucket and an irrigation system.[198] Still, the welfare state is only one of the problems in a new mix, a refurbished Swedish model.

Whatever the options, the welfare state is there. It has a history, and reached its first zenith only ten years ago, during the hung Parliament and the Haga negotiations between government, opposition and all the major interest organizations.[199] Therefore, it is not particularly likely to disappear overnight. Much more probable is the start of a *longue durée*. The maturation process may prove more difficult. If the welfare state will turn out to be that "whistle stop of the road to socialism", as the old Minister of Finance Ernst Wigforss once claimed, or just a dead end street, remains to be seen.[200] Although the workings of its destiny are largely unknown, for the foreseeable future the welfare state is definitely here to stay.

IV. The Dialectics of Decentralization and Privatization

1. Introduction: Decentralization and Privatization – Alternatives to the Welfare State Paradigm?

The welfare state – a state which assumes responsibility for citizen welfare in the context of a market economy and a plural polity – grew rapidly in the 1960s in the overwhelming majority of the developed market countries and matured in most of them a decade later.* For a short while, the welfare state looked like an integral element of Western Society, the outcome of a harmonious marriage between capitalism and democracy. Thus, a non-conflictual relationship between state and civil society was assumed in the early postwar discussion on the development of the welfare state (cf. Briggs 1961). An all-embracing state of this type generally consists not only of a broad system for income protection in connection with illness, disability, unemployment, childbirth/rearing, and old age – transfers constituting a social security state – but also of a variety of public goods or a social consumption sector – the social service state of education, health, housing, personal social services etc. In a few of these countries, these domains of state activity were enlarged even further with an institutionalized commitment to full employment, keeping unemployment at a very low level.[1]

At the turn of the 1970s, however, the shifting and amorphous boundaries of the welfare state came under attack from various directions: social reform through state intervention in the process of distribution – the welfare state *strategy* – became troublesome in conjunction with weak economic growth and mounting public deficits. The early prophesy of James O'Connor – the breakdown of state finance – was suddenly not an exaggerated scenario even for advanced Western countries (O'Connor 1973). Real growth in social expenditure had for most of the postwar period been financed from the increment of real national income often without making the re-distributional conflicts or policy trade-offs in resource allocation explicit. For most of these countries and for most of the first postwar decades, there was often a balance between income and expenditures in the public budget, or at least the balance between the two was under control. Already in the mid-1960s, Harold Wilensky talked about the possibility of a "welfare backlash", but he had to wait a decade until the tax revolts started (Wilensky & Lebaux 1965; Wilensky 1975). During the 1970s with low economic growth the increased need for social expenditure had to confront questions about the tax capacity of the Nation, the impact on the labour market of unemployment benefits, the role of old age pensions in altering saving habits, etc. From the late 1970s onwards, both left and right-wing governments started to make tougher economic decisions concerning welfare. Several authors have argued that the current trend to curb public expenditure has been universal and largely uniform. It was initially carried out by governments lacking an outspoken neo-liberal ideology (Tarschys 1985). In contrast, the new governments of 1979 and 1980 in the United Kingdom and United States respectively, had a fundamental belief in the need to shift the boundaries of public and private activity. They saw these measures as not only necessary but also as positively desirable (O'Higgins & Ruggles 1985). To many observers, the postwar welfare state carnival was over.

Although O'Connor's prophesy has so far not been fulfilled, social security and other public commitments have been pruned in many highly industrialized Western democracies in the 1980s. The crucial full employment target, for example, has in several countries been downgraded on political priority lists, and has had to give way to the anti-inflation goal or similar governmental redefinitions (Therborn 1985, Esping-Andersen 1986). This has given rise to a major debate on the "crisis", "end" and "future" of the welfare state (OECD 1981). Many social scientists have pointed to the profound conflicts and contradictions between an ever-expanding state sector (for example in terms of GDP, personnel, legislative regulations, etc) and the workings of civil society in general and the competitive market sphere in particular (Mommsen 1981, in particular part IV). Although the question of *limits* has accompanied the welfare state ever since its modest beginnings, social

246

scientists seem to be much more aware of them from the early 1980s (Flora 1981a).

Authors close to mainstream economic theory, have often argued that there exists a critical threshold, beyond which lies dangerous territory: increased state regulation of economic life threatens to destroy the very foundations of the well-being of the welfare state, the efficiency of the economic system, i.e. economic growth potentials. The high level of taxation that is necessary to finance a burgeoning public sector is a threat to the smooth functioning of the market mechanisms. In particular high marginal tax rates – decreasing wage differentials – drain resources from high-tax to low-tax sectors, and act as barriers to GDP growth. Examples of such negative or "disincentive" effects are the tendencies to choose leisure instead of work for payment, do-it-yourself work, pursuance of – legal – tax evasion, etc. Although authors in this tradition have changed the exact point of no return through the years, the public spending levels observed in welfare states in the 1980s, such as the Low countries and Scandinavia, are recognized as being on the threshold of darkness (Lindbeck 1981). Furthermore, organized interest groups like unions interfere in the free play of the market forces to such an extent that economic efficiency is retarded. This power of special-interest groups hinders overall growth, making the economy unproductive and the political system ungovernable (Olson 1982). A general slow-down in adaptation to changing conditions characterizes the centralized decison-making procedures of advanced welfare states. Apart from this "institutional sclerosis", another idea prevalent in these circles is that the growth of the public sector "crowds out" investments and labour supply from the private sector. In a normative discourse, authors in this tradition have argued that increased incentives for private initiatives and a limitation of state activities would be a solution to the crisis of the welfare state.

If "less state – more market" is a brief summary of the first approach, a second approach – typical for the German critical tradition especially – shares some but not all of the basic characteristics just mentioned, and can be abstracted to "less state – more civil society". Claus Offe and Jürgen Habermas no longer paint the future of the welfare state as a happy marriage between democracy and capitalism, but as the condition for their painful and conflict-filled divorce. According to Offe – as well as Christine Buci-Glucks-mann (1982) – the days of the Keynesian welfare state are numbered due to the same negative effects that the traditional economists point out: the welfare state is undermining both the incentive to invest and to work, and in it, undisciplined organized interests take command over economic reason. Analytically, the limits of the welfare state should be defined as those points at which either capitalist societies turn non-democratic, or democratic regimes turn non-capitalist (Offe 1984:80). Habermas poses the problem slightly less revolutionary: it is not only the problems caused by the recent economic recession that endanger the future of the welfare state, but also its very success – the work society utopia or social state project in the words of the Frankfurt theorist (Habermas 1985). In the process of distribution political intervention has changed on a qualitative level from being a successful mean towards the end of equalization, to an instrument of deceptive rationalization which depopulates the competitive business sector of jobs. By enlarging the activities of the state through political intervention in the process of job creation, another negative effect of the welfare state strategy is highlighted. The lives of individuals become even more regulated by the state bureaucracy, and, as the impossibility of full employment in advanced Western societies has been shown during the 1970s and 1980s, the progressive potential of the social state project is depleted. Instead of making people more dependant on the bureaucracy, Habermas and Offe have argued for the necessity to overcome the work society utopia by de-bureaucratization and by strengthening the everyday life-spheres. Increased solidarity in these life-spheres of civil society can give a new, less work and state-centered, welfare paradigm legitimacy. A new social state with street level bureaucrats or social networks appears as an alternative to welfare-state management (Eräsaari 1986). These ideas are quite close to a perspective on the welfare state put forward by Durk-heimian-inspired sociologists like Morris Janowitz (1976), who argue that a swelling public bureaucracy weakens the integrative functions of intermediary structures like the family and the local community, promotes anomic tendencies by inflating expectations, and by individualizing benefits also encourages selfishness. To Janowitz, increased self-regulation and a greater citizen participa-tion is required to avoid a drift towards reliance on coercive control. Otherwise, the welfare state will transcend into a control state with increased reporting, inquiry, and control of the lives of the citizens, and where the burden of proof of innocence will increasingly lie with the individual himself.

A third approach puts the boundary question very differently: despite the fact that the welfare state came into the critical forefront during the economic recession from the mid-1970s – switched from being a "solver" to a "generator" of crisis – and despite the fact that "the growth party is over", this type of state is today an irreversible element of advanced modern societies which is highly unlikely to disappear. Although not a fixed entity, the welfare state has drawn up fairly clear demarcation lines against the competitive market sphere, which of course vary between countries but are unlikely to change considerably. At least as long as democracy prevails, it is impossible to build an anti-welfare coalition that can carry out the promised cuts in public expenditure and public bureaucracies (Therborn & Roebroek 1986). The Reagan Revolution failed before the end of the Reagan presidency – the lame duck hypothesis once again proved to be truth!

These three hypotheses have a certain functionalist flavour in common, an inherent determinism in the logic of the development of the welfare state. But their divergence points to the analytical necessity of distinguishing on one hand between the state and the market, and on the other between the public sector and the private sphere, the latter including much more than work for payment and similar commodified social relationships. These distinctions are much more important to make as there is a tendency in the present controversy over the welfare state to pose its "crisis" in a dichotomous way (Mishra 1985). In particular, the internal cleavages, both on the right and left spectrum of politics, are ignored. The focus on the dramatic aspects of the New Right challenge, the political rhetoric of Thatcher and Reagan, and the theoretical anti-keynesianism associated with such names as von Hayek and Friedman, tends to reduce the alternatives and policy responses (Miller 1986). In particular in an article that like the present focusses on decentralization and privatization as alternative modes of welfare administration, this is obviously necessary to emphasize.

The starting-point of this article is none of the above-mentioned three hypotheses, but a power resource perspective, or a "political class struggle approach" (Hedström 1986). Responding to the dominant pluralist paradigm of the 1950s and the neo-marxist challenge of the 1960s, this approach denies both the consensual balance-of-power-perspective of the former, and the state-power-monopoly-idea inherent in the latter, and emphasizes the possibility of affecting state policies and state institutions by collective, unified action. Thus, the state is not only conditioned by changing social power relationships, but also regulates and legitimizes the execution of power – whether visible or not – in various sectors of civil society. According to the political class struggle approach, the major types of basic power resources in capitalist democracies are, on the one hand, control over capital and the means of production, and, on the other, control over "human capital" and the ability of wage-earners and other subordinated social stratas to form industrial and political organizations which make possible collective action. Because the basic nature of their power resources is different, a fruitful hypothesis is that in comparison with employers and business interests, wage-earners are generally at a disadvantage with respect to power resources but that, through their capacity for collective action, the extent of their disadvantage may vary over time as well as between countries (Korpi 1986). The activities of the state thus reflect the actual distribution of power resources between the major collectives or classes in society, and the state is consequently seen as an arena of political class struggle, and not only as an instrument of class interest (Himmelstrand et al. 1981). In this perspective, the role of political factors in the shaping of governmental intervention in protection from the insecurities and hardships of an unrestrained market economy is underlined. The welfare state is neither seen as a gift from above by the well-to-do in prosperous nations, nor as a functional necessity in an advanced capitalist society. The role of politics in the making of the welfare state has been there from its very first beginning. The famous example is of course the two-legged strategy employed by Prince Otto von Bismarck in Imperial Germany in the last quarter of the nineteenth century: repressive measures against the means for working class collective action – the political party (Social Democracy) – but on the other hand the institutionalisation of a, for its time, generous but selectivist social insurance program (for the industrial working class). The present-day universalistic or institu-

250

tional welfare state model is in this article regarded as the result of a more or less conscious – but not everywhere achieved – political strategy employed by the left spectrum of Occidental politics, but influenced by the overall distribution of power resources in these societies (Titmuss 1974, Korpi 1980).

In contrast to the universalistic model, both *decentralization* and *privatization* have been launched as alternative strategies to the prevailing mode of organizing social security, social services, and full employment in most Western democracies in the last quarter of the 20th century (Friedmann et al. 1987). What do these notions actually stand for? None of them have a precise definition, and it is important to emphasize, that both of them are overloaded with ideological symbolism. Throughout the Western World, privatization – sometimes reprivatization – is the well-known theme of the New Right. The public sector is indicted as the root of most social evils in affluent but crisis-ridden societies. It is too big and ungovernable, overburdened with obligations, responsibilities and expectations. Supposedly a problem-solver, it is now creating more problems than it solves. The strategy of privatization – the answer to these new problems according to these spokesmen – implies the deregulation and commercialization of previously publicly provided goods, services and transfers, all of which should be switched from bureaucratic agencies to competitive private enterprises. According to this view, such a turn will promote a revival of work ethic and a resurgence of traditional values.

Superficially, the strategy of decentralization is less politically partisan and consequently less controversial. But it can be interpreted in very different ways. The advocates of privatization have tried to sequester it, too. They regard the old hegemonic etatist welfare state strategy as highly centralized (bureaucratic) and see the market as a consumer-oriented instrument for decentralized, individual freedom of choice and action. For example, when decreased private savings are substituted by an increase in centralized social security funds, this may have discouraging effects on the emergence of private entrepreneurship as the availability of local supply of credit may disappear. In this perspective, pluralism in culture and society is encouraged by a decentralized economic decision-making.

Other outspoken friends of decentralization do not at all share the privatizer's view. In Western Europe at least, decentralization is more often equated with the emerging social movements of a more or less "green" character – of ecological, environmentalist, and feminist ad hoc groups and constellations. To them, big business is as centralized as the welfare state, and modern market liberties imaginary. To use the language of T.S. Marshall (1964), it was not necessarily property rights which were lost with the advent of the centralized welfare state, but civil and political rights. In the "green" perspective, the state is too remote and unsuitable as an organization for catering for the needs of the local citizenry. In a feminist perspective, the present-day welfare state is an oppressing force acting against its low-paid female employees as well as disfavouring its women beneficiaries (Wilson 1977, Land 1986).

Democratization, de-bureaucratisation, participation, voluntarism, self-management, mutual aid, and local decision-making are key-words for the strategy of the new social movements. Decentraliz-ation is given a non-commodified meaning, and thus a strategy embedded in civil society. For example, under the provocative slogan of "the progressive potential of privatization", Donald Donnison in a single strike tries to grab the notion of privatization out of the hands of the privatizers, and simultaneously attack the "conservative" defenders of the welfare state. The self-interest of the providers of public goods, services, and transfers is pitched against the interests and needs of welfare consumers, claimants, clients, tax-payers and even sovereign voters. Private profit, not private initiative, is the main demarcation line between the two new strategies. Many old-style state services are in need of a stronger economic orientation (equity and efficiency), area focus and com-munity base. Too often, different public services are badly co-ordinated, and show insufficient sensitivity to local needs and feelings. These services are in the hands of the producers, while the influence of consumers is low. If their opponents do not like the – real – Conservatives' medicine for these ills, they should be pre-pared to suggest alternative remedies, not only a restoration of the previous regime. They must find new solutions if their association with the welfare state is not going to lead to declining popularity. Decentralization is a more constructive response to the major defects to which the neo-liberal theme of privatization initially was addressed concludes the author (Donnison 1984).

Thus, as is illustrated in *graph 1*, both the notion of decentralization and of privatization point to a change within the welfare state which is signified by a movement from the central to the de-central. Furthermore, they point towards changing boundaries of the market economy as well as between and within the private and public spheres.[2] By looking at these tendencies from the angle of the central state, the discussion of decentralization will primarily focus not on the non-etatist life-spheres of civil society singled out by authors like Offe and Habermas, but, as Donnison suggests, on a shift of formal responsibility within the (Swedish) state, from

Graph 1. Spheres of change: Decentralization and privatization as tendencies within the welfare state/society context. The (central) welfare state

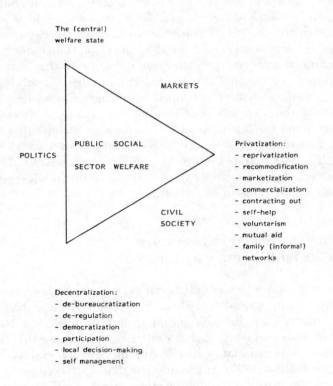

The (central)
welfare state

MARKETS

POLITICS

PUBLIC   SOCIAL

SECTOR   WELFARE

CIVIL
SOCIETY

Privatization:
- reprivatization
- recommodification
- marketization
- commercialization
- contracting out
- self-help
- voluntarism
- mutual aid
- family (informal) networks

Decentralization:
- de-bureaucratization
- de-regulation
- democratization
- participation
- local decision-making
- self management

253

central to local government (section four). The kind of intermediary structures that are in the forefront of the German discussion, will be considered to be within the private sphere, although at a kind of border-zone between private and public (section five). When discussing privatization (section three), the focus will be on attempts to privatize earlier public tasks and to do so in a commercialized form, i.e. marketization. But we will also look for the possibilities that facilitate private initiatives, when the public sector imposes limits on its own activities (apart from section three, see especially four/one).

The emphasis on both decentralization and privatization make possible a discussion of various developments in the wake of the crisis for the centralist welfare state strategy. But as decentralization and privatization appear simultaneously at a moment when the welfare state is said to be in crisis, the oldfashioned and outmoded Hegelian concept of dialectics has been employed in the title of this article in order to stress the interaction between the two tendencies. With the ambition to avoid the above-mentioned dichotomy threat, decentralization and privatization throughout this article will nevertheless be treated as separate trends, as distinct developments in the welfare society. This must be strongly emphasized, in particular as the advocates of privatization consider that their strategy incapsulates the other one (decentralization), a claim that at most is a half-truth. First of all, however, the actual course of the Swedish welfare state itself in the 1980s will be considered (section two). This can be regarded as a follow-up of the trends reported in earlier studies (Olsson 1986, 1987b).

2. Swedish Social Expenditure and Social Programs in the 1980s

In general, advocates as well as critics have pointed out Sweden as the very best example of where the welfare strategy has reaped triumphs (Childs 1936; Tomason 1970; Huntford 197). No other welfare state can boast such a perfect concordance with Titmuss' famous "institutional redistributive model of social policy" as Sweden (Mishra 1977). For a little less than half a century, Sweden was almost uninterruptedly governed by a Labour cabinet drawn from a party closely affiliated with a well-organized blue collar trade union movement. However, for most of this period, the government needed support in Parliament from either a party to the right – most often the Agrarian Center Party – or the small Communist party to its left. But it was under a Social Democratic Premier the welfare state was built up, and the party came to be identified with this development. However, in 1976, this exceptional political stability came to an end, and during six years, up till 1982 when the Social Democrats regained the helm, Sweden was ruled by four consecutive bourgeois cabinets. What has happened to the welfare state during these recent years of relative instability?

The institutional social framework that was built up over some four decades is still a living reality. Broad sectors of society regard and defend this framework as an irreversible achievement of late 20th century Sweden, providing employment and benefits in kind and cash according to universalistic principles (LO 1986). It is indicative, for instance, that transfer income corresponded to one quarter of total private consumption in 1984 (Regeringens proposition 1985/86:00). Most residents draw on this pool, although some groups – singles and couples who are healthy and have no dependent children – may only pay in taxes and social payroll contributions to the social security network. But sooner or later most of them will also receive benefits from either the health insurance system or the pension programs.

The major change connected with the Swedish welfare state is the halt at the turn of the 1970s in social expenditure's rising trend (*graph 2*).[3] Since 1980, total outlays on social programs have stagnated in real terms. As a share of GDP, social expenditure has been fairly constant at just over thirty per cent. In this (limited) bookkeeper-perspective the Swedish pattern is not that far from the overall development of western welfare states, but it is characterized by stagnation, not decline. (The graph includes most welfare programs at central and local levels, major exceptions being public spending on education and some housing items, mainly 'tax expenditures'.)

A breakdown of social expenditure reveals a varied picture. Some small items, like occupational injury insurance, follow the overall trend but otherwise the differences are considerable. *Graph 3*

Graph 2. Social expenditures 1950, 1960-1985 and their financing. Billion SEK. Constant (1950) prices. Source: "The Cost and Financing of the Social Services in Sweden 1985, Statistics Sweden S 42 SM 8701.

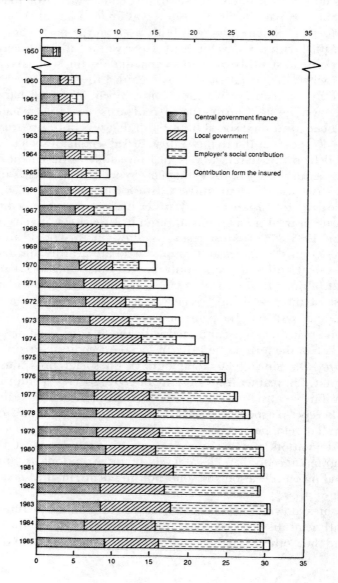

illustrates the development in the 1980s of the major social security programs – mainly highly centralized cash benefit programs that have scarcely been affected by privatization and/or decentralization. It concerns current price outlays on most social insurance programs – except unemployment and family support. The only sizeable changes in this half-decade are the growing share for the National Superannuation Pension scheme (which covers the total labour force), and a decline for partial pensions (early part-time retirement from the age of 60). The latter is actually one of the few apparent consequences of cuts in social insurance programs: as of 1981 the benefit level was reduced from 65 to 50 percent of previous earnings, and from 1980 to 1985 the number of partial pensioners has diminished from 27 to 10 percent of those eligible. This benefit will be restored to its initial level in 1987.

The growth of Superannuation Pension expenditure reflects the maturation of this system, as well as the growing number of persons, women in particular, with pension rights. Rising superannuation payments lead automatically to falling expenditure on municipal housing allowances (decreased from over 800 000 beneficiaries to an estimated 600 000 pensioners in 1986) and on the general increment to the basic pension (paid to retired persons with little or no superannuation entitlement – see below). In real terms, the average annual expenditure growth rate in the first half of the 1980s is well above 5 percent. This program is entirely financed with fees from employers.

Outgone payments from the basic pension scheme, which included a variety of benefits including the housing allowance and the general increment and covers the entire population resident in Sweden, thus show a decline in real terms (1980 prices), from 33 billions to 31.6. Just under three-quarters of the total outlay goes to old-age pensions (*graph 4*), an indexed, flat-rate benefit (different for singles and couples) generally paid from the retirement age of 65. Roughly two million people received a basic pension in early 1987, out of a total population of 8.3 million. A majority of these, 1.5 million, are old-age pensioners and one million also received a Superannuation pension. Some 745 000 persons got the general pension increment, which indicates that almost a quarter of a million old-age pensioners had a rather small Superannuation entitlement. Other major benefits in the basic pension scheme are

Graph 3. Social insurance excl. family support 1980-1985. Source: The Swedish Budget 1986-87.

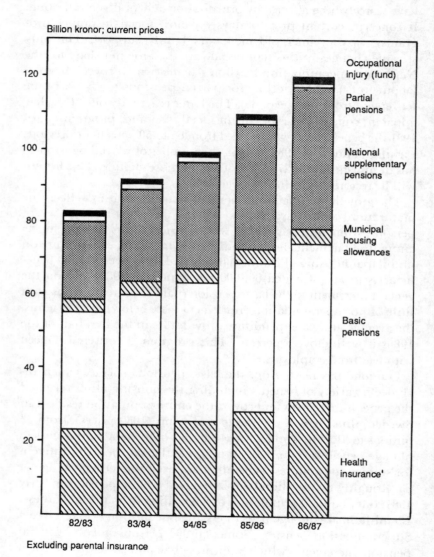

Billion kronor; current prices

Occupational injury (fund)

Partial pensions

National supplementary pensions

Municipal housing allowances

Basic pensions

Health insurance'

82/83   83/84   84/85   85/86   86/87

Excluding parental insurance

Graph 4. Basic pension system 1985/86, m.kr. Total expenditure; 45,353 (current prices). Source: The Swedish Budget 1985-86 p. 86.

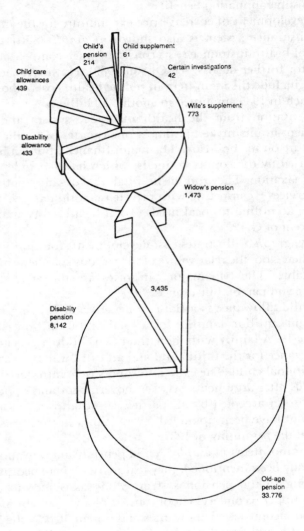

the disability pension and the family (widows and orphans) pension. Disability pensioners number some 300 000, of whom 270 000 receive a superannuation benefit.

The development of current price expenditure for the universal health insurance system is also shown in *graph 3*. Roughly 55 percent of health insurance costs consist of wage compensation for illness (for further details, see Olsson 1989). However, the graph does not include the main item in public health costs – hospitals, etc – which in 1985 amounted to another 50 billion.

Compensation from the health insurance system and direct government grants make up almost one-quarter of public health expenditure on medical care. The major financial burden is, however, carried by the county councils, which have an independent power of taxation. They run the hospitals and organize out-patient health services – competing with private practitioners, see part 3.4 and 3.5 – according to local needs. Total health costs amount to nine percent of GDP.

Finally, *graph 5* illustrates cost-developments for family allowances. There, too, the relative size of the various sub-items has been rather stable. The two major categories are the general child allowance and parental insurance.

The child allowance is a flat-rate benefit and is being paid to roughly one million families for a total of 1.6 million children under age 16. A family with more than two children gets an extra half allowance for the third child and an extra full allowance for each additional child. The extra allowances were introduced in the early 1980s after arguments between government and opposition but were soon accepted by all parties. Child allowances are not indexed but have been upgraded several times in the 1980s, most recently at the beginning of 1987.

Of the minor items in *graph 5*, child pension and care allowance have already been mentioned; they feature twice here because they also belong to the pension system. Study assistance to pupils attending upper secondary school consists of a variety of universal, means and income-tested allowances and is regulated by the Ministry of Health and Social Affairs. The Ministry of Education and Cultural Affairs administers similar economic support to students both in secondary and tertiary education – mainly in the form of long-term loans with a low, fixed rate of interest but also some

Graph 5. Government support for families 1982/83-1986/87.[1] Billion kronor; current prices. Source: The Swedish Budget 1986-1987.

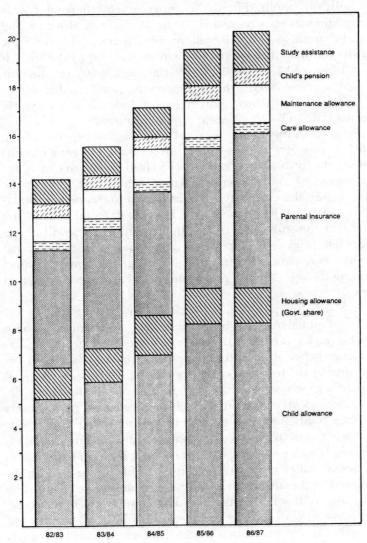

1. In addition, a grant-in aid is provided for child-minding facilities.

universal grants; the total exceeds 7 billion SEK in 1986/87 (not shown in the graph). Their repayment has in recent time created some political unrest. Finally the government share of family housing allowances is regulated by the Ministry of Housing and Physical Planning but distributed by municipal social authorities. With the municipal share (not shown in the graph) the total is some 3 billion SEK in 1986/87. Well above 300 000 low-income households were receiving this income-tested benefit (a decrease by half since the mid-1970s), which is not indexed but is yearly augmented, when both income and rent ceilings are also raised.

Parental insurance is the second largest family expenditure in *graph 5*. It provides income protection for a total of nine months following the birth – or adoption – of a child at the same earnings replacement rate as the parent's sickness cash benefit, and is to be utilized before the child's fourth birthday (plus some additional benefits which can be utilized up to age 12). Parental benefits are financed in the same way as health insurance. Expenditure on day-care facilities – financed out of general central and local taxation – is not included in *graph 5*. Altogether family support (including the municipal share) is almost twice the level shown in the graph.

Have Swedish social welfare benefits been characterized by less generosity and harsher tests in the 1980s? Has more emphasis been placed on the recipient's willingness to work? More generally, has the balance between growth and welfare tipped in favour of the former during the long recession from the mid-1970s? Must social outlays now give a better return than in the years of affluence?

Of course, social expenditure has been scrutinized more closely than when public revenues were continuously rising. But in one sense, these questions are wrongly phrased for Sweden. The fact is that Swedish welfare policy has always been keen on readiness to work. Social policy must pay at all times. This has to do with the part played by the unemployment question, and more recently, by employment policy in Swedish politics. Comparatively speaking, unemployment cash support has been rather low and hard to get. From early this century, state support has been provided primarily for municipal job creation rather than being disbursed to individual recipients. Responsibility for unemployment lay with the state, not the individual. This was further developed and strengthened by the Left when the Social Democrats began to manage state finance, and employment policy came to be dominated by the trade unions.

When a Labour-led cabinet started almost half a century of government in the early 1930s, its main program concerned employment issues. In a decade or two these concerns were transformed into a full employment policy, known as the Rehn-Meidner plan after the trade union economists who drafted it against the Social Democratic cabinet's income policy. This policy has been expanded since the 1960s, and, particularly during the recession in the late 1970s and early 1980s has its contribution to the low Swedish unemployment level been significant. As a consequence, the boundary between economic and social policy was transcended. Simultaneously, a Protestant work ethic was integrated with the egalitarian aims of Socialist Labour ideology. The right-to-work ideology of Swedish social democracy is miles away from the right-to-laziness vision of Paul Lafargue and the Second International.

In quite another sense, the questions posed above highlight some pertinent problems in Swedish society. For a long time the development of social assistance – the last resort in the welfare system – followed unemployment fairly closely. In the 1980s, however, unemployment has decreased but social assistance has continued to rise. For almost two decades recipients of social assistance made up roughly four to five per cent of the relevant population, depending on the employment situation. Since 1980, the number in need of social assistance has risen by more than 180 000 persons to over seven per cent. Disbursements have more than doubled. Cuts in and more restrictive rules concerning housing allowances have been singled out as one explanation. Singles without children have been deprived of their entitlements. And this category is the one that has grown remarkably among recipients of social assistance in the 1980s according to two different public investigations (Ds Fi 1986; Ds S 1986). Part of the rapid increase is probably a consequence of the difficulties that have beset the Swedish economy since the mid-1970s. Many people were forced into unemployment or retraining. Many others with parttime jobs, who for financial reasons would have worked longer hours, had no opportunity of doing so. They may still have problems because the recovery of employment since 1984 has consisted entirely of full-time jobs, and an adjustment to the new situation takes time. Some improvement in real earnings has occurred since then, but for many part-time workers – such as single mothers – this has probably not sufficed to reduce outside support.

3. The Absence of Privatization in Sweden

Privatization as a general theme has been preached in Sweden during the 1980s as a general alternative to the old and – according to New Right or neo-liberal spokesmen – outdated Swedish model. Outside Parliament, one of the chief partners in Sweden's "historical compromise", the Employers Confederation, conducted a major ideological onslaught on the principles behind the welfare state from the late 1970s. The background was the changing political climate. Six months after the installation of the first Center-Right cabinet in almost half a century, the business community swiftly reacted to the changing balance of forces. In bargaining negotiations with the Trade Union Confederation in early 1977, the Employers Confederation took a hawkish, rigid stand under a new and more determined leadership, unprecedented since the early 1930s not only with regard to wage demands but also on recently legislated issues. Revisions of the rules governing sickness cash benefits, as well as on working and vacation time, were demanded by the Employers (Himmelstrand 1982). The Employers were also provoked, of course, by the Trade Union Confederation's proposal to introduce wage-earner funds. Socialism, even in the mild and friendly form presented by Swedish Social Democrats, has never been popular in the eyes of capitalists.

After the September election in 1979, which left the Center-Right parties with a majority of one in Parliament, the Employers Confederation started to publish a series of preparatory documents for its Congress in late 1980 (Westholm 1979-80). Experts closely affiliated with the organization presented solutions that, in the Swedish context, are highly controversial, such as competition in protected areas like childcare, privatization of sickness insurance, and a reinforcement of the role of private practitioners in health services. With these proposals, and the translation of books like Henri Lepage's *Demain le capitalisme* (1981) and von Hayek's *The Road to Serfdom* (1984), the Employers succeeded in engendering a major debate on the future of welfare and social institutions. A libertarian ideology has deliberately been distributed by the Association which has succeeded in influencing a growing number of dissatisfied intellectuals, in particular former old and new leftists and young new rightists. A few days before its Congress began, a senior official of the Confederation published a chronicle in the leading Stockholm morning paper, the independent, left-liberal *Dagens Nyheter*, in which he suggested a complete "minimal state" in Nozick's sense, responsible only for defence, law and order – a scenario quite unfamiliar to Swedish customs (1980-11-04). This marked the culmination of the campaign although it was further fuelled when the Moderates adopted a new party program in 1984, which contains clearly neo-liberal elements. The ideological campaign was never implemented on any scale but a few models of new private welfare have consciously been instituted. As these are the most discussed signs of privatization in an otherwise etatist welfare society, these cases will be scrutinized in the coming pages.[4] In doing this, we will follow the terminology adopted by Titmuss (1958) and distinguish between occupational, fiscal and private welfare as alternatives to social (etatist) welfare. First, however, we will discuss less organized developments on the pension insurance and housing markets.

3.1 Private Pension Insurance: The Rise of Occupational Welfare

Private alternatives for old age and invalidity have not been that rare in Sweden, and have a history that parallels the development of state pensions. Life insurance companies were set up in the 19th century; the largest one today, *Skandia*, is the only listed company to have survived from the opening of the Stockholm exchange in 1853. At the turn of the last century, senior civil servants and some other public employees were guaranteed an old age pension, marking a break from the earlier system of various benefits "in kind" (Nilsson 1984). Later on these programs were merged into one pension program for central state employees and another one for personnel employed by regional and local authorities.

When private white collar unionization got under way early in

265

this century, wage demands tended to be regarded as improper, subversive, and an intrusion on the domain of the employer. The issues at stake instead became financial security in the event of illness, old age or bankruptcy of the firm. In a joint effort in 1917, the Employers Confederations and several white-collar unions set up an insurance company (SPP), which came exclusively to administer and valorize collective insurance contracts for pensions and sick pay. When the National Superannuation program was introduced in the early 1960s, after bitter political strife between blue collar and non-socialist political forces, these contracts were renegotiated and brought into line with the public scheme (Mohlin 1965). After some years, the blue collar Trade Union Confederation also negotiated a collective pension and sick pay contract with the Employers in addition to the national programs. This, too, is administered by the SPP but also by other companies like the Social Democratic owned Folksam. In the 1980s, most employees in Sweden are covered by these occupational pension programs and some three quarters of a million Swedes receive a pension benefit of this kind (Ståhlberg 1985). Thus, it is fair to say that the Swedish pension system consists of at least three levels: the basic pension scheme, the Superannuation system and a few nation-wide negotiated programs (some big firms – like the major commercial banks and the Coop – still had, and have, their own funds, too).

A fourth major level should be added from the 1980s (Olsson 1987c). As part of the debate about the fiscal crisis of the state, doubts have been cast upon the National Superannuation system's ability to meet its commitments for future generations of pensioners. The opportunity to contract an individual pension with a private insurance company has always existed in Sweden, but in the 1980s the private pension market has been booming, particularly at year-ends. Taxation rules for pension insurance are, comparatively speaking, rather favourable (Hort 1987). The purchase of pension insurance almost trebled between 1980 and 1985, whichever way it is calculated (numbers, premiums, yearly total, etc). From 40 000 new policies in 1980 the number shot up to 120 000 in 1985. From 1980 to 1985 the total stock of pension insurance grew from some 620 000 to 820 000, i.e. roughly one person in ten in Sweden has private pension insurance. Among the two million Swedish pensioners, the same proportion receives a return from their private premium. In the first half of 1986 there was actually a break in this sales trend, caused by the threat of a tax on real rates of interest; if imposed, this would have hit private insurance companies directly and private pension savings indirectly. However, after an intensive campaign against the tax proposal, the insurance companies and their organizations defeated the forces behind the State Commission that drafted it. Instead, the Government chose a temporary tax on the capital of insurance companies, which was approved by the combined Social Democratic and Communist majority in Parliament. Of course, the insurance companies also attacked the latter tax, but silently admitted that it would not hurt the market prospects for pension policies. Actually, the number of sold policies in 1986 was slightly higher than the year before.[5]

Private pension insurance is still only for a relatively wealthy minority, but its attraction points to the feasibility of what in nearby Denmark is referred to as the dual welfare state: good quality – and quantity – for the well-to-do, and meager benefits for the less well-off (Kampmann, Henriksen & Rasmussen 1987, Vesterö-Jensen 1984). But the state and negotiated pension schemes are still in such good condition that this scenario is far from being an immediate threat in Sweden.

3.2 Housing: The Rise of Fiscal Welfare

Of all welfare policies, housing policy is probably the one that most often has attracted criticisms in public opinion. The housing sector seems to be the most complicated area to regulate according to social welfare aims and the one that has the most shaky balance between market and politics, between private and public (Affärsvärlden 1987). Repeated housing crises have succeeded each other on both arenas.

State intervention in the housing sector takes an extremely complicated form: production subsidies (a lower value-added tax on most housing construction material, long-term repayment loans as well as interest subventions on public housing loans), price regulation (again interest subventions, direct rent regulation, housing allowances to low-income families), and finally tax deductions on the mortgage interests (Olofsson & Hort 1986).

Rent regulation was an instrument used from World War II but phased out until 1975. Housing allowances as well as production subsidies have been used throughout the postwar period. In particular from the mid-1960s, a concerted public program for the construction in a decade of one million apartments was decided, and implemented, too. Housing standards improved considerably, measured in persons per room, as well as in modern facilities such as running water and drains, sanitation, own bathroom, central heating, equipments like modern cooker and refrigerator. Nevertheless, many newly erected suburbs, and public housing as well, got a bad stamp albeit these apparent improvements.

After the implementation of the one million program, the construction of public multi-dwelling almost ceased, whilst that of owner-occupied single-family houses boomed. In the late 1960s, ordinary tenants made up the majority in the housing stock, while in the 1980s there is a clear dominance for owner-occupied single-family houses and tenant owner-apartments (Frykman 1987). Furthermore, this has changed the balance between the various forms of state support. In particular the visible support in public budgets to low-income earners and pensioners (housing allowances) has declined in relative importance, while interest subventions and invisible public expenditures like tax deductions have increased rapidly from the mid-1970s onwards. Thus, fiscal welfare – in the language of Titmuss – has grown in importance in recent years. The latter tendency is reflected in the growing role of private ownership in the housing sector, i.e. a marketization of one of the most important and necessary "social goods".

3.3 "Manikin Ltd": Encouraging Commercialized Welfare

One outcome of the above-mentioned privatization campaign organized by business interests was a private company for the provision of child day-care, *Pysslingen AB* ("Manikin Ltd"). It was founded by a small lobby group headed by the budding leader of the Liberal People's Party, and financed by big business (the Employers Confederation and the Swedish Federation of Industry jointly). Later it was transferred to one of Sweden's major multinationals, *Electrolux*, producer of home appliances (since the mid-1980s also owner of Italian Zanussi and the American company *White Consolidated Industries*).

Pysslingen has become a symbol of efforts to privatize public services in the 1980s (Küng 1983). Some initial problems arose for this company because the Social Democratic cabinet in 1983 changed the rules for central support to municipalities and publicly condemned profitability in the handling of human beings. For a while, some Right-governed municipalities hesitated and withdrew their interest, but since early 1986 the company operates two day-care centers on contract in a rather wealthy Stockholm suburb. During 1987 the capital of Stockholm will promote the establishment of this type of day care centers, too. The intake is still based on the same queuing system as in all other municipalities, but the internal organization of the centers is different: staffing is lower but better trained. Only white collar pre-school teachers are employed, and thus no nurse maids, who are unionized in the blue collar, Social Democratic Trade Union Confederation! As the centers are so new, it is too early to predict whether the company will go bankrupt or be listed on the exchange. The quarterly accounts from *Electrolux* say nothing about the profitability of its latest operating subsidiary. But its establishment has created a heated political debate.

3.4 Private Health Insurance

With the exception of two small units, in Stockholm and Gothenburg respectively, all hospitals in Sweden are run by public authorities (county councils). Moreover, since the mid-1950s there is public health insurance for the entire population (see part 2). But universal access to medical services is another problem, because demand for health services is difficult to define. And even where demand is obvious, resources are scarce, which may generate queuing. Furthermore, the regional responsibility for public health, creates major organizational differences that affect the allocation of available resources. For some complaints – in particular those that affect the elderly – the queue exceeds two years in some counties while it is less than a month in others.

In an attempt to bypass the queues in public health, since 1984 the insurance company *Skandia* offers private health insurance in co-operation with the only private hospital in Stockholm *Sophia-hemmet*. Initially, this was part of an economic reconstruction of this old institution which still is chaired by a member of the Royal Familiy. However, the settlement between the insurance company and the hospital led to a number of conflicts, and in early 1987 the former together with some major investment companies made a successful hostile take-over. Although publicly presented as a non-profit initiative, the new organization behind the hospital points towards a growing general interest from the business community in Sweden in health for profit.[6]

The new private health insurance is designed for corporate management and is tax deductible for the enterprises. But self-employed persons can also use this facility through their firms. The basic idea is that the hospital shall provide clinical and in-patient treatment within 24 hours. Many specialists at this little hospital work part-time on contract, combined with a regular post at a public hospital. The insurance is only offered to healthy persons, so the average yearly premium is comparatively low (around SEK 4000). In 1986 roughly 3000 persons had subscribed since the start and the potential is estimated to some 30-50000. Using Richard Titmuss' terminology, this benefit should probably be labelled 'occupational welfare', as it is a fringe benefit of a type hitherto quite rare in Sweden (of course other fringes exist). In contrast to "Manikin Ltd", this new private opportunity has aroused little controversy so far, and there seems to be no attempts to change the rather favourable tax roles so far.

3.5 "City Clinic Ltd"

A rather controversial initiative was the start in 1983 of an emergency out-patient center in downtown Stockholm.[7] It was promoted by a number of physicians, some of whom had a regular appointment at one of the capital's public hospitals.[6] During the 1970s Stockholm county council, like all other county councils, had set up a number of out-patient centers with the double aim of reducing cost-pressure on in-patient treatments (in particular hospi-

270

tals), and giving everybody access to immediate medical service. Although this type of service encroached on the market for private practitioners, it was accepted by the medical profession, some of whose members formed joint "doctors' houses", providing a variety of specialist services. These "houses" merged into a company, *Praktikertjänst* (owned by the participants/practitioners) in order to cut administrative costs, benefit from tax deductions, and support the establishment of new "houses". The company has been quite successful; in the field of dental care where it is also very active its share of the total "adult" market is in the mid-1980s roughly 50 per cent.

The start of "City Clinic Ltd" differed from the earlier pattern in that it lay outside the mutual understanding between public health authorities and private practitioners. The City Clinic explicitly competes with the public out-patient centers, which operate along territorial lines. Situated in downtown Stockholm, the City Clinic served a new market of commuting professionals who wanted to avoid queuing half the day for a consultation in their suburbs. As the City Clinic was to observe the rules in other respects, it was subsidized by the health insurance system (the fee paid by the patient is only slightly higher than at a public center).

Still, the county council and the health insurance system managed to impose a ceiling on the number of subsidized consultations. Each year in early December the City Clinic has had to close temporarily to avoid exceeding the annual limit. The controversy also concerned the fact the the doctors were – and are still – working in their leisure time, in many cases together with a full-time specialist post at one of the public hospitals in the capital. So far, this private experiment has been a success; in 1985 it was incorporated by the aforementioned practitioners' company, and a second clinic opened in Gothenburg. The competition between private and public health has thus been made more explicit in recent years. It is sometimes said, even by left politicians, that the City Clinic has stimulated efficiency at the public health centers and promoted cost consciousness among their employees.

3.6 Private Experiments and Alternatives:
A Preliminary Summary

To talk about the absence of privatization in Sweden – as is done in the introductory sub-title to this part of the chapter – may be interpreted as an exaggeration and somewhat provocative after the empirical investigation of attempts to privatize parts of the Swedish welfare system. In particular the developments on the housing and pension insurance markets point at a growth for what Titmuss has labelled occupational and fiscal welfare – in contrast to the social welfare of the universalistic policy model. However, if cutbacks would occur in the general social insurance system, the most likely result would be an increase in nation-wide, negotiated solutions rather than an increase in individual solutions (Edebalk & Wadensjö 1987). Private alternatives in health and child day care point toward the possibilities for commercialized welfare, for market solutions. But so far, there has been no major privatization of existing public services. Savings in public commitments to social welfare have involved changes that might be termed social dismantling, but this has not led immediately to a crop of private alternatives. Futhermore, fees have probably been introduced in the public sector to a somewhat greater extent than earlier.

Nevertheless, privatization as an ideological theme has been popular in the media, elaborated by opponents as well as adherents. The pro-welfare ideology has also demonstrated its strength, in particular in the national elections in the 1980s. But above all, the actual establishment of examples of private welfare alternatives has illustrated the feasibility of solutions that differ from the traditional norm in Sweden. The viability of these newly established companies and products has yet to be proven but they manifestly compete with long established welfare state products, which in turn are showing signs of a willingness to heed a swelling grassroot chorus.

4. Decentralization – in the Public Sector

The division of tasks and responsibilities between the central, regional and local levels of government have constantly been reviewed and debated in Sweden. There exists an old tradition – predating modern industrial, democratic, welfare society – of local self-government and a division of labour between various levels of government. The local state has been of considerable importance since centuries. A little more than hundred years ago, the basic administrative structure was established, and a line of demarcation between secular and ecclesiastical authorities was drawn. Local self-government is since then exercised by elected representatives at the local level in the municipalities, and at the regional level in country councils. These authorities have from the very outset had, and still have, their own tax-raising power, and fairly well-defined areas of responsibility.

The number of country councils has since the 1860s been constant, while the number of municipalities has decreased tremendously since the early postwar period: 2 500 small units, generally parishes in origins, were eliminated from the early 1950s and replaced by roughly 280 big ones in the mid-1970s. The number of local representatives was reduced by two-thirds from 200 000 to some 70 000 (Gustafsson 1988:32).

The aim was to create economically viable units, in order to implement the large-scale postwar social policy and educational reforms all over the country. This goal was achieved. However, for less than 25 years a major centralization process occurred in the public realm with important social and political-ideological repercussions. In the first phase, this boundary reform was introduced gradually and on a voluntary platform. Later on, a number of small municipalities opposed amalgamation, and the plan was made compulsory in the late 1960s. This decision became very controversial and was made at a time when the Social Democrats had a majority of their own in Parliament. In particular their former ally, the Agrarian Center Party, vehemently criticized the proposal as part of their stress of decentralization as a major ideological theme (Fryklund et al. 1973). In office in the late 1970s, that party contributed to the partition of a few local authorities, with the result that the number of municipalities in 1987 is 283. Otherwise, there were few signs of a return to the previous form of local self-administration.

In the 1980s, basically two decentralization tendencies in Sweden are noteworthy: 1) something we may label "fiscal decentralization", caused by central government budgetary cutbacks on transfers to local governments; and 2) administrative decentralization created by a major ideological campaign from central authorities.

4.1 Fiscal Decentralization: Towards Privatization?

In the early 1980s, public spending and welfare policy finally became politically controversial in Sweden. The state budget deficit – as well as the national debt – became a major political issue during the second term of bourgeois governments. During the first (1976-79), the deficit had grown from one to over ten percent of GDP. The cabinet chose the method of trimming the budget from the expenditure side, rather than putting up taxes to boost public revenue. From mid-1980, all major state authorities were subject to an annual two percent cut in outlays (after compensation for inflation) (Regeringens proposition 1979/80:100). Towards the end of 1980, the first clear-cut austerity bill was presented. Out of a central state budget of almost 200 billion SEK, six were to be cut out; mostly transfers and benefits in kind to households (Regeringens proposition 1980/81:20). A second major austerity bill was presented one and a half years later. This time, the government proposed a decrease in earnings-replacement from 90 to 87 percent in sickness cash benefits, and increased direct contributions from the insured in unemployment insurance. Altogether, the estimated savings amounted to some four percent of the 1982/83 central government budget (Regeringens proposition 1981/82:30).

This retrenchment policy was severely criticized by the Social Democratic opposition, a critique that contributed to their return to power after the September election in 1982 (Holmberg 1985). During the Labour reign in the mid-1980s, direct cuts in household transfers have generally been avoided, but budgetary policy has continued to be restrictive. However, the cabinet has chosen different avenues from its predecessors', and concentrates on transfers from central to local government, thereby putting the pressure on local politicians. However, the overall financial situation of local government has been very good in the mid-1980s, and a major financial surplus is foreseen towards the end of the decade. Municipal liquid assets are high, and the National Association of Local

274

Authorities has estimated that a tax cut of some five percent on average is feasible. Of the 1986/87 state budget, which amounts to around 336 billion, some 60 billion go to the municipalities and county councils. A five percent cut was suggested by the Ministry of Finance (Regeringens proposition 1985/86:100). Local politicians have swiftly reacted to the new situation, and demonstrations – in particular by public employees – have taken place outside many city halls. This has probably created an atmosphere of uncertainty in parts of the public sector, at a time when the private market sector is booming. In particular, wage negotiations in the public sector have been extremely complicated in the mid-1980s.

4.2 Administrative Decentralization: Towards Debureaucratization?

Decentralization is not only – nor even essentially, I would argue – an aspect of privatization and greater freedom of choice in the consumption sphere in a limited sense: the market. It is much more the very opposite of the unifying element of civil society: the central state and its enlarged domain in recent decades. Centralization and decentralization presuppose each other, like the two sides of a coin. Even for its former adherents, the comprehensive welfare state strategy has diminished in magnificence and popularity. The possibility of a just bureaucratic rule has been seriously questioned by an increasing number of persons, organizations and institutions concerned with the individual social and civil rights.

When the Social Democrats returned to power in 1982, they immediately tried to usurp the theme of decentralization – formerly one of the jewels of the Agrarian Center Party, but seriously tarnished after six years in office. The Social Democrat cabinet was reshuffled and a new Ministry of Public Administration was set up, headed by a young, energetic former county council chairman, known for his preferences for new solutions to the organization of social welfare. A concerted program for the renewal and revitalization of the public sector was soon presented, and in 1983 Parliament passed what hitherto has been regarded as the culmination of the decentralization strategy: several municipalities and a few county councils were declared "free zones for administrative experimentation".

The aim of the Social Democratic decentralization program is to make public authorities still more accessible to inspection, influence and participation by the citizenry. The problems of the present public sector have been defined in the following way in a recent government document:

...as things now stand, individual persons having dealings with public authorities experience formidable difficulties. Those difficulties are becoming more and more palpable to persons coming into increasingly frequent contact with the authorities. Procedures of application, notification, deposition, and appeal are not infrequently complicated and time-consuming, added to which many people find it difficult to understand the impact of official decisions. Not only is it very important for official language to be plain and lucid, but individual persons frequently also need information, guidance, advice, and other assistance in order to secure their rights. It is often the authority handling a case which can render the best and cheapest assistance. But public authorities do not always support the individual to the extent desirable...(Regeringens skrivelse 1984/85:202; English summary p. 1).

Measures have been taken for better services and information, deregulation and less bureaucracy – often attitude campaigns aimed at certain groups of public employees, including the directors-general of major state agencies, and similar categories. The content of public activities has been changed to obtain a better match between what people need and want. Great importance has also been attached to rendering public administration still more effective by simplifying or abolishing administrative and other regulations in order to make routines smoother and quicker.

Of the main central welfare agencies, the National Board of Health and Welfare has not been much affected, as it was thoroughly reorganized and pruned in the late 1970s. Neither has the National Social Insurance Board been much influenced by the renewal program.[8] And it is even said that at the ministerial level, it is the two main welfare ministries, those for Health & Social Affairs, and Education & Cultural Affairs, that have been least co-operative in the revitalization program (Mellbourn 1986). At least one of the Ministers was a typical representative of the traditional Social Democratic centralist welfare state strategy, a former party secretary.

But a third important welfare agency, the powerful National Labour Market Board, led by a new and dynamic director-general close to the Prime Minister, has coopted the program and decided to prune head office and transfer 500 employees to the field service, the employment offices. This sub-program is still in its infancy.

The general revitalization program also concerns the regional apparatus of central government administration. At mid-1986 a pilot project started in the northernmost region, the County of Norrbotten, in order to test a more co-ordinated State County Administration. All regional state agencies, with the exception of the regional labour market board, are to be merged into a single board. Paradoxically, in the rest of the country the tax departments of the State County Administration has been transformed into separate regional authorities at the beginning of 1987. It seems that the decentralizers have not yet decided whether the new program stands for integration or diffusion.

Most attention has been paid to the pilot project for greater local autonomy in nine municipalities and three county councils. The basic targets for these "free zones" are more local influence over activities, improved quality of service, better use of resources, and services that are more compatible with the user's needs. As geographical and social conditions vary greatly, a further target is to let each municipality take advantage of and strengthen its uniqueness. Certain regulations have been curtailed and local authorities participating in the project have greater freedom to define their own priorities, choose their own ways of achieving the specified objectives and plan their own activities. Programs for improving information, access and services, for revising and decentralizing controls, and experimental schemes for user influence in child care, care of the elderly, schools and cultural activities, are the most important aspects of the process of renewal at local level. But it has taken some time to get the program off the ground in the face of many obstacles and impediments.

Also municipalities outside the pilot project have taken steps in a similar direction. For example, Stockholm municipality has decentralized its social welfare and school administration into eighteen district social welfare boards and fourteen school district boards, and – simultaneously – tried to cut down the number of officials at City Hall. Nevertheless, the future of the capital's decentralization program and efforts is uncertain. Two social welfare districts are already threatened with integration and the whole school decentralization program will be abolished, as a new City Hall majority was created in late 1986.

As all these measures have generally started quite recently, it is too early to evaluate their performance. But it seems as if the central agency of change – the new Ministry of Public Administration – after four years in operation has lost its public appeal and its chief is regarded as a rather weak executive. Nonetheless, those institutions that have acquired some measure of independence through the decentralization program often implement the intentions in their own, decentralized ways. One example is decentralized budget responsibility – including bonus to the manager and personel if a budget surplus is achieved – to those who actually produce the public services; a kind of producers' co-op within the public sector.

5. Excursus:
Between Public and Private: Voluntary Co-operatives

In the international discussion on a new welfare model or even "paradigm", decentralization is not primarily associated with a renewal of the public sector itself, but of a growing role of what has loosely been called the "informal sector" in the production and distribution of welfare. Most of the development hitherto discussed can be captured in a Titmussian terminology, either as trends on the continuum between various social policy models (universalistic vs. residual, etc), or as developments inside different welfare sectors (fiscal, occupational, etc). However, the new kinds of organizational mixes that have been put forward by the new social movements cannot directly be grasped with Titmuss' notions. He seems to have no concept for the pre-welfare state organization or strategy as it emerged under the coordination of the old social movements, friendly societies, trade unions etc. It was neither a residual social policy model, nor private charity. This is particularly evident when we reach the decentralized, autonomous sector of civil society, where market relations are more or less absent (Ascoli 1986). Less bureaucracy and more self-determination on a smaller scale is seen as an alternative to the centralized, technocratic organization of human reproduction. The welfare state should be replaced by a welfare society separated from both the state and the market – comprising both consumption and production and covering such activities as unpaid community work, neighbourhood co-operatives, self-help, and even squatter action. The rhetoric of the collectivizers in the new social movements concurs with that of the conservative privatizers .

In Sweden, however, the terrain of social movements is still dominated by the old social movements (Olofsson 1986). For example, co-operatives have been fairly strong in the private consumption market (retailing) and in the agrarian production process. Two million Swedish consumers belong to the retail Co-operative Society, and most farmers to the Swedish Federation of Farmers, both of them nation-wide, rather highly centralized organizations. In principle they are not partisan but in reality affiliated with the Social Democrats and the Center Party respectively.

However, in Sweden too a new "autonomous sector", mainly consisting of various new forms of co-operative and other types of self-help organizations, has appeared in the 1980s. It is still extremely small. In some respects these endeavors can be interpreted as a reaction to the established co-operative organizations, but mostly they have wider ambitions in their social critique, seeing themselves as alternatives on a small but determined scale to an increasingly anti-ecological, technocratic, and competitive society (Friberg & Galtung 1985).

But some of them have grown up as more immediate responses to problems confronting people with other ambitions than to be "alternative". This is often the case as regards child care, where parents in the public queue unite to solve their child-minding problems. In some cases they also take an educational stand and establish nursery schools with an alternative approach. But in many instances the main objective is to find someone to look after the children. As part of the decentralization program mentioned earlier and in an effort to stop the abovementioned "Manikin Ltd", in 1983 the Social Democrats decided to provide state support for non-profit day-care co-ops run by parents. These "consumer" co-ops have to follow the general rules for public day-care centers, but the municipal authorities do not intervene in the administrative matters. As municipalities often contribute to the salary of the co-op's employees, they can control the quality of the staff.

Since the provision of state grants for parents' co-operatives, the traditional Co-operative Movement has also been alerted to the new phenomena. At the central level, the Co-op set up a development project with the aim of supporting local initiatives by parents outside and inside the Co-operative movement (the retail business, the cooperative building societies, the co-operative insurance company, and similar nation-wide associations). This project can of course be seen as the entrance of the old Co-op into new service production. But it can also be interpreted as an attempt to find a meeting point between the new "autonomous sector" and the old, well-established co-ops (Palmer & Persson 1985). As it is fairly complicated to launch a parents' day-care co-operative – many municipalities do not encourage the idea – another aim of the development project is to help parents without the necessary bureaucratic skills to overcome public authorities and their regulations (Persson & Svensson 1986). So far, this is just a tentative venture but in the long run it might yield a nation-wide organization of local parents' day-care co-operatives (KF/Folksam 1986). In the mid-1980s, some 125 parents' co-ops exist in the whole of Sweden, most of them state supported.

Finally, small buds also put forth in the employment area. As a kind of micro-employment policy, support has been given to Youth Cooperative Enterprises (YCE) in order to combat youth unemployment, which is quite severe in particular in the sparsely populated areas. In some cases YCEs have been started by young people themselves, but generally they are initiated jointly by local governments and local trade unions in areas where youth unemployment is high. At the start, the Cooperatives get financial assistance (subsidies) from the public, but the ambition is to create competitive co-ops operating on the open market. In 1984 the Swedish Government's Children and Youth Delegation instituted a special "start your own enterprises" grant and decided to support information and education concerning cooperative ideas. Since then about 40 new YCEs have started. Some 300 persons have been involved. The average size of an YCE is 5-6 persons and they exist both in the service and in the industrial sector. The majority of them are still subsidized, but only a few of them have managed to become competitive (Schröder & Sehlstedt 1987). This kind of experimentation has undoubtedly challenged the traditional producers of public welfare, and those who have tried to start such cooperatives have encountered many obstacles to overcome. Nevertheless, the legal informal economy appears to be an important field of modelling in particular for youngsters between schooling and a "normal" work career. Thus, a very different kind of mixture between social and occupational welfare – voluntary welfare?

6. Summary and Conclusions: Why is There so Much Talk about Decentralization and so Little Actual Privatization in Sweden?

In this essay, the relative stagnation of social expenditure and social programs in Sweden, as well as the challenges posed by privatization and decentralization to the welfare state paradigm, have been considered. But how can all the pieces that have been picked up in these pages be put together into a coherent mosaic?

The theoretical approaches discussed in the introduction to this article sheed some light over welfare development in Sweden in the 1980s. The halt at the turn of the 1970s of social expenditure's postwar rising trend seems, at least on the surface, to confirm the idea prevalent in mainstream economic theory of a "critical threshold". The welfare state has reached its limits. No major expansion of social security and social services have occurred (with one exception that will be pointed out below). Civil society in the shape of the competitive market sphere has succeeded in safeguarding and even expanding its operative territory even within the national frontiers of an established welfare society. Secondly, the Habermas-Offe thesis is partly confirmed in that a major attempt to de-bureaucratize the central welfare state has taken place in recent years. More dubious is if – in Janowitz' perspective – citizen participation really has grown. There is no indication that the everyday life-spheres of civil society have been radically strengthened in recent years despite the fact that new types of cooperatives have emerged. But local government has definitely increased its autonomy, while central authorities have tried to deregulate their activities. The Habermas-Offe idea of a breakdown for the work society utopia must in the case of Sweden with its adherence to the full employment policy – and low rates of unemployment during the recent crisis – be rejected. But their scenario is not completely out of touch with reality: public concern for work and employment has thus been combined with public de-bureaucratization and a growing emphazis on local decision-making. Finally, the welfare state can be regarded as an irreversible aspect of late 20th century Sweden. No national welfare backlash has occurred, and so far the possibility of an anti-welfare coalition is less likely. Commitment to welfare has been upheld, although not enlarged. Social expenditure is not rising anymore, but has not declined in relative terms. Nevertheless, in particular in pension and housing non-etatist welfare solutions have shown their viability. However, these theories only give a partial picture of the Swedish case.

In order to evaluate the new trends against the actual performance of the old strategy it is necessary to grasp the outcome of distributional conflicts and negotiations over the "social contracts". Thus, it is important to look at the power structure, and the power alternatives as viewed by various actors when making strategic decisions. In the Swedish context, the relative equilibrium between capital and labour has been singled out as the background to the well-established productivity of Swedish industry, the absence of major industrial disputes (with a few exceptions), and the build-up of the welfare state. Industrial capital is highly concentrated in Sweden and in the hands of a few private groups, in particular the Wallenberg dynasty and the Volvo conglomerate. Trade unions as well as the organizations of private enterprise are extremely centralized, and generally make binding national wage agreements. Comparatively speaking, unionisation is very high, and the blue-collar Trade Union Confederation forms the backbone of the Social Democratic Labour Party, which from 1932 for a period of 44 years (until 1976) alone or in coalition governed the country and came to be identified with the building of the centralized welfare state. Thus, when the first non-socialist government in almost half a century entered the stage in the mid-1970s, welfare policy had a strong backing in Swedish society, and the first cabinets did not even try to challenge this position. On the contrary, the new cabinets dominated by the Center and Liberal parties, were as eager as their predecessor to safe-guard and even encourage social security, social services and especially full employment. However, the recession of that decade undermined the economic balance of the public household, in particular as the government choose foreign borrowing instead of increasing domestic leavies or decreasing public expenditure. And on the fringe of Swedish politics, one of the partners in the new majority, the Conservative Party, actively worked for lower taxes and stopped attempts to achieve sound public finances. That party also promoted the earlier mentioned privatization campaign organized by Big business.

After the failure of the bourgeois parties, and the return to power of the Social Democrats, in particular two issues have dominated public debate on social welfare. Health expenditure, in particular sickness cash benefits, has fostered a major political controversy in the 1980s (Svallfors 1987). Six months before the 1982 general election, as part of central government economies, the Center-Liberal cabinet suggested cutting the earnings replacement from 90 to 87 percent and reintroducing two qualifying (waiting) days. The changes were enacted only three months before election day, to be effective as of 1983. The proposal would in particular have hit the privately employed blue collar workers who – unlike all public employees as well as most private white collar employees – had no collective sick-pay agreement with their employers. The Social Democrats, backed by the Trade Union Confederation, fiercely attacked the new law during the election campaign and this definitely contributed to the government's defeat. Nonetheless, in the run-up to the 1985 election the Center-Right parties continued to suggest further cuts in sickness benefits: the Moderates (Conservative) a reduction of earnings replacement from 90 to 60 percent for the first ten days of sick leave, thereafter only 80 percent, while the Center and Liberal parties proposed 80 percent from all sick leave. Once again, the Social Democrats attacked these 'Thatcherist' proposals in their electoral campaign and were returned for another three years term.

In the mid-1980s, the political parties are debating the future of support to the youngest members of society and their up-bringers. When the Social Democrats won the 1982 election they launched the strategy of expanding day-care by providing generous state support to municipalities that set up new facilities. The public day-care program may be regarded as the sole exception – at least in the field of welfare – from an otherwise cautious and restrictive budgetary policy. According to this program, every child over 18 months shall, not later than 1991, have a statutory right to a pre-school place, i.e. in a day nursery, a municipal "family day nursery", a part-time group, an open pre-school or a publicly sponsored parents' co-operative, depending on whether the parents are gainfully employed, in education or at home. The number of places in public day-care has increased considerably in the 1980s, although it has fallen short of the target. In 1986 it is estimated that about 65 percent of all children below schoolage are involved in the municipal childminding program.[9] But demand continues to exceed supply, and as the birth rate has gone up unexpectedly in the mid-1980s, the problem will persist into the 1990s.

Furthermore, the cabinet has recently been investigating the possibility of prolonging parental insurance up to eighteen months so as to coordinate it with the day-care program, but no firm proposal has been presented yet. Nevertheless, the prevailing policy can be said to indicate that the Swedish Labour Movement is still relying on the traditional, centralist welfare state strategy. Economic support to parents' cooperatives is an exception but in other respects the day-care program is definitely etatist in essence. In contrast, the non-socialist parties and social forces far into the Social Democratic camp have opposed what they regard as a one-sided emphasis on public day-care facilities, and instead suggested tax deductions for children, private day-care, and a special care allowance to the guardian, in order to improve freedom of choice in child minding. Although no coherent program has been – and probably will not be – presented, these proposals touch upon the guiding ideas behind both the strategy of privatization and decentralization. But it would definitely be an exaggeration to say that a breakaway from the traditional Swedish model has occurred. The attempts to find compromises between government and opposition point in a different direction: these proposals ought to be interpreted as complements, not alternatives.[10] The welfare state strategy has been institutionalized for so long that its transformation would not be accomplished over night. At least as long as the balance of social power is in favour of the forces to the Left.

In Sweden, as elsewhere, privatization as an ideological theme is identified with the upswing of the social and political Right from the late 1970s, i.e. the Employers Confederation (the major business pressure group) and its affiliates, and among the political parties in particular the Moderates (Conservatives). The domestic political climate has obviously been affected by thunder storms that do not stop at national frontiers. Privatization is undoubtedly a major feature of the welfare state debate in the 1980s, but its application in Sweden remains marginal. Internationally, it seems that many advocates are pessimistic about the chances of a real withering away of the welfare state. In Sweden, too, a libertarian ideologist has complained about the possibility to change the mind even of liberal and conservative Swedes (Langby 1985). However, a few successful examples have been born out of these considerations, and in the business press there exist a handful of heroic welfare entrepreneurs (Veckans Affärer 1986). But in many sectors of Swedish society, they operate on the margin of a broad public organization, and the market possibilities created must be regarded as complements, not alternatives, to the basic structure.

The trajectory of decentralization is rather different. Already from the mid-1960s onwards, it became the slogan of the rising 'old' Swedish Greens, the Agrarian Center Party that was success-fully moving into the towns at that time. As an oppositional political project this was the most successful non-socialist alterna-tive in half a century, but it collapsed with the simultaneous demise of a credible Center-Right power block in the early 1980s. Since then, decentralization has changed hands and become – at least on the surface – the new strategy of the earlier longstanding, etatist power holder, the Social Democratic Labour Party (cf. Carlsson & Lindgren 1978). After six years in the political wilder-ness, the Social Democrats regained the helm in 1982 and were reelected in 1985. In both elections, their defence of existing welfare achievements *and* their new decentralist strategy for improving the public alternative were pitched against the adherents of privatiz-ation, who so far have not succeeded in capturing the theme of decentralization.

Thus, the national elections in the 1980s have been over welfare issues, but so far the pro-welfare forces have succeeded in defending existing public provisions. But in at least one case, the pension insurance issue, the privatization campaign – although not explicitly under that banner – might create a real threat to the public programs, as the recent controversy over a real interest tax indicated.

285

However, the major emphasis must be put on the decentralization theme, which has well-established, deep roots in Swedish society and history as the competition over the ownership of that theme suggests. In one sense, its strength must be seen in the light of the autonomy of the municipalities: after a period of growth in central administrative planning, local authorities are regaining some degree of administrative freedom concerning public commitments built up over a period of several decades. In another sense, however, decentralization may create space for private initiatives in the future: the fiscal pressure from the Ministry of Finance may force the local authorities to prune some of their activities. One alternative is that these are overtaken by innovative private enterprises. Another possibility is the non-governmental organizations (NGO), in the Swedish case most likely the popular movements, which may regain some of their earlier importance. Finally, nothing has been said about the growing role of fees in the budget of local authorities, which point to a marketisation of publicly provided goods and services. Likewise, the alternative of contracting out public commitments to private firms has only been touched upon. This is a topical phenomenon in, for instance, refuse collection. A further possibility would be a commercialized "contracting within" the public sector, for instance between municipal authorities responsible for personal social services for the disabled and elderly, buying home medical services from the producers of health care, i.e. the county councils. Thus, if one were to believe Georg Friedrich Hegel, the dialectic between decentralization and privatization may give rise to a synthesis on a new and higher order of social welfare.

Overall, the role of social and political power – in particular the political and syndical left – has been stressed in this essay, above all in blocking the privatization of public welfare commitments. As indicated in the foregoing sections, the prospects for social welfare are rather favourable in Sweden, especially as the economy is recovering in the mid-1980s. For the first time in ten years, the public sector will show a surplus, still the national debt and foreign loans cast shadows over a prospering nation. But so far, neither decentralized NGOs nor private enterprises may be viewed as guiding principles for the future of a welfare society so closely bound up with its central but decentralized state. At least one local welfare backlash has occurred, still the national backlash seems far away.

Footnotes

Introduction

1. For example, commenting on a text closely related to the ones included in this volume, Wolfe has argued that although the Scandinavian welfare state is a post-World War II phenomenon, it has been transformed into an even more recent "new" welfare state emphasizing the internal and external strength of public welfare institutions designed to carry out tasks once assigned to civil society, a caring or enabling state (Wolfe 1989:151-2; cf. Gilbert & Gilbert 1989). The latter work is one of the few books in this field that includes a full chapter on agriculture from a social policy perspective.

2. On the general problems related to the case study as method in the social sciences, cf. Rothstein (1986:59-63). Apart from his methodological skills as well as his novel approach to welfare bureaucracies, this author has also been a source of inspiration regarding the actor-structure relationship (1988); cf. Anderson 1980 and Stephanson 1989.

3. The main tombstone reflecting the centennial celebrations of the institutionalization of Bismarckian-type social insurance schemes is Köhler-Zacher (1981-2). The dominant perspective there is on the evolution of laws, programs and institutions – not social expenditure – within the ambience of social insurance, which is underscored by the book being written by social law scholars and legal historians. The point of departure in their study is the 1880s. However, even for a class perspective on social policy, the time perspective is similar, although the spacial starting point is the organized working class movement (cf. Therborn 1986).

4. This way of codifying the welfare state is clearly visible in such documents as the ILO Studies and Reports series from the 1920s, summarized in the two major international surveys from the 1930s but extended into the early 1940s (ILO 1925-42; cf. Perrin 1969), as well as in the global overview of social security programs published by the US Department of Health and Human Services (earlier Health, Education and Welfare) on behalf of the International Social Security Association (1937-86). Even a cursory glance in one of the latest volumes of the latter catches the empty boxes at the bottom of most pages ("family and child allowances"). Furthermore, the notion of family benefits does not take into consideration tax deductions for children (cf. Olofsson and Hort 1986). Thus, the definition of the welfare state in the dominant research tradition within the social sciences has had its kernel in these four social security programs (occupational injury insurance, pensions, sickness and unemployment insurance), while child and family benefits have been neglected. One exception is Kaim-Chaudle (1973), who devotes a full chapter to "family endowment".

5. Internationally, social insurance was primarily aimed at industrial workers – men and women, but in particular men. Even in the first universal social insurance systems, men and women were treated differently. For a feminist critique of the Swedish social insurance system, not least the 1913 pension reform, cf. Abukhanfusa (1987). The radical change in the structure of the welfare state associated with the increase of female labour force participation and the expansion of child and family cash and in-kind benefits, has not yet been an object of comparative welfare state research (cf. Flora 1986:XXVI). To my knowledge, there exists no overview of the feminist critique of social policy and welfare state. On the absence of a "gender dimension" in welfare state research, cf. Sainsbury (1989), Acker (1988), Hernes (1987), Sassoon-Showstack (1986), Land (1986) and Wilson (1977).

6. There was also more historically oriented comparative research that tried to delineate the various roads to state welfare (cf. Rimlinger 1971). If we take Rimlinger's work as the starting-point of the "comparative welfare state research growth", which I do not consider appropriate, only a few more titles would be included from Shalev's list (1983). Wilensky's study was on the one hand more provocative, on the other closer to mainstream sociological research designs.

7. Although 64 nations make up Wilensky's total data set, only 22 are included in most of the analyses. Among these rich countries, two belong to North America (Canada and the US), fourteen to Western Europe (in rank order: Sweden, Iceland, Switzerland, Denmark, West Germany, France, Norway, Belgium, Finland, the UK, the Netherlands, Italy, Austria and Ireland), three to Eastern Europe (Czechoslovakia, East Germany and the USSR), two to the Pacific Islands (Australia and New Zealand) and two to Asia, (Israel and Japan, although the latter country was only no. 23 (!) on the list). Luxemburg was excluded from the analysis of "leaders" and "laggards" among the rich nations (1975:121-34).

8. Released the same year as Wilensky's work was Jackman's Politics and Social Equality (1975), and a year later the former published a sequential work The "New Corporatism": Centralization and the Welfare State (1976)

9. The following countries are involved: Austria, Australia, Belgium, Canada, Denmark, France, Finland, Germany (West), Ireland, Italy, Japan, the Netherlands, New Zeeland, Norway, Sweden, Switzerland, the US and the UK.

10. There were of course other projects of a similar type. Of a very different kind are Dixon's 55 nation project on social welfare (1986-9) and Estes global survey of well-being (1982).

11. This article, the only one of these four studies that has not appeared in print earlier, is part of an on-going project on "Alternatives in Swedish Social Policy" financed by the Swedish Delegation for Social Research. An early draft was presented at the IV Nordic Research Conference on Social Policy, Hässelby, 1984.

12. In view of the existence of a well-developed network of social policies, for a very long time there has been surprisingly little institutionalized research in this field. Social policy as well as labour economics have existed on the fringe of established academic disciplines. Even with the early postwar expansion of social science research in general, social policy issues did not become a major

289

concern for academic imperialists in Sweden (cf. Sellberg 1950:8 and Elmér 1960:1). At the semi-academic schools of social welfare/work, research was on the agenda but took off only in the late 1970s (Svensson 1962:336-7; Berglind 1987). It is noteworthy that up to 1988, only one chair in social policy has existed in Sweden: the first one from 1921 at the newly established School of Social Work/Welfare (Socialinstitutet) in Stockholm as part of a chair in economics at the university there. The notion of social policy was in effect dropped when its third incumbent was installed in 1953. Formally, this disappearance can be dated to 1978, when the fourth appointment was prepared. By that time, a new chair had been set up at the Swedish Institute for Social Research (established in 1972). At the schools of Social Welfare, now part of the system of higher learning, the chairs that were set up in the late 1970s and early 1980s were labelled "social work" or "care", and geared towards the professionalization of work in this field.

13. The second article included here was first published in 1989, in International Review of Social History, and its final version was discussed in plenum at the Bergen Conference of the Research Group on Social Policy, Poverty and the Welfare State of the International Sociological Association, together with an enlarged version of its much more provocative counterpart (Baldwin 1988). This text is an outgrowth of, on the one hand of one of the short "case studies" included in the third article (pp. 81-2 in the original version), and on the other a presentation of the Swedish basic pension system at a "Parliamentary hearing" in Bonn, organized by the German Green party (Olsson 1987c).

14. The main objective of the Florence project was to strengthen empirical research in this area and establish a sound basis for future comparative research and teaching. Each participant was to produce a chapter on her/his own country, following relatively standardized guidelines that specified a variety of questions in a strictly comparative way, as well as the empirical information to be studied. The other countries are: Denmark, Finland, Norway (volume I incl. Sweden), Germany (West), Ireland, Italy, and the UK (vol. II, in which France was to have been included according to the initial plan), Austria, Belgium, the Netherlands, and Switzerland (in a forthcoming vol. III). In an appendix volume (IV) covering all the above-mentioned countries, another sixty pages deal with the institutional characteristics of the Swedish welfare system in 1980, along with a bibliography and background data on social expenditure, the financing of the welfare system (i.e. taxation), the welfare clientele (i.e. the Swedish population) etc. This information has not been included here, and the social policy addict will have to consult the original source (Flora 1987).

15. The basic framework of this project still bears the signature of its director (Flora 1986:XII-XXXVI), who plans to publish one or two concluding volumes in the early 1990s.

16. As the time period covered in the Florence project took 1945 – rather than 1932 – as its point of departure, it was most natural for me to amalgamate "arguments within Swedish marxism": the emphasis on the role of class power, parliamentary politics and industrial relations developed by Korpi (1978 & 1983) and Johansson (1974), and insights from the discussion in the late 1970s about class and state (Therborn et al 1978; Olofsson 1979). On the other hand,

local marxist analysis of social policy from that time was not particularly convincing, whereas the domestic handbook literature were often informative (Olsson 1988; cf. Persson 1978 & 1980 for a critique of the former perspective). In the early days of both the Florence study and the project "Social Policy in an International Perspective" at the Swedish Institute for Social Research, of which I was a participant for several years (cf. Korpi, Olsson and Stenberg 1982), Hans L Zetterberg painted a gloomy picture of the situation in welfare state research in Sweden: "It is amazing that a holistic social scientific analysis of the welfare policy has never been attempted in Sweden. We have many excellent detailed investigations and evaluations, but no overarching theory or universal view (totalåskådning). Economists and sociologists have ignored something essential, and those in research funds who should have pointed this out, exhibit their cowardice" (1979; my translation). At the time of Zetterberg's polemic, in a review essay the grand old man of the Swedish social adminis-tration school basically agreed, although he added that during the 1970s a few books with theoretical ambitions had been published in Sweden (Elmér 1981); another leading local expert devoted a full chapter to social research, research institutes and research funds within the domain of social welfare, although this author admitted the existence of manifold unresolved theoretical and empirical problems (Lindblom 1982). In the 1980s in Sweden a number of projects and studies have focussed on various aspects of welfare state developments, in sociology as well as in political science, economics, history of economics, etc. Besides the "power resources" project at the Swedish Institute for Social Research mentioned above., major studies – all within the "new orthodoxy" of agency but some definitely more structure-oriented – with objectives similar to those included in this book, have been conducted in particular at the Sociology Department at the University of Umeå (Furåker 1987 and Furåker at al 1989; Marklund 1982 and 1988; Marklund & Svallfors 1987), as well as by Swedish sociologists in exile (Olofsson 1984; Therborn 1986). From the mid-1980s, most of these studies have been discussed at the regular and lively meetings of the Working Group on Social Policy and the Welfare State of the Swedish Socio-logical Association.

Furthermore, it seems pertinent to point out that Sweden in the early 1980s was a "model" in a more general and slightly different sense in the social scientific literature: an example of a peaceful transformation from capitalism to socialism through wage-earner funds. In the welfare state literature, Esping-Andersen in particular emphasized economic democracy as an answer to the crisis of the welfare state and as a mean of rebuilding the class coalition behind a solidaristic social policy (1985; cf. Himmelstrand et al 1981; Abrahamson & Broström 1980, and the critical overview by Pontusson 1984).

17. The fourth study is a follow-up to an article not included here (Olsson 1987b). The present text is the second outcome of an international ad-hoc study group on trends in welfare state developments that first met in Haifa in 1985 (Friedmann et al 1987). The papers for this meeting were similar to the main outline of the Florence project but a few non-European countries were in-volved (the US, Japan and Israel as well as the borderline-case Jugoslavia). However, the time perspective was slightly shorter, 1960-1980. The ambition of the second and latest meeting – in Boston 1986 – was to penetrate trends in the

1980s, in particular the common phenomena of privatization and decentralization. Furthermore, when the paper presented there was printed, the theoretical introduction was omitted without my knowledge (Morris 1989).

18. Although the 1968 election was not a clear-cut "welfare election", it took place only three weeks after the invasion of Czecho-Slovakia. However, the theme of equality had reached the top of the political agenda, and 1968 is the only year in the postwar era when a majority rejected the proposition that "social reform has gone too far" in the election survey (cf. table 40 in the third study in this boo).

19. As Tarschys has pointed out, cost control has been achieved by most Western governments, irrespective of political colour (1986).

20. These are not the only social programs were changes have occurred in the second half of the 1980s. For instance, in unemployment insurance, initial no-benefit days have been completely abolished (cf. Elmér 1989). Another significant welfare reform – as of 1993 – is the extension of the statutory right to holidays (from five to six weeks, while a six hour work day for parents with pre-school children has been dropped from the political agenda).

21. In early 1990, the Social Democratic government proposed the introduction of an initial period of employer responsibility for sickness insurance, which the non-socialist parties have favoured for some time (cf. Lindqvist 1990).

22. Furthermore, in the late 1980s and early 1990s, the idea of a "maturation" of the welfare state has been a popular theme in psycho-analytically inspired speeches by the Swedish Budget Minister (since March 1990 Vice-Premier).

23. A typical example in Sweden is the decisive superannuation pension battle in the late 1950s (cf. Rehn 1989; Marklund 1988).

24. However, in early January 1990, a "super minister" of social welfare – with eight other cabinet members below – was appointed. If this is more than a cover for the relative failure of the Ministry of Public Administration, the future will answer.

Chapter I

* I would like to thank the participants at the IV Social Policy Research Conference, Hässelby, Oct. 1984, and the members of the Workshop of the Research Group on Social Policy and the Welfare State, Skytteholm, Oct. 1989 for most helpful comments on two different drafts for this essay. In particular P G Edebalk's critical remarks on the final draft were most useful.

1. References to most of these two types of works are included in the other articles included in this volume.

2. Of course, both the above-mentioned articles have to be situated in their specific polemics: Holmberg was at that time a secretary of the controversial Low Income Commission, while, Zetterberg wrote for the Employers' Confederation in a period when it for the first time since the late 1950s – the superannuation battle – vociferously attacked "the Swedish model".

3. This search for a domestic theory stems from an earlier attempt to come to

terms with the (postwar) Swedish textbook literature within this field of policy. Theoretically the inspiration came from Kuhn (1962; cf. Brante 1980) and his emphasis on the role of textbooks as important paradigmatic signifiers, but this topic will be dealt with only marginally here. Furthermore, early on Bernt Hagtvet pointed out the possibility of cross-national studies of intellectuals (1973), while Anderson (1968) had provided an example of a empirical case study of a specific "national culture".

4. Here, I think it is important to make a brief note about the concept of the state in relation to local government in Scandinavia. The specific autonomy of the local authorities makes it pertinent to analytically distinguish them from the central state. Long before the introduction of modern democracy, self-governing parishes, later on municipalities and county councils, were important mediating institutions between rulers – most often landowning farmers composing the Fourth Estate in Parliament from the birth of the Nation-State, later the majority of the Second Chamber – and the ruled, basically rural population. Thus, for centuries an important segment of the rural population did not feel itself to be outside the political system, which probably is one explanation for the lack of interest in the public-private dimension in Scandinavia (cf. Allardt 1984; Therborn 1989a). The implication of this note is not a triangle but, as Kuhnle (1989) has made visible, a quadrangle. However, as the role of local government in welfare policy is not the main object of this text, I will not extend this figure but stick to the umbrella of civil society.

5. Titmuss is one of the most imaginative thinkers within the social policy tradition. However, there are enormous problems involved in applying his brief general models highly visible in particular in the attempts to develop the other famous Titmuss proposal, the distinction between residual, industrial achievement-performance and the institutional redistributive models (1974).

6. Alan Wolfe has argued for the centrality of the concept of civil society – counterposed to market and politics – in sociology (1989). Although there is no reason to underestimate the atomistic and competitive nature of contemporary society, which Wolfe in no sense does, I am in favour of his "social" interpretation of this concept without underwriting the moral pretention he ascribes to sociology as a discipline. However, my own preference for the concept of civil society has a very different, "italian" origin (cf. Forgacs 1989). Rather surprisingly, this theoretical tradition is not at all alluded to by Wolfe.

7. Furthermore, civil society's philological roots point towards bourgeois society as a reasonable alternative (cf. Colletti 1972), but this would one-sidedly stress societal human relationships at the expense of close ties of friendship and hate as well as overemphasize the monetary nature of human relationships, i.e. markets as cultural dominants. Furthermore, in a Swedish context, bourgeois society would a priori underestimate one social force with hegemonical pretensions at the expense of another.

8. This is a full research project which will not be undertaken in this short paper basically because this is in many senses a voyage into an uncharted territory. This piece of research will necessarily be brief and cursory, a tentative and explorative mapping of a landscape not known in its full details.

9. Thus, as a starting point I take for granted that social insurance is at the "core", or the "essence", of (modern) social policy (cf. Wilensky 1975; Flora

1981). This is of course not an indisputable fact in particular not in Sweden, where the /un/employment question also has been on top of the social agenda. However, as will definitely follow from the coming pages, I have tried to stretch the boundaries of this discourse during its formative decades as social insurance was in no sense the obvious answer to the social question, and, as indicated, never really became the full answer in Sweden.

10. However, medieval recepies like repressive poor laws – although for a while refreshed in particular in England with the Speenhamland system – and charity were to dominate the scene for almost a century after the storming of the Bastille (Rimlinger 1971).

11. Cf. Heidenheimer on education as an alternative to social insurance (Heidenheimer 1981:269-304). I have already indicated "full employment" as an alternative to social insurance in Sweden.

12. As an alternative to the state as active interventionist in modern society, the popes during the second half of the 19th century actively emphasized the wordly role of the – Catholic – Church (cf. esp. Leo XIII's encyclica "Rerum Novarum" 1891). This initiative was crucial for the formation of christian-social political parties in central Europe, and of major importance for example in a country like Belgium where there was a deep cleavage between two kinds of "state minimalists": secular liberal-capitalists vs catholic corporatists (cf Kossman 1978).

13. In mid-19th century Germany, Prussia played the role of "modernizer", but in 1918 this process came to an halt, and Prussia/Germany did not fully manage to transcend its feudal-absolutist legacy (Anderson 1974).

14. To portray the social policy tradition as a reaction to laissez-faire thought, one has from the start to add that the classical mood of socio-economic thinking never was a monolithic corpus of thought. There was a wide variety within this tradition: from the Scottish Enlightenment to the Manchester School, the latter together with social Darwinism half a century later, being only the most extreme representatives of free individualist and self-regulating competition in almost every sphere of society, the natural laws of the invisible hand and the survival of the fittest, and consequently characterized by a strong emphasis on the absence of state involvement in civil society. Nonetheless, in a developmental perspective – in terms of "progress" – one has to stress that the priority of the "free market" became hegemonical thought associated with the emerging bourgeois class.

15. On the one hand, the bureaucracy should promote the existence of a politically loyal middle class composed of independent farmers and 'small' businessmen. On the other hand, the threat of working class insurgency should be bought off by social reform.

16. During these decades, German replaced Latin as first foreign language at institutions of higher learning in Sweden, a change that was contested by francophiles like Adolf Hedin (Kihlberg 1972:93-6) Thus Germany became Sweden's main spiritual trades partner. And, as among others Franco Moretti (1987) have pointed out, Germany was indispensable in the spread of avant-garde Scandinavian culture of that time (Ibsen and Strindberg). For at least half a century German remained the first foreign language taught in secondary schools in Sweden.

17. In 1882, a brief proposal had been put forward in Parliament by a farmer from the North (Berggren 1965). Two years earlier, a County Governor who had violently defeated a worker strike in 1879 had, on behalf of the sawmill owners of this district, proposed social legislation as a means of ameliorating the situation of the workers (Träffenberg 1880).

18. Eli Heckscher characterized Forssell's view of the state as "doctrinaire", and throughout his life, Forssell opposed the introduction of state supported social insurance (cf. Elvander 1961:96-7).

19. Theres was a certain gentleman's respect between Forssell and Hedin, although they had clashed a number of times (Kihlberg 1972:72,81, & 123). For instance, when Hedin was under severe personal economic pressure in the late 1870s Forssell, as Minister of Finance, appointed him member of the Royal Tax Commission, although Hedin was known for his poor capacity for cooperation.

20. Hedin was brought up in a rural environment characterized by lively agitation for political reform in the late 1840s and early 1850s. As a student, he wrote with admiration about Polish and Italian nationalism, and met with the anarchist Bakunin in Stockholm 1863. In 1867, Hedin wrote the most far-reaching democratic manifesto Sweden witnessed during the 19th century. He never became satisfied with the representative reform of the 1860s but was a steadfast democrat and passionate anti-royalist; a secular reformer and a member of the jury ("Giftas") that found August Strindberg (1849-1912) not guilty in late 1884 (cf. Lagercrantz 1979); an outspoken and active adherent of military reform but in no sense an anti-militarist as well as a stubborn defender of the Norwegian constitutional right within the dynastical union (cf. Spång-berg 1926).

21. Hedin was a "free" intellectual without any wealth apart from his meagre salary as an MP and what he earned from writing in the press. Only reluctantly did he accept material support from friends when his economy was severly strained. Among his supporters was a wealthy Norwegian capitalist and left politician, Astrup, a fact that created hard feelings among Swedish nationalists (Kihlberg 1972:254; cf. Sevåg 1967).

22. Kihlberg's book is written in an attempt to firmly situate Hedin within the liberal tradition (1972:9 and 230). Hedin's first biographer, his younger colleague and the left liberal publicist Spångberg, is more ambiguous in his early Verdandi booklet as well as in his fullscale biography; in the latter citing several orbituaries by socialists including Branting (1901 and 1926 respectively). On the socialist left, perhaps most outspoken in his admiration, however, was the young Per Albin Hansson who at that time was editor of the paper of the Social Democratic Youth League (cf. Gunnarsson 1970:146).

23. As indicated Hedin who was a francophile but fluent in several European languages including Italian had closely followed the development of social thought throughout Europe. Brentano was his main source of inspiration among the German Kathedersozialisten (Kihlberg 1972:110).

24. Hedin, who had been extremely critical of state involvement in the build-up of the Swedish railroad network in the 1860s and 70s, changed his mind at the height of the first business cycle crisis affecting Sweden in 1879. Forssell, then Minister of Finance, actively opposed "keynesianism of that

time" and only reluctantly accepted public interventions to support important infrastructural private capitalist investments like railroads (Berggren 1965).

25. As always, Hedin feared his antagonists in the more conservative upper house, where his bill quite surprisingly had passed through without any opposition (as mentioned, Forssell was a Senator).

26. The logic in the preceeding text in the bill is slightly different: it starts with occupational injury insurance (A – pp. 2-7), followed by employer's liability, work accidents and factory inspection (B – pp. 7-10) and old age insurance (C- pp. 11-22).

27. It is definitely true, that it took several decades before most of the proposals by the first as well as by other royal workers commissions were transformed into effective legislation (Kuhnle 1978). The results from the first Workers Commission were published and debated at the beginning of the last decade of the 19th century. New commissions continued this work and a number of legislative initatives were enacted under both conservative and liberal Premiers, most important a work safety law in 1889 (amended and revised in 1900 and 1912), a law regulating voluntary sickness insurance in 1910, the universal pension act of 1913, the occupational injury insurance of 1916, a revised poor relief law in 1918, and the eight-hours day in 1919. A new child welfare act had to wait until 1924. Administratively, a public factory inspectorate was set up in 1889, a National Insurance Board in 1901, a Social Board in 1913, a Pension Board in 1914 and in 1920 at the cabinet level, a Ministry of Social Affairs was separeted from the Ministry of Civil Affairs. This is a period of decline for independently organized agrarian interests in Swedish politics, nevertheless the farmers – conservatives as well as liberals but in most cases always close to home – managed to put their imprint on social legislation throughout these years (cf. Baldwin 1989).

28. Nevertheless, the symbolic value of Hedin was definitely lost hundred years after the bill was written: in Sweden, the absence of any centennial celebration of social insurance in 1884 is amazing. Apart from a short editorial in Dagens Nyheter (Kleberg 1984), Hedin was almost completely forgotten that year. This was in sharp contrast to the many articles following the publication of Kihlberg's biography in 1972, as well as the celebration of Hedin in the early postwar years by such different authorities as the Swedish TUC (LO) and the Swedish Academy. In particular the biography (Hellström 1948) published by the latter aroused some controversy (cf. Thermaenius 1950). Furthermore, in the aftermath of the appointment of a Workers' Commission in Sweden, the king proposed the Norwegian (left) government to establish a similar committee.

29. In contrast to the insurance expert Englund, who stresses the in no sense insignificant technical role of the insurance experts within the Commission (1976:66), I think it is necessary to underline Hedin's prolific diffusion of foreign social insurance experience as well as his steadfast rebuttal of conservative attempts to take over the social insurance issue, in particular the King's initiative in 1888, in Parliament as well as in the press and at public meetings throughout his life.

30. I owe this phrase to Francis Mulhern, who in turn paraphrases Walter Benjamin (1979:304).

31. "When changing economic conditions and new modes of communication shook the old local order and when a thin central state establishment loosened the repressive powers of the Church, there appeared a cultural and social void which relatively resourceful farmers and farmers' sons, artisans, small business-men and skilled workers could fill with organizational skills" (Therborn 1989a:199).

32. In his study of the historical development of work safety laws in Sweden, Sellberg makes the distinction between the "urban-liberal" years of 1884-1907, and the mixed "social democratic-urban liberal" period of 1908-1919, which – although overemphasizing the theoretical novelty of Social Democracy – is applicable to the social policy discourse as a whole, but also directs attention to a point of transition in the latter part of the period (cf. Montgomery 1932:186-199 and Höjer 1952:39-41).

33. Among the co-sponsors were the labour leaders Branting and Thorsson and several liberals close to the poor law reform circles (Beckman, Jacob Pettersson and Edvard Wawrinsky – see below). In a preceeding bill, Hedin had also proposed a separate – secular – Ministry of Education. Popular education was another reform field close to Hedin (cf. Lindensjö 1989).

34. For an illuminating local example, cf. Ericson 1987.

35. Its foundation was inspired by a courageous and strongly contested anti-clerical speech in a free church meeting hall by an overdue student, the budding economist Knut Wicksell. In *Verdandi*, the tiny radical youth gathered, and its founding generation included the first Liberal as well as the first Social Democratic Prime Minister: Staaff (1860-1916) and Branting respectively.

36. This bibliography was published on the initiative by the National Association of Social Work, and consequently its published material is most likely overrepresented. Thus the role of G H von Koch made visible in table 1 below is somewhat exaggerated, not to speak of Hirsch, Pettersson and Palm-stierna (see table 2 with sequential footnote). Thus, Gustaf Steffen (see below sec. 8.a) is a possible candidate for inclusion on the top ten list.

37. As mentioned the role of von Koch, Hirsch and Pettersson is somewhat exaggerated. Of the earlier mentioned authors, Forssell appeared four times in the bibliography, and Hedin five; one of the latter's pieces published in the first volume of *Social tidskrift*. Of other male social policy thinkers mentioned in this text, Steffen scored (14), Palmstierna (13), Beckman and Elmquist (both 10), Nyström (9), Fahlbeck, Heckscher (both 8), Huss (6), Beskow and Branting (both 5), Danielsson, Kjellberg, Carl Lindhagen, and Marcus (all 4), Bagge, Lindstedt, Spångberg, and Wawrinsky (all 2), Blomberg, Hamilton, Henrik Hedlund, Palm and Staaff (all 1) while Bergegren as well as Eriksson, Gyldén, S A Hedlund, Järte, Löfgren, Lennstrand, Raab, Rydberg and Öhrwall all zeroed. Of the female social policy authors to be briefly considered later, several of whom were urban social-christian philantropists, Broome scored (1), Fjäll-bäck-Holmgren (1), Hesselgren (5), Anna Lindhagen (5), Meyerson (6), Mon-telius (8), Pauli (7), Stahl-von Koch (9), Bugge and Whitlock (0). In particular Raab should have been included, and the omission of his pension booklets is symptomatic: he wrote on social insurance, not on poverty and poor relief. Likewise, Branting had during that period been a more frequent writer on socialism than the bibliography indicates. In identifying these and other

297

persons mentioned in this essay, I have frequently consulted *Svenska män och kvinnor* and *Svenskt biografiskt lexikon*.

38. Wicksell's first article in *Social tidskrift* – on taxation – appeared in 1909. His late appearance is an indicator of the controversiality of this neo-malthusian.

39. Both Leffler and Raphael belonged to the late 19th century reform community at least partly spatially gathered in the garden city adjacent to the Swedish capital, Djursholm – another project of modernity with Beckman as CEO (see section 7). Leffler also edited a two volume piece on "society and economic life" to which Raphael was a frequent contributor.

40. In Lund, from the 1890s, there was of course Bengt Lidforss, a biologist who shocked the conservative worldview but the participation of the academic community in the spread of popular education had to wait until early this century (Beyer 1968).

41. After the untimely death in Leipzig in 1885 of a *Verdandi* student – Christian Lorén – this fund, controlled by people living in Djursholm, was established with the explicit aim of sponsoring the study of the social question.

42. In another context, an attempt has been made to outline the intricate problem of selecting intellectuals (Olsson 1985). Throughout this section, I will point out alternative candidates to the ones selected for inclusion.

43. The inclusion of an eccentric soldier among a band of scholars may seem erratic and incidental. However, in Sweden the birth of this discourse appears to have been basically extra-academic. Furthermore, the composition of these sub-sections is, however, inspired by the biographer of one of these proponents of social reform – Steffen – who in that biography is contrasted with three other social policy thinkers: Wicksell, Fahlbeck and Cassel (Lilliestam 1960:95-123). Fahlbeck and in particular Cassel wrote early general treatises that can be regarded as forerunners of the textbook literature that was to appear from the 1940s onwards.

44. In a Swedish version of this article, I will tackle the theoretical problem posed by the "Chicago school of historical social policy analysis" (Castles 1989) and include a prominent state official, who was part of this reform community at least from the 1890s but made his major achievements in the first decades of the 20th century: Anders Lindstedt (1854-1939), an astronomer, mathematician and insurance expert, who was "omnipresent" in social insurance reform (Heclo 1974:212). He was also dean of the Technical University in Stockholm and as such an educational reformer. An early alternative to Lindstedt would have been Hugo Gyldén (1841-1896), a member of the first Worker's Commission and the head of the Stockholm Observatory, where Branting was a favourite student.

45. Svensson (1986) gives an comparative survey of the phenomenon of paternalistic welfare and welfare capitalism. According to his summary, the 1890s seems to be too early for a clearcut proponent of modern welfare capitalism. However, as a forerunner in the Swedish case, he points out the existence of both an urban type of late 19th century paternalism (at the Lindholmen shipyard-community in Gothenburg) as well as a rural paternalism (for example at Jonsered factory-community close to Gothenburg, whose patrician family in 1910 had an MP who wrote the first member bill asking for compulsory sickness insurance – cf. Edebalk 1989). Under the

sub-heading rural paternalism, Svensson also mentions Sandviken, where the Göranssons were proponents of welfare capitalism with social-christian undertones in the 1920s. Here, the reading list for the social policy study circle consists of roughly the same intellectuals as discussed in sections 6 and 8.2 with the exception of Raab (cf. Sunesson 1977:44).

46. I have deliberately chosen not to include Leffler or Raphael in the section on "independent spirits". They definitely belong to this category, but were secondary to both Wicksell and Cassel, and did not share the social conservatism of Fahlbeck. Furthermore, here it is important to emphasize that the topic of this essay is social policy. Had it been "public mass education", it would not have been possible to pass by Anton Nyström (1842-1929), a positivist, phycisian, and founder of the liberal Workers' institute.

47. This section is mainly based on the excellent biography by Gårdlund (1956, engl. ed 1962), and the latter's short article in the *International Encyclopedia of Social Science* (1968). Of course, I have also consulted the more recent biography on his cohab, the Norwegian suffragette Anna Bugge (1862-1928) (cf. Nordkvist-Wicksell 1986). Possible alternatives to Wicksell would have been Bergegren or the radical atheist Victor Lennstrand (1861-1895), but both were more distant from the core of the social policy discourse.

48. From his student years Wicksell had a close friend and intimate collaborator in the controversial atheist physiologist Hjalmar Öhrwall (1851-1929), the editor of the *Verdandi* series of booklets and the translator of John Stuart Mills (Gårdlund 1956:69; cf. Jonsson 1986 & 1987). Likewise, from the late 1880s, Anna Bugge, whom Wicksell first met at a women's lib-conference in Copenhagen in July 1888, was of course also instrumental in practical as well as theoretical support (cf. Nordkvist-Wicksell 1986). Outside this close circle, this thought was spread within the emerging popular movements. Furthermore, the Wicksells had close contacts with both Liberal and Social Democratic MPs.

49. In the first half of the 1880s, Wicksell was also actively involved in a radical newspaper project in Stockholm (*Tiden*), and an organizer in Uppsala in the emerging – liberal – workers' movement. In the second half of that decade, supported by the Lorén foundation, Wicksell spent several periods abroad, in London, Paris, Strassburg, Vienna and Berlin and met people in academic as well as in radical circles. In Strassburg, he followed courses by Brentano, in Vienna by Menger and in Berlin by Wagner. However, the population question was still at the heart of his thought, and although this turned him towards monetary theory, where he did his lasting work, he always remained deeply engaged in this problem. Throughout the century, Wicksell mixed journalism and public lectures with a bohemian life-style and a somewhat erratic self education (cf. ibid 1956:88-9).

50. Thus, Wicksell came to argue various theoretical and socio-economic matters from marxism to the normal working day with his friends and sometimes rather reluctant supporters in the mainstream socialist movement. Sometimes, when he provoked the throne, the sword, the altar and the moneybag, he was enthusiastically hailed by in particular the marginal anarchist left. Although a May Day speaker and a contributor to its still marginal newspapers, he never joined Social Democracy. He never managed to convince a

broad majority that birth control was the ultimate solution to the poverty problem, and like Strindberg, Wicksell always remained a lone star. For a long time he was an outsider, a man without a job, only supported by the Lorén foundation. But finally in 1901 the University of Lund after heavy infighting overcome its hesitation to employ a heretic as professor in law and national economy and employed Wicksell. However, he remained a drop-out even after he got an academic position, and continued to shock prevailing dominant values whether private-ethical or public-political. His personal life style – non-married cohabitation with children – and his public intrusion in private life through propagating birth control was throughout his life deemed a sin. He had a hard time to avoid provocations, and in 1908, his public jokes with sacred christian values sent him to jail for two months for blasphemy.

51. In 1897, he was one of the founders of *Statsvetenskaplig tidskrift* (the Political Science Review) – to which he later donated a part of his fortune – and its sole editor for several years (1899-1918). For eight years (1903-11), he was a member of the Senate, and from 1909 a full professor in political science and statistics. The latter subject was in no sense a subsidiary: from the early 1890s Fahlbeck lectured on the official statistics of Sweden and soon published a textbook in this field (1897, French ed. 1900).

52. Vallinder (1987:13-4) points out the close theoretical and methodological relationship between *Stånd och klass* and Fahlbeck's magnum opus, the statistic-demographic *Sveriges adel* (The nobility of Sweden; two vol., 1898-1902; German ed., one vol. 1903). At the end of his life, Fahlbeck planned a three volume work on the types of classes in history. However, only one volume on classes in antiquity was published (1920, German ed. 1921). An alternative to Fahlbeck is hard to suggest, but Harald Hjärne was not too far from *Kathedersozialismus* (Elvander 1961).

53. For example, Fahlbeck dismisses Pope Leo Encyclica on social affairs as wishful thinking. Sooner or later, hopefully the latter, the working classes in its struggle for equality, will be in such a position that they can take command of a new socio-economic order. In the mean-time, the educated classes can adjust their "standard of life" in anticipation of the more or less marxian needs- and work-principles which will govern income and consumption in the next society (1892:163-79).

54. Raab belonged to a noble family in which several members had supported representative and military reform – in the latter case in close cooperation with Adolf Hedin – during the 19th century (cf. Kihlberg 1972:68-73). There is no good alternative to Raab, the only one would be his speechwriter Henrik Hedlund (see note 56).

55. This section is based on Elmér (1957:749-52; cf. Elmér 1960:24-6).

56. Henrik Hedlund was the editor of GHT 1896-1916, an MP in 1891-93 and 1900-05, as well as the nephew and successor of Gothenburg's leading 19th century publisher, S A Hedlund (1821-1900). The latter, with interruptions an MP between 1867 and 1889, was one of the few who had the ability and tenacity to consistently cooperate with Adolf Hedin in Parliament, and Hedlund supported the 1884 social insurance bill although he preferred a combination of private and municipal initiatives (Kihlberg:1972:106). As a member of the town council 1862-91, he became the brain behind the so called Gothenburg

system, a forerunner to the national alcohol distribution (Bratt) system from 1922 onwards. Some of Hedlund's initiative has even been characterized as "socialist-utopian" (Berggren 1965). Hedlund was also the patron of non-orthodox christian author and aestethician Victor Rydberg (1828-95), a frequent contributor to GHT, the outstanding personage in Swedish culture in the epoch immediately preceeding Strindberg, and at the end of his life a mildly conservative university professor. Both Hedlund and Rydberg should be included in a overview of the environment in which Hedin played a key role. (On the impact of Rydberg on a later generation of radicals, cf. Beyer 1985:49 & 206 regarding Branting and Wigforss 1950:71 & 104-8).

57. Raab in vain sent out questionnaires to county governors and municipalities to investigate the level of living among the frailed elderly. When no answers arrived, he visited a number of Swedish towns and parishes, and apart from propagating he collected information about the situation of the poor and destitute. This way, he managed to present an overview of poverty among the elderly in Sweden based on a non-representative sample of a tenth of its population, which formed the basis of his calculations of necessary levies as well as pension benefits.

58. For Raab, this meeting ended in catastrophe: his resolution was not adopted, and he was called to give an account of his collection of money, which he failed to deliver. At this time, he had also started to show signs of mental self-absorbtion, and at the end of his life took for granted that he would become Director-General of the State Pension Board (Elmér 1957:752).

59. Rather surprisingly, there exists no biography on Cassel, although his secretary Ingrid Giöbel-Lilja wrote a book about her former employer in the "life-and-letter" tradition (1948). For a thorough presentation of Cassel's – and Eli Heckscher's – social policy positions during their lives, Carlson's dissertation is extremely useful (1988:145-80). However, the most reasonable alternative to the early Cassel would be the economist Davidson.

60. While still in Copenhagen, he competed with his arch-rival Wicksell for the open position in economics at the University of Lund, Sweden, but withdrew, according to Cassel's own version, as he did not wanted to be a means in the hands of the clerical-academic reaction who despised Wicksell's views on contraception and prostitution (Cassel 1940:33-5; cf. Gårdlund 1956:206-10). The polemic between the two, which Wicksell had started in 1899 with a comment on Cassel's dissertation continued throughout their lives. For example, in 1910 Cassel attacked Wicksell's anti-patriot population theory while in 1919 Wicksell published a critique of Cassel's whole system of economic thought. Furthermore, on religion as well as international security, their opinions completely clashed (Gårdlund 1956:350-1).

61. From 1897 to the early 1940s, Cassel was a frequent contributor on socio-economic matters to one of the main Stockholm dailies, Svenska Dagbladet – an outstanding career that ended if not as tragic as that paper's main literary critic during these decades, Fredrik Böök, at least in disgrace (Anderson 1965; Forser 1976; Carlsson 1987).

62. These were Bagge in the Conservative party, Wohlin in the Farmers' League, Ohlin in the Liberal party and Gunnar Myrdal among the Social Democrats.

63. At the centennial of the birth of Cassel, Gunnar Myrdal wrote: "During his Uppsala days in the late 1880s he had come into contact with contemporary youthful radicalism. Had he also come into contact with the popular movements, which at that time really were 'movements' and not yet 'apparatuses' to the extent that they are today, then his future life and work would no doubt have taken a different turn. Instead he came to identify himself with the romantic and nationalistic currents of *fin de siècle*. His excursions into unconventional behaviour were confined to becoming a vegetarian, the cultivation of folk music and dancing, and an experimental approach to spelling. He also returned the Northern Star – which arrived encouragingly early, before the days of an automatic 'ten years after the appointment' – and never accepted foreign awards. A more significant observation is that throughout his life he held on – from the radicalism of the 1880s – to a belief in development, rationalism and anti-religiousness (Myrdal 1972:305).

64. In these preliminary notes, I have deliberately decided to leave the work of an important royal commissions from early this century, that was the result of a CSA-initiative, the Emigration Commission, outside the boundaries of the present study (cf. footnote 44).

65. Apart from a fair number of wellknown upper or upper middle-class urban liberals, two lower middle-class teetotallers were on the first board of CSA. Otto Järte – see section 8) was probably the first Social Democrat on the board of CSA (1909-34).

66. Broomé was a teacher, peace and franchise acticist, and liberal member of the Stockholm town council 1911-24. She became managing director of CSA, 1904-14, and was a member of the controversial Employment Commission 1914-22 (Björklund 1929). Fjällbäck-Holmgren was CSA's first managing director, 1903-04 and later also 1918-29, and also a liberal suffragett. Hesselgren was the first female labour inspector and also became the first female (left-liberal) MP in Sweden (1922). Meyerson who belonged to the tiny jewish community in Stockholm, in 1898 sat up a home for female workers in the capital, and became the founding secretary of CSA. Agda Montelius, the oldest in this group of female charitans, was not only a founder of CSA, but had in 1889 started *Föreningen för välgörenhetens ordnande* (the Association for Coordination of Charity) of which she was the managing director 1892-1910. Whitlock was principal of an avantgardist girl school in the capital. With the exception of Hesselgren, none of them came to occupy a position within the new welfare bureacuray. However, in 1913 Broomé became a member of the Social Council, a corporatist instituion affiliated from its start affiliated with the National Board of Social Welfare (cf. Rothstein 1988b) as well as a member of the Employment Commission a year later, and in 1912, Montelius was appointed to serve on the public marriage law commission. However, most important as a social welfare theoritician was Ebba Pauli (see section 7.2).

67. Anna Lindhagen was also important in a movement that sponsored the set up of allotment-gardens/cottages, as its national chairman from its inception in 1906 onwards. In 1910, she joined Social Democracy, where she became editor of the paper of its womens' association.

68. Here, in particular Hirsch together with von Koch became leading organizers. Hirsch, who came from a wealthy jewish family in Stockholm, was

302

managing director for some thirty years, editor of its journal, and main financier of the association.

69. Of the five top officials in the National Board of Social Welfare in 1914, at least five (Elmquist, Huss, Markus, Sjöstrand and Järte) were or had been members of the board of CSA.

70. Chairman of CSA during its first thirteen years was one of the elderly statesmen in the liberal party, the travelled publicist, chief executive of the garden city Djursholm, christian humanitarian and MP Ernst Beckman (1850-1924) who had been a deputy of Hedin in the first worker's commission. He was succeeded by another liberal celebrity, Knut Kjellberg (1867-1921) – professor in anatomy, teetotaller, and an MP – who had not belonged to the board of CSA but for a similar period of time been a chairman of the Association of Popular education, another organization set up by von Koch early this century. Among the younger CSA activists, Palmstierna was an MP 1908-20, von Koch 1915-26, Hesselgren 1922-44, Löfgren 1910-32 (various years), and Bagge 1932-1947.

71. Formally, von Koch was an ordinary board member until 1909, when he for a year was its secretary. In 1926, he became vice chairman, and a few years later chairman for ten years (1930-40). Cf. Palmstierna (1951:27) regarding von Koch's significant roles behind the scene in a number of voluntary organizations within the orbit of the early CSA. However, CSA's memorials written by its secretary general Fjällbeck-Holmgren, especially pointed at Emilia Broomé's key role in CSA (1928).

72. At the age of sixteen he left school for farming, and in 1892, he had completed a higher agricultural degree and worked a few years as an estate supervisor, which acquianted him with the miserable conditions among agricultural labourers in Sweden, in particular in Scania. There, he became a convinced teetotaller, and sobriety remained throughout his life a backbone of his welfare ideology. Back in Stockholm in the late 1890s he became involved in a liberal organization, "Students and Workers", which strived for social peace and harmony between the social classes.

73. Apart from being editor of Social Review and secretary of the national co-op association 1899-1905, von Koch was in charge of *Centralbyrån för folkupplysning* (the Central Bureau for Popular Science Lectures, 1901-08), and held a number of positions in CSA as well as connected organizations. In 1913, he became a member of the Social Council and from 1914 of the Employment Commission. In 1918 he joined the civil service as the first state inspector for poor relief and child welfare, a position that two years later was coupled to a high-ranking position in the Ministry of Social Affairs. Temperence welfare and care of alcoholics were other major concerns. Furthermore, von Koch was a liberal member of the City Council of Stockholm, as well as a Senator (1915-1926).

74. This is a statement concerning the relative importance of CSA as a lobbyist compared to the earlier mentioned Raab pension movement. CSA emphasized poor relief reform but was in no way critical of social insurance as an idea, rather the contrary.

75. Closest to such a position, I would argue, came *Tiden* the theoretical monthly of the Social Democratic Party, which already in its first issue in 1908

published a major programmatical article on social insurance by the party's leading social politician, Branting.

76. However, in his speech at the first CSA Poor Relief Congress, von Koch stressed the double strategy of poor law reform and a new pension insurance system. He also wrote a pamphlett on the German workers' insurance for the CSA-series poor relief and people's insurance (1906). Oddly enough, his wife from 1906, Carola Stahl-von Koch, who also became a frequent contributor to the review, and after their honeymoon trip wrote about old age insurance in France.

77. At the 1906 convention, the leading Social Democratic trade unionist and MP Ernst Blomberg – a teetotaller – gave the main speech on unemployment. At the convention, where also the economist Heckscher spoke (Carlsson 1987:294), a decision was made to send a letter to Parliament asking for an investigation. It was in favour of the state subsidized but voluntary so called Ghent system. In a subsequent move, Wawrinsky during 1908-10 presented a member bill in Parliament, which was finally expedited by the 1911 Liberal cabinet (see section 8 below).

78. Her father was a principal of a school, and civil servant in the capital of Sweden, and as a teenager she came to participate in her mother's charity work in a rural parish outside Stockholm.

79. Between 1929 and 1937, Pauli was a member of the board of CSA at a time when the association had lost most of its clout.

80. Already at this time, Pauli was inspired by Natanael Beskow, the unorthodox preacher in the garden city Djursholm, and a radical freethinker within the State Church. Beskow recommended christians to study the Verdandi booklets by the Swedish social democrats and in a speech to christian students in 1901 outlined a new strategy for cooperation between workers and christians based on a positive attitude to Social Democracy (cf. Beskow 1901). In the 1920s and '30s, although fiercely anti-Bolshevik, Pauli intimately worked with a female social volunteer in Stockholm with deep sympathy for the organized work of unemployed communists (1953).

81. In Parliament, Carl Lindhagen was the main ciritical voice concentrating on the differential treatment of men and women. For a penetrating critical account of the Swedish social security system from a feminist perspective, cf. Abukhanfusa 1987.

82. In his obituary, von Koch wrote about Ebba Pauli: "Many also expected that she would become one of the leaders of state control and consultation. But Miss Pauli stayed in the voluntary sphere. (SvD 29/7 1941 reprinted in *Ebba Pauli* 1953:20.) Instead, von Koch left voluntary social work and in 1918 became the first National Poor Law Inspector.

83. Together these activists deliberately chose an established working class community in the northern part of downtown Stockholm to set up their first "settlement" and, in cooperation with the local socialist working class movement, a folk high school (cf. H-E Olson 1982 for a fine, detailed overview of the latter movement). In this area, workers' priests were also instrumental in the foundation of sport clubs, e.g. *Matteuspojkarna*.

84. Heckscher (1879-1953) came from a wealthy background and got his Ph D in economics in Uppsala 1907. For a while he was associated with the Univer-

sity of Stockholm only to become professor at the Business School there in 1909. Heckscher contributed early on to *Social tidskrift* and was a CSA board member, though only for a few years (1906-08) but was replaced on the board by his wife for another three years (1909-12).

85. Like most of the other CSA activists, Bagge came from the upper middle class in the capital. An endowment from his mother was, together with the money from CSA's funds, instrumental in setting up the chair. However, in particular the experienced female philanthropists in CSA were sceptical towards Bagge, and the fact that he had been a conservative member of the town council made him suspicious in female reform circles (Andrén & Boalt 1987).

86. In power during the latter part of the first decade of the 20th century the Conservatives had become more active on social issues and even moved towards an elaborated social-conservative position. Minister of Civil Affairs, still responsible for social issues, under Admiral Lindman was the "red count" Hugo Hamilton (1849-1928) who during the late 19th century had belonged to the liberal camp and worked with Hedin in the first Workers' Commission.

87. Apart from writing in *Svensk tidskrift*, Heckscher actively participated in public debate – like the well publicized battle with Branting and other leading socialists in the Stockholm People's House in 1908 (cf. n.a. 1979) – although he had to wait a decade before he got a tribune in *Dagens Nyheter* similar to Cassel's in *Svenska Dagbladet* (cf. Carlsson 1987:156-7).

88. Wadensjö emphasizes in particular Bagge's role as a transitional figure in the community of economists (cf. Wadensjö 1987, 1988 and 1989). Bagge was instrumental in the early establishment of the "Stockholm School" of Economists, in which in particular Gunnar Myrdal and Alf Johansson became devoted social policy analysists (see section 8.2 below). Furthermore, it is noteworthy that despite that Bagge got the first chair in social policy, he never published a major work in this field. However, a manuscript to a "general treatise" or a text-book exists (1930-1).

89. As mentioned, the 1913 pension bill was the offspring of thirty years of investigations, commission reports, cabinet and members' bills, a rather spontaneously organized one man social movement, and the deliberate work of outspoken welfare reform politicians and opinion makers like Hedin and Branting as well as early "social engineers" like the astronomers Gyldén and Lindstedt.

90. Throughout the 1920, this became the major bone of contention between the liberal welfare intelligentsia and the new generation of Social Democratic social policy makers. The "Swedish system of workfare" was run by welfare intellectuals like von Koch, and Järte, supported in the media by the leading economists (cf. Lindeberg 1968, Öhman 1970, Unga 1976; Rothstein 1983).

91. In Sweden, although ambiguous toward this concept, from the start 'social policy' was also a catch-word in socialist circles in Sweden. For example, in 1886 it was used – most likely by Axel Danielsson (1863-1899) – as the equivalent of the 'higher' organization of society, synonymous with Social Democracy (cf. 1972:175). Apart from Branting, in the first generation of Social Democratic leaders, Danielsson, the editor of Arbetet and the local party leader in Southern Sweden, was the most articulated and sophisticated intellectual and the sharpest pen of the early movement (cf. Zennström 1983). Outside the

Labour press, he was published in the Verdandi series (1894). At the end of his life he wrote a booklet with the title *Social självhjälp* (Social self-help; 1898), which in its composition shows a striking resemblance to Cassel's above-mentioned *Socialpolitik*: a treatise on wage policy, trade unions, coops, volunterism, public social initiatives, etc (1972:163-172). But to Möller in retrospect, these pages were probably rather poor.

92. Bernhard Eriksson (1878-1952) belonged to the pioneer generation of the Swedish labour movement (cf Cohn 1983). He was a blacksmith who entered Parliament in 1906, and after a few years on the National Pension Board, he became the first Minister of Social Affairs ever in 1920 (for only four months, though). Early this century, he seems to have been affiliated with the tiny "Students and Workers"-movement – his local chapter in Dalecarlia being the only one outside the main urban areas (Wirén 1980:80) – and for many years he was an activist in the voluntary sickness benefit societies. In 1924, Per Albin Hansson on his road to power replaced him as chairman of the SD Parliamentary group, but in 1928 Eriksson became Speaker of the House. A few years later he became the first Social Democratic County Governor ever. At the age of 59, Gustav Möller in the late 1930s made him chairman of the Royal Commission on Social Services that continued its work throughout the 1940s and whose tasks consisted of reforms in most areas of social affairs except unemployment, housing and family policy. Throughout his adult life Eriksson was very active in friendly societies and wrote several handbooks about social insurance, in particular on pensions and sickness insurance. However, his views on social reform were framed within the constraints of early Social Democratic parliamentary positions and did not match Möller's far-reaching goals.

93. In the early working class movement there seems to have been a contradiction in style between the missionary agitator or provocative orator, and the guarded but assiduous organizer or tenacious negotiator. The individual trade unionist should not be a drunkard but a exemplary working class hero, whose proper and prudent behaviour should be spread to all working men, thus preparing them to be able to sustain a hostile siege by their exploiters and rulers.

94. In a similar moderating move, Branting managed to disarm the religious questions to an individual choice for party activists to the great disappointment of the staunch Labour atheists.

95. Järte was also a frequent contributor to Social Review from 1908 onwards, and a year later became the first Social Democrat on the board of CSA. But it was above all in Bagge's and Heckscher's *Svensk Tidskrift*, where he first came to combine an authoritarian state approach with economic liberalism, later as chief editorialist in Svenska Dagbladet (Andersson 1965).

96. Hedin of course never appointed a successor, but during his last years Lindhagen at least among the MPs was the one closest to him. Their special relationship is illustrated by the fact that Lindhagen was the main speaker at the funeral of Hedin, a major public event in the capital of Sweden in which approximately one hundred thousand persons participated.

97. Apart from teetotalling, Wawrinsky was an expert on in particular employment issues and a proponent of maternity benefits, while Palmstierna

306

through his work in CSA, was knowledgable on municipal poor relief. Lindhagen may be regarded as an innovator as he had an overarching utopian social program manifested on several issues related to social policy: apart from the women's question (see his position regarding the pension proposal), on agriculture and on the colonization of the Far North of Sweden.

98. It is very hard to point out an alternative Social Democratic *Katheder-sozialist*, in particular if we add roots in the 1880s Uppsala student circles as a second criterion. Apart from Branting, C N Carleson (1865-1926), editor-in-cheif of Social-Demokraten 1892-96 and 1908-10, is a possible choice. However, his social policy writings belong to the 1920s when he was an independent left voice.

99. In 1886, only two years after *Giftas*, Steffen had approached August Strindberg and became almost immediately assigned to the duty of secretary-treasurer on the *Journey among French peasants*. After a fortnight on trains and roads their partnership suddenly ended, Steffen being fired as a simple "thief" by the erratic Grand Homme-Auteur who had just made his first inroads into obscurantism (Lagercrantz 1979:182-5). Steffen then turned to journalism and was a foreign correspondent of the radical-liberal *Göteborgs Handels- och Sjöfartstidning* in London and Rome. In this way he managed to finance his social science studies at foreign universities above all in Germany, and wrote several lengthy articles for Swedish journals on subjects like anarchism, consumer cooperatives, the crofter-question in Scotland, the normal working day, the history of the wage system in England etc. Steffen was also supported by the Lorén Fund.

100. In particular, "The presuppositions and tasks of social policy" from 1906 must be seen in light of Cassel's earlier work. Here, Steffen tried to delimit and clarify the concept of "social".

101. In 1915, Steffen and Järte were stripped of their party memberships because of their active support of Imperial Germany in World War I. But in contrast to Järte, who changed completely from being a lieutenant of Branting to a similar position in the Conservative party, Steffen rejoined the SAP and became a state commissioner on industrial nationalization. Nyström has characterized the late Steffen as a fabian (1989b).

102. During these years also Wigforss wrote on unemployment.

103. Jungen was a carpenter who in 1918, at the age of 28, got his teaching degree. For many years a leading Labour politician faithful to his hometown and chairman of the town council (1934-1962). In the latter year, the University of Gothenburg awarded him an Honorary Ph D (after serving on its Board of Trustees for eightteen years (1936-54). Furthermore, he became vice chairman of that town's School of Social Welfare from its start in 1944 (until 1960). Quite remarkably, this leading local politicians has not been included in *Svenskt biografiskt lexikon*.

104. "Social policy can practically be taken as far as possible, but it doesn't reach a principal transformation of private capitalism". However, as part of a realization of economic and social security, it can cause the "class law character to disappear, as it becomes a component in society's normal function to furnish protection in case of social or individual invalidity for socially and economically equal groups of citizens (1931:478).

105. Although Swedish unions in a comparative perspective from the start worked fairly close with the main Labour party, not least due to the close organizational bonds (cf. Olofsson 1979), and the fact that the unions early-on had a say in the formulation of social policy (the second Swedish Minister of Social Affairs was a former trade union leader, a pattern close to the continental model) during Moller's long period of office, social policy in many senses became more of a party task compared to what happened in the postwar decades (cf. Kassman 1989:216-45).

106. These articles were simultaneously published in the Danish review "Socialt tidskrift". The first article by Myrdal was published in the same issue as Erik Mesterton's novel study of T S Eliot's method. The brain behind this journal was the poet Karin Boye.

107. "The dilemma of liberal social policy is profound. It has been admitted that property distribution is a result of occasional institutions which could be changed, if it were considered beneficial for society...when social policy reaches a size, where redistribution becomes feasible, a conflict of interests is exposed but is not ackknowledged... in this situation there is a circumstance which affords a comfortable road to rationalize a conservative retreat from the annoying declarations about the benefits of a more equal distribution of property. I refer to the possibility that social policy inhibits individual initiative" (4-16).

108. In an article focussing on these early Myrdal articles, Nilsson (1990) has emphasized another startingpoint for Myrdal: the low level of taxation in Sweden in the 1930s.

109. Recently, Hirdman has emphasized the utopian-socialist background to the writings of the Myrdals (1990).

110. Also in their "limitlessness" regarding the role of the state, they stand out as good pupils to the early Cassel but also to his contemporary Wicksell, whose radicalism on social issues was both provocative and ahead of its time.

111. Despite the fact that Hedin early on left the countryside for the capital while von Koch through several years of daily agricultural supervision learned the plights of the people, in terms of timing it was the radicalism of the 1880s that anticipated the later red-green social hegemony. Thus, the early social policy breakthrough ended in stagnation, to use the Höjer's terminology (1952), before a new social policy saw the light of day in the 1930s: the etatism and potential universalism of Hedin was replaced by von Koch's and Pauli's potential residualism and more restricted state interventionism.

Chapter II

* This article is part of the project "Developments and alternatives in Swedish Social Insurance Policy" funded by the Swedish Commission for Social Research (DSF 87/91). I am indebted to Åke Elmér, Olli Kangas, Rafael Lindqvist, Per Nyström, Gunnar Olofsson, Joakim Palme, Gösta Rehn and Stefan Svallfors for their helpful comments and criticisms on the draft for this text. Jarl Hjalmarsson generously shared his time for an interview. I am also

grateful for the critique at the Sociology Department Seminar, University of Stockholm. Suzanne McMurphy corrected the draft and Patrick Hort made the final language corrections.

1. Therborn, G. (1983): The Working Class, the Welfare State and Sweden. Paper presented at the Social Policy seminar of the Swedish Sociological Association, Ladvik, (1985) p. 37, reprinted in P. Kettunen (ed), *Det nordiska i den nordiska arbetarrörelsen* (Helsinki 1986) pp. 1-75. Baldwin follows in the footsteps of Therborn and indeed singles out major contributors to the development of the Swedish welfare state in addition to those who are usually honoured. Although an appropriate foundation, considering we are approaching 1989 – the centenary of the foundation of the Social Democratic Labour Party in Sweden – I think it is important to see the true proportions of this narrative. Thus, these pages may be labelled, to paraphrase Therborn, "a respectful *Festschrift* contribution" (p. 28).

2. Å. Elmér, *Folkpensioneringen i Sverige* (Malmö, 1960).

3. *International Review of Social History* (Vol. XXXIII, No. 2, pp. 121-147 (1988). Hereafter Baldwin, IRSH. Cf. P. Baldwin, "The Scandinavian Origins of the 'Social Interpretation of the Welfare State", *Comparative Studies in Society and History*, Vol. 31, No. 1 (1989) pp. 3-24.

4. P. Baldwin, (1987): "The Politics of Social Solidarity and the Class Origins of the European Welfare State 1875-1975". Harvard University, Department of History (mimeograph). Hereafter Baldwin, PSSCOEWS.

5. Productivity at American universities, in particular the production of dissertations from the elite schools, has created a fundamental problem in the scientific community at large. The need to make a career in an extremely competitive academic market place, where success is founded on making a 'break through' in an overwhelming publishing milieu, forces the dissertation authors to press their points to the extreme as well as to adapt them to the theoretical conjuncture of the day. Invisible academic proof-work is superficially transformed into visible articles in scientific journals, the most prestigious form of publishing and the best means for providing advertisement for forthcoming books. Thus, while simplistic viewpoints are spread all over the field, the indispensable 'Socratic' dialogue between scholarly minds is put aside. Too much competition can be turned into a disadvantage. The threat of anti-intellectualism based on this orientation cannot be overlooked, sacrificing the generally high quality of American research, in particular historical research. I would like to add, that these remarks reflect my own ambiguity towards a system I had an extremely rewarding firsthand experience of as a Fulbright visiting scholar during academic year 1987/88 at Mount Vernon College and the Brookings Institution, Washington D.C. Commenting upon these remarks, Per Nyström reminded me that Gunnar Myrdal early on had noticed another bad habit in the US academic community: the abuse of citations from best friends and close colleagues (letter to the author 1989-01-26).

6. Concerning the astonishment among social policy experts at the apparent progressiveness of the bourgeois parties, it is important to note that Baldwin misreads Elmér, ibid., IRSH, p. 137 n45. Elmér does not say that the Right's attitude "is the most difficult to explain", only that it is not possible for him to conclude whether it was purely tactical or a matter of principle (pp. 118-27).

Elmér also stresses that he is speculating on this issue, but pays considerable attention to the principal arguments. However, he does not analyze in terms of rationality (a great merit in Baldwin's article), makes no reference to the Right's advocacy of white-collar pension interests, and does not investigate the sources to which Baldwin has had access (especially the archive of the Right party).

7. Baldwin, IRSH, p. 128: "The universality and apparent solidarity of some of the most conspicuous and celebrated postwar reforms were not the result of the Left's strength, but were due to the immediate and direct interests the bourgeois classes and their parties developed in such social policy". Indeed, these "interests" are of course *part* of the policy process that made possible the unanimity in Parliament when welfare reforms were enacted in Sweden in the mid-1940s. Cf A-K Hatje, *Befolkningsfrågan och välfärden* (Stockholm, 1974) esp. pp. 222-4.

8. Baldwin, PSSCOEWS, pp. 27-8. For references to proponents of the 'Social' interpretation, see Baldwin, IRSH, p. 127 n18 and n20. For a recent overview of alternative schools of thought, see T. Skocpol and E. Amenta "States and Social Policies" in *Annual Review of Sociology*, vol. 12 (1986), pp. 131-57.

9. Baldwin, PSSCOEWS, pp. 77-9. This "counter-criticism" is *not* made in order to apologize for the frequent use and abuse of Sweden as an implicit yardstick in recent welfare state research, just to bring out the underlying methodological problem in Baldwin's article.

10. It would have been interesting to know whether the Right Party's pretention that its new social policy stance was the equivalent of the Beveridge Plan, had any repercussions outside the party. However, it seems that this was mainly an "internal argument". Cf. Baldwin, IRSH, p. 134. Already in 1943 a presentation of the Beveridge Plan had been written by Sven Larsson – a social policy expert on the secretariat of the Population Commission – as a result of active intervention by Gustav Möller. This booklet was published by the Social Democratic publishing house *Tiden*.

11. Of course, both the British Labour Party and the Swedish Social Democrats belong to the European Labour Movement and definitely share certain general values. Nevertheless, despite their internationalistic rhetoric, each labour party has first of all to be seen in its national context, in particular when it is in a position to influence the broader political spectrum. To see Alarik Hagård and Martin Skoglund, the junior and senior Conservatives on the Social Welfare Committee, as two Swedish "Beveridges" – which in effect is what Baldwin does – would be a tremendous exaggeration. Hagård was the son of a farmer, worked as a teacher but ended up as General Manager of the Borås Public Hospital. He entered Parliament in 1941 and was a MP until his untimely death in 1956. Throughout his Parliamentary career, his main interest was social policy. (Information provided by Åke Elmér in a letter to the author 1988-08-11.) Skoglund was a wealthy farmer and later Speaker of the Upper House (see also note 39). Actually, Skoglund advertised the lack of a "Swedish Beveridge" at a meeting of the Social Welfare Committee. See Riksarkivet (hereafter RA) 11853/3, minutes, 2 Oct., 1944, p. 5 (cf. p. 1 in the drafts for these minutes, RA 11853/3, 2-5 Oct).

12. See the forthcoming works by G. Esping-Andersen, "The Three Political

310

Economies of the Welfare State", in J.E. Kolberg (ed) *Between Work and Social Citizenship*; and S. Svallfors, *Vem älskar välfärdsstaten?* (Lund, 1989). To be fair, Baldwin hints at this problem in his dissertation: PSSCOEWS, pp. 481-495.

13. For example, it is very unlikely that a book like Ronald Fraser's *In search of a Past* (London, 1984) could have been written in Sweden. The way class differences changed between pre- and postwar Britain and Sweden, respectively, differs strikingly. A book akin to Fraser's, Tom Nairn's recent *The Enchanted Glass* (London, 1988), with its analysis of the form of the British state, indirectly highlights the difference between the two countries in the relationship between monarchy and democracy.

14. The workers' movement as the inheritor of the egalitarian and democratic traditions in Swedish society, earlier upheld by the peasantry, is elaborated in G. Therborn, "Socialdemokratin träder fram", *Arkiv för studier i arbetarrörelsens historia* (English edition in *Annalli Giangiacomo Feltrinelli 1983-84*) no. 27-28 (1984). A similar idea for Scandinavia as a whole has been put forward by Stein Rokkan. Cf. *Stat, nasjon, klasse* (Oslo, 1987).

15. This is stressed in a letter to the author from Per Nyström, Möller's Under-Secretary of State 1945-50 (17.8.1988). Cf P. Nyström, *Historia och biografi* (Lund, 1989), B. Rothstein, "Att administrera välfärdsstaten: några lärdomar från Gustav Möller" in *Arkiv för studier i arbetarrörelsens historia* no. 36-37 (1986) pp. 68-84, and J. Hermansson & T. Svensson, "Möller och socialpolitikens principfrågor" in *Tiden* Vol. 81, No. 1, (1989) pp. 59-65.

16. Elmér, ibid, esp. pp. 54-75. Cf. H. Heclo, *Modern Social Policies in Britain and Sweden* (New Haven, 1974) esp. pp. 211-226. Heclo emphasizes the "informed defence" put up by *the administrators* of pension policy – the Director-General of the National Pension Board – against the intense Conservative attacks on the disastrous effects of public pensions, but also stresses the role of Möller's *learning* as Minister of Social Affairs in the 1920s for later developments.

17. Baldwin has a short paragraph on this dilemma but does not draw the full implications, IRSH, p. 145. The resistance from Wigforss as Minister of Finance against the more costly pension alternative (III) had a clear background not only in the necessity to finance this and other expensive social policy reforms (child allowances, sickness insurance, etc.) but also in the fact that the Liberal and Conservative parties combined their backing for reforms with active efforts for lower taxation immediately after the war. Cf. Elmér, ibid, p. 88, and E. Rodriguez, *Offentlig inkomstexpansion* (Uppsala, 1980), esp. pp. 112-23.

18. Baldwin, PSSCOEWS, pp. 153-68.Cf. K. Englund, *Arbetsförsäkringsfrågan i svensk politik, 1884-1901* (Uppsala, 1976), esp. pp. 126-9 and ch. 14, and Elmér, ibid, pp. 16-54, 116-146 and 149. The 1913 pension system had a dual character: universal contributory pensions based on premiums paid, and tax-financed, means-tested supplementary pensions.

19. Income testing was discussed a great deal in the Ministry of Social Affairs in the mid-1940s, in particular regarding housing support. Cf. Möller's speech in Minutes from the Nordic Meeting of Ministers of Social Affairs 1947, (mimeo) pp. 7-17, and P. Nyström, "Goda bostäder åt alla", *Arkiv för studier i arbetarrörelsens historia* no. 41 (1989) pp. 83-90. Nyström has also stressed that

the inspiration behind the shift in principle from means- to income-test goes back to the Danish social policy expert K.K. Steincke, who may be described as a mentor for Gustav Möller in this field of policy. P. Nyström. "Välfärdsstaten och dess styrningsmekanismer" in A. Björnsson (ed.), *I folkets tjänst* (Stockholm, 1983) pp. 221-34.

20. Public expenditure on poor relief was greatly reduced as a share of total social expenditure between 1900 and 1940: from 60 to well below 20 percent. By 1950, after the 1948 pension payouts, poor relief costs had dropped to below five percent, see graph 2 in S.E. Olsson, "Sweden" in P. Flora (ed), Growth to Limits. *The Western European Welfare State Since World War II*, Vol. 1 (Berlin & New York, 1986) p. 6.

21. Hatje, A-K., ibid. esp. pp. 32-4 and 209-13.

22. Baldwin gives in his article the impression that the pre-1948 pension system was limited to the poorest, defined very narrowly. See pp. 129 ("the poor alone"), p. 136 ("cover more than the most indigent in any but the most miserly fashion"), p. 143 ("targetted at the poorest"). In 1939, more than 93 percent of the over-67s were entitled to a pension benefit. Of these, more than a third (37 percent) received only the non means-tested benefit, based on previous premium payments. All these benefits were obviously meager – before the war on average 10 percent of an industrial worker's wage – but every Swede could claim them. Thus, to a significant degree, "vertical universalism" had already been achieved before World War II (see also *graph 1*). Cf. S.E. Olsson "Svensk socialpolitik i internationell belysning: Old Age Pensions 1930-1985", Institutet för social forskning (Stockholm, 1985), mimeo, and J. Palme, "Rätt, behov och förtjänst – ålderspensionerna i välfärdsutvecklingen." Institutet för social forskning (Stockholm, 1987), mimeo.

23. Alternative I from the Social Welfare Committee, definitely the proposal closest to the old pension system, also included a uniform flat-rate benefit (although rather small compared to the other two alternatives), but this proposal was never seriously considered outside the Committee. Cf. G. Möller "De planerade socialreformerna", *Tiden*, Vol. 38, No. 2 (1946) pp. 70-85.

24. SOS (Sveriges Officiella Statistik), *Allmän folkpensionering 1939-1950* (Stockholm, 1951) p. 36.

25. Or, in terms of the Titmussian social policy model as developed by Mishra and Korpi, it is *not* the subdimensions "Range of statutory services" or "Population covered by statutory programs" (Mishra) or "Proportion of population affected" or "Dominant types of programs" (Korpi) that is at stake, but rather "use of means-test" (Mishra) or "importance of social control" (Korpi). See in both cases *table 1* in R. Mishra, *Society and Social Policy* (London, 1981) p. 101 and in W. Korpi, "Social Policy and Distributional Conflict in the Capitalist Democracies. A Preliminary Conceptual Framework" p. 303 in *West European Politics*, Vol. 3, No. 3 pp. 296-316 (1980).

26. Svensson, G., "Utländska bilder av Sverige. Bespeglingar i det moderna" in U. Himmelstrand & G. Svensson (eds), *Sverige – vardag och struktur* (Stockholm, 1988) pp. 139-161. This rather uneven exposition of "Sweden as a world model" is quite explicit regarding the slow take-off of the export of this image after World War II, p. 148.

27. Cf. the lively appreciation of social welfare and daily life in a report from

a journey to Sweden, as well as critical comments on C.A.R. Crosland *The Future of Socialism* (London, 1956), by the young Perry Anderson: "Sweden: Mr. Crossland's Dreamland", *New Left Review* no. 7 and no. 9 (1961). Cf. D. Strand "Välfärd och apati" in T. Erlander et al. Idé och handling. Till *Ernst Wigforss på 80-årsdagen* (Stockholm, 1960). Furthermore, the continental European refugees in Scandinavia during World War II – for instance Willy Brandt and Bruno Kreisky – came to power in the 1960s.

28. The 'strong society' was a concept used by Prime Minister Tage Erlander to characterize the Swedish welfare state. See T. Erlander *1949-54* (Stockholm, 1974) esp. pp. 369-388.

29. Wigforss' remarks on Bagge's unsuccessful ambition to play the role of deputy prime minister – as leader of the largest non-socialist party – in the wartime national coalition government hints at the issue of hegemony. See E. Wigforss, *Minnen*, part III (Stockholm, 1954) pp. 278-9. The regrouping within the Swedish party system is discussed from the other (i.e. Social Democratic) angle by G. Therborn, "Den svenska socialdemokratin träder fram", ibid, esp. pp. 34-5. From a conservative insider's perspective, Ivar Andersson has written several admirable works – both in the "Life and Letters"-tradition and auto-biographical – that cover this era of conservative decline: see *Arvid Lindman och hans tid* (Stockholm, 1956) esp. chs. XVI-XVIII, *Otto Järte – en man för sig* (Stockholm, 1965), *Åsyna vittne* (Stockholm, 1967) and the work cited by Baldwin, IRSH, p. 145, n71.

30. Lewin, L., *Planhushållningsdebatten* (Uppsala 1967) esp. pp. 186-240.

31. SOU 1945:46 Socialvårdskommitteéns betänkande XI: *Utredning och förslag angående lag om folkpensionering* (Stockholm, 1945) p. 276. Cf. SOU 1944:15, *Utredning och förslag ang allmän sjukförsäkring*, (Stockholm, 1944) p. 353 and Elmér, ibid, p. 86. Here, it is appropriate to add that the Right party's final decision to support alternative III was taken *after* the Employer's Confederation (SAF) and the Trade Union Confederation (LO) had delivered their support for the same proposal.

32. D. Sainsbury, *Swedish Social Democratic Ideology and Election Politics 1944-1948* (Stockholm, 1980) p. 61. Cf. P. Nyström, "Gustav Möller i Marx-sällskapet" in *Meddelande från Arbetarrörelsens arkiv och bibliotek* no. 2/3 (1977) p. 67. and, on white-collar unionization, T. Nilsson, *Från kamratföreningar till facklig rörelse* (Lund, 1986).

33. However, in the same breath as the Conservative party leader mentions the middle class, he pitches the elderly against the young and active generations arguing for a *productive* (emph. in orig.) social policy. RA, Moderata samlingspartiet, partiledarna, Domö/5, ms for a speech, 3 Oct 1945 (cf Baldwin, IRSH, p. 134 n35).

34. Zetterberg, K., *Liberalism i kris* (Stockholm, 1975) esp. pp. 142-45.

35. SOU 1945:46, ibid. Cf. Elmér, ibid, pp. 81-2. This division within the Social Welfare Committee is simplified by Baldwin into pure party lines: he omits the fact that alternative III was supported by one Social Democrat and one civil servant (as well as the fact that the other civil servant on the Committee supported alternative II). See Baldwin, IRSH, p. 132. This is only one example of the disturbing "non-Socratic", "American" habit of "stressing points" and painting in black and white. Likewise, Baldwin fails to mention

that Elmér twice in his *magnum opus* gives credit to the secretary of the Social Welfare Committee (and partly to one of the civil servants) as the originator of alternative III (ibid, pp. 81 and 126, n13) – in marked contrast to Baldwin's unproven suggestion that the Conservative representatives had this role. For example, none of the Conservative representatives were present at the meeting when the Committee took the decision to work out alternatives II and III, see RA 11853/3, minutes, 14 Sept, 1945. Furthermore, from the minutes of the Social Welfare Committee, where the discussion was very open-minded, it seems that one of the civil servants (Höjer) early on opted for income-tested housing allowances as the sole 'tested' part of the pension benefit. See RA 11853/3, minutes, 1 June 1944, p. 3-4. The role of the experts – "state managers" – is a reminder of the potential of Theda Skocpol's theoretical approach. Cf. M. Weir, A.S. Orloff & T. Skocpol (eds) *The Politics of Social Policy in the United States* (Princeton, 1988).

36. Governmental power and Parliamentary strength are not the sole variables for the strength and weakness of the Left and Right. However, it is instructive to compare the parliamentary situations in Sweden in connection with the two major pension decisions. In *1913*, just after the change to universal male suffrage, the Social Democrats were still outnumbered by both the Liberals and the Conservatives. In *1946*, the Social Democrats had as many seats in the Lower Chamber as all the other parties combined (including the Communists) and outnumbered them in the Upper Chamber. This highly relevant fact is omitted in Baldwin's article. Cf. G. Carlsson, "Partiförskjutningar och tillväxtprocesser", *Statsvetenskaplig tidskrift*, Vol. 66, No. 2-3 (1963). Furthermore, unionization had increased considerably between 1913 and 1946. Cf. W. Korpi *The Working Class in Welfare Capitalism* (London, 1978) and A. Kjellberg *Facklig organisering i tolv länder* (Lund, 1983).

37. A lot of research hints at this decisive relative shift of the Agrarians in the Swedish party system, although no monograph has covered this process in terms of hegemony and political dominance. There is still no authoritative biography of the party leader Bramstorp. However, this essential hegemonic shift from right to left is considered briefly in G. Therborn "Den svenska socialdemokratin träder fram", ibid, pp. 30-2. Cf. B. Fryklund et al., "Från bondeförbund till centerparti", *Zenit* no. 34 (1973) pp. 4-23, and B. Fryklund and T. Peterson, *Populism och missnöjespartier i Norden* (Lund, 1982) esp. ch. 12. On the more recent Agrarian shift in the other direction – from left to right – see also the autobiography by the former Conservative party leader G. Bohman *Maktskifte* (Stockholm, 1984) esp. pp. 59-69. On Nordic agrarian pension policy, see also O. Kangas "Politik and ekonomi i pensionsförsäkringen", Swedish Institute for Social Research, Occasional papers No. 5, Stockholm, 1988, G. Olofsson & J. Rasmussen, "Det svenska pensionssystemet: historia, struktur och dilemmor", University of Copenhagen, Institute of Sociology, 1988 (mimeo), and the discussion on this issue in the articles by S. Kuhnle, L. Nörby Johansen, M. Alestalo and H. Uusitalo in P. Flora (ed), ibid.

38. Sainsbury, ibid, p. 57.

39. Lewin, ibid, p. 190-1.

40. Elmér, ibid, pp. 124-5. However, the Conservative MP Hagård did not give any indication of the direction of change. See *Riksdagens Protokoll* AK

1944:11, March 22 1946, pp. 90-1. On this occasion the senior Conservative argued for changes in the income-testing procedure in order to encourage the expansion of entrepreneurial pensions, ibid. pp. 86-7.

41. When analyzing a singular political event, the *Fingerspitzgefühl* of the main actors also needs to be considered. According to another leading conservative – Ivar Anderson in *Åsyna vittne* – nature had bestowed this important political gift generously on the senior conservative in the Social Welfare Committee, p. 190. A Conservative attempt similar to that on the pension issue was made with the aim of taking over the child allowance question, but this time another conservative politician failed. See Hatje, ibid, ch. III esp. p. 97 n51. According to the retrospective view of the leader of the Liberal party, Bertil Ohlin, it was the senior Conservative representative who first presented the idea of a completely non income-tested pension benefit. In the same breath, Ohlin complains about the prestige of Gustav Möller on social policy issues. See *Memoarer 1940-1951* (Stockholm, 1975) p. 133. Cf Ohlin's appreciation of Möller in Parliament when the pension decision was taken. AK 1946:27, 20 June 1946, pp. 43-4.

42. See also note 35. The first written document in the archives of the Social Welfare Committee is a memorandum by the secretary. However, the Committee's secretariat informed Möller about the content of "alternative III" early on. When the Ministry took over work on the bill after the Committee's report had been published, this was the main alternative from the start, although Möller had some ideas of his own and was prepared to give way to the majority of the Social Democratic leadership, which supported "alternative II". Möller's main ambition was to increase the benefits for the poor and needy, not to extend pension benefits to the well-to-do. But there is no indication that he actively wanted to keep the income-test alive, quite the contrary. Cf. Elmér, ibid, p. 81, pp. 86-90, and Möller's retrospective remarks in "Inkomstprövade pensioner?", *Arbetarrörelsens årsbok 1971* (Lund, 1971) pp. 180-2. According to the latter document, the cabinet was seriously split and Möller managed to get the issue transferred from the leadership circle to the Parliamentary group.

43. Elmér ibid, p. 126 n13. On the remarkable career of the Agrarian on the Social Welfare Committee – a scandalized Social Democratic entrepreneur who in 1932 became an Agrarian MP and subsequently displayed strong pro-nazi sympathies – see G. Hellström, *Jordbrukspolitik i industrisamhället* (Stockholm 1976) pp. 161-9.

44. Rather ironically, on this occasion the junior Conservative hailed the work of the chairman of the Social Welfare Committee – an old Social Democrat who had supported income-tested pensions. *Riksdagens protokoll*, AK 1946:27, 20 June 1946, p. 26.

45. Cf. note 42 above. Baldwin gives an overview of the tensions within the labour movement on this issue IRSH (p. 137-9). This is the only occasion in the article where Baldwin really takes issue with Elmér's thesis. However, I cannot share his view that Elmér's underlying assumption is that the Social Democrats of course "supported the reforms that eventually resulted" (p. 138 n49) if this means "alternative III". Elmér thoroughly scrutinizes the process that led to this position – although he did not investigate one of the sources that has been available to Baldwin, the archives of the Right Party.

46. According to the retrospective view of Gösta Rehn, Per Albin Hansson from the start envisaged the advantages of alternative III (oral communication). However, the written documents indicate that the Social Democratic Party Chairman supported alternative II when the leadership circle discussed the pension reform.

47. One explicit reason for not accepting Möller as the heir of Per Albin Hansson was that Wigforss considered that Möller limited himself to social policy issues instead of regarding the totality of the party's policy positions. See *Minnen* Part III (Stockholm), 1954) p. 296. Cf. A. Gjöres, *Vreda vindar* (Stockholm, 1967) p. 163, T. Erlander, *1940-49* (Stockholm, 1973) p. 254 and *1949-54* (Stockholm, 1974) p. 246, G. Jonasson, *Per Edvin Sköld 1946-1951* (Uppsala, 1976) pp. 11-24, 56-70, 135-8, 152-4, 185-6, T. Nilsson, *Männniskor och händelser i Norden* (Stockholm, 1977) pp. 112-117, and S. Andersson, *På Per Albins tid* (Stockholm, 1980) pp. 276-289. Andersson is also very detailed about the tensions within the cabinet after 1946, ibid. pp. 292-301. Cf. G. Möller, "Dyrtidstilläggen" in *Arbetarrörelsens årsbok 1971* (Stockholm 1971) pp. 187-9. Already in early 1946, however, Möller had responded to this state-financial criticism and stated that maybe alternative II had to be accepted in view of the strain on public resources. See *Tiden*, February 1946.

48. On the tensions between the elderly editorialists at *Svenska Dagbladet* and the new generation of Conservatives, see E. Sandlund, *Svenska Dagbladets historia, part III* (Stockholm, 1984) pp. 204-7. Cf. I. Anderson, *Från det nära förflutna* (Stockholm, 1969), esp. pp. 216-19.

49. Elmér, ibid, pp. 86-90.

50. Elmér, ibid, pp. 76, 126 and 170. The lobbying by the emergent pensioners' associations is not discussed at all by Baldwin.

51. Elmér, ibid, p. 171.

52. Elmér, ibid, p. 86.

53. Arbetarrörelsens arkiv och bibliotek, Partistyrelsen, Minutes, 5 March 1946. Cf. Elmér, ibid, p. 90.

54. For a recent illuminating essay on this topic, see R. Ambjörnsson, *Den skötsamme arbetaren* (Stockholm, 1988). For a contrasting perspective, cf. M. Franzén, "Ölkaféet och det folkliga drickandet", *Arkiv för studier i arbetarrörelsens historia*, No. 43-44 (1989).

55. Elmér, ibid, pp. 146-156.

56. (Minneapolis, 1983). For a critical review from a neo-liberal perspective of this fairly non-partisan account of Swedish social democratic social policy, see E. Langby, "Sweden: Libertarianism on Rocky Soil" in *The Public Interest* No 80 (1985), pp. 100-103.

57. Heckscher, ibid, esp. pp. 41-52. Heckscher's contributions to the social policy discussions of the 1940s are included in RA, Igor Holmstedts Samling om Högerpartiet, 2. The conservative claim – not repeated by Heckscher – that their representatives in the Social Welfare Committee made a major contribution to the abolition of means- and income-testing in the basic pension system has been repeated continually since the inception of the new pension system. Apart from the sources mentioned by Baldwin, see also *I frihetens tjänst* (Stockholm, 1979) p. 58.

58. On the long route from voluntary to compulsory sickness insurance cf. R.

Lindqvist, "Konflikt och kompromiss vid den allmänna sjukförsäkringens tillkomst", *Arkiv för studier i arbetarrörelsens historia* no. 41-42 (1989) pp. 52-81, and, on unemployment insurance, P.G. Edebalk, "Från motstånd till genombrott: den svenska arbetslöshetsförsäkringen 1935-54", *Arkiv för studier i arbetarrörelsens historia*, No. 45 (1990).

59. Baldwin, PSSCOEWS, pp. 496-521. Cf. S. Marklund, "Welfare State Policies in the Tripolar Class Model of Scandinavia", *Politics & Society*, Vol. 16, No. 4 (1988), pp. 451-68.

60. O. Kangas and J. Palme, "The Public-Private Mix in Pension Policy" in J.E. Kolberg (ed), ibid.

Chapter III

*I am most grateful to Peter Flora for his constant encouragement, skilful editing and scholarly guidance during the writing of this chapter.

(This chapter is published with the kind permission of Walter de Gruyter & Co., Berlin.)

1. Höjer, K.J., *Svensk socialpolitisk historia*. Malmö, Norstedts, 1952; see also Berggren, H. & Nilsson, G.B., *Liberalsocialpolitik*. Uppsala, Norstedts, 1965; and Sellberg, H., *Staten och arbetarskyddet 1850-1919*. Uppsala, Almqvist & Wiksell, 1950; Montgomery, A., *Svensk socialpolitik under 1800-talet*. Stockholm, Kooperativa förbundets förlag, 1934.

2. Isling, Å., *Kampen för och emot en demokratisk skola*. Stockholm, Sober, 1980; Richardsson, G., *Kulturkamp och klasskamp*. Göteborg, Akademiförlaget, 1963.

3. Hammarström, I. et al., *Ideologi och socialpolitik i 1800-talets Sverige*. Uppsala, Acta Universitatis Upsaliensis 1978, Almqvist & Wiksell Internationel; see also Heidenheimer A. & Elvander, N., *The shaping of the Swedish health system*. London, Croom Helm, 1980.

4. Kihlberg, L., *Folktribunen Adolf Hedin*. Stockholm, Bonniers, 1972; see also Elmér, Å., *Folkpensioneringen i Sverige*. Lund, Gleerups, 1960; Wirén, A., *G.H. von Koch*. Ystad, Rabén & Sjögren, 1980; Boalt G. & Bergryd, U., *Centralförbundet för socialt arbete*. Karlskrona, CSA, 1974; and Englund, K., *Arbetarförsäkringsfrågan i svensk politik 1884-1901*. Acta Universitatis Upsaliensis, Uppsala, 1976.

5. Unga, N., *Socialdemokratin och arbetslöshetsfrågan 1912-1934*. Kristianstad, Arkiv, 1976.

6. Casparsson, R., *Saltsjöbadsavtalet*. Stockholm, Prisma, 1970; see also Korpi, W., *The Working Class in Welfare Capitalism*. London, Routledge and Kegan Paul, 1978.

7. Most of the reforms in the 1930s are covered in Hatje, A-K., *Befolkningsfrågan och välfärden*. Stockholm, Liber, 1974.

8. On the costs of social reforms, see also SOU 1944:33 and SOU 1945:14, both written for the State Commission on Population headed by Tage Erlander.

9. Friberg, L., *Styre i kristid*. Stockholm, Allmänna förlaget, 1973.

10. On the impact of World War II on social policy in Sweden, see Molin, K.,

Försvaret, folkhemmet och demokratin. Stockholm, Allmänna förlaget, 1974.
11. Samuelsson, K., *Från stormaktsvälde till välfärdsstat.*
Stockholm, Bonniers, 1968; Tarschys, D., *Den offentliga revolutionen.* Falköping, Liber, 1978. A critical discussion of the 'continuity thesis' in Sunesson, S., *Byråkrati och historia.* Malmö, Arkiv, 1981.
12. Therborn, G. etal., "Sweden before and after social democracy", *Acta Sociologica,* Vol. 21, supplement, 1978.
13. Girvets, H.K., "Welfare State", *International Encyclopedia of the Social Sciences.* Vol. 16. New York, MacMillan, 1972. The Bismarckian model is taken as a starting point in most Swedish literature on social policy, see Nasenius, J. & Ritter, K., *Delad välfärd.* Stockholm, Esselte Studium, 1974.
14. Kuhnle, S., "The beginnings of the Nordic welfare states". *Acta Sociologica.* Vol. 21, supplement, 1978.
15. Johansson, S., *När är tiden mogen?.* Karlskrona, Tiden, 1974; English edition, *When is the time ripe?,* Stockholm, Swedish Institute for Social Research, 1979. mimeo.
16. Korpi, W., *The Democratic Class Struggle.* London, Routledge and Kegan Paul, 1982.
17. Myrdal, G. & A., *Kris i befolkningsfrågan.* Stockholm, Tiden, 1934; see also *The Annals of the American Academy of Political and Social Science,* "Social Problems and Policies in Sweden", Ohlin B. (ed.). Philadelphia, 1938.
18. Kuhnle, S., "National Equality and Local Decision-Making", *Acta Sociologica,* Vol. 23, 1980.
19. Therborn, G. etal., Ibid, 1978; see also Marklund, S., *Klass, stat och socialpolitik,* Lund, Arkiv, 1982; English edition, *Capitalism and Income Protection.* Umeå, Department of Sociology, University of Umeå, 1983, mimeo.
20. Parts of this history are covered in Hatje (1974) and Elmér (1960).
21. Jörberg, L., "Svensk ekonomi under 100 år" in Södersten, B. (ed.), *Svensk ekonomi.* Stockholm, Rabén & Sjögren, 1970; for private ownership of Swedish industry see SOU 1968:7 "Ägande och inflytande i det privata näringslivet"; see also the works by C.H. Hermansson – particularly *Koncentration och storföretag.* Stockholm, Artbetarkultur, 1959, and SIND 1980:5 "Ägande i det privata näringslivet", Statens Industriverk.
22. Korpi, W., *The Democratic Class Struggle.* London, Routledge and Kegan Paul, 1982; see also Elvander, N., *Skandinavisk arbetarrörelse.* Helsingborg, Liber/Publica, 1980.
23. Forsman, A., *En teori om staten och de offentliga utgifterna.* Uppsala, Acta Universitatis Upsaliensis, 1980.
24. Elvander, N., *Svensk skattepolitik.* Uppsala, Rabén & Sjögren, 1972.
25. Johansson, R. & Karlberg, B., *Bostadspolitiken,* Stockholm, Publica/Liber, 1979; see also Franzén, M. & Sandstedt, E., *Grannskap och stadsplanering.* Uppsala, Acta Universitatis Upsaliensis, 1981; Broberg, K. etal., *Bostad och kapital,* Stockholm, Prisma, 1975: Ståhl, I. & Sandbergs, N-E., *Svensk bostadspolitik,* Stockholm, Prisma, 1976.
26. Furåker, B., *Stat och arbetsmarknad,.* Kristianstad, Arkiv, 1976; see also Rothstein, B., "AMS som socialdemokratisk reformbyråkrati", in *Arkiv för studier i arbetarrörelsens historia,* No. 18, 1980.

27. Elmér, Å., *Folkpensioneringen i Sverige*. Lund, Gleerups, 1960.

28. Broberg, R., *Så formades tryggheten*. Stockholm, Försäkringskasseförbundet, 1973; see also Eckerberg, P., 'Medborgarnas behov av trygghet' in Nilsson, F. (ed.), *Gunnar Sträng*. Stockholm, Tiden, 1981; Lindeberg, G., *Den svenska sjukkasserörelsens historia*. Lund, Svenska sjukkasseförbundet, 1949; and Moberg, K. et al., *Utvärderingsforskning: från yrkesfarelag till arbetsmiljölag*. MURA report, Lund, 1982.

29. Mohlin, B., *Tjänstepensionsfrågan*. Göteborg, Akademiförlaget, 1965.

30. Borgenhammar, E., *Hälsans pris*. Kristianstad, Studieförbundet Näringsliv och Samhälle, 1981.

31. Marklund, S., *Skolsverige 1950-1975*. Uddevalla, Liber, 1980; on education see also SOU 1974:53, Skolans arbetsmiljö.

32. Vinde, P. & Petri, G., *Swedish Government Administration*. Lund, Prisma, 1978.

33. GDP figures are taken from the OECD National accounts, Vol. I, Paris 1982 and 1981 (for the year 1950, which for reason of space seems to be excluded in the former edition). Public and welfare expenditure figures are taken from Höök, E., *Den offentliga sektorns expansion*, Uppsala, Almqvist & Wiksell, 1962 (up to 1956) and the follow-up of Höök's major investigation in Forsman, A. (1980), *En teori om staten och de offentliga utgifterna*. Forsman's calculations end in 1974 and for the remaining years, 1976 and 1978, I have tried to follow Forsman's coding scheme using the same sources (see Forsman p. 127). Problems related to measuring the public sector both in Sweden and in general are discussed in Gustafsson, B. (ed.), *Den offentliga sektorns expansion – teori- och metodproblem*, Uppsala 1976, Almqvist & Wiksell, and in an essay by E. Höök in Gustafsson, B. (ed.), *Post-Industrial society*, London, Croom Helm, 1979.

34. The disaggregation according to economic categories has been done solely using data from the abovementioned OECD volume for the period 1962-1978. We have not been able to construct a series for the whole postwar period with the help of Höök's and Forsman's studies. However, for the period prior to 1960 some material can be found in the above-mentioned books and also used data from Forsman, A. et al. in Gustafsson, B. (ed.), *Post-Industrial Society*; Waara, L. et al., Offentlig sektor, Falköping, Esselte, 1978; and Meidner, R., *Den offentliga sektorns expansion*. Stockholm, Arbetslivscentrum (German edition, Berlin, Wissenschaftszentrum, 1981).

35. There is no source giving consolidated public expenditure figures by the four levels of government. Figures on local and regional government expenditure are found in SOU 1960:6 (The State Commission on Public Activities and Regional Welfare). Here, for social insurance figures on income maintenance have been taken as an approximate indicator from Table 3 in the Appendix volume. Central government expenditure is deflated here as total government expenditure (see Table 1, Appendix volume) minus local, regional and social insurance expenditure.

36. In this paragraph we follow closely Höök's investigation and Forsman's follow-up. For the years 1976 and 1978 we have made our own calculations according to Forsman's coding scheme. All purposes are according to Forsman's summary of Höök's more detailed account, with the exception of the

319

concept of welfare, which is constructed as an amalgamation of the three categories (1) education, (2) health including sickness insurance, and (3) social services and social insurance, of course with the exception of sickness insurance already counted under health (2). For example, in Flora, P. (ed.), *State, Economy and Society in Western Europe 1815-1975 − a data handbook*, the figures for the three categories are given separately (see also graph 8 and 9) in section (under the subheading of social expenditure).

37. There is no reliable and detailed investigation of the development of public employment in Sweden, during the whole postwar period the most recent discussion of any length seems to be the State Commission's "Offentlig verksamhet och regional välfärd" (Public activity and regional welfare) SOU 1980:6, Arbetsmarknadsdepartementet/ERU. The figure mentioned in the text for 1950 is taken from Waara et al., which does not include state business enterprises; see also Tarschys, D., *ibid.*, which seems to include state business employees for 1950. The figure given in SOU 1980:6 for 1950 is 475 600, approximately 15 percent of the labour force, and for 1977 1 290 000 − the latest figures given. State business enterprises included. The table is mainly taken from the Statistical Yearbook of Sweden for 1981, when a new series was introduced: "Government employees and employees in local authorities 1960-1979", though no figures appear for the earlier years. For reasons of comparability state business enterprise employees are not included.

38. The social expenditure item used in this part is, as a summary, derived from two sources. Firstly, the investigations made by Höök and Forsman, mentioned in note 33, which was solely the basis for the equation made i part II.1, and is used here as source for educational expenditure. Secondly, we use the 'social expenditure' figures given yearly in Statistical Yearbook, which are approximately the same as those for 'health and sickness insurance' and 'social services and other social insurance' in Höök and Forsman. As described in the Appendix, the figures differ somewhat more for the latter part of the period under investigation. As mentioned in the text, housing costs part fall outside this calculation. The traditional concept of 'social expenditure' is derived from the Swedish Statistical yearbook with an almost unbroken series from 1948. Almost the same figures appear in the biannual Nordic Social Statistics (or similar titles going back to the early 1950s). The following subheadings are used:

− Disease (further subdivided into health, sickness insurance, temperance welfare and dental service et al.).

− Industrial accident insurance and workers' protection (two subitems).

− Unemployment et al. (four subheadings); insurance, employment service, retraining and relief work).

− Old age and invalidity pensions, etc. (giving basic pension, supplementary pension (from 1963), care of the handicapped, old people's homes and home-help services (entailing some small changes).

− Family and child welfare (with several, and changing subitems including child allowances, housing allowances, parents insurance etc.).

− Public assistance (formerly relief and in the latter part of the period including some small items not counted here).

− Compensation for injuries incurred on military service and war casualities.

- Criminal care was added to the series in the early 1970s but we have consequently withdrawn these figures.
- Central administrative costs.

39. The figures given in Statistical Yearbook for unemployment and employment programme, are not easy to breakdown in terms of cash benefits versus benefits in kind (education etc.). Besides unemployment insurance, the three remaining subheadings given in Statistical Yearbook under unemployment and employment programme include large sums of cash benefits, particularly various kinds of educational allowances during the 1970s.

40. As indicated above, income maintenance gives a rough picture of cash benefits, though not all schemes are included. On the contrary, not all of sickness insurance consists of cash benefits. The problem in 1974 was that in particular some taxes were included in sickness insurance, because of the change in replacement from net to gross earnings. It is however impossible to derive a correct estimation from present statistical sources. According to a special investigation made by the already mentioned State Commission on Social Insurance Integration (SOU 1979:94), the tax-figure for 1978 was estimated to 4 400 Mill. Sw.Kr. out of a total sum of 23 000 Mill. Sw.Kr. (as much as 20 percent!).

As regards the differences between the three types of income maintenance programmes SOU 1979:94 gives the following figures for 1978:
- Earnings-related schemes 48%
- Flat-rate benefits 42%
- Income- and meanstested programmes 10%

Recalculating our own figures for 1978 and withdrawing taxes will give the following percentages:
- Earnings-related schemes 48.3% (now 51.5%)
- Flat-rate benefits 40.6% (now 38.0%)
- Income- and means-tested programmes 11.1% (now 10.4%).

41. A. Hetzler, & K. Eriksson, *Arbetsskadeförsäkringens tillämpning*, Lund EKNA, 1983.

42. Öhman, B., *Svensk arbetsmarknadspolitik 1900-1947*. Stockholm, Prisma, 1970; see also Rothstein, B., "Fanns det en arbetsmarknadspolitik före AMS?", in *Arkiv för studier i arbetarrörelsens historia*, Nos. 23-24, 1982. The doctrine of active manpower policy explained in Rehn, G. & Lundberg, E., "Employment and Welfare: Some Swedish Issues" in *Industrial Relations*, Vol. 12, No. 2, February 1963; see also Meidner, R. & Andersson, R., "The Overall Impact of an Active Labour Market Policy in Sweden", in Ulman, L. (ed.), *Manpower Programs in the Policy Mix*. Baltimore, John Hopkins University, 1973; Critical evaluation in Furåker, *op. cit.*

43. SOU 1978:45, *En allmän arbetslöshetsförsäkring*.

44. Information in Section III, is based on calculations derived mainly from the Statistical Yearbook series 1950-82/83, with some references to 'National Insurance', 'Local Government Finances' and 'Social Welfare', Official Statistics of Sweden.

45. Rodriguez, *Offentlig inkomstexpansion*, Uppsala, Gleerups, 1980; Forsman, A., 'Orsakerna till de offentliga utgifternas expansion under 1900-talet', in Lindqvist, A., *Skatteforskning*, Stockholm, Riksbankens jubileumsfond

1980:6; Hansen, B. *Fiscal Policy in Seven Countries 1955-65*, Paris, OECD, 1969. Concerning local government, Hansen means that 'from a practical point of view the economic activities of local authorities are in many respects directly and indirectly controlled by central government', p. 340.

46. Hansen, *op. cit.*, p. 351.

47. Rodriguez, *op. cit.*, in particular Ch. VII. For a discussion on taxes and welfare state development, see Wilensky, H., *The 'new' corporatism: centralization and the welfare state*, Beverly Hills, Sage, 1976; and the critique in Korpi, W., 'Social Policy and Distributional Conflicts in the Capitalist Democracies' in Heidenheimer, A., *West European Politics*, 1980, Vol. 3.

48. Elvander, *Svensk skattepolitik*, Uppsala, Rabén & Sjögren, 1972.

49. Esping-Andersen, G., *Social class, social democracy and state policy*, Köpenhamn, New Social Science Monographs E8, 1980; and Fryklund, B. & Peterson, T., *Populism och missnöjespartier i Norden*, Lund, Arkiv, 1981.

50. See fn 14.

51. See fn 4.

52. SOU 1978:45. See also Edebalk, P.G., *Arbetslöshetsförsäkringsdebatten – en studie i svensk socialpolitik 1892-1934*. Lund, Departments of Economic History, 1974 (Diss).

53. The American Journal Deadulus, in spring 1984, is summing up the Welfare State debate in Scandinavia as a whole.

54. Erikson/Åberg: *Välfärd i förändring* is the summary report from the level of living investigation – a panel study – giving detailed information about the situation at the three interview occasions (1968, 1974 and 1981). Income figures refers to the forgoing taxation year in this panelstudy. The level of living investigation does not cover pensioners over 74 (half a million persons out of the total Swedish population of eight million in 1980). Many of these oldest pensioners have little or no supplementary pension – but a minority has sizeable private pensions – and thus clearly diminish the overall increase reported in the text, but the pattern is still one of improvement.

Since the mid-1970s the National Bureau of Statistics also carries out a level of living investigation each year focussing on different aspects of welfare development (ULF). Many of their findings are summarized in Reports No. 27 and 33.

55. Jonsson, J. & Lundberg, O., *De äldre i välfärden*. Institutet för social forskning, Stockholm, 1984.

56. SCB, *Välfärdsbulletinen* 1983:4.

57. OECD, *Tax/Benefit position of a typical worker*. Paris 1982.

58. Reported in "Kan vi lita på ATP", LO, Stockholm 1982 (mimeo).

59. The official household income survey is since 1972 carried out by the National Bureau of Statistics annually and started as a part of an international project sponsored by the United Nations. The two main reports are "Inkomstfördelningsstudien 1972", Official Statistics of Sweden, Stockholm 1976 and "Våra inkomster", Official Statistics of Sweden, Stockholm 1982 (covering 1979 and some datas from the years immediately before). Peter Hedström at the Swedish Institute for Social Research introduced me to the 1981 survey.

60. Figures for invalidity pensions in relation to other household incomes are taken from Wadensjö 1984 table 8.8: "De arbetshandikappades arbetsmark-

nadssituation och åtgärder för arbetshandikappade" (Swedish Institute for Social Research, March 1984).

61. The Trade Union investigations are "Kan vi lita på ATP?" and "Pensionärernas inkomster 1981", LO, Stockholm 1982 and 1984 – the latter one using income statistics from taxation sources (Official Statistics of Sweden – "totalräknad inkomststatistik"). Välfärdsbulletinen 1:1984 (National Bureau of Statistics): "Stora inkomstklyftor beroende på typ av pension" differentiates pension benefits according to the different basic, supplementary and occupational schemes.

62. SCB, Levnadsförhållanden, nr 25: Handikappad. Delaktig eller jämlik? 1977/78.

63. SCB, *Levnadsförhållanden nr. 33*, Perspektiv på välfärden.

64. SPRI, *Äldreomsorg och ekonomi*, Stockholm, 1984.

65. For references, see note 55.

66. On these questions, see the penetrating sociological analyses by Francesco Alberoni, for example *Förälskelse och kärlek* (Sw. translation 1983, Korpen, Göteborg).

67. No medical certificate is required for reimbursements for sickness lasting less than a week but payout starts after the first day.

68. SOU 1981:31, "Sjukersättningsfrågor".

69. Regeringens proposition 1983/84:73, *Reformering av efterlevandepensioneringen m m*.

70. Riksförsäkringsverket, "Allmän försäkring 1963-81", Stockholm.

71. SOU 1981:2 "Ohälsa och vårdutnyttjande". See also SCB, "Levnadsförhållanden" No. 15, "Arbetsförhållanden och sjukfrånvaro" and Eriksen, T.E., "Den ökade sjukfrånvaron – en statistisk analys". DSF, Stockholm 1981.

72. SCB, "Levnadsförhållanden" No. 27 and No. 12, "Arbetsmiljö 1975". For a discussion of the progress occurred in working environments the last fifteen years, see Erikson/Åberg (eds) ch. 7.

73. Kjellström, S. and Lundberg, O., "Hälsa och vårdkonsumtion" in Erikson/Åberg, ibid. (ch. 5).

74. SCB, "Levnadsförhållanden", No. 33 ch. 8.

75. SCB, "Levnadsförhållanden", No. 27 ch. 12.

76. See note 64.

77. See note 74.

78. Erikson/Åberg (eds) ch. 5.

79. Ibid. ch. 4.

80. "Ekonomisk debatt" 7/1979, which among other articles includes a translation of Victor R. Fuchs "The Economics of Health in a Post-Industrial Society" from The *Public Interest*, No. 56, Summer 1979.

81. Marklund, S.: "Skolan och svångremmen". Liber, Stockholm 1982.

82. SCB, "Levnadsförhållanden" No. 33, ch. 2 and SOU 1981:31.

83. Yearbook of Nordic Statistics 1982 and 1978.

84. SCB, "Levnadsförhållanden" No. 39.

85. SCB, "Levnadsförhållanden", No. 33, ch. 2.

86. SCB, "Levnadsförhållanden", No. 40.

87. Skandinaviska Enskilda Banken: "Dina Pengar", 1984:1.

88. SOU 1978:45 *"En allmän arbetslöshetsförsäkring"*. Erici, *Arbetslöshets-*

försäkringen i Sverige 1935-1980. Arbetslöshetskassornas samorganisation, Stockholm 1981.

89. Elander, I., *Det nödvändiga och det önskvärda*, Arkiv, Kristianstad 1978. See also Åberg, R. "Flyttarna och arbetsmarknaden". Prisma, Borås 1980.

90. Leiniö, T-L, *Inte lika men jämlika?*, Institutet för social forskning, Stockholm 1984. Vogel, J., *Levnadsnivå och ojämlikhet i Norden.* Nordiska rådet och Nordiska statistiska sekretariatet, Göteborg 1983.

91. Jonung, Ch., "Kvinnorna i svensk ekonomi" in Södersten, B. (ed.): *Svensk ekonomi*, Rabén & Sjögren, Borås 1982. See also *Sociologisk forskning* no. 3/1978 ("tema: kvinnoforskning") and no. 2/1981 ("Patriarkat och kvinnoforskning").

92. SCB, "Levnadsförhållanden" No. 36 ("Arbetslöshetens offer"). See also Björklund, A. and Persson-Tanimura, I: Youth Unemployment in Sweden in Reubens, B. (ed) Youth at Work: an International Survey, Totowa, N.J.: Allenheld, Osmun & Co 1983.

93. AMS Verksamhetsberättelse, various years 1974-.

94. SCB, "Levnadsförhållanden", No. 33, ch. 1.

95. Recent research results indicate, however, that many immigrant groups prefer to live among their compatriots before better housing standards. See Anderson-Brolin, Lillemor, *Etnisk bostadssegregation.* Department of Sociology, University of Stockholm 1984 (Diss.).

96. SCB, "Bostads- och byggnadsstatistisk årsbok 1982".

97. The Swedish Government, prop. 1982/83:100 app. 13. - education.

98. Frykman, Tofte, "Boendeförhållanden 1968-81" in Erikson/Åberg (eds) (see note 55). SCB, "Levnadsförhållanden", No. 27, ch. 6.

99. Frykman, ibid.

100. SCB, Levnadsförhållanden, No. 33 ch. 1, and Frykman, ibid. Overcrowding might also be a problem for the growing number of divorced parents with joint responsibility for their children, who live with them alternately (every fortnight, every second week, etc.).

101. Frykman, ibid.

102. SCB. Levnadsförhållanden, No. 27.

103. Jonsson, I., "Utbildningsresurser" in Erikson/Åberg, ibid. See also Jonsson/Lundberg/Tham (eds.) *Tabeller och figurer.* Rapport nr 8. Institutet för social forskning, Stockholm 1984.

104. SCB, "Levnadsförhållanden, nr 40".

105. Bentzel, R., *Inkomstfördelningen i Sverige.* Stockholm, IUI, 1952. SOU 1964:25, Nytt skattesystem; and the comments upon it in SOU 1965:28 (remissvar). See also, Ortmark, Å., *Maktspelet i Sverige.* SOU 1971:39, Den svenska köpkraftsfördelningen 1967; Spånt, R., *Den svenska inkomstfördelningens utveckling*, Uppsala, Nationalekonomiska institutionen, 1976; and "Den svenska inkomstfördelningens utveckling 1920-76" by the same author, Ds E 1979:4 (Ministry of Economy); Åberg, R., Selén, J., and Tham, H., "Ekonomiska resurser" in Erikson, R. and Åberg, R. (ed), ibid (see note 55). See also the studies made by Statistics Sweden on Income distribution both surveys and collected taxation statistics.

106. SCB, *Våra inkomster*, SOS, Stockholm 1982.

107. Åberg et al., ibid.

108. SCB, Be 1983:4.1, *Inkomstfördelningsundersökningen*. SOS, Stockholm 1983.

109. Ibid.

110. Hewitt, Ch., "The Effects of Political Democracy and Social Democracy on Equality in Industrial Societies: a Cross-National Comparison" in American Sociological Review, Vol. 42 (1977), pp. 450-464; Wilensky, H., The Welfare State and Equality. Berkley, University of California Press, 1975. Lindbeck, A., *Swedish Economic Policy*. MacMillan, London 1975; Uusitalo. H., *Income and Welfare*. *A Study of Income as a Component of Welfare in the Scandinavian Countries in the 1970's*. Research Group for Comparative Sociology, University of Helsinki. Research Reports No. 8, 1975; Sawyers, M., *Income Distribution in OECD Countries*. OECD, Paris, 1976; Spånt, 1979; Schnitzer, M., *Income Distribution*. New York 1974; Schnitzer, M., *The Economy of Sweden: A Study of the Modern Welfare State*. Praeger, New York, 1976.

111. SCB, Levnadsförhållanden No. 40.

112. SCB, Levnadsförhållanden No. 39 and the debate following Sten Johansson's article "Förslag till revision av familjepolitiken" ("A proposal to a revision of the family policy") in the social-democratic theoretical journal Tiden 1980-1981.

113. Arnman, G. & Jönsson, I., *Segregation och svensk skola*. Arkiv, Lund, 1983. (Diss.)

114. Blomdahl, U., *Erfarenhetsverkstaden*. Stockholm, Stockholms fritidsförvaltning, 1984.

115. Spånt, R., "Den svenska förmögenhetsfördelningens utveckling" in SOU 1979:9.

116. SCB, Levnadsförhållanden nr 27.

117. Åberg et al., ibid.

118. With the major exception of Volvo, nine out of the ten largest multinationals are in the hand of the Wallenberg dynasty; see the books cited on ownership in note 21, and the article in the *Financial Times* on the death of Marcus Wallenberg, 'The financier of the welfare state', Sept. 1982. See note 21. I have also benefitted from a so far unpublished paper by Therborn, G.: "The Bourgeoisie: Limitations of a Success Story." Lund, 1981.

119. Affärsvärlden No. 38/1983.

120. SCB, Levnadsförhållanden nr 39, *Hushållens förmögenheter* årsskiftet *1981/82*. SOS, Stockholm 1984.

121. Poverty is a highly complex concept, with many ramifications. For a discussion of it see for example Korpi, W., "Approaches to the Study of Poverty in the United States: Critical Notes from a European Perspective" in Covello, V. (ed), *Poverty and Public Policy – An Evaluation of Social Science Research*. Cambridge, Mass., Schenkman, 1980. Problems on measurement are discussed in Ringen, S., "Towards a Third Stage i the Measurement of Poverty", Swedish Institute for Social Research, Stockholm, 1984 (mimeo).

122. SCB, Levnadsförhållanden, No. 16, *Låginkomstfamiljerna – vilka de är och hur de lever 1975/76*. Stockholm, 1979; Sundbom, L., *De extremt lågavlönade*. Allmänna förlaget, Stockholm, 1971; Tengvald, K., *Samhällets krav och de fattigas resurser*. Sociologiska institutionen, Uppsala, 1976, (Diss.)

123. SCB, No. 27, ibid.

124. Rowntree, S., *Poverty – Study of Town Life*. MacMillan, London, 1901, and, by the same author, *Poverty and Progress – A Second Social Survey of York*. Longmans, London, 1941.

125. Gustafsson, B., *Socialhjälpens bestämningsfaktorer*. DSF Projekt 1983:1, Stockholm and "Fattigdom", Nationalekonomiska institutionen, Göteborg, 1983 (mimeo). See also Szulkin, R. "Socialhjälpsfrekvensen och dess bestämningsfaktorer" in *Sociologisk forskning*, Vol. 18, No. 4 (1981); and Korpi, W., "Social Policy and Poverty in Postwar Sweden" in *Acta Sociologica*, Vol. 18, No. 2-3 (1975).

126. Lundeqvist, K. *Socialhjälpstagande*. Acta Universitatis, Upsaliensis, Uppsala, 1976 (Diss.); and Korpi, W., 1973, ibid.

127. Stenberg, S-Å, *Vem vräks?*, Institutet för social forskning, Meddelande nr 3/1984, Stockholm.

128. Korpi, W., *Fattigdom i välfärden*. Tiden, Stockholm, 1973. Sunesson, S., "Maktlöshet och socialhjälpstagande" i Nordiskt *Socialt Arbete*, Vol. 3/4 No. 1-4 (1983) is discussing social assistance from a social anthropologian perspective in a very interesting way. See also his book *När man inte lyckas*. AWE/Gebers, Stockholm, 1981.

129. Erikson R. et al. (eds), *The Scandinavian Model. Welfare States and Welfare Research*. New York: M.E Sharp, 1987.

130. A rough indicator is table 5.1 in Holmberg, S., *Svenska väljare*, Liber, Stockholm, 1981. According to this no social democratic voter had a negative opinion about employment policy and an overwhelming majority only positive attitudes towards this aspect of the party's policy. Also communist voters appreciated manpower policy.

131. Erikson, R. and Tåhlin, M., "Samgång mellan välfärdsproblem" in Erikson/Åberg (eds), ibid.

132. For a stimulating discussion on social problems and social science see C.W. Mills, *People, Privilege and Power*.

133. Sainsbury, D., *Swedish Social Democratic Ideology and Electoral Politics 1944-1948*. Almqvist & Wicksell, Stockholm, 1980 (diss.).

134. Guteland, G. et al., *Ett folks biografi*. Liber/Publica, Stockholm, 1981. (Available in English as the Swedish government report to the UN-population conference in Bucharest 1974, "The Biography of a People – Past and Future Population Changes in Sweden, Conditions and Consequences", Ministry of Foreign Affairs, Stockholm, 1974.) For the earlier period see also C. Winberg, *Folkökning och proletarisering*. Cavefors, Lund, 1977.

135. L. Jörberg, *op. cit.*

136. P. Kuusi, *1960-talets socialpolitik*. Kuoppio, Söderströms, 1964.

137. Korpi, W., *The Democratic Class Struggle*. Routledge and Kegan Paul, London, 1983; Berglund, S. & Lindström, U., *The Scandinavian Party System(s)*. Studentlitteratur, Lund, 1978; Therborn, G., "The rule of capital and the rise of democracy" in New Left Review, no. 103, 1977.

138. Back, P-E. & Berglund, S., *Det svenska partiväsendet*. AWE/Gebers, Stockholm, 1978; Hadenius, S., Molin, B. & Wieslander, H., *Sverige efter 1900*. Aldus, Stockholm, 1972.

139. Therborn, G., "Socialdemokratin träder fram" in *Arkiv för studier i*

arbetarrörelsens historia, no. 27-28, Lund 1984; Hagtvet, B., "Sweden – fascism on the fringe" in *Who were the Fascists?*. Universitetsforlaget, Oslo, 1981; Kennerström, B., *Mellan Två Internationaler: Socialistiska Partiet 1929-1939*. Arkiv, Lund, 1974; Olsson, S.E. (ed), *Från SKP till VPK*. Cavefors, Lund, 1976.

140. Holmberg, S., *Väljare i förändring*. Liber, Stockholm, 1985 and *Svenska väljare*. Liber, Stockholm, 1982.

141. Hirdman, Y., *Vi byggde landet*. Tiden/Pogo, Stockholm, 1978; Tingsten, H., *Den svenska socialdemokratins idèutveckling I-II*. Aldus, Stockholm, 1967. *The Swedish Social Democrats: Their Ideological Development*. Bedminnster Press, Totowa, 1973; Bäckström, K., *Arbetarrörelsen i Sverige I-II*. Arbetarkultur, Stockholm, 1963.

142. Olofsson, G., *Mellan klass och stat*. Arkiv, Lund, 1979.

143. Hellström, G., *Jordbrukspolitiken i industrisamhället*. LT, Stockholm, 1976 and Thullberg, P.,

144. Cf. Myrdal, G., *Jordbrukspolitiken*. Tiden, Stockholm, 1938.

145. Elvander, N., *Intresseorganisationerna i dagens Sverige*. Gleerups, Lund, 1969.

146. Westerståhl, J., *Svensk fackföreningsrörelse*. Tiden, Stockholm, 1945; Sunesson, S., *Politik och organisation*. Arkiv, Stockholm, 1974 (Diss.); Hadenius, A., *Facklig organisationsutveckling*. Rabén & Sjögren, Stockholm, 1976.

147. Szulkin, R., "Politiska resurser" in Erikson/Åberg (eds) 1984, ibid.

148. Kjellberg, A., *Facklig mobilisering i tolv länder*. Arkiv, Lund, 1983 (Diss.); Nilsson, E.T., "Tjänstemän och arbetsdelning" in *Zenit*, no. 57, 1978; Sandberg, P. "Tjänstemannarörelsen". Stockholm, Tiden, 1969.

149. Szulkin ibid.

150. Szulkin ibid.

151. Flink, I., *Strejkbryteriet och arbetets frihet*. Acta Universitatis Upsaliensis, Uppsala, 1978 (Diss.); Otter, C. v., "Lockouten i kampen mellan arbete och kapital" in Dencik, P. & Lundvall, B-Å., *Arbete, Kapital & Stat*. Zenit/Rabén & Sjögren, 1974. Söderpalm, S-A., *Direktörsklubben*. Zenit/Rabén & Sjögren, Stockholm, 1976.

152. Casparsson, R., *Saltsjöbadsavtalet*. Prisma; Söderpalm, S-A., *Arbetsgivarna och Saltsjöbadspolitiken*. Svenska Arbetsgivareföreningen, Stockholm, 1980.

153. Bresky, T., Scherman, J. & Schmid, I., *Med SAF vid rodret*. Liber, Uddevalla, 1981.

154. So far, there exists no coherent overview of pressure groups in the welfare sector. The figures mentioned in the text are provided by the respective organizations.

155. Hatje, ibid.

156. The system of "child supplement" on the wages survived however in some industries, in particular in the Textil industry. See Nordlöf, S: "Textilfabrikerna hade ofta ledare som ärvt nå'n djäkla tysk anda" in Hermansson, C-H., *Kommunister II*. Arbetarkultur, Lund, 1980.

157. Erlander, T., *1901-1939*. Tiden, Stockholm, 1972.

158. Abukhanfusa, K., *Beredskapsfamiljernas försörjning*. Stockholm, Liber, 1975; see also Marklund, S., *Klass, stat och socialpolitik*. Lund, Arkiv, 1982.

159. SOU 1946:43 See also Erlander, T., *1940-1949*. Tiden, Stockholm, 1973.

160. Mainly based on Elmér (1960). See also Heclo, H., Modern *Social Policy in Britain and Sweden*. Yale U.P., New Haven, 1974.

161. Wigforss, E., *Minnen III 1932-1949*. Tiden, Stockholm, 1954.

162. Wigforss, ibid. Erlander in his self-biography devotes only a few pages to this question; see Erlander T., *1940-1949 and 1955-1960*.

163. Mainly based on Molin (1965).

164. Söderpalm (1980) ibid.

165. Erlander, T., *1950-1954*. Tiden, Stockholm, 1975.

166. Söderpalm (1980) ibid.

167. A typical example is the right (effective 1979) of parents with children below age 8 to reduce their work-time to six hours a day without compensation for loss of income. See *Svensk författningssamling* (SFS) 1978:410

168. One outcome of this critique was the establishment of a private company to organize daycare, *Pysslingen*, which has become the symbol of efforts to privatize public services in the 1980s. Westholm, C.J. (ed): *Skapande eller bevakande Sverige?* Vol. I-III. Svenska Arbetsgivareföreningen, Stockholm, 1979; See also Küng, A., *Låt Pysslingen leva*. Stockholm, Timbro, 1984.

169. *Regeringens Budgetförslag 1980/81 - sammandrag*. Budgetdepartementet, Stockholm 1980.

170. Regeringens proposition 1980/81:20, *Besparingar i statsverksamheten, m m*. Stockholm, 1980. For a critique of mainstream economic thought, see Erixon, L. & Frazer, N. "Tränger den offentliga sektorn undan den privata?" i *Häften för kritiska studier* no. 3-4 1984.

171. *Regeringens budgetförslag 1982/83 - sammandrag*, Ekonomi och budgetdepartementet, Stockholm 1982. See also *Regeringens proposition 1981/82:30*.

172. *Regeringens proposition 1982/83:40*.

173. See for example *Regeringens proposition 1984/85:40*.

174. *Regeringens proposition 1983/84:73*. During the first year after the partner's death, all widows and widowers would have been entitled to a "transformation benefit". Thereafter, special meanstested survivor supplements would have been paid out if the remnant lacked opportunities to maintain him/herself.

175. Before their Congress in September 1984, the Social Democrats mentioned that if the budget situation became better, then the benefit level in the part-time pension program would be restored to its initial level. In early 1985 it is not very likely that this will be the one and only Social Democratic election promise concerning welfare, although rumour have circulated to this effect. See Socialdemokraterna: *Sverige på rätt väg!* No. 11 Socialförsäkringar, Stockholm, 1984.

176. See for example Riksdagen 1984/85. *Motion no 1582, 1644, 997, 852 and 823*.

177. Moderata Samlingspartiet: *Möjligheternas samhälle*. Falun 1983. See also Burenstam-Linder, S. *Den hjärtlösa välfärdsstaten*. Stockholm, Timbro, 1983.

178. Riksdagen 1984/85. *Finansutskottets betänkande no. 10*, Reservation no. 1. See also Riksdagen 1984/85 Motion no. 2295, 2298, 2431 and 2799. The drastic reduction of sickness cash benefits in the Conservative proposal (no. 2431) concerns only the first ten days of sickness. For the rest of the period, the reduction is the same as in the Centre and Liberal proposals.

179. Of course, various 'catastrophic scenarios' have been suggested, but during the growth years these warnings were largely ignored. In particular, suspicion has been cast upon the National Supplementary Pension System's promises to provide for future generations of pensioners. Already before the first pension decision in 1913, extremely pessimistic model calculations were presented (see Elmér 1960). In the postwar period, a notable example of this type is Rappaport, E. *ATP-sveket.* Stockholm, Affärsförlaget, 1980.

180. OECD: Social expenditure 1960-1990. Paris, 1985. See also J. Gidlund et al., *Choosing Local Futures* Stockholm, Swedish Council for Building Research, 1985.

181. Ståhlberg, A-C.: *Transfereringar mellan den förvärvsarbetande och den äldre generationen.* Expertgruppen för Studier i Offentlig Ekonomi (ESO). Ministry of Finance, Forthcoming, Stockholm, 1985.

182. SCB: *Sveriges framtida befolkning.* Information i prognosfrågor 1983:2, Stockholm 1983. The demographic assumptions are the following: after a slight increase between 1983 and 1988, fertility will remain constant. Slight declines in mortality are forecasted between 1985 and 1988, thereafter a fairly constant pattern. Net immigration will thus be the only source of population growth throughout the present century. From the mid-1990s onwards, however, the total Swedish population will decrease (see table below). As a matter of fact, the absolute number of men have been diminishing since 1981. In the mid-1980s, the absolute numbers of live births and deaths are almost equal, and as of the late 1980s, it is assumed that the number of deaths will be larger for the first time since 1757 when statistics first became available.

183. Riksförsäkringsverket: *Angående avgiftsuttag för allmän tilläggspensionering 1985-1989*, GD nr. 420/82, Stockholm 1982 (mimeo).

184. See note 64.

185. Recent projections towards the next century are summarized in Snickars, F. & Axelsson, S., *Om hundra år.* Ds SB 1984:2 (a report from the Council of the Prime Minister).

186. Crozier, M., Huntington, S., & Watanuki, J., *The Crisis of Democracy.* New York, 1975; See also Mishra, R.: *The Welfare State in Crisis.* Wheatsheaf Books, Brighton, 1984. Offe, C. *Contradictions of the Welfare State.* Hutchinson, London, 1984; Habermans, J., *Legitimation Crisis.* London, Heineman, 1976.

187. *Outline of the Results of the Third International Survey on Youth Attitudes.* Prime Minister's Office, Tokyo, 1984. In 1977, "Social welfare" ranked first among Swedish youths. In the replication of the same survey in 1983, "social welfare" lost its top position and became third after "nature" (71 percent) and "standard of living" (66 percent). Science, history, culture etc occupied the lower positions among the ten items to choose between. See also SIFO 85109-19 and Zetterberg, H.S., "En politik för åttiotalet" in Westholm, C-J., *Skapande eller bevakande Sverige?* Vol. II, Svenska arbetsgivareföreningen, Stockholm, 1979.

188. *Variabler och koder för LNU 81.* Institutet för social forsknig, Stockholm, 1984, and Johansson, S. *Välfärdsförändringar vid sidan av inkomster 1968-1974-1981.* Institutet för social forskning, Stockholm, 1981 (mimeo). The concept of "political resources" was in Sweden developed by the Level-of-living

survey. It is concentrated on the individual's opportunities to defend himself by political activity taken in a broad sense (activity in trade unions and other interest organization, ability to express oneself in speech and writing, etc.). See Johansson, S. *Politiska resurser*. Stockholm, Allmänna förlaget, 1971, and Szulkin, R., "Politiska resurser" in Erikson, R. & Åberg, R., *Välfärd i förändring*. Stockholm, Prisma, 1984.

189. Holmqvist, H-E. & Pettersson L-O.: *Svenska folket tycker om den offentliga sektorn*. LO, Borås, 1985.

190. A preliminary analysis presented by the Umeå research group in sociology and social insurance. See R. Lindqvist, 'Legitimitet och legitimitetskrig i svensk socialförsäkring', paper presented at the meeting of the Social Policy Group of the Swedish Sociological Association, Skytteholm, Sept. 1984, and S. Marklund, "Is the welfare state irreversible?" and S. Svallfors, "Vem älskar välfärdsstaten?". The latter two papers presented at the annual meeting of the Swedish Sociological Association, Lund, 1985 (mimeos to be published in research reports, Department of Sociology, University of Umeå, 1985). The papers try to distinguish between various aspects of legitimacy. See also G. Therborn and J. Roebroek, 'The Irreversible Welfare State'. Paper presented at the conference on 'The Future of the Welfare State', European Centre for Work and Society, Limburg University, the Netherlands, December 1984 (mimeo); M. Gilljam and L. Nilsson, *Svenska folket och den offentliga sektorn*, Forskningsrapport 1984:2, Statsvetenskapliga institutionen, Göteborgs universitet (Paper presented at the annual meeting of the Swedish Association of Political Scientists, Umeå 1984); and U. Himmelstrand, 'Opinioner, sakfrågor och förtroende', *Sociologisk Forskning* 1985.

191. Holmqvist & Pettersson op. cit.

192. See for example, Riksdagen 1984/85. *Motion no. 1505* (the Liberal People's Party proposal on freedom and democracy) and Carlsson, I., *Frihet och framtidstro*. Göteborgs arbetarekommun, Göteborg, 1983.

193. Arvidsson, H. & Berntson, L. *Makten, socialismen och demokratin*. Lund, Zenit, 1980; Ehnmark, A., *Arvsskiftet*, Stockholm, Norstedts, 1984.

194. *Regeringens proposition 1983/84:152*.

195. Hedborg, A. & Meidner, R., *Folkhemsmodellen*. Stockholm, Rabén & Sjögren, 1983; Hansson, S.O., Åberg., R. & Holgersson, L., *Hur ska vi ha det med jämlikheten?* Stockholm, Tiden, 1984, and Rehn, G. "På väg mot valfrihetens samhälle", Delegationen för arbetstidsfrågor, Arbetsmarknadsdepartementet, Stockholm, 1985 (mimeo). The latter text is the outcome of an OECD Conference on "New patterns of working time" in 1972 and published in English, French as well as German. See "Towards a Society of Free Choice" in Wiatr, J.J. and Rose, R. (eds), *Comparing Public Policy*, Wroclaw, Ossolineum, 1977; "Beiträge zu einer Theori der Sozialpolitik" in *Festschrift in honour of Elisabet Liefmann-Keil*, Berlin, Duncker & Humbolt, 1973; "Vers une société de libre choix" in *Droit Social* No. 7/8, 1978.

196. The environmentalist alternative was in the 1970s mainly under the banner of the Centre Party, but has in the 1980s become a ballot of its own. In the 1982 election, the "green" Environment Party got 1.7 percent of the votes. In the 1980 Referendum, the green alternative (termed no. 3, which opted for no further construction of nuclear power stations and liquidation of the in

1980 existing ones during a ten years period), backed by the Centre Party and the Left Party Communist together with various other independant organizations including associations inside the Liberal and Social Democratic parties (which on the top level backed alternative no. 2), got 38.7 percent against 39.1 for alternative no. 2. Alternative nr. 1, backed by the Conservative Party and by Swedish Industry and in phrasing similar to no. 2 except concerning public ownership of nuclear power stations (both alternatives opted for a 25 years liquidation period and the built-up and maintenance of the initially planned 13 nuclear power stations), got 18.9 percent of the votes. See Holmberg, S. & Asp, K., *Kampen om kärnkraften.* Stockholm, Publica/Liber, 1984. See also Gahrton, P. *Det behövs ett framtidsparti.* Stockholm, Prisma, 1980.

197. *Riksdagen. Andra Kammarens protokoll 1897.* Band 1. Stockholm, 1897.

198. Korpi, W., "Economic growth and the welfare state: leaky bucket or irrigation system?" in *European Sociological Review* Vol. 1 No. 2 (1985). See also Therborn, G. & Roebroek, J., "The Irreversible Welfare State". Paper presented at the Conference on "The Future of the Welfare State", European Centre for Work and Society, Limburg University, the Netherlands, December 1984 (mimeo).

199. During the election period 1973-76 the non-socialist parties had as many seats in Parliament as the Social Democrats and the Communists taken together (see Appendix, table 19). Two important round-table meetings were held at the Haga castle in the Stockholm surroundings between government, opposition and the major interest organizations.

200. Wigforss, E., *Skrifter i urval.* Tiden, Stockholm, 1980. See also Tilton, T.A., "Utopia, Incrementalism, and Ernst Wigforss Conception of Provisional Utopia" in *Scandinavian Studies*, Vol. 56 No. 1, and Higgins, W., "Ernst Wigforss and the Renewal of Social Democratic Theory and Practice" in *Political Power and Social Theory* 1985 (forthcoming).

*

References to *Appendix* throughout this text and in the footnotes above, cf. Flora 1987 pp. 1-64.

Chapter IV

* I would like to thank the organizers and members of the International Study Group on Trends in the Welfare State, which gave me opportunity to present the ideas put forward in this article. In particular Ram Cnaan, Neil Gilbert and Robert Morris read and commented upon the final draft.

1. This article is not about the theoretical notion of the welfare state. In itself, this is a wide-ranging debate with many ramifications. The empirical approximation of the welfare state used in the text, is of course not unrelated to this debate and in no way unproblematic as it stands. However, it is out of touch nor with the common-sense notion of the welfare state, neither with the empirical discussion on the welfare state in many books with scientific aspirations. For example, Robinson and le Grand (1984) use the following em-

pirical description of the welfare state:

"Although there is no precise definition of the bounds of the welfare state, it is possible to specify the main programmes that are normally identified as parts of it. First, there is the social security system, which makes income transfers from taxpayers to benefit recipients in the form of cash payments. These include the social insurance system based on programmes emphasised in the Beveridge report (1942), through which individuals' contributions provide entitlement to benefits (i.e. sickness benefits, short-term unemployment benefits and retirement pensions) and also increasingly – in the face of continuing high levels of long-term unemployment – non-contributory payments such as supplementary benefits. Second, there are benefits in kind, which are provided via free health care, education and various personal social services (e.g. the services of social workers, home-helps, meals-on-wheels, etc). Third, there is a range of price subsidies designed to reduce the cost to consumers of certain commodities deemed socially desirable. These include rent subsidies, housing improvement grants and public transport subsidies." (p. 2)

Apart from the similarity between our social security and social service "states", (Olsson 1987b) Robinson and le Grand emphasize price regulation, while I tend to focus on the central state in job creation programs. This perhaps partly reflects the difference between the British and the Scandinavian welfare state, although there is a lot of price regulation in both housing and agricultural policies in Sweden.

2. However, this shift of responsibility can occur on several level, and in particular when discussing privatization it is important to make a distinction between the organizing, the financing, and the production of various welfare provisions (Kielland 1986).

3. The data on social expenditure in this section is taken from various official statistical publications: *Social Welfare* (Socialvården) published by Statistics Sweden, *National Insurance* (Allmän försäkring) by the National Social Insurance Board, and the *Swedish budget* published by the Government (all yearly publications). See also Olsson (1987a). For a more detailed account of various social programs and social expenditure items in the 1980s, see Nasenius, J., and Veit-Wilson, J. (1985). On the reforms of social security in recent years, see Sjöberg (1985).

4. In the 1985 election, the Social Democrats for the first time in 68 years lost power in the municipality of Malmö, the third biggest local government in Sweden, and its major southern city (across the Channel to the Danish capital of Copenhagen). After a fierce attack by the non-socialist parties, in particular by a new, pro-NATO, anti-immigrant and anti-tax party led by a member of one of the most important, well-established financial families in the area, the Chicago-styled Labour leadership (relatively speaking) had to resign (Fryklund & Pettersson 1987). This is not an indication of a future liberation of the former Danish province Scania, and thus not an indication of a "break-up of Sweden" in Nairn's Scottish sense (1978). However, it points towards Harold Wilensky's (1975) discussion of recent developments in the welfare state. It is definitely true, that no general welfare backlash has occurred in Sweden. But the outcome of the 1985 election in this major Swedish municipality can be labelled a *local* welfare backlash.

The new mayor of Malmö belongs to the young and hawkish neo-liberals – liberal-conservative according to their own terminology – which seems to have taken command over the Moderate Party in the mid-1980s. Shortly after taking office, he announced the so far most articulated privatization program from any local government in Sweden. In particular the difference with the program of the Moderate Mayor of Stockholm from the late 1970s is striking – a Mayor who in the first half of the 1980s became the national leader of that party. According to the Malmö program, municipal monopolies shall be abolished altogether, and the public service sphere privatized, in particular child care, health and education. A new private hospital will also be initiated and supported by the local authorities. However, very little has so far been materialized, and after one hundred days in office, the Mayor of Malmö admitted that many obstacles to the fulfillment of the election promises remained (*Dagens Nyheter* 1986-04-07).

The most apparent signs of a new political regime in the capital of Scania is – apart from the spectacular breakthrough for the new right populist party – a tax decrease and some cuts in the municipal budget, which in particular have hit the public child care program in the town. Also other personal social services will be affected, in particular home help services to the old and handicapped.

5. Information provided by Försäkringsbranschens Service AB. Pressmeddelande 12/85 and directly from Ulf Norman, FSAB. (FSAB, Kvartalsrapport 1/1986 presented in *Dagens Industri* 3.6.1986.) See also Tarras-Wahlberg, B. "Största skattehöjningen" in Dagens Nyheter 24.5. 1986, and the debate that followed during the summer of 1986 in *Dagens Nyheter*. For an interesting overview of the campaign against the tax proposal, see Rossander, O. "Kritiken mot realränteskatten informationstekniskt toppnummer" in *Dagens Nyheter* 7.9.86. On September 12th 1986, the proposal was withdrawn and replaced by an exceptional tax on the wealth of insurance companies.

6. The weekend before the take-over of the hospital was presented in the press (*Dagens Nyheter* 1987-02-04), I met with one of the managing directors of hospital, who silently remarked that according to Swedish law, insurance companies must make profits in order to safe-guard the savings of their clients. The investment companies involved in the hostile take-over of this private hospital are *Investor, Providentia* – the cornerstones of the Wallenberg empire – and Carnegie (owned by a new successful financial tycoon Penser, who controls the *Nobel Industries*, too). Peder Bonde – a cousin of Peter Wallenberg – is acting vice president of *Investor* and *Providentia*, vice chairman of the insurance company *Skandia*, and a longstanding member of the board of Trustees of the foundation that runs *Sophiahemmet*.

The information about private health insurance is otherwise based on information kindly provided by the *Skandia* insurance company (personal communications as well as their annual reports for 1985 and 1986 and some brochures). See also *Pockettidningen R*, "Skattjakten", No. 4, 1985, and *Dagens Industri* 26.8.86 (in the latter also information about a competing private health insurance company – *Trygg-Hansa*).

7. This part is based on information from *Praktikertjänst AB* (the annual report and other material) generously provided by Mikael Albinson. See also

Veckans Affärer (1986). In a recent issue of *Statsvetenskaplig Tidskrift*, No 1, 1986 – several articles discuss new orientations in health policy (service culture, budgetary politics, private versus public etc.)

8. Like the National Labour Market Board, this agency has carried out its own decentralization programme.

9. In 1980, 120 800 children were in day nurseries, 77 900 in family day care, and 107 900 in part-time pre-school groups. By 1985, these numbers increased to 184 700 and 108 800 for "day" and "family" care, but declined to 78 600 for pre-school part-time care (Statstical Yearbook of Sweden).

10. Party differences concerning family policy, in particular child minding are discussed in Sidebäck, G. & Sundbom, L. (1984). See also Lamb, M.E. & Levine, J.A. (1983). In the summer of 1986, a major debate on the organization and provision of child care took place in *Dagens Nyheter* provoked by some articles by leading Social Democratic politicians and intellectuals who opted for less public intervention. See also the debate in *Tiden* in 1980-1 on family policy.

References

Abrahamson, B. and Broström, A. 1980. *The Rights of Labour*. Beverly Hills: Sage.

Abukhanfusa, K. 1987. *Piskan och moroten*. Stockholm: Carlssons.

Acker, J. 1988. "Class, Gender and the Relations of Distribution". *Signs* Vol. 13, no. 3.

Affärsvärlden. 1987. "Vår feltänkta bostadspolitik ett totalt misslyckande efter 45 års regleringar", *Affärsvärlden* (weekly business magazine), No. 15.

Alber, J. 1982. *Vom Armenhaus zum Wohlfartsstaat*. Frankfurt a M: Campus.

Alapuro, R. 1987. "De intellektuella, staten och nationen" in *Historisk tidskrift för Finland*, 1987:3.

Alapuro, R. Alestalo, M., Haavio-Mannila, E. and Väyrynen R. (eds.). 1985. *Small States in Comparative Perspective*. Oslo: Norwegian University Press.

Alestalo, M. and Kuhnle, S. 1987. "The Scandinavian Route: Economic, Social and Political Developments in Denmark, Finland. Norway and Sweden" in R. Erikson et al (eds.).

Alestalo, M., Flora, P. and Uusitalo, H. 1985. "Structure and Politics in the Making of the Welfare State: Finland in Comparative Perspective" in R. Alapuro et al (eds.).

Alestalo, M. and Uusitalo, H. 1990. "Social Expenditure: A Decompositional Approach" in J.E. Kolberg and G. Esping-Andersen (eds.) *Between Work and Social Citizenship*. New York: M.E. Sharpe.

Allardt, E. 1984. "Representative Government in a Bureaucratic Age", *Daedalus* Vol. 113, No. 1.

Ambjörnsson, R and Gaunt, D. 1984. *Den dolda historien*. Stockholm: Författarförlaget.

Amenta, E. and Skocpol, T. 1986. "States and Social Policies" in *Annual Review of Sociology* Vol. 12. Palo Alto Annual Reviews.

Anderson, B. 1983. *Imagined Communities*, Verso: London.

Anderson, I. 1972. *Otto Järte - en man för sig*. Stockholm: Bonniers.

Anderson, P. 1968. "Components of the National Culture". *New Left Review*, No. 50.

-, 1974. *Lineages of the Absolutist State*. London: New Left Books.

-, 1980. *Arguments within English Marxism*. London: Verso.

Ascoli, U. 1986. "The Italian Welfare State between Incrementalism and Rationalization" in L. Balbo and H. Nowotny (eds.), *Time to Care in Tomorrow's Welfare Systems*. Vienna: European Centre for Social Welfare and Training.

Bagge, G. 1935. *Socialpolitik*. Stockholm: Socialinstitutet. Ms.

Baldwin, P. 1989. "The Scandinavian Origins of the Social Interpretation of the Welfare State", *Comparative Studies in Society and History*, Vol. 31, No. 1.

-, 1988. "How Socialist is Solidaristic Social Policy? Swedish Postwar Reform as a Case in Point", *International Review of Social History*, Vol. XXXIII, No. 2.

Berggren, H. 1961. Nationalist i det nya riket – Politikern S.A. Hedin debuterar", Samfundet Örebro Stads- och Länsbiblioteks Vänner, *Meddelande N:o XXVII*.

-, 1965: "För rättvisa och trygghet" in H. Berggren and G.B. Nilsson, *Liberal socialpolitik*. Uppsala: Acta Universitatis Upsaliensis.

Berglind, H. 1987. "Social Problems and Social Work – Practice and Research in Social Work in Sweden" in U. Bergryd and C.G. Jansson (eds.), *Sociological Miscellany. Essays in Honour of Gunnar Boalt*. Stockholm: Department of Sociology.

Berman, M. 1983. *All that is Solid Melts into Air*. London: Verso.

Beyer, N. 1968. *Bengt Lidforss – en levnadsbeteckning*. Stockholm: Norstedts.

-, 1985. *Den unge Hjalmar Branting*. Stockholm: Norstedts.

Boalt, G. and Bergryd, U. 1974. *Centralförbundet för socialt arbete*. Stockholm: CSA.

-, 1975. *De socialpolitiska centralförbunden*. Stockholm: CSA.

Brante, T. 1980. *Vetenskapens struktur och förändring*. Lund: Doxa.

Briggs, A. 1961. "The Welfare State in Historical Perspective", *European Sociological Archive*, No. 2.

Buci-Glucksmann, C. 1982. "Socialdemokratin och keynesianismen", *Zenit* No. 78.

Carlsson, I. & Lindgren, A-M. 1978. "Centerns omöjlighet – socialdemokratins möjlighet", *Tiden*, No. 1.

Carlsson, B. 1988. *Staten som monster*. Lund: Ekonomisk-historiska institutionen.

Carlsson, C. 1986. *Kvinnosyn och kvinnopolitik*. Lund: Arkiv.

Cassel, G. 1902. *Socialpolitik*. Stockholm: Gebers.

Castles, F. 1985. *The Working Class and Welfare*. Wellington: Allen & Unwin.

-, 1989a. (ed.), The Comparative History of Public Policy. Cambridge: Polity Press.

-, 1989b. "Book Review: The Politics of Social Policy in the United States", *American Journal of Sociology*, Vol. 95.

Childs, M. 1936. *Sweden – the Middle Way*. New Haven: Yale University Press.

Classon, S. 1984. *Med otryggheten som drivkraft*. Stockholm: Försäkringskasseförbundet.
-, 1988. *Kampen för tryggheten*. Stockholm: LO.
Colletti, L. 1972. *From Rousseau to Lenin*. London: New Left Books.
Cohn, H. 1983. *Profiler i svensk socialpolitik*. Värnamo: Skeab.
Cutright, P. 1965. "Political Structure, Economic Development and National Social Security Programs", *American Journal of Sociology*, Vol. 70.
Daedalus. 1984. "The Nordic Enigma" 113, No. 1 (Winter), and "Nordic Voices", No. 2 (Spring).
Danielsson, A. 1972. *Om den svenska revolutionen*. Stockholm: Arbetarkultur.
Davidson, A. 1989. *Two Models of Welfare*. Uppsala: Almqvist & Wiksell International.
Debray, R. 1981. *Teachers, Writers, and Celebrities*. London: Verso.
Dixon, J. and Scheurell, R. (eds.). *Social Welfare in Developed Market Countries*. London: Routledge.
Donnison, D. 1984. "The Progressive Potential of Privatization" in J. le Grand & R. Robinson (eds.).
Ds Fi. 1986. *Socialbidrag*. Stockholm: Expertgruppen för studier i offentlig ekonomi, Ministry of Finance, Report No. 16.
Ds S. 1986. *Socialbidrag – en faktaredovisning och probleminventering*. Stockholm: Ministry of Health and Social Affairs, Report No. 7.
Edebalk, P.G. 1975. *Arbetslöshetsförsäkringsdebatten. En studie i svensk socialpolitik 1892-1934*. Lund: Ekonomisk-Historiska institutionen (diss.).
-, 1989. "Gustav Möller och sjukförsäkringen". Paper presented at the Workshop of the Research Group on Social Policy and the Welfare State, Swedish Sociological Association, Skytteholm, Oct.
Edebalk, P.G. and E. Wadensjö. 1987. "Social Insurances – Public and Private". Paper presented at the symposium, "The Political Economy of Social Security". Fiskebäckskil.
Ebba Pauli. Stigfinnare – övervinnare. Stockholm: Svenska kyrkans diakonistyrelses förlag.
Elmér, Å. 1989. *Svensk socialpolitik*. (First ed. 1943.) Malmö: Liber
-, "Svenska bidrag till socialpolitisk teori" in Statsvetenskaplig tidskrift, Vol. 63, No. 1.
-, 1960. *Folkpensioneringen i Sverige*. Lund: Gleerups.
-, 1957. "Den raabska pensionsaktionen – en utomparlamentarisk opinionsrörelse", *Sociala Meddelanden*.
Elvander, N. 1961. *Harald Hjärne och konservatismen*. Uppsala: Almqvist & Wiksell.
Englund, K. 1976. *Arbetarförsäkringsfrågan i svensk politik 1884-1901*. Uppsala: Acta Universitatis Upsaliensis.
Ericson, H-O. 1987. *Vanmakt och styrka*. Lund: Arkiv.
Erikson, R., Hansen, E.J., Ringen, S and Uusitalo, H. (eds.). 1987. *The Scandinavian Model Welfare States and Welfare Research*. New York and London: M.E. Sharp.

337

Erikson, R. and Uusitalo, H. 1987. "The Scandinavian Approach to Welfare Research" in R. Erikson et al (eds.).

Erikson, R. and Åberg, R. (eds.). 1987. *Welfare in Transition*. Oxford: Clarendon.

Eräsaari, R. 1986. "A New Social State?", *Acta Sociologica* Vol. 29 No. 3.

Esping-Andersen, G. 1985. *Politics Against Markets*. Princeton, N.J.: Princeton University Press.

-, 1986. "Institutional Accomodation to Full Employment: A Comparison of Policy Regimes". in H. Keman and H. Palohe (eds.), *Coping with the Economic Crisis*. Beverly Hills: Sage.

-, 1989. "Jämlikhet, effektivitet och makt – socialdemokratisk välfärdspolitik" in Misgeld et al (eds.) 1989.

European Journal of Political Research. 1989. Vol. 17. No. 4. Special issue. *The political economy of people's welfare*, F. Castles & R. Wildenmann (eds.).

Eyerman, R. 1985. "Rationalizing Intellectuals – Sweden in the 1930s and 1940s", *Theory and Society*, Vol. 14.

Fahlbeck, P. 1892. *Stånd och klass: en socialpolitisk översikt*. Lund: Collin and Zicherman.

-, 1910. *Arbetarfrågan. Villa och verklighet*. Lund: Gleerups.

Flora, P. and Heidenheimer, A. (eds.). 1981. *The Development of the Welfare State in Europe and North America*. New Brunswick: Transaction.

Flora, P. 1981a. "Solution or Source of Crisis?" in W. Mommsen (ed.), *The Emergency of the Welfare State in Britain and Germany*.

-, 1981b. "Stein Rokkans Makro Modell der Politischen Entwicklung Europas: Ein Rekonstruktionsverzuch". *Kölner Zeitschrift für Soziologie und Socialpsychologie*, Vol. 33, No. 3.

-, et al. 1983. *State, Economy and Society in Western Europe 1815-1975*, Vol. 1. Frankfurt a M Campus.

-, ed. 1986. *Growth to Limits: The West European Welfare States Since World War II. Vol. I & II*, Berlin & New York: Walter De Gruyter.

-, ed. 1987. *Growth to Limits*, Vol. IV. Berlin & New York: Walter De Gruyter.

Folkpartiet, *Liberal ideologi och politik 1934-1984*, Stockholm.

Forgacs, D. 1989. "Gramsci and Marxism in Britain", *New Left Review*, No. 176.

Forser, T. 1976. *Bööks 30-tal*. Stockholm: Norstedts.

Friberg, M. & Galtung, J. 1986. *Alternativen*. Stockholm: Akademilitteratur.

Friedmann, R., Gilbert N. and Sherer M., (eds.). 1987. *Modern Welfare States*. London: Wheatsheaf Studies in International Social Policy.

Fryklund, B. et al. 1973. "Från bondeförbund till centerparti", *Zenit*, No. 34.

-, & Peterson, T. 1987. "Skånepartiet AB". Paper presented at the Annual Meeting of the Swedish Sociological Association, Hassela.

Frykman, T. 1986. "Housing Conditions" in R. Erikson and R. Åberg (eds.), *Welfare in Transition*. Oxford: Clarendon Press.

Furåker, B. 1986. *Stat och offentlig sektor*. Stockholm: Rabén & Sjögren.

-, 1989 (ed.), *Välfärdsstat och lönearbete*. Lund: Studentlitteratur.

Gesser, B. 1985. *Utbildning, jämlikhet, arbetsdelning*. Lund: Arkiv.

Gilbert, N. and B. 1989. *The Enabling State*. New York: Oxford UP.

Girvetz, H.K. 1972. "The Welfare State", *International Encyclopedia of the Social Sciencies*. London: MacMillan.

Giöbel-Lilja, I. 1948. *Gustav Cassel*. Stockholm: Norstedts.

Gough, I. 1975. "State expenditure in advanced capitalism", *New Left Review*. No. 92.

-, 1979. *The Political Economy of the Welfare State*. London: MacMillan.

Gunnarsson, G. 1965. *Arbetarrörelsens genombrottsår i dokument*, Stockholm: Prisma.

Gustafsson, A. 1988. *Local Government in Sweden*. Stockholm: The Swedish Institute.

Gårdlund, T. 1956. *Knut Wicksell – rebell i det nya riket*. Stockholm: Tiden.

Habermas, J. 1984. "Die Krise des Wohlfartstaates und die Erschöpfung utopischer Energien", Sw. transl. in *Ord & Bild*, No. 3, 1985.

Hagtvet, B. 1973. *Intellectuals, Party Structure and Factional Power: The Norwegian and Swedish Labour Party Elites in Comparative Perspective*. New Haven: Yale University. Ms.

Hayek, F. 1984. *Vägen till träldom*. Stockholm: Timbro.

Heckscher, G. 1984. *The Welfare State and Beyond*. Minneapolis: University of Minnesota Press.

Heclo, H. 1981. "Towards a New Welfare State?" in P. Flora and A. Heidenheimer (eds.).

Hedin, A. 1884a. "Motion No. 11". *Riksdagstrycket* (reprinted in *Tal och skrifter*, del I & II, Bonniers, Stockholm (published by Valfrid Spångberg)).

-, 1884b. "Tal i riksdagen". *Riksdagstrycket.*

-, 1884c. "Det tyska sjukförsäkringsförslaget". *Nationalekonomiska föreningens handlingar.*

Hedström, P. 1986. "From Political Sociology to Political Economy" in U. Himmelstrand (ed.), *Sociology: from crisis to science?*. London: Sage.

Heidenheimer, A. 1981. "Education and Social Security Entitlements in Europe and America" in P. Flora and A. Heidenheimer (eds.).

-, Heclo, H. and Adams, T. 1975. *Comparative Public Policy*. New York: St. Martin's Press. (2nd ed. 1983.)

Hellström, G. 1948. *Adolf Hedin*. Stockholm: Norstedts. (Svenska Akademiens minnesteckningar.)

Hernes, H. 1987. *Welfare State and Woman Power*. Oslo: Norwegian University Press.

Himmelstrand, U., G. Ahrne and L. Lundberg. 1981. *Beyond Welfare Capitalism*. London: Heinemann.

339

-, 1982. "Sweden: Paradise in Trouble" in I. Howe (ed.), *Beyond the Welfare State*. New York: Schocken Books.

Hirdman, Y. 1990. *Att lägga livet till rätta*. Stockholm: Carlssons.

Holmberg, P. 1974. "Socialpolitik" in B. Södersten (ed.), *Svensk ekonomi*. Stockholm: Rabén & Sjögren.

Holmberg, S. 1985. *Väljare i förändring*. Stockholm: Liber.

Hort, K. 1987."Välfärdsstat och marknadsekonomi", *Zenit*, No. 94.

Huntford, R. 1971. *The New Totalitarians*. London: Allen Lane.

Höjer, K. 1952. *Svensk socialpolitisk historia*. Stockholm: Norstedts.

Jackman, R.W. 1975. *Politics and Social Equality*. New York: Wiley.

Janowitz, M. 1976. *Social Control of the Welfare State*. Amsterdam: Elsevier.

Johansson, S. 1974. "Marknaden, politiken och privatsfären", *Sociologisk Forskning*, No. 4.

Jonsson, K. 1985. *Vid vetandets gräns*. Lund: Arkiv.

Jungen, E. 1931. "Socialpolitik och socialism", *Tiden*.

Kaim-Chandle, P.R. 1973. *Comparative Social Policy and Social Security. A Ten-Country Study*. London: Martin Robertson.

Kampmann, P., Henriksen, J. & Rasmussen, J. 1987. Arbejdsmarkedspensioner og Pensionspolitik". Oplaeg til seminariet "Pensionssystem og pensionspolitikkens dilemmaer i Norden", Sociologisk Institut, Köpenhamn. *Mimeo*.

Kassman, C. 1989. *Arne Geijer och hans tid 1910-1956*. Stockholm: Tiden.

KF/Folksam 1986. "Vårat dagis – en möjlighet för alla? Project report. Stockholm. *Mimeo*.

Kielland, E. 1986. "Privatisering – troll med mange hoder", *Tidskrift för samfunnsforskning*, No. 3/1986.

Kihlberg, L. 1972. *Folktribunen Adolf Hedin*. Stockholm: Bonniers.

Kleberg, O. 1984. "En gammal folktribun", *Dagens Nyheter*, 24-4-1984.

von Koch, G.H. (ed.), 1908. *Social handbok*. Stockholm: CSA (2nd ed. 1923.)

Korpi, W. 1978. *The Working Class in Welfare Capitalism*. London: Routledge & Kegan Paul.

-, 1980. "Social Policy and Distributional Conflicts in the Capitalist Democracies". *West European Politics*, Vol. 3, No. 3.

-, 1983. *The Democratic Class Struggle*. London: Heinemann.

-, 1985: "Economic Growth and the Welfare State: A Comparative Study of 18 OECD Countries" in *Labour and Society*, Vol. 10, No. 2.

-, 1985a. "Power Resources vs. Action and Conflict: On Causal and International Explanations in the Study of Power" in *Sociological Theory*, Vol. 3

-, 1989. "Power Politics, and State Autonomy in the Development of Social Citizenship: Social Rights during Sickness in Eighteen OECD Countries Since 1930", *American Sociological Review*, Vol. 54.

-, Olsson S.-E. and Stenberg S.-Å. 1982. "Svensk socialpolitik" i B. Södersten (ed.), *Svensk ekonomi*. Stockholm: Rabén & Sjögren.

-, and Esping-Andersen G. 1984. "From Poor Relief towards Institutional Welfare: The Development of Scandinavian Social Policy. Swedish Institute for Social Research. Occ. Papers No. 5.

Kossman, E.H. 1978. *The Low Countries*. Oxford: Clarendon.

Kuhn, T. 1962. *The Structure of Scientific Revolutions*. London: The University of Chicago Press.

Kuhnle, S. 1986. "Norway" in Flora (ed.) 1986.

Kuhnle, S. 1989. "Scandinavien im Wandel", *Journal für Sozialforschung*, Vol. 29, No. 1.

-, 1978. "The Beginnings of the Nordic Welfare States", *Acta Sociologica*, Vol. 21, (supplement).

Küng, A. 1983. *Låt pysslingen leva!* Stockholm: Timbro.

Köhler, P. and Zacher H., hrsg. 1981. *Ein Jahrhundert Sozialversicherung*. Berlin: Duncker & Humbolt.

-, (eds.). 1982. *The Evolution of Social Insurance 1881-1981*. London: Frances Pinter.

Lafargue, P. 1883. *Le Droit á la Paresse*, Henry Oriol (ed.). Paris. (Sw. transl., "Rätten till lättja", *Fri press*, Göteborg, 1980.)

Lagercrantz, O. 1979. *August Strindberg*, Stockholm: W&W.

Lamb, M.E. & Levine, J.A. 1983. "The Swedish Parental Insurance Policy: An Experiment in Social Engineering" in M.E. Lamb and A. Sagi (eds.), *Fatherhood and Family Policy*. London: Lawrence Erlbaum Associates.

Land, H. 1986. "An Analysis of the Meaning of Women's Work as Manifested in the British Income Maintenance Schemes", *International Sociology 1*, no. 3.

Langby, E. 1985. "Sweden: Libertarianism on Rocky Soil", *The Public Interest*, No. 60.

Le Grand, J., & Robinson, R. (eds.). 1984. *Privatization and the Welfare State*. London: Allen & Unwin.

Lepage, H. 1981. *I morgon kapitalism*. Stockholm: Ratio.

Lilliestam, Å. 1960. *Gustaf Steffen*. Göteborg: Akademiförlaget.

Lindbeck, A. 1981. "Work Disincentives in the Welfare State", *National-ökonomische Gesellschaft Lectures 79-80*. Vienna: Manz.

Lindblom, P. 1982. *Socialpolitiken och den problematiska välfärden*. Stockholm: Rabén & Sjögren.

Lindensjö, B. 1989. "Från liberal bottenskola till allmän grundskola" in Misgeld et al (eds.).

Lindkvist, R. 1990. *Från folkrörelse till välfärdsbyråkrati*. Lund: Arkiv.

Lipset, S.M. 1960. *Political Man*. London: Mercury Books.

Livijn, C. 1893. *Om moderna socialpolitiska lagar och lagförslag angående arbetarklassens betryggande mot de ekonomiska följderna av s.k. olycksfall i arbetet*. Stockholm: Beckman.

LO. 1986. *Fackföreningsrörelsen och välfärdsstaten*. Jönköping.

-, (Swedish Trade Union Confederation) 1986. *Fackföreningsrörelsen och välfärdsstaten*. Jönköping. (Summary in English).

341

Lundquist, L. (1967). *Fattigvård och folkförsäkring*. Lund: Statsvet. inst. *Mimeo*.

Marklund, S. 1982. *Klass, stat och socialpolitik*. Lund: Arkiv

-, 1988. *Paradise Lost? The Nordic Welfare States and the Recession 1975-1985*. Lund: Arkiv.

-, and Svallfors, S. 1987. *Dual Welfare – Segmentation and Work Enforcement in the Swedish Welfare System*. Umeå: Department of Sociology.

Marshall, T.S. 1964. *Class, Citizenship and Social Development*. New York: Doubleday.

Maurer, A. 1981. "Landesbericht Schweiz" in Köhler & Zacher (hrsg) 1981.

Maury, L. 1951. *Sveriges metaformos – minnen och intryck 1900-1950*. Stockholm: Bonniers.

Mellbourn, A. 1986. *Bortom det starka samhället*. Stockholm: Liber.

Merton, R. 1948. "The Position of Sociological Theory", *American Sociological Review*, Vol. 13.

Miller, S.M. 1986 "New Welfare State Models and Mixes", *Social Policy*, Fall, 1986.

Misgeld, K., Molin, K., & Åmark, K. (eds.), 1989. *Socialdemokratins samhälle 1889-1989*. Stockholm: Tiden.

Mishra, R. 1977, 1981. *Society and Social Welfare*. London: MacMillan.

-, 1985 "Public Policy and Social Welfare: the Ideology and Practice of Restraint in Ontario", Paper presented at the Second Conference in Provincial Social Welfare Policy, Calgary, Alberta. *Mimeo*.

Mohlin, B. 1965. *Tjänstepensionsfrågan*. Göteborg: Akademilitteratur Göteborg (diss.).

Mommsen, W. ed. 1981. *The Emergence of the Welfare State in Britain and Germany*. London: Croom Helm.

Montgomery, A 1934. *Svensk socialpolitik under 1800-talet*. Stockholm: Kooperativa förbundets bokförlag.

Moretti, F. 1986. "The Moment of Truth", *New Left Review*, No. 159.

Morris, R. 1989. *Testing the Limits of Social Welfare. International Perspectives on Policy Change in Nine Countries*. Hanover & London: The University Press of New England.

Mulhern, F. 1979. *The Moment of 'Scrutiny'*. London: New Left Books.

-, 1981. "Introduction" in R. Debray *Teachers, Writers, Celebrities*. London: Verso.

Myrdal, G. 1932. "Socialpolitikens dilemma", *Spektrum*, Vol. 2. No. 3 & 4.

-, 1972. *Vetenskap och politik i nationalekonomin*. Stockholm: Rabén & Sjögren.

Myrdal, A. & G. 1934. *Kris i befolkningsfrågan*. Stockholm: Bonniers.

Möller, G. 1959. *När vi började*. Stockholm: Tiden.

Nairn, T. 1976. *The Break-Up of Britain*. London: New Left Books.

-, 1988. *The Enchanted Glass*. London: Radius.

Nasenius, J. & Veit-Wilson 1985. "Social policy in a cold climate: Sweden in the eighties" in C. Jones and M. Brenton (eds.), *The Yearbook of social policy in Britain 1984-85*. London: Routledge & Kegan Paul.

Nationalekonomiska föreningens handlingar 1882-1885, (1883-86), Stockholm.

Nordkvist-Wiksell, L. 1985. *Anna Bugge-Wiksell: En kvinna före sin tid.* Malmö: Liber.

Nilsson, G. B, 1990. "Den sociala ingenjörskonstens problematik", *Nytt Norsk Tidskrift.*

Nilsson, T. 1985. *Från kamratföreningar till facklig rörelse.* Lund: Arkiv.

Nozick, R. 1974. *Anarchy, State, and Utopia.* New York: Basic Books.

Nyström, P. 1983. *I folkets tjänst.* Stockholm: Ordfront.

-, 1989. *Historia och biografi.* Lund: Arkiv.

O'Connor, J. 1973. *The Fiscal Crisis of the State.* New York: St. Martins Press.

O'Higgins, M. & Ruggles, P. 1985. "Retrenchment and the New Right: A Comparative Analysis of the Impacts of the Thatcher and Reagan Administrations", in G. Esping-Andersen, L. Rainwater and M. Rein (eds.), *Stagnation and Renewal in Social Policy.* New York: ME Sharpe.

OECD. 1981. *The Crisis of the Welfare State.* Paris.

OECD. 1985. *Social Expenditures 1950-1990.* Paris.

Offe, C. 1984. *Contradictions of the Welfare State.* London: Hutchinson.

Ohlin, B. 1974. *Ung man blir politiker.* Stockholm: Bonniers.

Olofsson, G. 1979. *Mellan klass och stat.* Kristianstad: Arkiv.

-, 1984. "Den svenska modellen", *Zenit,* 84.

-, 1984a. "Den svenska socialdemokratin: en rörelse mellan klass och stat" i Ambjörnsson, R. och Gaunt, D. 1984.

-, 1986. "Efter arbetarrörelsen?", *Zenit,* 93.

-, 1987. "After the Working class movement?", *Acta Sociologica,* Vol. 31, No. 1.

-, and Hort, K. 1986. "Bidrag, skatter och avdrag inom bostadssektorn". Paper presented at the Annual Meeting of the Swedish Sociological Association.

Olson, H.-E. 1982. *Från hemgård till ungdomsgård.* Stockholm: RSFHs förlag.

Olson, M. 1982. *The Rise and Decline of Nations.* New Haven: Yale UP.

Olsson, S.E. 1987a. "Comparative tables: Sweden" in P. Flora et. al. (ed.), Vol. IV.

-, 1987b. "Towards a transformation of the Swedish Welfare State?" in Friedmann et al. (ed.).

-, 1987c. "Die Volks-Altersrente in Schweden – einst, heute und künftig". In Opielka (ed.), *Die Grundrente diskutieren.*

-, 1985. "Perry Anderson – en ny typ av västerländsk marxist?", *Arkiv för studier i arbetarrörelsens historia,* No. 31.

-, 1975. "Hamnarbetarna och Transportarbetareförbundet", *Arkiv för studier i arbetarrörelsens historia,* No. 7-8.

-, 1988. Bookreview: "Åke Elmér, Svensk socialpolitik" in *Ekonomisk Debatt* Vol. 16 No. 7.

Opielka, M., (ed.), 1987. *Die Grundrente diskutieren: Politische und wissenschaftliche Auseinandersetzungen mit dem Rentenreformvorschlag der Grünen*. Essen: Klartext Verlag.

Orloff, A. and Skocpol, T. 1984. "Why Not Equal Protection? Explaining the Politics of Public Social Spedning in Britain 1900-1911 and the United States, 1880-1920", *American Sociological Review*, Vol. 49.

Palmér, A. & Persson, A. 1985. "Etablerad kooperation på nya vägar" in *Kooperativ årsbok 1985*. Stockholm: Föreningen kooperativa studier.

Palmstierna, E. 1951. *Ett brytningsskede*. Stockholm: Tiden.

Pauli, E. 1904. *Socialförsäkringen i Schweiz*. Stockholm: CSA.

Perrin, G. 1969. "Reflections on 50 Years of Social Security" in *International Labour Review*, Vol. 99, No. 3.

Persson, A. & Svensson, A. 1986. "Vårat dagis" in *Kooperativ årsbok 1986*. Stockholm: Föreningen kooperativa studier.

Persson, G. 1986. "The Scandinavian Welfare State Anatomy, Logic and Some Problems", Suntory Toyota International Centre for Economics and Related Disciplines, Welfare State Programme, London School of Economics and Political Science, Discussion Paper, No. 22.

-, 1978. "Socialpolitiken, marknaden och marxismen", *Zenit*, No. 58.

-, 1980. "Till socialpolitikens försvar", *Zenit*, No. 65.

Polanyi, K. 1944. *The Great Transformation*. Boston: Beacon Press.

Pontusson, J. 1984. "Behind and beyond Social Democracy in Sweden" in *New Left Review* No. 143.

Proposition (Government bill) 1985/86 100, *The Swedish Budget*, Summary, Ministry of Finance, Stockholm.

-, 1984/85 302. *Skrivelse*, Ministry of Public Administration, English summary p. 1, (Government report to Parliament).

-, 1982/83 152, *Besparingar i statsverksamheten*.

Raab. G. A. 1905. *Förslag till lag angående allmän pensionering af behöfvande jämte motiv m.m*. Göteborg: Kommittén för allmän pensionering.

Rehn, G. 1985. "Swedish Active Labour Market Policy: Retrospect and Prospect", *Industrial Relations*, Vol. 24, No. 1, University of California at Berkeley.

-, 1939/1988. "Socialpolitik och lönepolitik", *Full sysselsättning utan inflation*. Stockholm: Tiden.

-, 1989. "En rättvis och flexibel tilläggspension". Stockholm: Swedish Institute for Social Research. Occ. Papers No. 7.

Richardsson, G. 1963. *Kulturkamp och klasskamp*. Göteborg: Akademiförlaget.

Riksdagens protokoll 1882-1906.

Rimlinger, G. 1971. *Welfare Policy and Industrialization in Europe, America and Russia*. New York: Wiley.

Ringer, F.K. 1969. *The Decline of the German Mandarins*. Cambridge: Harvard University Press.

Roebroek, J. and G. Therborn. 1986. "The Irreversible Welfare State: its Recent Maturation, its Encounter with the Economic Crisis, and its Future Prospects", *International Journal of Health Services*, Vol. 16, no. 3.

Ronnby, A. 1982. *Socialstaten*. Lund: Studentlitteratur.

Rose, R. 1986. "State, Markets and Households" in R. Rose and R. Shiratorei (eds.), *The Welfare State East and West*. Oxford: Oxford UP.

Rothstein, B. 1982. "Fanns det en arbetsmarknadspolitik före AMS?", *Arkiv för studier i arbetarrörelsens historia*, No. 23-24.

-, 1986. *Den socialdemokratiska staten*. Lund: Arkiv.

-, 1985. "Administring the Welfare State: Some Lessons from Gustav Möller", *Scandinavian Political Studies*.

-, 1988a. "Struktur-aktöransatsen – ett metodiskt dilemma", *Statsvetenskaplig tidskrift*, No. 1.

-, 1988b. "Sociala klasser och politiska institutioner: den svenska korporatismens rötter", *Arkiv för studier i arbetarrörelsens historia*, No. 40.

Sainsbury, D. 1989. "Welfare State Variations, Women and Equality". Paper prepared for the ECPR Workshop on 'Equality Pinciples and Gender Politics'. Paris.

Schmidt, F. 1945. "Från franska revolutionens rättighetsförklaring till Beveridgeplanen", *Statsvetenskaplig tidskrift*, Vol. 27.

Schmidt, M. 1989. "Social Policy in Rich and Poor Countries: Socioeconomics Trends and Political Institutional Determinants", *European Journal of Political Research*, Vol. 17. No. 4.

Schröder, L. & Sehlstedt, K. 1987. "Local Job Creation Programs for Youth in Sweden", Paper prepared for the Expert Meeting on the Role of the Social Economy in the Creation of Local Employment, European Centre for Social Welfare, Vienna, April 1987.

Seip, A. 1984. *Sosialhjelpsstaten blir til*. Oslo: Gyldendal.

Sellberg, H. 1950. *Staten och arbetarskyddet 1850-1919*. Uppsala: Almqvist & Wiksell.

Sevåg, R. 1967. *Statsråd H. R. Astrup*. Oslo: Dreyers.

Shalev, M. 1983. "The Social Democratic Model and Beyond. Two generations of comparative research on the welfare state". *Comparative Social Research*, Vol. 6.

Showstack-Sassoon, A. 1986. *Women and the State*. London: Hutchinson.

Sidebäck, G. & Sundbom, L. 1984. "Agents of change". Paper presented at the ECPR, Joint session of workshops, Barcelona.

Sigg, R. 1985. "Sociology and Social Security: A Fresh Approach", *International Social Security Review*, No. 1.

Sjöberg, B. 1985. "Reforming the Swedish social security system", *International Labour Review*, Vol. 124, No. 1.

Socialismens grundvalar. En diskussion å Folkets Hus den 7 februari 1908. Lund: Arkiv (reprint 1981).

Southern, D. 1987. *Gunnar Myrdal and An American Dilemma*. Baton Rouge: Louisiana State University Press.

345

Spångberg, V. 1901. *Adolf Hedin – Väktaren och föregångsmannen*. Uppsala: Verdandi (no. 100).

-, 1926. *Adolf Hedin i liv och gärning*. Stockholm: Almqvist & Wiksell.

Steiger, O. 1971. "Till frågan om den nya ekonomiska politikens tillkomst i Sverige" i *Arkiv för studier i arbetarrörelsens historia*, No. 1.

Stephanson, A. 1989. *Kennan and the Art of Foreign Policy*. Cambridge MA: Harvard University Press.

Strindberg, A. 1879. *Röda rummet*. (Ny utg. 1981). Stockholm: Norstedts.

Ståhlberg, A-C. 1985. *Public and Negociated Pension Wealth in Sweden*. Institutet för social forskning, Stockholm.

Sunesson, S. 1977. "Onsdagsklubben och klasskampen – från tjugotalets arbetarrörelse i Sandviken", *Arkiv för studier i arbetarrörelsens historia*, No. 11-12.

Svallfors, S. 1987. "Vem älskar välfärdsstaten?", *Zenit*, No. 94.

-, 1989. *Vem älskar välfärdsstaten?* Lund. Arkiv.

Swedberg, R. 1990. "Introduction" in G. Myrdal *The Political Element in the Development of Economic Theory*. New Brunswick: Translation.

Svenska män och kvinnor. 1944. Stockholm: Bonniers.

Svenskt biografiskt lexikon. 1922- . Stockholm.

Svensson, B. 1962. "Primärkommunerna och undervisningsväsendet". *Hundra år med kommunalförfattningarna 1862-1962*. Stockholm: Svenska Landskommunernas Förbund.

Sörlin, S. 1988. *Framtidslandet*. Stockholm: Carlssons.

Tarschys, D. 1985. "Curbing Public Expenditure: Current Trends", *Journal of Public Policy*, Vol. 5. Part 1.

-, 1986. "From Expansion to Restraint: Recent Developments in Budgeting", *Public Budget & Finance*, (Autumn.)

Taylor-Gooby, P. 1989. "Current developments in the sociology of welfare", *British Journal of Sociology*, Vol. 40. No. 4.

Therborn, G. 1983. "Why are some classes more successful than others?", *New Left Review*, No. 138.

-, 1985a. *Why Some People are More Unemployed than Others*. London: Verso.

-, 1985b. "Karl Marx Returning". *International Political Science Review*, Vol. 7.

-, 1986. "The Working Class and the Welfare State" in P. Kettunen (ed.), *Det nordiska i den nordiska arbetarrörelsen*. Helsinki: Finnish Society for Labour History.

-, 1987. "Klassernas språk och klasskampens spår" in U. Bergryd (ed.), *Den sociologiska fantasin*. Stockholm: Rabén & Sjögren.

-, 1989a. "'Pillarization' and 'Popular movements'. Two Variants of Welfare State Capitalism: the Netherlands and Sweden" in F. Castles (ed.), *The Comparative History of Public Policy*. Cambridge: Polity Press.

-, 1989b. *Borgarklass och byråkrati i Sverige*. Lund: Arkiv.

-, 1989c. "Nation och klass, tur och skicklighet" i Misgeld et al (eds.).

Therborn, G., Kjellberg, A., Marklund, S. and Öhlund, U. 1978. "Sweden Before and After Social Democracy", *Acta Sociologica*, Vol. 21 (supplement).

Thermaenius, E. 1949. "S A Hedin i Sv. Akademiens minnesteckningar", *Statsvetenskaplig Tidskrift*, Vol. 31.

Thunberg, S. and Herlitz, N. 1907. *Svensk socialpolitisk litteratur*. Stockholm: Ekmans.

Tingsten, H. 1941. *Den svenska socialdemokratins idéutveckling*. Stockholm: Tiden.

Titmuss, R. 1958. "The Social Divison of Welfare", in *Essays on the Welfare State*. London: Unwin.

-, 1974. *Social Policy: An Introduction*. London: Allen & Unwin.

Tjäder, P-A. 1982. *'Det unga Sverige'*. Lund: Arkiv.

Tomason, R.F. 1970. *Sweden – Prototype of Modern Society*. New York: Random House.

Townsend, S. 1989. *Mr Bevan's Dream*. London: Chatto & Windus.

Treffenberg, C et al. 1880. *Betänkande angående åtgärder till förbättrandet af de vid sågverken i trakten af Sundsvall anstälde arbetarnes ställning afgifvet af den för sådant ändamål af sågverksegarne nedsatta Komité*. Sundsvall: Boktryckeri AB.

Wadensjö, E. 1989. The Committe on Unemployment and the Stockholm School. Stockholm: Swedish Insitute for Social Research (*Occational papers* No. 9).

-, 1988. "Gösta Bagge – ett ekonomporträtt", *Ekonomisk Debatt*, Vol. 16, No. 7.

-, 1987. "Före Stockholmsskolan – arbetslöshetsutredningen, Gösta Bagge och Ernst Wigforss", *Ekonomisk Debatt*, Vol. 15., No. 4.

Vallinder, T. 1987. "Pontus Fahlbeck – en statsvetenskaplig klassiker", *Politologen*.

Veckans Affärer. 1986. "Det privata alternativet", *Veckans Affärer*, No. 26-28.

Vennström, E. 1984. "Folkhemmets födelse" in Ambjörnsson, R. and Gaunt, D.

Vesterö-Jensen, C. 1984. *Det tve-delte pensionssystem*. Roskilde: RUC.

Weir, M. and Skocpol, T. 1985. "State Structures and the Possibilities for 'Keynesian' Responses to the Great Depression in Sweden, Britain, and the United States" in P.B. Evans, D. Rueschmeyer and T. Skocpol (eds.), *Bringing the State Back In*. Cambridge: Cambridge University Press.

Weir, M., Orloff, A. S. and Skocpol, T. (eds.) 1988. *The Politics of Social Policy in the United States*. Princeton N.Y.: Princeton University Press.

Westholm, C-J. (ed.), 1979-80. *Skapande eller bevakande Sverige?* Vol. 1-4, Stockholm: Svenska Arbetsgivareföreningen.

Wilensky, H.L. & Lebeaux, C.N. 1958. *Industrial Society and Social Welfare*. New York: Russell Sage Foundation (enlarged paperback ed. 1965.)

Wilensky, H.L. 1975. *The Welfare State and Equality*. Berkeley: University of California Press.

347

-, 1976. *The "New Corporatism". Centralization and the Welfare State.* California: SAGE.

Wilson, E. 1977. *Women and the Welfare State.* London: Tavistock.

Wittrock, B. 1989. "Social Science and State Development: Transformations of the Discourse of Modernity". *International Social Science Journal,* Vol. XLI, No. 4.

Wolfe, A. 1989. *Whose Keeper? Social Science and Moral Obligation.* Berkeley: University of California Press.

X. 1884. "Nya försök till förbättring af arbetsklassens vilkor", *Nordisk tidskrift för vetenskap, konst och ekonomi,* Årg. 6, (later published in Forsell, H 1888, *Studier och kritik,* II, Stockholm.

Zennström, P.O. 1983. *Axel Danielsson.* Lund: Arkiv.

Zetterberg, H. 1979. "En socialpolitik för åttiotalet" in C-J Westholm (ed.), *Skapande eller bevakande Sverige.* Stockholm.

-, 1979. "Maturing of the Swedish Welfare State", *Public Opinion,* (Oct. Nov).

Postscript:
Crisis, Crisis, Crisis – 1990-92

Fellowship and solidarity are the very foundation on which the home is built. The good home does not know of privileges nor of neglect, there are no favourites or stepchildren. Equality, consideration, cooperation and helpfulness prevail in the good home. Applied to a larger people's or citizens' home, this would mean breaking down all social and economic barriers that would divide people into privileged and underprivileged, rulers and dependents, rich and poor, the landed classes and the destitute, plunderers and plundered ... Swedish society is not yet the good home for its citizens. To be sure, formal equality in political rights prevails here, but in the social area the class society remains and economically the dictatorship of a minority prevails.

Per Albin Hansson (PM of Sweden 1932-1946), 1928

In his unsentimental way, Mr Bildt is setting a new tone in Swedish politics. Gone is the familiar rhetoric about solidarity, equality and collectivism in what became known as the Social Democratic People's Home. Instead, here is a Swedish prime minister enthusing without guilt about the profit motive, private enterprise and competition.

Financial Times Oct 7 1991

1. Introduction:
A Crisis of a Welfare Model – or Policy Regime?

The conclusions with which the first edition of this book opened – and closed – must inspire certain reservations not quite three years

349

after its initial publication. In view of recent events, the non-apocalyptic tone is itself a suspect sign of difficulties resolutely evaded or ignored, and might even be interpreted as an ambition to play problems down. The book's perspective on Swedish social policy is long-term. The present state of affairs goes back to the early transformation by radical intellectuals – with crucial support from the free peasantry – of the German industrial and selective social insurance model, or in the words of Richard Titmuss the "industrial achievement-performance" model, into a universal policy regime, also assisted by the active intervention of, not least, the Swedish labour movement. This century-long perspective is contrasted with the crisis or even doomsday perspective of the 1980s: the dismantling or withering away of the welfare state. Several conceptual entrances/frameworks were applied – consolidation, maturation, stagnation – but none of them proved fully satisfactory. Instead, the notion of transformation was employed – with some reluctance. Today, when the heartland of this welfare model more seriously than a decade ago is invaded by the threat of crisis, the question remains: transformation – into what? A new welfare model or policy regime? Is there a third domain of welfare capitalism? Or is Sweden's once celebrated welfare state (model) deteriorating as did for instance the egalitarian model in New Zealand in the 1980s?[1]

In my introduction I briefly surveyed the model-building in this field of social research, from British social administration onwards. Since then the most popular dichotomies, such as residual vs institutional, have been scrutinized far more critically (cf. Sainsbury 1991 & Therborn 1989). In recent years, this discussion has taken a new turn with the growth of empirical cross-national or comparative research on advanced welfare states conducted by scholars such as Peter Flora and Walter Korpi (cf Allardt 1989). In this context it is appropriate to add Peter Baldwin's *The Politics of Social Solidarity* (1990), a fine example of the historian's craft (cf Orloff 1992 & Esping-Andersen 1991).

Following in particular the release of Gösta Esping-Andersen's *The Three Worlds of Welfare Capitalism* (1990), the notion of "policy regime" has become a fancy way of contrasting the experience of the Social Democratic or Scandinavian – especially the Swedish, sometimes also refered to as the (neo-)Corporatist (following Rothstein, Möllerian ought to be added) – welfare states with the Liberal (on and off also named Anglo-Saxon, or Beveridgean) model on the one hand, and the Conservative (Catholic, Corporatist, Continental or Bismarckian – the labels are many) model on the other (cf Kolberg 1992a & Cnaan 1992). This work has also inspired badly wanted feminist scholarship in the intersection of historical sociology and comparative policy analysis (cf Lewis 1992; Kolberg 1992c; Bergqvist 1990; Shaver 1990; Siim 1990).

Here, some initial comments are pertinent. First, there is the obvious problem of labels – Conservative, Liberal, Socialist or Social-Democratic – with a considerable variation in meaning across national political cultures. For instance, in the US, Liberal – including a Liberal Welfare State – has very different connotations from in Europe. As has the notion of welfare as such. Furthermore, Esping-Andersen's regimes rely heavily on Karl Polanyi's view of the long-term historical transformation of Western society into a monetarized exchange economy. However, what seems to be the most critical threat to the national welfare states – the hyperfluidity of an international money market almost totally freed from the impediments of industrial production and household consumption – is not discussed in terms of the necessity of embeddedness in order to have functioning markets. Making national policy priorities working in a globally integrated economy has become a tremendous problem, not least for left-leaning governments (cf. Glyn 1992 & Noterman 1991).

Esping-Andersen also adds two new dimensions to the debate about welfare models or policy regimes: decommodification and stratification. Both are related to discussions about the welfare state in terms of equality, security, poverty, and solidarity, but in particular the first notion – decommodification: the withering away of labour's commodity form or "the alpha and omega of the unity and solidarity required for labour-movement development" (1990:37) – is closely linked to the Polanyian scheme. Sceptical reviewers of Esping-Andersen have pointed out the dual nature of the relationship between wage-earners, state and market. What he analyzes is more a recommodification – better functioning labour markets – than a decommodification of labour power.

Stratification is more common sociological goods, but still significant for a discussion of the outcome of welfare state activities on

351

the distribution of life-chances. In terms of comprehensiveness and total social spending, welfare states can be similar yet they can have entirely different effects on the social structure. Each case produces its own unique fabric of social solidarity: "one may cultivate hierarchy and status, another dualisms, and the third universalism" (Esping-Andersen 1990:58). Despite my partial scepticism in particular towards the notion of decommodification, I think it is illuminating to show the clustering of nations that results from these two dimensions (table 1). One reason is, of course, that examples from other countries are referred to when changes in welfare system reach the political agenda.

Table 1. Decommodification and stratification in various policy regime types according to Esping-Andersen.

Decommodification

Low	Medium	High
Australia	Italy	Sweden
United States	Japan	Norway
New Zealand	France	Denmark
Canada	Germany	Netherlands
Ireland	Finland	Belgium
United Kingdom	Switzerland	Austria

Stratification

Liberal	Conservative	Socialist
Australia	Austria	Denmark
Canada	Belgium	Finland
Japan	France	Netherlands
Switzerland	Germany	Norway
United States	Italy	Sweden
United Kingdom	Ireland	New Zealand

Source: Esping-Andersen pp. 52 and 74
Note: All nations above scored "strong" on their respective stratification label, apart from Ireland, United Kingdom and New Zealand, which scored "medium".

Thus, Esping-Andersen ends up with roughly the same location of countries as other researchers before him. Workers in this field, often inspired by the position of their country in the wrong box, have slightly extended this approach. Castles (1990) has made a qualification in the form of two types of liberal policy regime – the market-oriented (US, Japan) and "radical", "lib-lab" (UK, Australia, New Zealand) – while Leibfried, confining himself to the European scene, distinguishes between four types of welfare state: the modern universalistic (Scandinavia), the liberal free market-based (UK, Ireland), the continental based on labour market participation (Germany, France, Austria, the Netherlands, Belgium), and the Latin rim with rudimentary welfare institutions (Italy, Spain, Portugal). Habermas has added a communitarian model based on the experience of an alternative culture – self-help and ecological responsibility – in central Europe (Abrahamson 1992). More than the others, this model has close links to the idea of a civil society of both distant and intimate obligations circumjacent to both the state and the market. The latter may also be true for those libertarians who emphasize modern urban individualism at the expense of traditional family-values (cf. Arvidsson, Berntson & Dencik 1992). In the introduction, I have tried to outline a somewhat different perspective on civil society based on the interwoven historical experience of the local communities and the popular social mass movements of the Far North (cf Mahon 1991). To fully explore the advantages of this approach would need a book-length manuscript. Here I would only like to point out its usefulness in analyzing changes currently taking place in the Swedish social service sector (section 5:3 below).

Esping-Andersen's regime-types basically correspond to Titmuss' three-fold typology of welfare models: the residual, the industrial-performance, and the institutional models of social policy. Thus, second, the problems that apply to Titmuss are also relevant in a critical review of the concept of policy regime, which is defined in terms of the priorities given to state, family, and market, with no allowance for the many and varied sets of voluntary, non-governmental or semi-official intermediary institutions and organizations with significant welfare functions (Kuhnle & Selle 1992). These models or regimes are ultimately ideal-type classifications of empirical cases (countries). Although Esping-Andersen does propose an interactive model of the relationship between actors and structures – of institutions and systems – and includes various attempts

353

at macro-economic steering into his definition of what makes a state in a given society a "welfare state-complex", his regime-types run the risk of becoming a broad set of static analytical categories. As a partial, ad-hoc solution, in the concluding section I will employ another typology used by Titmuss: the distinction between (1) social (or state provided) welfare, (2) fiscal welfare (financed through "tax expenditures" or tax deductions), (3) occupational welfare (from schemes negotiated and jointly administered by the main "social partners", employers and employees, to fringes benefits provided on an enterprise level), and, finally, (4) private welfare or charity. This typology will be combined with another model which originates from the post-Titmussian discussion.

From a Swedish perspective, the basic questions are whether the policy regime or welfare model of the Far North has started to move in the direction of one or the other of the two – or three – alternatives that seem to be available in the comparative welfare state literature, and to what extent state welfare has been replaced by fiscal, occupational (or corporate), and private welfare? These questions are further scrutinized in the concluding pages of this postscript in the light of a survey of the most recent domestic events. To explore in both theory and practice contemporary problems and present difficulties adequately – not to speak of ultimately solving or transcending them – would require another book. Hence, I will only add some significant facts of recent date, and relate them to the intense theoretical discussion on welfare models or policy regimes.

In 1990-92, four dramatic events have raised questions about the viability of Sweden's famous welfare state. Three of them are commonly labelled as "crises": the first was a cabinet crisis in January-February 1990, the second a threat of devaluation in the autumn of 1990, the third another but much more spectacular economic crisis two years later including an unprecedented hike in the central bank's lending rate to 500 per cent. Between the second and the third of these crises came the departure from the helm of the nation-state's traditional 20th century political ruler, Social Democracy, when the election result in September 1991 turned out to be its worst result since 1928 and the first time since then that the party received less than 40 per cent of the vote. In its place came a right-centre government with the outspoken aim of bringing about a "freedom-of-choice revolution" in welfare policy, headed by the chairman of the Moderate or Conservative party, Carl Bildt. These events point to three major problems all related to the nature of the model or policy regime: the implications of reorganization, cuts and austerity measures for the future of this model; the social basis of the welfare state; and the nation-state as the foundation of the welfare state. These issues will be addressed after a brief look at the three crises of the Swedish welfare state.

2. Crisis Number One

For the first time since 1957, in February 1990 a Social Democratic Prime Minister resigned without a previous electoral defeat or a vote of non-confidence in Parliament. Most important, the once powerful Minister of Finance, Kjell-Olof Feldt, resigned as well. For a large part of the Labour movement, not least the trade union movement and the Social Democratic Women's movement, he had become a symbol or scapegoat of adaption to non-social democratic or bourgeois values due to his role as the man behind the comprehensive tax reform of 1988-89 (jointly worked out with the Liberal Party) which considerably lowered marginal tax rates. This reform remained extremely controversial within the Labour movement throughout parliament's three-year term 1988-91. The previous tax system had been described by the chairman of the blue collar trade union confederation (LO) as both perverse and rotten, yet LO maintained that two million low-income employees would be losers when indirect taxes, in particular value-added tax (VAT), were extended and taxes were increased on housing and petrol. Increased selective, income-tested housing allowances for pensioners as well as low-income employees – once again not only to families with children (cf pp. 140 & 225) – failed to quieten the trade union protest, mainly because such measures were regarded as a threat to the universal or institutional welfare model.

Otherwise, the background to the first crisis was the failure of the government to manage the aftermath of the devaluations in 1981-82 as well as the sudden change from an economic boom in the late 1980s to a recession in the early 1990s. In January 1990, the Social Democratic party and the blue collar union movement did succeed in joining forces behind a remarkably austere package that included a strike ban, a freeze on wages, prices and local income tax, and other non-traditional or, rather, anti-union measures. But a revolt soon spread inside the Labour movement and the strenuously achieved unity lasted only a few hours. The cabinet handed in, and the struggle within the Labour movement over economic and social policies continued. Popular support for the Social Democratic party slumped: opinion polls indicated a level below 30 percent – the lowest since polls started in the early postwar period.[2]

In the absence of a clear non-socialist parliamentary majority, the leader of the Moderate Party refused to take over the helm eigtheen months before the next election. Within a few days the former PM and chairman of the Social Democratic Party, Ingvar Carlsson, reappeared at the head of a Cabinet. He was accompanied by a new Minister of Finance, the former Director-General of the powerful National Labour Market Board, who was also rapidly catapulted to a top party position in a way familiar to postwar continental Social Democracy but rather untypical for the local section of the Socialist International. Meanwhile, a Parliamentary accord had been worked out between the Social Democrats and the Liberal Party. Fighting inflation became a top priority among the major policy goals (Olsson Hort 1993), and in its wake followed a principal hard currency policy. Furthermore, this agreement raised VAT to 25 per cent, but for welfare policy the main items were a delay in the increase of the general child allowance (agreed as part of the tax reform engineered by the two parties the year before), a halt to an extended right to parental leave, and a reversal of a decision to lengthen the annual holiday – the two latter reforms being Social Democracy's most expensive promises in the 1988 election campaign. Furthermore, sickness insurance was reformed, forcing the Social Democrats to accept employer administration of short-term sick leave – a proposal advocated for some time by the non-socialist parties but resisted by the trade unions (cf. p. 31).

3. Crisis Number Two

Only half a year after the first major crisis, the Swedish Government, faced with the first of a series of devaluation threats, had to vigorously defend the Swedish krona and work out a new economic recovery package. In order to gain the confidence of international money markets, the Social Democratic Minister of Finance – not the PM – announced in a footnote to this package that Sweden would apply for full membership in the European Community. This issue had been carefully avoided by the leadership at the party Congress only three weeks before. For more than a year, the party leadership had chosen to play the EES – European Economic Space (Area) – card together with other reluctant Social Democrats in the countries of the Eurpean Free Trade Association (with the Austrian Social Democracy being the main exception). In Sweden, the Moderate and Liberal parties, together with business interests, had been actively pushing for EC membership, while the Labour movement had adhered to the traditional neutrality line, though the latter had lost ground as the cold war came to an end. As might be expected in a small industrial economy geared to exports, business interests in Sweden have always tried to bring the country closer to its southern and western neighbours. The Labour movement, on the other hand, has put security first, i.e. relationships with and between Finland, NATO and the Soviet Union. Although Sweden has had a free trade agreement with the EC since the early 1970, as recently as 1988 a government bill stated that "EC membership is incompatible with the policy of neutrality" (Prop 1987/88:66). The Autumn 1990 package meant that for the first time ever, a Social Democratic government lowered benefit levels: daily sickness benefits were reduced from 90 to 65 (75) per cent for short term absence. Benefits had been eroded earlier by inflation (see for instance child allowance pp 135, 158, 198-200 in ch. 3); this time a labour government proposed direct cuts. The accord also included rather weak hints about a reform of work injury insurance, which since the mid 1980s had been running a growing deficit (Mikaelsson & Lister 1992). Another point to note is that resistance from welfare traditionalists within the Ministry of Social Affairs postponed the inauguration of a new sickness insurance system. The internal cost of reducing benefit levels was a retreat from the Spring agreement with the liberals on an initial employer period in sickness insurance. This is just one example of the difficulties that Social Democracy and the traditional welfare administration experience in the implementation of changes in welfare policy – a phenomenon already present in the mid-1980s and discussed in chapter four of this book.

Besides the attempts to come to terms with problems in the social insurance systems, this package also included a controversial solution to the queues in municipal child day care: lowering the school entry age from seven to six. This proposal had for long been resisted by various organized interest groups in the welfare sector: by both pre-school teachers and schoolteachers, who belong(ed) to two distinct apparatuses within the welfare administration (social welfare and education, respectively – in the early 1990s some municipalities merged). A concluding comment on the Swedish model is that rapid consensual crisis packages have replaced slow consensus-building in royal commissions as Sweden has become more republican after the constitutional changes in the early 1970s (the latter relationship is of course purely coincidential).

4. Crisis Number Three

Problems did not end there even though an economic "turning point" was heralded by the Social Democratic Minister of Finance in early 1991. After the September election and the new coalition government's first economic policy bill came the Finnish Devaluation of November 1991 and considerable speculation against the Swedish krona. This time, however, the Bank of Sweden raised interest rates without further intervention from the cabinet. But the domestic financial crisis worsened – real estate companies, banks and insurance companies went more or less bankrupt – accompanied by rising unemployment as industries closed down or laid people off.

The third major crisis occurred a year after the earthquake election of 1991 (cf Rothstein 1992b). In the shadow of the break-up of the infant European monetary union, with major devaluations in the UK, Italy and Spain, the Swedish krona in the wake of yet another Finnish devaluation, again came under serious threat. After a series of spectacular increases of the Bank of Sweden's lending rate, the new government and the Social Democratic opposition joined forces twice in a fortnight. The government-opposition agreements involved further cuts in welfare benefits, a major reorganization of welfare administration and increased taxes, but also a halt to some of the main new ideas from the bourgeois cabinet for the rest of the election period: no privatization of state firms and no changes in labour or social legislation without previous consultation with Social Democracy. However, disagreements and quarrels broke out before these packages were tabled as bills in Parliament. The Social Democrats declared there would be no third package until the disputes had been settled, and when the government presented such a package just a few hours before the autumn of the krona on November 19th 1992, the main opposition did not support the latest proposed measures. However, the Social Democrats remained firmly behind the two former packages, and in their aftermath gained an absolute majority in opinion polls. It remains to be seen whether these concessions from the political opposition at a crucial moment in the first year of the new coalition government will be to the advantage of Sweden's habitual ruler. But there is no doubt that the internal coherence of the 1991 government is seriously wounded.

The autumn 1992 package is the first major cooperation between the Moderate Party and the Social Democrats as the principal partners. In one sense these packages are a departure from the "new start for Sweden" program the Moderates and Liberals proposed before the election, yet in another they are close to the tone of that program. This illustrates the ambiguity on both sides of Swedish politics, both the differences and the common grounds of the main political parties. And how they join forces to persuade the labour market organizations to avoid industrial disputes that may further erode the economic potential. While this cooperation did break down with the end of the hard currency policy in mid November 1992, only six weeks after the second Autumn-1992 package had been announced, it is a sign of the way the Swedish political culture operates, or has been operating for most of this century: conflictual, yet mostly consensus seeking, although in a new direction as was noted above. History will tell whether the events of the Autumn of 1992 represent the beginning of another era of "historical compromises" similar to those in the 1930s. It is conceivable, though unlikely, that a snap election will provide an initial, temporary answer. In the meantime, new crises with far-reaching implications for the welfare state may see the light of day.

5. The Swedish Welfare State – What's Left?

In terms of benefit cuts and welfare policy reorganization in Sweden, how is one to summarize the measures in the early 1990s? Of course, this is a complex question with many ramifications. Overall, it is probably fair to say that benefit levels – and social rights in general – have been rolled back to the situation in the late 1980s, i.e. only minor changes so far. But there are also signs of more significant changes summarized below in terms of the welfare state components described in the introduction to this book (p. 26).

(1) As regards active labour market policy, a whole array of measures has been taken to counteract the rapid increase in unemployment. The National Labour Market Board is working at full capacity, a capacity that was created to cope with unemployment up to four per cent, but which in 1993 is having to handle some five per cent of the labour force. Furthermore, the NLMB is operating a youth program that is fairly successful (in terms of the number activated) with work at less than the market wage, inaugurated against the wishes of the trade union movement, as well as not so impressive infra-structural projects for roads and railways. Even so, open unemployment has gone on rising – in late 1992 the level is expected to reach six percent – and the worst scenario from the NLMB foresees well above ten percent despite an increase in the capacity of the Board and related agencies for training and retraining, including a larger intake in higher education. Thus, it is the overall economic situation that is the heart of the problem, and no increase in selective measures can eliminate that problem in an open economy. An economic recession, moreover, imposes financial constraints on state intervention in this as in other fields, such as those discussed below, and the more so with global economic integration and penetration. But it is important to underline that apart from the Social Democratic government's reluctance in 1990-91, the major socio-political actors have still not shown any sign of abandoning the commitment to full employment. This statement includes also the Employers who have not deliberately attacked this policy goal, although they have left the NLMB as part of their general turn against neo-corporatist representation. Of course many labour politicians, trade union leaders and other sceptics explain this consensus on the Rhen-Meidner model as

whitewashing by one or more of the bourgeois political parties. Fighting inflation still has top priority in economic policy. If the implication of this shift of emphasis among the major policy goals is that Swedes cannot afford to work, then a major paradigm shift has occurred in Swedish social and economic policy (cf Korpi 1989).

(2) It is in the field of social security that it is most valid to talk of a decrease in benefit levels (eg. the general child allowance) to levels in the late 1980s. This is also evident in other regulations, such as the statutory annual holiday (two additional days from the 1988 election are to be cut) and social insurance qualifying days: one day is to be reintroduced in sickness and occupational injury insurance, and most likely a return to five days in unemployment insurance (in the latter case, thus, back to the 1987 level). In some cases the regression is more pronounced. This applies in particular to short-term daily sickness benefits; in early 1991 the replacement level was cut from 90 to 65 (75 in reality) per cent for the first three days, followed by 80 percent up to the nineteenth day. Employer-run sickness pay for the first fourteen days was introduced as of 1992. Furthermore, the "coordination period" between sickness and work injury insurance, which means that the lower levels of benefits in the first type of insurance are paid, has been prolonged from 90 to 180 days.

As of 1993 there are to be more substantial reductions primarily as regards long-term sickness benefits: instead of 90 percent reimbursement for an unlimited period (if not rehabilitated – as was the idea in the late 1980s – sooner or later those people who go for an "unlimited period" end up on some form of pre-retirement scheme) there will be 80 percent for most of the first year and 70 percent thereafter. These – decreased – benefits are supplemented for most (full-time) employees with negotiated occupational sickness benefits, but the Social Democratic government had already imposed a ceiling (90 per cent of previous wage in order to come to terms with the supposed problem of over-insurance.

Moreover, the general retirement age is to go up in stages from 65 to 66 starting in 1993. A further increase has been openly discussed, though not yet directly proposed, in a key document from the 1991 government (1991/92:38). This type of initiative illustrates a general problem in austerity policy: the government –

in this case together with the main opposition – calculated the amount saved directly in billions in order to please the money markets. What is not discussed openly is the effect on other social security programs: the higher pensionable age is likely to result in more people on the pre-retirement rolls, which even if it does not amount to an overall increase in pension expenditure, will at least mean that the total amount saved is smaller. The austerity packages of September 1992 also included a general cut in pension benefits, but before this could be effected it had been overtaken by the indexation rules. Overall, the technicalities of social insurance create if not insoluble at least tremendous problems for political manoeuvering (cf Isaksson 1992). Of long-term importance is the idea of introducing a larger element of savings in the pension system. This had been presented by the previous Social Democratic government in its 1990/91 budget bill (cf. also SOU 1992:19 app. 12).

The most important feature of the Autumn 1992 packages was the proposal to remove sickness and occupational injury insurance from the state budget. While this proposal does point towards a more corporatist pattern, a considerable amount of universalism is likely to remain. The intention is to let employers and employees jointly administer and finance a coordinated, statutory insurance. First, however, a state commission will be appointed to construct the new system and the necessary legislation. State financing is to be phased out. As of January 1993, the financial burden will be shared by leavying a – tax deductable – social contribution on employees. A similar contribution in the Swedish system was abolished in 1974 (see p. 145). Also in unemployment insurance, the employee contribution, never completely cancelled, is to be substantiall increased. Thus, there is both an attempt, in particular from the Social Democrats, to strengthen the trade unions, and, from the parties of the "middle", to increase their responsibilities. At the same time there have been some minor attempts to universalize unemployment insurance, which can be interpreted as an attempt to weaken the unions. There are also areas which so far have remained stable. Most important are the benefit levels in parental insurance, which used to be coordinated with daily sickness benefits but are currently higher. Because this is a self-reporting system with very little administrative control, this may result in some "perverse effects" as parents declare their children sick instead of themselves in order to receive better benefits. That could create a pressure for "coordination", a euphemism for lower benefit.

(3) Personal social services have featured most explicitly in changes proposed by the 1991 government. In this area, Sweden now has its first programmatically revolutionary government, offering a "freedom-of-choice revolution" in medical, educational and other personal social services, above all for children, the handicapped and the elderly (cf Johnsson 1992). Public production is not to be directly replaced by private services, but more alternatives are being encouraged. These areas of social action will continue to be regulated and financed mainly by the public purse, although the role of fees will increase, as is already the case with the general medical fee (Olsson Hort & Cohn 1993). The current tendency for services is the voucher alternatives, i.e. a measure on the border between social and fiscal welfare, and for public organization also an attempt to separate financial and productive agencies. The latter aspect includes a type of deregulation, from the central state to local authorities, and in some areas also from local authorities to non-governmental agencies/producers, i.e. institutions on the borders of state, market, and civil society. So far, with the partial exception of general education and homes for young criminals, there have been no proposals to increase the possibility of central state control or inspection (Olsson Hort 1992). Overall, however, developments in these sectors can be interpreted as a continuation of the earlier decentralization movement, described in chapter 4 of this book. The difference compared to the 1980s lies in more private alternatives, and higher and more diversified fees. These developments have their impetus in the strengthening of the local public level and were centrally reinforced by the advent of Social Democracy in the early 1980s (Olsson 1992; Montin 1992; Premfors 1991).

(4) Regulation of and subsidies to housing and agriculture have been another object of reform. The general pattern in the housing sector is deregulation and some reduction in subsidies. The deregulation of housing was already in progress under the Social Democratic government, with a new planning and construction law in 1988. The 1991 cabinet quickly abolished a number of what were considered cost-augmenting regulations for residential construc-

tion, and cut investment subsidies. The municipal housing sector, historically closely affiliated with Social Democracy, was hit in particular by these moves. The 1992 Supplementary Budget Bill (Prop. 1991/92:150) explicitly stated that "this denoted the end of the special status enjoyed by SBAB (State Housing Finance Co-operation) on the credit market. SBAB now works in competition with other housing loan institutions" (p. 30 English translation). This occurred at a time when housing construction had slowed down. The new government's proposals accentuated the crisis tendencies in this sector: unemployment rose considerably, real estate prices fell, and construction companies went bankrupt. The government simultaneously enlarged the opportunities to form housing cooperatives out of existing municipal rented housing, but few such initiatives were taken by tenants.

An important re-interpretation of the historical closeness between agricultural policy and social welfare policy in Sweden, which challenges in particular the thesis advocated by Korpi and Therborn, has recently been published (Rothstein 1992c). Today, this relationship is more ambiguous but still part of most political bargaining. Agricultural reform, aiming at partial marketization, had proceeded in the late 1980s despite considerable resistance from the farmers (Wetterberg 1991). Growing consumer protest was manifested not least as part of the build-up of a right-wing populist political alternative (see section 6 below). Finally, an agreement on agricultural reforms was reached which the Centre party and the farmer producer cooperative also accepted. Rationalization grants were scaled down, while subsidies to fisheries were halved as of 1992/93 and to be terminated a year later. However, with EC membership in sight, and the possibility of a still largely regulated – albeit at a European level – sector within reach, the farmers' organizations tried to block the domestic reforms. Thus, this opens up for new types of socio-political coalition-building.

(5). Finally, taxation and the financing of the welfare state: as mentioned in chapter 3, from the early 1980s even the Social Democratic party became more sceptical towards enlarging the public sector. The tax agreement between the Social Democrats, the Liberal and Centre parties that split the bourgeois government in 1981, was another sign of the Left's reluctance to increase taxes. Unlike the Thatcher government, for example, during the 1980s

Swedish Social Democracy managed to lower total public expenditure relative to GDP. Only a redistribution of public expenditures was permitted. In 1989, after numerous investigations and negotiations, the Liberal party and the ruling Social Democrats together decreased marginal tax rates as part of an agreement on a general tax reform (implemented in 1990-91). Lower overall taxation of earned income was financed – at least on paper – by a broadening of the tax bases and limitations on the possibility of making tax deductions. Fringe benefit – or "occupational welfare" in the terminology of Titmuss – became more heavily taxed. Uniformity between tax bases was a declaried aim. The 1991 government abolished turnover tax on shares, and cut capital income tax as well as other taxes that were said to be hampering small and medium-sized entreprises. The abolition of wealth tax was also announced but the four parties had to withdraw this promise when the pact with the Social Democrats was made a year later. In conjunction with EC membership, the 1991 government made it clear from the start that "tax pressure in Sweden will not be able to deviate appreciably from the rest of the world. A downward adjustment of various tax rates is important for these reasons but also because the high tax pressure in Sweden has tended to weaken the potential economic growth" (Prop 1991/92:38). If such ideas are implemented, a considerable downscaling of the welfare state is a quite likely consequence. On the other hand, several experts have pointed to the possibility of increasing taxes that are not sensible to labor unit costs or trade at national borders. Finally, the role of payments of the public debt should be mentioned in this context. Despite the decrease of this item during the 1980s, what has been labelled a "structural budget deficit" remains and creates problem for the overall financing of the welfare state. Thus, if the competitive edge of the welfare state is firm enough, is yet an open question (cf Phaller et al 1991).

6. A Crisis of the Welfare State or a Crisis of Social Democracy?

As pointed out repeatedly in the preceeding essays, the Swedish welfare state has had strong backing in particular from the farmers and the labour movement. Other socio-political forces also sided with or in some cases even actively pushed for an enlargement of the social welfare sector (see especially the discussion in ch. 2). Furthermore, attitudinal data from the last decades point at considerable popular support for universal welfare programs. Thus, it is important to distinguish between the "crisis of Social Democracy" and the "crisis of the welfare state", which may or may not coincide. In any case, major changes have occurred in the strength and structure of interest group representation in Swedish society and these changes are definitely related to the social backing of the welfare state: there has been a clear decline in the role of farmers and rural interest groups, and a clear fragmentation of interest representation based on the labour market, in particular on the trade union side. The partial breakdown of central negotiations and similar aspects of industrial relations, including a higher level of strikes in the 1980s, are of course relevant for the future development of the welfare state. Thus, there is a great need of bringing in particular capital back in, also in the analysis of welfare policy. So far, big business has primarily appeared as an outside threat, and not as an inside player. However, this crucial issue cannot be elaborated in a short overview (cf Pontusson & Swenson 1993; Ahrne & Clement 1992; Hernes 1991; Swenson 1992a, 1992b & 1991; Therborn 1991a).

Another factor is the diversification of the political system; in the 1994 election there could be as many as nine or ten parties seriously competing for parliamentary representation. Besides the eight mentioned in table 2, a womens' party is certainly a possibility – fairly radical and in terms of gender and family welfare policy the antithesis of the Christian Democrats. As is well-known, most working women are employed in the public sector and despite class cleavages among women, they generally favour the present type of welfare regime. Whatever effects such an eventual party might have, inside and/or outside Parliament, its appearance is a sign of the vigour of the gender backing of the Swedish model (cf. Jensen & Mahon 1992). More generally, here it is appropriate to add that not least in the context both of intimate and distant gender relations, the discussion about social citizenship has taken a new departure (cf Taylor-Goody 1991).

Another possibility is the emergence of a more openly racist,

366

anti-immigration party than New Democracy. Racist candidates have already done quite well in some local elections (cf. Bergström 1991 & Fryklund & Peterson 1989). Traditionally, social policy and immigration policy have been closely connected in Sweden, and immigrants have quickly been included in the fairly generous welfare system. In the early 1990s, this contributes to the inherently explosive potential of the issue from a welfare state perspective. Since the late 1980s, both central and local authorities have tended to be more restrictive and exclusive as regards social benefits in-kind and cash.

However, it was outside the realm of politics that the basis of welfare policy was first openly attacked. In the mid 1970s, the powerful and centralized Employers Confederation began to question the viability of a large public sector, and paved the way for more private enterprises in the welfare sector. But the centre-right cabinets at that time did not yield to this pressure. In particular the Centre and Liberal parties adhered – and still adhere – to the guiding principles of the universal welfare state. Thusm it is correct to say that the present non-socialist coalition has not subscribed to the persistent challenges from this – the most internationalist or transnational – sector of Swedish society, despite support among factions of the Moderate party. Neither the 1976-81 governments nor the 1991 government have, however, been particularly inclined to raise taxes, which mainly due to the overall economic situation has created considerable difficulties in reconciling economic and social policies. The legacy of the 1976-81 cabinets was deficit spending (see ch. 3) and it is a fairly safe bet that this may also apply to the 1991 government. But this government is in no sense programmatically an anti-welfare cabinet. On the contrary, its first budget statement officially proclaimed the adherence to the principles of a universal welfare policy:

Everyone benefits from welfare policy but its significance is greatest for those who are alone, poor or ill, as well as for all those who are not in a position to create a reasonable standard and have no one to care or take responsibility for them. The state must be ultimately responsible for ensuring that all citizens have basic security in relation to unemployment, illness, old age and disablement. These efforts must largely continue to be publicly financed ... The alternative to the welfare state is a selective system, aimed at supporting only those suffering under the worst conditions. Such a system has many disadvantages. It presumes considerable means-testing and social control. It has to determine who has the right to public support and who has not. The consequence is liable to be more bureaucracy and more of intrusive investigations. A selective system also creates marginal tax effects. Benefits decrease as income rises. Many people are at risk of being caught in this poverty trap. The basic ideology of the universalist welfare state, therefore, will continue to provide guidance in the future. (Government Bill 1991/92:100. Supplement 6, p.4-5)

In particular the chairman of the Liberal party, who is also Deputy Premier and Minister of Social Affairs, has more than once underlined the importance of social rights and the continuing relevance of a general welfare policy, a theme that has not been well received at least in neo-liberal circles on the borders between the Moderate party and the Employers' Confederation. Together with the present female Liberal Minister of Finance, he has also underlined that a universal welfare state demands a fairly high tax level thereby undermining the hopes for drastic tax cuts among non-socialist followers. The Christian Democrats, despite their un-Swedish or anti-modernist view of family policy, and the Centre party (farmers) are also more or less in favour of the universal model.

Although Moderates are generally more prepared than others to accept a larger element of selectivity in the welfare system, most social conservatives within the Moderate party, in particular political pragmatists in municipalities and county councils, are closer to the "welfare statism" of the late Gunnar Heckscher than to the neo-liberalism of the 1980s (cf chapter 2). This deserves to be stressed. In the top Moderate circles, however, there has for some time been a desperate seach for a new welfare policy regime or social state model (Zetterberg 1992). Instead of Friedmannian economic neo-liberalism, more emphasis has been put on catholic social ideas about subsidiarity (cf Spicker 1991) mixed with a return to secular – Tocquevillian – ideas about a civil society counterposed to the state (but less so to the market), both concepts having more local peculiarities than their present proponents seem willing to accept (cf. the introduction and chapter 1). So far, these ambitions have not become politically feasible.

Even such a former out-and-out neo-liberal as the present social policy advisor to the 1991 Prime Minister, does not propose a fundamentally new model in the second of a series of books from the "Social state project" of the abovementioned privately – big business – launched Stockholm City University. In the end, he retreated to Popperian piecemeal social engineering having at great length criticized the deficiencies of the present universal social welfare system: "The study does not propose any new blue print for the welfare system but pleads the need to reconsider the present policies one by one with openness for the failures and undesirable incentives which the present solutions bring" (Borg 1992:86).

Of course, the Swedish Thatcherites have not disappeared but are seriously wounded. For instance, an MP and chairman of the Young Moderates accused his mother party of being one-sided in its critique of the tax state: the party saw only the financial aspects and had no vision of an alternative on the benefit-side, i.e. it was not critical enough of the welfare state as the modern version of serfdom. He presented the idea of an "individual welfare policy" – intimately resembling the Titmussian residual model – as an alternative to the ruling Swedish consensus (Olsson Hort 1992). As long as the Moderate party remained in opposition, this idea was still within the confines of established Swedish conservative discourse. When he also dared to criticize his party leadership, including the PM, after the Autumn-1992 packages – from a principal Hayekian position – he definitely played with fire and was almost immediately removed from the chairmanship of the party's youth organization.

As has been demonstrated more than once in the past decade, universal welfare programs have across-the-board support in Swedish public opinion (Svallfors 1993 & 1991). There are thus strong institutional impediments to form a viable social policy alternative to the present regime. Welfare citizenship has become the "obvious solution" to the normative problem of social justice that is hard to argue against in democratic national policy-making (Rothstein 1992a; Elster 1987). Nonetheless, there also seems to be a more open attitude towards shrinking the public sector, including cuts in welfare benefits. The present macro-economic situation and the unanimity behind the austerity programs have, of course, contributed to this. But the Social Democrats probably paved the way with their cuts in transfers to local government, as well as with their general policy after 1982 of not raising taxes (cf Korpi 1992). The expansion of public child day care was the only explicit exception to the Social Democratic restraint on public sector expansion. Can this general reluctance to increase taxes be interpreted as an answer to a (new-)middle class tax revolt? Is the 1991 election an indication of such an insurgency?

The 1991 election was a major defeat for the Social Democrats – from 43 per cent to 38 – as well as for its junior partner to the Left, the former Swedish Communist party (see table 1). Departing from their usual stance, the Social Democrats, hesitated to put more money and effort into its key policy area: active labour market measures. A business slowdown was definitely under way and unemployment clearly rising. This position seriously damaged the Social Democratic party's possibility of developing a successful election campaign and further eroded popular support, even within the blue collar union movement, in particular among young men, for whom New Democracy proved attractive.

In their joint program for a new government – published a year ahead of the election – the Liberal and Moderate parties vociferiously reiterated their support for full employment policy. The Social Democrats never fully retreated from their parsimonious treatment of the Labour Market Board, and in summing-up the election campaign even the Moderate party leader was a more outspoken champion of anti-unemployment measures than traditional Social democratic defenders of full employment. Even the new right-wing populist party, New Democracy, was in favour of more money for state organized labour market measures, and in Parliament it has hesitated to propose deep cuts in universal welfare schemes.

The first really new party in Parliament since the democratic breakthrough of the 1920s, the Green Environment party (in its own view outside the traditional ideological spectrum of western politics), which had managed to climb over the magic four percent threshold in 1988, fell short of that limit only three years later (see table 1). The rise of this party can be interpreted as a middle-class revolt, but in no sense against social rights and welfare universalism (cf. Sulkunen 1992). As mentioned earlier, there is a possibility that at least one and perhaps two new parties will enter Parliament in 1994. Once a breakthrough has occurred, the flood is hard to stem, but of course there is also the possibility that all or most of the smaller parties will – temporarily? – disappear from the political map. In any event, two new, but this time explicitly non-socialist parties, entered Parliament in 1991: the traditionalist or culturally conservative Christian Democrats, which immediately joined the government, and the populist New Democracy. Only the latter party can be considered a programmatic proponent of considerably lower taxes, although since the election it has done its best to support costly welfare programs that the 1991 government wants to abolish (eg. the part-time pension scheme). The possibility of finding a political support for reforming (i.e. diminishing but in no sense abolishing) expsensive welfare programs is of crucial importance for the future viability of these programs particularly in the present gloomy economic situation. Here, the Christian Democrats have proved to be yet another welfare party, despite their adherence to the depolitization of family policy. However, the Social Democrats have not yet flirted with this party.

What about the three traditional non-socialist or bourgeois parties in this more fragmented political system? The parties in the middle, the Centre and Liberal, have benefitted least, and all the three parties have lost supporters to the two newcomers. In 1991 the three oldies together received only 39.9 percent of the vote compared to 41.9 percent in 1988 and a high of 45.4 in 1985. The backing behind the 1991 government amounts to 47 per cent. Thus, it is a fairly shaky minority government and its long-term prospects do not appear particularly bright. Of course, the neighbouring Danish Conservative Prime Minister has managed to hold together a bunch of non-socialist parties against a Social Democratic party for more than a decade. In Denmark, however, the two main non-socialist parties, the Conservatives and the Liberals, have had fairly similar electoral support, while except in 1991, the Social Democrats have been considerably weaker than their Swedish sister party. The Danish scenario is of course appealing to the Swedish Conservatives but less so for Liberal and Centre politicians who are not prepared to be swallowed by big brother.

In the other neighbouring large-scale welfare state, Norway, dissension among the non-socialist parties has enabled the Social Democrats to create fairly lasting minority governments. A somewhat similar solution was adopted by Swedish Social Democracy in the late 1980s, but the party strategists seem reluctant to continue along this line. Of course, the Swedish labour movement will do its best to restore a fading hegemony, and here there are several alternatives. An outright majority is obviously preferable but would

371

probably be difficult to sustain. Both before the 1991 election and after the Autumn 1992 packages, the Social Democratic leadership paid its respects to the traditional parties in the middle. But these parties are reluctant to be swallowed by this big brother, too. The ink on the Autumn 1992 packages had scarcely dried, before Social Democratic headquarters began sniping at the Moderates, which returned the fire in due course. However, when the smoke clears, a new Swedish macro-constellation of an Austrian type – Social Democracy and Conservative – may emerge, particularly if a new set of industrial relations were to precede or follow the turnabout. Their common project is membership of the European Community and hence the salvation of domestic economic prosperity and growth. In view of the rather recent discovery – on both the left and the right of the political spectrum – of the existence of a Continental welfare state, both parties from different angles might be able to reach a modus vivendi also on social policy issues.

Table 2. Swedish elections 1985-1991 (per cent of electorate and seats in Parliament; cf graph 46 p. 208)

PARTY	YEAR					
	1985		1988		1991	
	Seats	%	Seats	%	Seats	%
SD	159	44.7	156	43.3	138	37.6
Moderate	76	21.3	66	18.3	80	22.1
Liberal	51	14.2	44	12.2	33	9.2
Centre	44	12.4	42	11.3	31	8.6
Left	19	5.4	21	5.8	16	4.5
Green	–	1.5	20	5.5	–	3.4
New Democ	–	–	–	–	25	6.7
Christian D	1	*	–	2.9	28	7.1

* In 1985, the Christian Democrats were on a joint slate with the Centre Party, which made their party leader an MP. Since 1991 he is a Cabinet member, and Minister of Foreign Aid and Human Rights Protection.

7. The National Welfare State and European Integration

The welfare state has been regarded as the last – or latest – phase in the process of nationbuilding and stateformation in Western Europe (Alestalo & Flora 1992). It is in this context of national welfare states that the Scandinavian model, the more or less full realization of the universal or institutional model, has evolved, geographically peripheral but for the theoretical discussion still central, though this may change. In all the Nordic countries, the Bismarckian model was adapted to the particularities of each nation-state. Throughout this century the effects of international economic integration have clearly contributed immensely to the feasibility of generous social programs in Scandinavia. But it is equally clear that the shape of this model has been largely overdetermined by the macro-constellations of domestic socio-political forces, in this sphere of social action under Social-Democratic leadership or hegemony since the 1930s. Is this model still of any central concern except as an example of a general deescalation of welfare efforts? More than ever, this model is being severely scrutinized abroad and from within: has the Scandinavian – and in particular the Swedish – welfare state reached its limits? In recent years this discussion has been conducted in the context of further European integration – the creation of a single market in the West and, it should be stressed, the appearance of new, fragile democracies in the East (Boje & Olsson 1993).

The future of the welfare state in the context of membership in the European Community has been one of the most hotly debated issues in Scandinavia since the late 1980s. A common argument against EC membership – not least from feminists – is that it will mean the end of the welfare model. Given Swedish membership, what are the possible effects of, in particular, economic and political integration in the EC? Does the Swedish welfare state have characteristics that will complicate integration with the EC? Or, as some tend to argue, is EC membership largely irrelevant to the future development of this welfare model? Are internal – and also perhaps other external – problems of greater relevance than European integration per se (Ervik & Kuhnle 1992)? Here are some – necessarily – speculative comments.

The fear of social dumping has been on the European agenda ever since the formalization of the Economic Community. France hesitated to sign the Treaty of Rome in 1957 because more generous French social legislation was supposed to make its industry vulnerable to less generous neighbours. Very little has occurred to support these fears (Leibfried 1991). The 1985 decision to create a single market vitalized the debate on social policy; the trade unions and social democratic parties, in particular, were afraid that national social provisions would be reduced to the lowest common denominator within the Community (Huber & Stephens 1992; cf Leibfried and Pierson 1992). This discussion has had more effects, for instance Jacques Delors' idea of an EC "social dimension" (cf Delors 1992) and the Maastricht social charter, signed by eleven member-states (Britain being the exception). In the meantime the European Community Court had started to intervene in social affairs, though only to a limited degree with regard in particular to migrant workers and construction companies moving from one country to another (Schulte 1992).

Thus, for the forseeable future, cooperation between EC member states will gradually grow most likely with several impediments and ruptures. In the years or even decades to come, however, it is highly unlikely that some kind of 'European state' will replace the existing sovereign member states. Still, a supra-national entity – with power derived from the nationstates – does exist and through the EC a wide range of economic and civil rights will be granted to EC citizens. Political and social rights, on the other hand, will play a minor role as long as the member states refuse to hand them over to Community institutions. Systems of social protection and social welfare will continue to be guaranteed at the national level (cf Berghman 1992).

In Sweden, however, the Social Democratic party's sudden swing in favour of EC membership was accompanied by an emphasis on European integration as a solution, in particular, to the financial problems of the welfare state. Overall, membership would give Swedish firms better access to their most important export markets and also enable Swedish authorities to have a say in European political affairs, not least on welfare issues. EC membership would be a precondition for better economic growth, which is considered to be essential for a generous welfare state. On the other hand,

374

calculations by government experts in the Ministry of Finance indicated the necessity of fairly substantial tax cuts, though other tax bases could be slightly enlarged (SOU 1990:14 and SOU 1992:19), and a consequential reduction of the public sector. Thus, there is a contradiction between the statements of politicians and their experts. Furthermore, if Sweden joins the single market through the European Economic Area agreement, which was approved by the Swedish Parliament in mid-November 1992 (but which requires the signature of all the other EFTA countries to be valid), Sweden will have to conform to most EC regulations without a say in the decision-making instances of EC. Thus, Sweden will become a half-member without the possiblity of voting on crucial issues. However, as long as social issues will remain national issues, also the financing of the welfare state will larlgely remain a domestic policy problem.

As is well-known, the Swedish public welfare sector is the largest one in Scandinavia and, indeed, in Europe (see table 3). The distinctively Swedish element, however, is not so much the social insurance – transfer payments – as the social services; in particular personal social services to the elderly, disabled and children are much more of a public (municipal) provision than in other European countries, using mainly female employees: doctors, nurses, schoolteachers, pre-school personnel, home helpers, etc (Kosonen 1993; cf Anttonen 1990). However, the ongoing shift of responsibility for welfare production may involve some reduction of state-provided services and an increase in private provision. But if the state retains its role as the main source of funds for such services, the latter will most likely be offered on a market and be visible in the national accounts. But there is also the likelihood that some of these services can be provided on a "black" market by cheap – mainly immigrant – labour.

The latter problem raises another aspect of European integration that has been overshadowed by the intense debate on EC membership: the appearance of new, fragile democracies in Eastern Europe with a labour supply that may weaken the willingness of the Swedish middle class to pay for others. With open borders and the possibility of three-months tourist visas as well as illegal immigration, a supply of temporary workers from the East can provide the fairly well-to-do with personal services that a system with high

Table 3. Total social expenditure as a percentage of GDP 1990 (1989)

	%		%
Sweden	35	Luxemburg	26
Netherlands	30	Italy	23
Denmark	30	United Kingdom	22
Norway	29	Ireland	21
France	28	Portugal	18
Germany	27	Iceland	18
Belgium	27	Spain	17
Finland	26	Greece	17

Source: Nosoko 1992:164 (after Abrahamson 1992). These figures do not correspond to the mode of accounting in *Growth to Limits*; i.e. chapter 3 in this book)

social contributions cannot afford. Such a possibility may tend to undermine the willingness to pay taxes for universal welfare programs. The prospect of a two-tier system of social services is at least conceivable.

Recent welfare developments in Sweden have been compared with similar countries, for good reasons in particular its Nordic neighbours (cf Kolberg 1992a-c) but also, as mentioned in the introduction to this book (p. 33), the geographically remote New Zealand. Denmark and New Zealand served successively as the model for the mid-century Social Democratic architect of the welfare state, Gustav Möller. Denmark has been called a "troubled welfare state" (Miller 1991) – unemployment in particular has been a problem well above the EC average – but in a European context it still has one of the most well-developed welfare systems, although the gap between haves and have-nots has widened (Abrahamson 1992). New Zealand examplifies a successful dismantling of a universal welfare state – carried out initially by a Social Democratic government – according to both friends and foes, and provides a senario for the future of the Swedish welfare state. One important difference between the two systems, however, is the absence in New Zealand of state-guaranteed corporatist solutions for income security. One should also invoke the ghost of Austria, another small country with a strong Social Democracy but a more segmented and partly corporatist or occupational welfare system. In the Esping-Andersen regime-type classification both Austria and New Zealand differ somewhat but not too much from the Scandinavian countries (Austria "conservative" stratification; New Zealand "low" on decommodification – otherwise close to both Denmark and Sweden). One interim conclusion is that the strength of the labour movement, as well as its potential allies, but perhaps even more the existing institutional set-up are of fundamental significance for future developments in this area.

8. Conclusions:
Towards a New Swedish Model of Welfare or Policy Regime?

The period I have dealt with is too short – scarcely three years – to provide a definite account of changes in the first half of the 1990s. The concluding question of the subtitle will therefore not be answered here. Three years do not yield the settled retrospect afforded by a century of history. Proportions and relations are liable to be foreshorted. Contemporary observers overestimate the rapidity of the present and are prone to interpret changes, which are forgotten tomorrow, as crucial events, aspects of a formative moment.

In the preceding section I emphazised the importance of global integration and the decreasing sovereignty of national welfare states. On the other hand, if West European integration were to involve a more impenetrable external frontier, it could leave more room for national policy-making in this field. Integration with the East, on the other hand, might be more deleterious for the long-term stability of the welfare state. At the beginning of this postscript I hinted at the absence of a discussion about the disembeddedness of the money markets. Since the mid-1970s, devaluations have been part of the Swedish pattern and, despite some critical voices, generally regarded as a means to economic recovery. With the advent of the short-lived hard currency principle, the disorderliness of the market has had a greater impact. With global economic integration and the growing importance of financial transactions unconnected with the real economy, Sweden has become much more vulnerable to external pressure. The absence of international institutional cooperation makes Polanyi's discussion about the necessity of embedded markets more apt that ever. This raises the issue of where to look for his countermovements. On a global scale, are there others than nation states, or clusters of nation states?

However, there is no doubt about the severity of the present economic crisis. Sweden is experiencing negative growth for three consecutive years. This has generated tremendous internal pressure on the welfare system in the form of constant political and institutional adjustments, not least in the form of hasty crisis packages, which, as mentioned, seem to have replaced slow investigatory commissions as consensus-builders. Political scientists in particular have stressed the importance of these commissions as a key element in the Swedish model (Ruin 1990). From the 1980s onwards, either sudden "crises" or the immediate post-election days or weeks have come to be seen as the only opportunities for long-term macro steering (cf Olsson & Therborn 1991 & Kaufmann 1991). This supposed diminishing steering capacity is also an aspect of the "crisis of the political system". Another aspect of this "crisis" is the fundamental regrouping of the socio-political constellation, i.e. whether the almost two-decade long campaign by the Employers Confederation will also result in a "new regime", or if the Swedish Left is still in a position to form new alliances and shape new "social contracts" on the labour market, in politics and in society at large. Here, the prospects of old and new Polanyian countermovements – from white collar unions to fairly ad-hoc feminist movements – are if not bright at least encouraging enough to block drastic moves towards an "individual welfare model".

The Employers Confederation has not influenced Swedish society, and above all the workings of the welfare state, from cabinet posts, and this may also prove to be the case for a fairly strong Social Democratic opposition in the future. In the latter case, the underlying assumption is that the strength of the parties in the middle will grow. But due to the instability of electoral support for all parties to the right of Social Democracy – the fragmentation of the bourgeois parties – this scenario is rather unlikely. It remains if the Social Democrats form minority governments from time to time, or if lasting coalitions can be established with either the Moderates, or two or three parties in the middle. Thus, it still remains open whether Sweden will get a Danish, a Norwegian, an Austrian or maybe even an Italian (a four- or five-party coalition cabinet dominated by one big party) solution to the question of government.

Hence, in this respect a transformation of the Swedish welfare state may be crucial for the outcome of such a process. The fit between the welfare model and the type of government is never exact. In the overview of developments in the early 1990s (section 5), I hinted at the possibility of a more mixed welfare system with, again in the words of Titmuss, more fiscal and occupational (corporate) welfare, and in the state sector a downscaling towards, paradoxically, both more universality and more selectivity. One way of transcending this paradox is to apply another model – so far employed only for one particular social insurance scheme, Palme's (1990) model of old age pensions – on a more general level of analysis. Combining Titmuss and several successors, including Esping-Andersen, Palme distinguishes between (1) a residual model with no or low social rights, (2) a universal basic security model with a fairly high degree of stateness in the form of statutory flat-rate, (3) a – selective but rather comprehensive – income security model with an emphasis on labour market participation and earnings records, and (4) an institutional model which combines the latter two. Thus, he ends up with the familiar sociological four-box table (see figure 1), and Sweden ends up in the fourth box: basic security, the old people's pension system dating back to 1913, was in 1969 linked with statutory income security – the general supplementary pension system from 1960 – via the pension increment (cf p. 130 in this book). Since then, on top of the statutory systems, occupational and private pension schemes have grown in importance (Olsson 1987). In chapter 4 I stressed such tendencies in other sectors of the social welfare system (cf Marklund 1992; Olofsson 1989).

This model-building has been applied to only one type of social insurance scheme, retirement pensions, but the distinction it makes between flat-rate and income-related social security systems, and the possibility of combining them, is a parallel to the decomposition of social expenditures carried out in chapter 3. It is of continuing relevance for our discussion here: with this typology in mind, universal and selective – but still comprehensive – models

379

Figure 1. Models of old-age pensions.

Basic Security

		No	Yes
Income	No	Residual Model	Basic Security Model
Security	Yes	Income Security Model	Institutional Model

Source: Palme 1990.

can be treated as two independent dimensions of variation besides the institutional. There is also the possibility of mixing them with the other Titmussian model: a residual model can have a strong element of not only private but also occupational and fiscal welfare. In particular the latter implies a large degree of state-guaranteed – tax relieved – "freedom-of-choice". The present statist mix of universal and selective but rather comprehensive social insurance schemes may for instance be partly replaced by a less statist mix with an all-encompassing universal flat-rate scheme at the bottom combined with various corporate or occupational – perhaps partly legislated or tax subsidized – schemes as well as blends of private and fiscal types of welfare provisions. Overall state responsibility will continue to be of greatest importance, but in the actual provision of benefits, in cash and in kind, there will be more plurality. The outcome is a more segmented welfare state, but not too unlike the present one. Whether such – potential – changes warrant a new label for the Swedish welfare state is still dubious. As a saying goes, "to remain the same, things have to change". After a hundred years in existence, the object is still moving – or transforming. The welfare state is not an end to history, but neither is it a dead end. At the close of my contribution to *Growth to Limits* (reprinted as chapter 3 in this book), I indicated that the welfare state's maturation process could turn out to be more difficult than the start of its *longue durée*, a safe bet also for the future prospects for the Swedish welfare model.

December 1992

Footnotes

1. According to one reviewer of my book (Stephens 1992), the answer to these and similar questions should be sought in Jonas Pontusson's forthcoming work *The Limits of Social Demcoracy* (1992), a book I have not yet had the opportunity to read.
2. The uncertainty of such polls for long-term trends should be underlined. In December 1992, the polls give the Social Democrats an overall majority. As pointed out by researchers in this field, the political opposition – even a responsible one such as Swedish Social Democracy – tends to do well when an election is far away.

References

Abrahamson, P (1992): "The Scandinavian Model: Myths and Realities." Paper prepared for the research conference "From European Societies to European Society: the National Welfare States and European Integration", St. Martin, Germany

Ahrne, G & Clement, V (1992): "A New Regime? Class Representation within the Swedish State", *Economic & Industrial Democracy*, Vol 13

Alestalo, M & Flora, P (1992): "Scandinavia: Welfare States in the Periphery – Peripheral Welfare States?" Paper prepared for the research conference "From European Societies to European Society: the National Welfare States and European Integration", St. Martin, Germany

Allardt, E (1989): "Recent Developments in Scandinavian Sociology". *Annual Review of Sociology* 15, 31-45

Anttonen, A (1990): "The Feminization of the Scandinavian Welfare State" in L Simonen (ed) *Finish Debates on Women's Studies*, University of Tampere

Arvidsson, H, Berntson, L & Dencik, L (1992): "Omtankar om omsorgen: efter välfärdsstaten – har civilsamhället någon chans?" Papper presenterat vid seminarium med projektet "Den svenska socialstaten – efter välfärdsstaten?", Cityuniversitetet, Stockholm

Baldwin, P (1990): *The Politics of Social Solidarity*, Cambridge University Press, Cambridge

Berghman, J (1992): "Social security and European Integration", *European Institute of Social Security Yearbook 1991*, Acco, Leuven

Bergqvist, C (1990): "Myten om den universella svenska välfärdsstaten", *Statsvetenskaplig tidskrift*, No 3

Bergström, H (1991): "Sweden's Politics and Party System at the Crossroads", *West European Politics*, Vol 14, No 3

Boje T P & Olsson Hort, S E (1993): *Scandinavia in a New Europe*, Scandinavian University Press, Oslo

Borg, A E (1992): *Generell välfärdspolitik – bara magiska ord?*, City University Press, Stockholm

Castles, F & Mitchell, D (1990): "Three worlds of welfare capitalism – or four?", Australian National University, Public Policy Program, Discussion Paper No. 21, Canberra

Cnaan, R (1992): Book review, *Acta Sociologica*, Vol. 35, No 2

Delors, J (1992): *Our Europe*, Verso, London

Esping-Andersen, G (1991): Book Review, *American Journal of Sociology*
– (1990): *The Three Worlds of Welfare Capitalism*, Polity Press, Cambridge

Ervik, R & Kuhnle, S (1992): "The Scandinavian Welfare States and the Limited Relevance of the EC". Paper prepared for the research conference "From European Societies to European Society: the National Welfare States and European Integration", St. Martin, Germany

Fryklund, B, Peterson, T & Stigendahl, M (1989): *Vi mot dom*, Lund University Press, Lund

Glyn, A (1992): "The Cost of Stability: the Advanced Capitalist Countries in the 1980s", *New Left Review*, No 195

Hernes, G (1991): "The Dilemmas of Nordic Social Democracy", *Acta Sociologica*, Vol. 34, No 3

Huber E & Stephens, J (1992): "Economic Internationalization, the European Community and the Social Democratic Welfare State, Paper prepared for the 1992 Annual Meeting of the American Political Science Association, Chicago

Isaksson, A (1992): *När pengarna tagit slut*, Brombergs, Stockholm

Jensen, J & Mahon, R (1992): "Representing Solidarity: Class, Gender and the Crisis of Social-Democratic Sweden". Paper prepared for the Eight International Conference of Europeanists, Chicago, Il, USA

Johnsson, A (1992): *Perestrojka på svenska*, SAF, Stockholm

Kangas, O (1991): *The Politics of Social Rights*, Swedish Institute for Social Research, Dissertation Series No 19, Stockholm

Kaufmann, F-X (ed) (1991): *The Public Sector – Challenge for Coordination and Learning*, De Gruyter, Berlin

Kolberg, J E (ed) (1992a): *The Study of Welfare State Regimes*, M E Sharpe, New York

– (1992b): *Between Work and Social Citizenship*, M E Sharpe, New York

– (1992c): *The Welfare State as Employer*, M E Sharpe, New York

Korpi, W (1992): "Ville väljarna ha systemskifte 1991?", Swedish Institute for Social Research, Stockholm (mimeo)

– (1989): "Can we afford to work?" in M Bulmer, J Lewis, & D Piachaud (eds) *The Goals of Social Policy*, Unwin Hyman, London

Kosonen, P (1993): "The Scandinavian Welfare Model in the New Europe" in T P Boje & S E Olsson Hort (eds)

Kuhnle, S & Selle P (eds) (1992): *Government and Voluntary Organizations*, Avebury, Aldershot

Leibfried S (1991): "Welfare State Europe", Paper prepared for the 1991 Workshop on Comparative Studies of Welfare State Developments, Helsinki

– & Pierson, P (1992): "Prospects for Social Europe", *Politics & Society*, Vol. 19, No. 3

Lewis, J (1992): "Gender and the development of Welfare Regimes", *European Social Policy*, Vol. 2, No.3

Marklund, S (1992): "The decomposition of social policy in Sweden", *Scandinavian Journal of Social Welfare*, Vol. 1, No. 1

Mahon, R (1991): "Book review", *Economic & Industrial Democracy*, vol 12 no 4

Mikaelsson, B & Lister, C (1991): "Swedish Occupational Injury Insurance: a laudable programme in need of reform", *International Social Security Review*, Vol. 44, No 3

Miller, D (1991): *Denmark – the Troubled Welfare State*, Westview, Boulder

Montin, S (1992): "Recent Trends in the Relationship between Politics and Administration in Local Government: the Case of Sweden", *Local Government Studies*, No 1

Noterman, (1991): "The Abdication from National Policy Autonomy: Why macroeconomic policy regime has become so unfavorable to labor", Paper prepared for the Annual Meeting of the American Political Science Association, Washington D C

Olofsson, G (1989): *Bostadskarriären som förmögenhetsmaskin*, Rapport till Expertgruppen för studier i offentlig ekonomi, Finansdepartementet, Stockholm (Ds 1989:29)

Olsson Hort, S E (1993): "Welfare Policy in Sweden" in Boje & Olsson Hort (eds)

– (1992): *Segregation – ett svenskt dilemma?*, Finansdepartementet, Stockholm (Appendix volume no. 9 to SOU 1992:19)

– & Cohn D (1993): "A small but growing slice of the pie?" in N Johnson (ed) *Private markets in Health and Welfare*, Bergh, Leamington Spa

Olsson, S E (1992): "The Freedom-of-choice Revolution in Welfare Policy", *Zeitschrift für Sozialreform*, December

– (1987): "The People's Old-Age Pension in Sweden: Past, Present and Future", *International Social Security Review*, Vol 40, No. 4 (also in French, German and Spanish)

– & Therborn, G (ed) (1991): *Vision möter verklighet*, Liber, Stockholm

Orloff, A S (1992): Book Review, *Contemporary Sociology*, Vol 42, No 3

Palme, J (1990): *Pension Rights in Welfare Capitalism*, Swedish Institute for Social Research, Dissertation Series No 14, Stockholm

Phaller, A, Gough, I & Therborn G (eds) (1991): *Can the Welfare State Compete?*, MacMillan, London

Pontusson, J (1992): *The Limits of Social Democracy*, Cornell University Press, Ithaka

– & Swenson, P (1993): "Varför har arbetsgivarna övergivit den svenska modellen?" *Arkiv för studier i arbetarrörelsens historia*, nr. 53-54

Premfors, R (1991): The 'Swedish Model' and Public Sector reform, *West European Politics*, Vol. 14, No 3

Proposition (various Government bills in general in official English translations – Economic Policy Bill 1991/92:38 being the exception)

Rothstein, B (1992a): "Just institutions matter – The moral logic of the universal welfare state", Paper prepared for the 1992 Annual Meeting of the American Political Science Association, Chicago

– (1992b) "The Crisis of the Swedish Social Democrats and the Future of the Universal Welfare State", Paper prepared for the Eight International Conference of Europeanists, Chicago

– (1992c): *Den korporativa staten*, Norstedts, Stockholm

Ruin, O (1990): *Tage Erlander – Serving the Welfare State*, University of Pittsburgh Press, Pittsburgh

Schulte, B (1992a): "The Role of the Court of Justice of the European Communities". Revised paper prepared for the Conference on "The New Europe(s)", Mannheimer Zentrum für Sozialwissenschaften

– (1992b); "The European Community and Social Assistance", Paper prepared for a Voksenåsen Research Seminar, Oslo

Seip, A-L (1992): "Velferdsstaten – en nordisk modell?", Oplaeg fra den nordiske konference 6-9 maj 1991 på Energicentret Nyköbing Falster, Selskabet til forskning i Arbejderbevaegelsens Historie

Shaver, S (1990): Gender, Social Policy Regimes and the Welfare State, Social Policy Research Centre, Discussion Paper No 26, University of New South Wales, Sydney

Siim, B (1990): "Feministiska tolkningar av samspelet mellan kvinnor och välfärdsstaten", *Kvinnovetenskaplig tidskrift*, No 2

SOU 1992:19, *The Swedish Medium Term Survey*, Ministry of Finance, Stockholm

SOU 1990:14, *The Swedish Medium Term Survey*, Ministry of Finance, Stockholm

Spinker, P (1991): "The Principle of Subsidiarity and the Social Policy of the Europan Community", *Europan Social Policy*, Vol 1, No 1

Stephens, J (1992): "Book Review", *Contemporary Sociology*, Vol 42, No 2

Sulkunen, P (1992): *A New Middle Class?*, Avebury, Aldershot

Svallfors, S (1993): "Policy Regimes and Attitudes to Inequality: A comparison of three European Nations" in Boje & Olsson Hort (eds)

– (1991): "The politics of welfare policy in Sweden: structural determinants and attitudinal cleavages". *British Journal of Sociology*, Vol. 42, No 4

Swenson, P (1992a): "The End of the Swedish Model in LIght of its Beginnings: On the Role of Engineers Employers and their Leaders", Wissenschaftzentrum, Berlin (mimeo)

– (1991b): "Managing the Managers: The Swedish Employers' Confederation, Labor Scarcity, and the Suppression of Labor Market Segmentation", *Scandinavian Journal of History*, Vol 16

– (1991a): "Bringing Capital Back in, or Social Democracy Reconsidered: Employer Power, Cross-Class Alliances, and the Centralization of Industrial Relations in Denmark and Sweden", *World Politics*, Vol. 43, No. 4

Taylor-Goody, P (1991): "Welfare State Regimes and Welfare Citizenship", *Europan Social Policy*, Vol 1, No 2

Therborn, G (1992): Social Europe 1945-1992, Gothenburg University, Department of Sociology (to be published by Einaudi, Torino)

– (1991): "Swedish Social Democracy and the Transition from Industrial to Post-Industrial Politics" in F Fox Piven (ed) *Labor Parties in Post-industrial Societies*, Polity Press, Cambridge

– (1989): "States, Populations, and Productivity: Towards a Political Theory of the Welfare State " in P Lassman (ed) *Politics and Social Theory*, Routledge, London

Wetterberg, G (1991): *Det nya samhället*, Tiden, Stockholm

Zetterberg, H L (1992): *Socialstatsprojektet*, City University Press, Stockholm